To: Alonzo & Gloria

My life time friend and his lovely wife, Gloria.

Carter

PILGRIMAGE
In
CLAY FEET

The Rev. Dr. Carlton Wadsworth Veazey

authorHOUSE®

AuthorHouse™
1663 Liberty Drive
Bloomington, IN 47403
www.authorhouse.com
Phone: 1 (800) 839-8640

Published by AuthorHouse 06/24/2019

ISBN: 978-1-7283-1654-3 (sc)
ISBN: 978-1-7283-1655-0 (hc)
ISBN: 978-1-7283-1656-7 (e)

Library of Congress Control Number: 2019908142

Print information available on the last page.

Any people depicted in stock imagery provided by Getty Images are models, and such images are being used for illustrative purposes only. Certain stock imagery © Getty Images.

This book is printed on acid-free paper.

Because of the dynamic nature of the Internet, any web addresses or links contained in this book may have changed since publication and may no longer be valid. The views expressed in this work are solely those of the author and do not necessarily reflect the views of the publisher, and the publisher hereby disclaims any responsibility for them.

PILGRIMAGE
In
CLAY FEET

THE REV. DR. CARLTON
WADSWORTH VEAZEY

About the Author

The Reverend Dr. Carlton Wadsworth Veazey was born on May 9, 1936 in Memphis Tennessee to Dolly C. and the Rev. Mertie G.F. Veazey, the sixth child in the family. He is also the third generation minister in his family. His grandfather, the Rev. George Veazey was born in slavery in 1860 and established his first church in 1890 in Arkabutla, Mississippi. He was educated in the public schools of Memphis and graduated in 1954 from the Booker T. Washington High School with honors and president of the class of 440 graduates representing the largest class in the history of the school up until that time. He later entered the Arkansas A.M. and N. College where he received scholarships in both instrumental music (trombone) and vocals, becoming a member of the outstanding Arkansas State Concert Choir directed by the renowned Dr. Ariel Lovelace. During his matriculation at Arkansas State, he became a member of the Alpha Phi Alpha fraternity and president of the John B. Watson Memorial Sunday School named after the first president of Arkansas State.

After receiving his B. A. Degree in Sociology, he received a full scholarship from the Howard University School of Religion in Washington, D.C. During his midler year, he interned at the historic Zion Baptist Church, one of the oldest Baptist churches in the District of Columbia. The church was founded in 1864 by seven freedmen and was established in southwest Washington where it remained for over ninety years. The Reverend Dr. A. Joseph Edwards was serving as pastor of Zion when the unfair and racist decision was made by the city to declare eminent domain requiring many churches and their memberships to be removed from southwest where they had built a very powerful and cohesive community. The city's decision led Zion to rebuild in northwest Washington rather than purchase a "white church" which had become available due to the "white flight" of white churches resulting from the 1954 Supreme Court decision that allowed Negroes to attend formerly all-white public schools.

The Phyllis Wheatley YWCA became Zion's church home for seven years and it was here that Dr. Veazey met Dr. Edwards in 1959 as an intern to fulfill the requirements for his Bachelor of Divinity degree. Rev. Edwards was one of the most pivotal persons in his internship at Zion which was definitely providential as many of the decisions were leading to this church. As assistant to Rev. Edwards, he was assigned to assist the superintendent of Sunday school, Miss Keturah Barnes who was definitely an important and pivotal person in his life as he entered another phase of his spiritual development. Miss Barnes introduced him to many of the leaders of the church along with many young leaders in Zion.

In September 1959, Dr. Edwards began plans for the ground breaking for the new church located at 4850 Blagden Avenue, N.W. that was to take place after the morning communion service held on the fourth Sunday in September. Dr. Veazey had also been appointed by Dr. Evans Crawford, dean of the Andrew Rankin Chapel, to serve as his student assistant. His responsibility to the dean was to take the guest speakers to breakfast and afterward to the chapel where he would prepare robes for both the dean and the guest speakers. This still allowed him time to fulfill his internship on Sunday which was to teach a teenage Sunday school class and asset the pastor at the eleven o'clock services.

On the fourth Sunday in September at approximately nine o'clock, Rev. Edwards stopped at the People's Drug Store to get an antacid because of his heart condition. The clerk in the store reported that before he could take the pill he fell and after the EMTs arrival, was pronounced deceased at the store. Dr. Veazey was sent by Dr. Crawford to the YWCA to provide spiritual support and subsequently became interim minister. This eventually led to him becoming pastor which was totally unexpected by him.

Dr. Veazey pastored Zion for thirty three years that included continuing to follow Rev. Edwards in building the new edifice on Blagden Avenue. This was truly a challenge at the age of twenty three. Dean Crawford, his mentor and friend, guided him through those years which ended with the erection of the church on Blagden, the first historic church built in many years. After a very effective ministry for thirty three years, dissent in the church arose and after a church meeting in August 1992, he was dismissed by a contested vote of which he would not allow a recount. In 1994, Dr. Veazey founded and pastored Fellowship Baptist Church. Seventeen years after leaving Zion he was invited back to preach which he accepted along with church members at Fellowship.

During his career Dr. Veazey received many honors and awards including: appointment to the D.C. City Council by president Richard M. Nixon in 1960-1964; selection as President of the Religious Coalition for Reproductive Choice (RCRC) in 1996-2011; the Gloria Steinim award by the Ms. Foundation; the Voters for Choice award by Gloria Steinim Foundation; being the first man honored by Women's Enews for his work as president of RCRC; and a Doctorate of Humane Letters from the Meadville Lombard Theological Seminary associated with the University of Chicago.

Foreword

The Rev. Carlton Veazey has written an autobiography that needs to be read by all who are believers in God and God's mercy. This book is not just for those who are preparing for ministry, who are in seminary, or those who have already been ordained and have been practicing ministry for many years. This book is also for laypersons and those who struggle with the realities of life on a day to day basis.

Pastor Veazey is brutally honest. He is open. He is transparent and yet there breathes from each page, each paragraph and each sentence he writes the warmth and love of a God who is always faithful and the God who has kept him and blessed him in spite of him!

If you have questions about the bible, this is the book for you.

If you have questions about God and where God was in the midst of chattel slavery, the holocaust, segregation, apartheid and raw racism, this is the book for you. If you have questions about sensuality, sexuality and wrestling with human feelings while living a life that is pleasing to God, this is the book for you.

I give thanks to God for Carlton Veazey. His book shows us a minister who is honest, a Pastor who is compassionate, a man of God who is also a man of clay with feet that are firmly and flatly on the ground of God's earth. Pilgrimage in Clay Feet is truly a "page-turner," and I recommend it to you. Enjoy Rev. Veazey's pilgrimage and walk along

with him as each chapter he writes carries you closer and closer to our
God who is always present.

The Rev. Dr. Jeremiah A. Wright, Jr.
Pastor Emeritus
Trinity United Church of Christ
Chicago, Illinois

Foreword

In his memoir, Pilgrimage in Clay Feet, Dr. Carlton Wadsworth Veazey welcomes us into his journey of life from the cradle to the threshold of completion and transition. With refreshing honesty and arresting transparency, he recounts his personal journey and allows us to walk with him through fidelity and failure; drama and delight; crisis and celebration; hurt and healing. Dr. Veazey shares both his stellar accomplishments and his dark valleys. As he narrates his heights and hurts, he does not mask those moments where he was a co-conspirator in wounding himself and others. The story emerges as testimony of authentic service, genuine faith, healing recovery, and coming promise.

Dr. Veazey's moving testimony concludes with the affirmation and the celebration that the good life is a journey characterized by growing intimacy with God, the true self, and all creation. Faithful living is not assent to static propositions about God, but rather a living relationship with God. This dynamic relationship is ever emerging through the evolution of the soul and growing intimacy with the eternal. Life does not end! Life is lived!

Dr. Veazey's living has given us greater life and may his journey continue. His feet may have been of clay, but how beautiful are the feet of those who bring redeeming news

The Rev. Dr. John W. Kinney
Virginia Union University
Richmond, Virginia

To my daughter Caron

"My father's journey of faith, failure,
forgiveness, and fulfillment."

Contents

Acknowledgments

I am grateful to God, who gave me life to work out the salvation of my soul and develop my future life through the spiritual development this life affords. Also, I must acknowledge Jesus the Christ, who was a unique son of God and also a "way shower," as He says in the book of John. The Greek of the verse uses the term *way shower*, which makes a great difference in interpretation. The inspiration of the spirit (Holy Spirit) has provided the impetus behind this book.

Thank you to the thousands of pilgrims to whom I have preached over these many years, although broken my preaching may have been.

Thank you to my parents, the Reverend Mertie G. F. and Dolly C. Veazey, who helped to shape and direct my life in its early stages and took seriously responsibilities as stewards of the life God gave to them in the person of Carlton Wadsworth Veazey. My mother was love, mercy, and grace in all her actions, and my father dedicated his life to others, which was passed on to me.

My wife, Jean, married me fifty years ago, and even though she knew I had "clay feet," she still loved and supported me in sunshine and rain. My brothers and sisters have been an integral part of my development as I make this pilgrimage, especially my brother Melvin. The Veazeys and the Jollys have been a great influence on my past because of their examples dating back to slavery and reconstruction. Isaac Jolly and Minnie Jolly, along with my paternal grandparents, Anna and the Reverend George Veazey, who were born into slavery, also left me the legacy of strength and pride, which has helped me on this pilgrimage. Thank you to them.

Thank you to my many friends and acquaintances I have met on the many roads of this pilgrimage. First, I'll mention my most recent friend,

Kimberly Jackson; providence brought us together for the many months of writing this book and debating its contents. Also, this book would not have been timely without the expert editing by a young lady I met when she was fourteen years old when I pastored Zion Baptist Church, Theresa Brockenberry Lee, who accepted the arduous task of reading and preparing my manuscript for the literary agent and publisher.

Thank you to my children: Gayle, who transitioned some years ago, made her mother and me very proud of the kind of woman she was and the service she rendered to many young people through the city's employment services. Katea continued the tradition of our family by fighting for justice for the many who had no voice in Washington, DC, through her work as program director of radio station WPFW. My youngest, Caron, made her mother and me proud of her stellar accomplishments as one of the outstanding women in the entertainment world through her management of musical icon Pharrell Williams, who acknowledges her indispensable value as partner in his company. Michael Vincent, my only son, who, despite his personal struggles, continues to demonstrate compassion for others.

Thank you to my grandchildren all make me proud in their chosen fields. My only great-grandchild, Zion Veazey, at age seven, shows great promise. And the many nieces, nephews, and cousins on both side of the Jolly and Veazey families have made outstanding contributions to society with the many skills they possess.

Thank you to the founding members of Fellowship Baptist Church, who through faith followed me in establishing God's church, especially Nannie Curtis, who was always curious about the afterlife and encouraged me to preach on it many times. Edmonia Johnson, a close friend to Jean, constantly reminded me of the fact that my ministry was not over even though I had left Zion Baptist Church. She never relented until I accepted the call to pastor Fellowship Baptist Church and kept the promise I had made to God over sixty years earlier when he'd healed my mother of cancer.

Thank you to the many friends who periodically inquired when the book would be completed and who motivated me to continue when I was weary of writing.

Finally, thank you to my friend and former colleague Sonya Crudup, who served as my chief operating officer at the Religious Coalition for Reproductive Choice and was instrumental in physically saving my life many years ago, for which I will be eternally grateful.

If there are those who were omitted, please know it was an omission of the head and not of the heart. To God be the glory!

Introduction

This book was inspired in 1998 in Cape Town, South Africa, where I was visiting with Frances Kissling, president of Catholics for a Free Choice, a pro-choice organization supporting Catholics' right to choose an abortion as provided by the Supreme Court of the United States of America. I had recently been elected president of the Religious Coalition for Reproductive Choice, representing twenty-six denominations and religious organizations that also supported a woman's right to choose. Frances invited me to come with her on this visit to learn more about the HIV/AIDS pandemic on the continent. While there, I heard President Mandela speak and was inspired by his life and the works, for which he had fought valiantly and been imprisoned for more than twenty-seven years.

In 1992, after I had pastored Zion Baptist Church for thirty-three years, a group of dissidents wanted to take over control of the church, which was rightly the province of the pastor. The dissidents developed an unholy alliance, raising issues that had been settled years earlier to form a corporate takeover as a disguise for their desire to control the church. On August 25, 1992, at approximately ten o'clock in the evening, the vote was tallied. The opposition won by seven votes, which many disputed because of irregularities in the voting procedure. Although there were those who wanted me to challenge the vote and procedure, I refused. I believed that God had a reason for allowing this to happen, even though I felt it to be unjust.

When I returned home, I found Jean was not dejected, although she felt my pain. I later learned it was her spirituality that gave her the calmness and serenity during this period. Later that evening as I reflected on what had occurred earlier, I received a call from Rev.

Dr. Walter Fauntroy, a close friend and former congressman for the District of Columbia. He was also a leading force with Rev. Dr. Martin Luther King in the civil rights movement. Walter's call came at exactly midnight, after I had received many calls of encouragement. Walter's words will always resonate in my spirit because they were prophetic, and they came through him, not from him. His exact words were, "Carlton, this is Walter. I tried to get in the church, but the guards would not allow me entry, saying that the trustee board under Mr. Christian's direction had directed the guards not to allow any of your friends to enter, even for observation and even if they were ministers. However, Carlton, you will never want for anything the rest of your life."

He hung up, and I was left to ponder those words. Somehow, there came over me an unusual quietness of spirit and calmness of mind. Walter's words, or more directly the words that had come through Walter, were prophetic. I will discuss this more in detail in *Pilgrimage in Clay Feet*.

God places people in your life for spiritual development, which is your sole purpose for coming to this planet. Many of the people I've met were placed in my pathway by God to assist me on my journey. None have been more important than Dr. Leon Wright, professor of New Testament at the Howard University School of Religion in 1958. It was prophetic that he had just returned from Burma after an extended sabbatical. Our paths crossed at the intersection of my lack of knowledge and the teacher who was supposed to help me on my pilgrimage. It is said, "When the student is ready, the teacher will appear." That is my testimony as to how I arrived at this place in understanding why I have "clay feet." Dr. Wright explained why we come here and how we must develop, which is the primary purpose of our existence. He introduced me to Edgar Cayce, who has also influenced my life, demonstrating the power and the possibilities of the human spirit. He was instrumental in helping me to read the scriptures with the third eye, which is the Holy Spirit. Dr. Gene Rice also helped me to exegete the scriptures, which made them come alive in my understanding.

Two references to clay in the scriptures influenced me. In 2 Corinthians, the apostle Paul explains, "We have this heavenly treasure in earthen vessels." Regardless of our givens, they are still encased in earthen vessels. In Daniel 2:31–45, he speaks of "feet of clay." All of Shakespeare's characters were referred to as having a "fatal flaw," which equates to feet of clay. Dr. Wright's extracurricular assignments, which included esoteric reading, helped to elucidate the meaning of clay feet.

During the months following the end of my tenure, I went over my life to see why and where I had failed. This required a very painful examination of my life, where honesty was the key. Although I had promised God many years ago that I would preach the gospel, I did not realize the cost of that commitment. Through the years, it became more apparent that I was not really prepared for this task. There were character flaws, pride, selfishness, and other negatives in my life, which helped me to understand why I had clay feet. Although I was hurt and discouraged about how my life had gone, I still believed that God found promise and purpose in me. As you read this book, remember I am trying to be as honest and forthright as I can so that some other pilgrims can find solace and encouragement.

My sixty-two years in ministry and fifty-five years in pastorate have taught me some valuable lessons about the church and some of the faulty theology that the church has embraced. Many will disagree with me, which is of course their right. All that I ask is that they give my words a fair hearing and formulate any criticism they desire. One thing I will assure the reader of—I have tried to be honest about my life; that means I've included some very hurtful and embarrassing times and times of failure that I work toward redeeming the remainder of my days.

Finally, we cannot make sense of this life if we do not understand the value and opportunities of spiritual development, which will assist us in our next level of spiritual enlightenment, where we will be challenged to improve even more. This makes what I do every day important because I am contributing to my future lives. It changes the meaning of death. Death is only the beginning of a new journey. As you read, think about your life and what progress you are making for your future spiritual existence. It is up to you to live up to your spiritual potential.

Chapter 1

THE BEGINNING OF
MY PILGRIMAGE

BIRTH THROUGH KINDERGARTEN

My pilgrimage began on the evening of May 8, 1936, after having resided in my mother's womb for almost nine months. This may sound strange to some people, but I believe we determine when we want to enter this world and by what channels we want to come. Kahlil Gibran said in *The Prophet* that our children are not our children; they come *through* us and not *from* us. Why I selected Mertie and Dolly Veazey to be my channel is a mystery, but I am convinced that our parents are uniquely selected for many reasons. The reasons are sometimes revealed in our pilgrimages and also those who are close to us such like our sisters and brothers. My sister Audrey chronicles the evening, describing the excitement at 1232 Beech Street in Memphis, Tennessee.

Dr. Coppage had arrived early in the evening to inform my father what needed to be done in preparation for my arrival. My sister described the moderate labor pains our mother was experiencing. They would grow severe as the hours passed. After midnight, the house was alarmed when my mother's pain became increasingly severe. Dr. Coppage returned around two in the morning to begin the procedure that would set me on my journey.

My father was very caring and reassuring to my mother during the last hours of her labor. At exactly 3:37 a.m. on May 9, 1936, I,

1

Carlton Wadsworth Veazey, joined my five siblings. My sister describes the moment with my father throwing open the French doors of their bedroom and announcing to my siblings, "You may come in and meet your brother Carlton."

Many people have commented that I have a unique name. All my sisters and brothers were given unique names. Our father was creative in naming us. My siblings, in order of their birth, were named Erwin Rhinehart Veazey, Melvin Aurelius Veazey, Audrey Celestine Veazey, Weldon Noyes Veazey, and Geraldine Loretta Veazey (Gerry).

My memory of my birthplace on Beech Street is vague because we moved when I was around three. I am told that Beech Street was a beautiful street on a high hill with large colonial homes. It was a middle-class community for the standards of that time. There were teachers, doctors, lawyers, and postmen who had federal jobs like my dad. There were also Pullman porters who commanded a middle-class income. Our street was near Lemoyne College, which was the only accredited black college in the city and was located only blocks from our home. The influence of the college was felt in the community by the aspirations of the children who grew up there. Lemoyne College was founded by the Quakers, who were known as champions of justice and equality. They were also pacifists, who neither believed in war nor accepted it. The Quakers were among those who kept the flame of hope alive in Memphis during the days of the Great Depression.

The Memphis culture was not unique for a Deep South city, since it was founded in 1826 and ruled by the Confederates during the Civil War. It still maintains some of the scars of that time, as evidenced by the statue of General Nathan Bedford Forrest, one of the revered Confederate generals. Memphis was named after the biblical city in Egypt that flourished under one of the major Pharaohs. Memphis sits on a bluff overlooking the mighty Mississippi River with all its majesty. We were taught that our river was the second longest in the United States, running from a little tributary all the way to the Gulf of Mexico. Much of the commerce of Memphis was around the river, which produced food and income for the residents.

Memphis was the throne of king cotton, in that we were surrounded by Mississippi and Arkansas, which were also great producers of cotton.

When I was growing up in the mid-1930s, I was always amazed when my father would take me to his job. We would walk along Front Street, which overlooked the great Mississippi, and see hundreds of bales of cotton that had been brought to Memphis to sell and to ship to textile mills around the country. Truly, cotton was king. It provided the livelihood on which the city depended during my years. I remember we celebrated king cotton with the annual festival called the Cotton Carnival.

Cotton made many white families rich, but we were not the recipients of any of this immense wealth. I remember people going to Mississippi and Arkansas to work for as little as four dollars a day for chopping and three dollars per hundred pounds for picking. It required a skilled person to pick three hundred pounds in a day, and you were in a class by yourself if you picked four pounds in a day.

Now you can see why cotton was king and we were the subjects. However, despite these inequities, we were able to feed and clothe our families and in many instances provide postsecondary education for them.

One can't talk about the culture of Memphis without including the name Edward Hull "Boss" Crump, who "ruled" Memphis from the late 1930s to the late 1950s. Boss Crump was to Memphis what Mayor Daley was to Chicago. Crump was known as the super-mayor of Memphis. He served for a short time as mayor but ruled Memphis government for many years. Every major officeholder was beholden to Boss Crump. If Crump said it, it was done.

When I was growing up, Boss Crump would sponsor a Fourth of July picnic for Negroes in Lincoln Park. He would provide food for hundreds—barbecued pig feet, greens, pies, and, of course, watermelon. My father would never take us and really despised black people for being so gullible. This was the culture of Memphis in my early years. We could also relate other disgusting things that happened during this segregated period, such as being made to sit in the rear of buses and drink from water fountains designated for "colored" people.

My earliest remembrance of education was when my mother enrolled me in the kindergarten program at Bethlehem Center, which was really the Head Start of that day. I was fortunate and blessed to have that opportunity, which only a few of us were able to have. Our teachers were Quakers who were kind and sensitive about our plight, and they never implied anything to cause us not to have confidence. My kindergarten education has remained with me through all the eighty years I have lived. I have several friends who also attended Bethlehem Center with me seventy-six years ago. I still have a picture of my class from 1942, and it means a lot to me.

When we "graduated" from Bethlehem Center, we were ready to go to the big school, Larose Elementary, which four of my siblings attended. This was exciting as well as challenging.

Chapter 2

EARLY EDUCATION

ELEMENTARY SCHOOL

I n kindergarten, my classmates and I had been treated as extensions of our mothers.

Everything changed at Larose. We were responsible for our conduct and assignments. There would be no more coddling or crying, although a few tried that. I grew up in an era when we were not allowed a long dependence, which means you accepted responsibility very young. When I visited my cousins in Mississippi, I was shocked to see my nine-year-old cousin, Irma Jean, plowing beside her brother Walter, who was at least sixteen. Although this may sound strange to today's youth, one must remember that we were only seventy-two years out of slavery and education was not universal. My Mississippi cousins attended school only four months a year, in a single room where children of all ages were being taught by one teacher. This environment did not lend itself to effective education.

Larose Elementary was exciting because there was so much to learn about our world, including new words, new ideas, and new people. I looked forward to and enjoyed going to school every day. One of the first persons I met was Curtis Bonds from my church. We became lifelong friends until his death in 1998. Curtis was smart and daring. It was years before I discovered he was three years older than I was, which accounted for his maturity even at a young age. He was also the oldest of nine children, which gave him a more mature outlook on things.

Our first teachers were combinations of our mothers, our grandmothers, and our Sunday school teachers. They were strict like most of our mothers; they were gentle like our grandmothers; and they were sweet like our Sunday school teachers. I remember Miss Raines, our first-grade teacher; Ms. Pritchett, our second-grade teacher; and Ms. Brown, our third-grade teacher. It is true that the important years of a child's life are the first three years of his or her educational life.

Enough cannot be said for today's Head Start program, but even in the early 1940s at Bethlehem Center, I now recognize how critical those years were leading into elementary school. Each year in elementary school was a challenge but also exciting. Although we were educated in a segregated system with inadequate buildings and books, we had what was most important—well-trained teachers dedicated not only to teaching us but also to preparing us for the segregated world we would inherit. That did not mean acceptance of the status quo; rather, it prepared us to challenge the system created in this horrible culture.

In the upper grades of elementary school, many things became attractive, mainly girls. Although we all found the opposite sex attractive, we were unsure how to approach each other. Walking a particular girl home from school was a major accomplishment that was noted by all your classmates. This led to visiting the girl at home if her parents permitted. We were permitted to sit on the porch as long as we were not too close. In the living room, we had to have at least the space of one person between us. As you can see, this made for real intimacy or whatever we called it.

In the latter years of elementary school, our real personalities began to form. There were those we did not like for whatever reason and those we liked without reservation. We formed cliques, even though we did not know what they were called. Some of us did not understand that kind of behavior, maybe because of our Sunday school teachers, who drilled in us the Golden Rule: "Do unto others as you would have them do unto you." This did not make us into angels; we had many other faults, which kept us humble.

Our final year in elementary school was one of elation and fear. We were finally leaving what we thought of as children's school and moving to the adult school. What would be the requirements? What would the classmates be like? Finally, what would the teachers be like? These and many other questions ran through our minds as we contemplated another chapter in our education. Booker T. Washington High School (also known as BTW) was the oldest and most renowned high school in Memphis, and we were on our way there. What an honor! We had heard so much about the teachers, the football team, the girls, and the beautiful big building that would be our home for the next four years.

Graduation from elementary school was very moving and emotional. Our ceremony was held at the Whitestone Baptist Church, which was large enough to hold the fifty-two classmates in our class. The church was an integral part of our culture, as Negro life in 1942 Memphis revolved around the church. There was not the separation of church and state that is so strictly held to in today's world. We started each day with the Lord's Prayer or the 23rd Psalm.

While it is not permitted in the schools today, it was not only allowed in the schools but also necessary in the black community. Our community was deeply rooted in biblical tradition, which made religion a part of our educational development.

The graduation ceremony was very impressive. We dressed in our Sunday clothes, and our parents invited relatives and friends to witness this event. We were given diplomas signed by the superintendent of public schools, Mr. E. C. Ball, and the principal, Mr. Brinkley. Our glee club provided the music, which was always comprised of Negro spirituals, such as "Swing Low, Sweet Chariot," or "Over My Head." I hear music in the air, which aroused my curiosity because they reminded us of another world, where things would be different. When the graduation exercise was over, there was a feeling of joy, excitement, and pride in what we had accomplished.

Next was our summer vacation, which lasted from early June to early September. This was also a very important time, which meant we had more time at home and with friends and relatives. My summer vacation, along with my sister Gerry's, was already determined. My mother's brother, Uncle Jesse, would come from Coldwater, Mississippi to pick us up and take us to our grandparents for the summer, which was our "summer camp."

This experience was accepted with mixed emotion because we were torn with not having the conveniences of running water and toilets to which we were accustomed. We also had to adjust to the darkness part of the rural experience. Every morning, our grandmother, whom we loved dearly, and my cousin Barbara Jean Jolly, who was the daughter of my uncle Macon and lived with my grandmother because her mother died in childbirth, would rise before dawn to prepare breakfast for all of us. That included my three uncles, my grandfather, and my cousins, who were preparing to go to the field to work for the day. I was amazed how my grandmother could prepare on a woodstove the most sumptuous breakfast I had ever seen. We would have biscuits, bacon, eggs, sausage, ham, grits, potatoes, and fish. This was also the biggest breakfast I had ever seen in my life.

When I first visited my grandparents, it was difficult for me to sleep. So at daybreak, I was tired. The first day I arrived at my grandfather's home, I refused to get up for the breakfast I just described. My grandfather told my grandmother not to insist that I eat breakfast but to prepare me to go to the fields with my uncles. I was overjoyed to know I could sleep longer and miss breakfast.

When we went to the fields that morning, my uncle assigned me to spread fertilizer to the cotton plants, which I saw when I surveyed the acres of field was a mammoth job. The sun was blazing around eight o'clock that morning and would continue to do so throughout the day. Let me tell you that you have not felt heat from the sun until you have felt the Mississippi sun. You can imagine I was not only hot but also hungry by ten o'clock that morning and pleaded with my grandfather to return to the house, but he refused. He informed me that Mama Jolly would be bringing dinner around noon, and we would just have to wait. What he said next were the cruelest words I thought he could utter. "Did you eat breakfast this morning?" I immediately understood his way of reminding me that I'd refused the breakfast Mama Jolly had prepared.

I have never experienced a more difficult two hours in my life. I was constantly watching for mama to come with our food, and the more

I watched, the hungrier I got. Finally, I could see dust from the road in the distance. I kept watch with great anticipation. Finally, I could make out the horses trotting at great speed toward us and Mama Jolly bringing us dinner for the day. I cannot describe the feeling of relief and gratitude I felt when I saw Mama coming to save us from "starvation."

Although I was near starvation, I was amazed, and I mean amazed, to see what she had brought by horse and wagon to feed us. Let me tell you first, the food was as hot as you would get in any restaurant today. We had for dinner. Remember that dinner was served midday in that time because we didn't eat heavy food before going to bed. We had supper just before bedtime. Now let me tell you what Mama brought. Everything was in molasses cans that were sealed and airtight. Those cans contained chicken, pork chops, ham, turnip greens, collard greens, mashed potatoes, sweet potatoes, corn bread, and apple pie from fresh apples. My grandfather had a large orchard of all kinds of fruit. As long as I live, I will never forget that dinner in the field.

That evening, I went to bed early, and I was the first person at the breakfast table. I had learned my lesson about missing breakfast and what to look for the next day. We labored for two months on my grandfather's farm; I remember that time in detail to this day.

Finally, the day arrived when Uncle Jesse would take us back to Memphis to prepare for the coming school year. I mean no disrespect to my sainted grandparents, but I know just how people feel when they are released from prison. On the positive side, it was the best motivation to get an education; I knew I didn't want to be a farmer. This is not to disrespect farmers or farming because it is honorable work that our forebears did to give us the opportunities we enjoy today.

Arriving at 623 Alston Street, where we had lived for several years after leaving Beech Street, felt like heaven. We were met by our friends in the neighborhood with shouts that "Carl and Gerry are back from the country." Although they teased us, there was a strange envy, which I detected, partly because they did not have people in the country they could visit. Gerry and I were very excited about going home to see our friends, but we saddened to learn that our mother and father had purchased a house at 1610 Arkansas Street in South Memphis. We had lived at 623 Alston most of our lives, and we were concerned about moving; August was over, and school would begin in three days. Although there was intense anticipation, there was also extreme reluctance to face that first day of high school, with its new friends, new teachers, new studies, and new rules.

September 4 arrived, and I, along with several of my friends on Alston, reported to the famous and historic Booker T. Washington High School at 8:30 sharp before the bugler blew his trumpet. Yes, you read correctly that we had a bugler from our high school band blow the bugle at exactly 8:30 a.m. on the orders of our revered and feared Rev. Dr. Blair T. Hunt, the principal of principals in Memphis. We found our way to our home rule class from 9:00 a.m. to 2:00 p.m. with Miss Mary Moore. It was exciting to meet students from other elementary schools, such as Porter, Florida Avenue, North Memphis, and Carnes Elementary. Children from Carnes had a choice between Booker T. Washington and our rival Manassas High School.

Sports, particularly football and basketball, were big in Memphis. Since my brother Weldon played for Booker T., as we called it, I was inclined to play also. I had shown some promise as an athlete by winning the tristate boxing championship the year before in my 112-pound weight class. I'd also demonstrated, in my community, the ability to throw a football a great distance at the age of twelve, so many thought I had talent to play high school ball. I went out for the football team with great enthusiasm, only to be told my 127-pound weight was not sufficient even though I had been playing with the same guys in the neighborhood the year before. I knew I was in great condition because of my boxing career. This was the first thing I was not allowed the opportunity to do, which was crushing. The memory has never left me to this day and makes me fantasize about what a great quarterback I would have become.

Before I finished high school, Coach Fowlkes, who lived down the street, saw me passing a ball and asked why I did not play football. After I told him the story, he asked me to come out and said he would work with my talent. However, by that time, I had developed an interest in music and had become a fairly good trombone player. When I asked Mr. McDaniel's, the band director, if I could play both football and be in the band, his prompt answer was an emphatic no! Since I was progressing so well in the band, and the lead trombonist was graduating, I would have the opportunity to become first trombonist for the Booker T. Washington marching band and possibly play in the local orchestra. In retrospect, this was the best path because my interest in music led to a very exciting and profitable high school career.

Chapter 3

HIGH SCHOOL DAYS

The first year of high school was rather uneventful, in that the routine of attending classes and preparing homework, along with extracurricular activities, made the year go by very quickly. During the year, we all had made a place in the high school relationships. Most of us were territorial in that our closest friends were those we had grown up with.

The most influential person in our high school was the Reverend Dr. Blair T. Hunt, who was nationally known as one of the premier black educators in the country. He was a native Memphian, a Harvard University graduate, and one of the outstanding orators in the south. People from every part of the south would come to hear him speak. We were fortunate because we had assemblies at least three times a week where he would speak and lecture us about our conduct. Although his words were harsh many times, we knew he was interested in helping us reach our goals and become productive citizens. He used words that caused us to keep a dictionary close at hand. During our many assemblies, he took the opportunity to stress how beautiful and brilliant we were. This was really the beginning of the "black is beautiful" period. Those of us who attended Booker T. believed we were the best scholars, the best football players, the best band in the south, and the best-looking in the city. Professor Hunt, as he was called, had a motto we all had to repeat: "We lead; others follow." This simple motto resonated in our spirits, to the point where losing or failing was not an option. Classmates all over the world attribute Professor

Hunt's motivating words to their success in their professional endeavors. Professor Hunt instilled in us the confidence to know that we could accomplish anything if we really believed in ourselves.

In retrospect, this was just as important as our studies because, without confidence, no amount of knowledge will make a difference. Not only did we have Professor Hunt; we also had the best faculty in the city. This was because of the influence of Professor Hunt, who had cultivated relationships with the power structure in Memphis, including Boss Crump. You may notice that I did not mention the mayor or the superintendent of schools; all of them reported to Boss Crump. Whatever Professor Hunt wanted for his school, he got.

However, this did not include the separate but equal doctrine, which would be challenged in the 1954 decision of the Supreme Court. We also did not have the best when it came to supplies, textbooks, and facilities. But we did have, thanks to Professor Hunt, the best teachers in the South, black or white. Some of our teachers had studied at Princeton, Harvard, Yale, and other major universities but had returned to Memphis to advance the race. Some of the nationally known educators in our school were Mr. Lowe, chemistry; Mr. Nat. D. Williams, history; Mr. Robert Wesley McGhee, Latin; Miss Hurd, trigonometry; and the most famous of all, the legendary educator and composer, Miss Lucie Campbell. She was respected not only as an educator but also as one of the most prolific composers of that day. Miss Lucie, as she was affectionately called, was a legend in the National Baptist Convention, the largest Negro church convention in the world. I was fortunate to have known Miss Lucie, who was the choir director in my church, the Central Baptist Church. There were many other legendary educators in Memphis to whom we owe a great debt of gratitude.

I have always been blessed with wonderful friends. Although I did not grow up with my brothers because they were away in the war during those years, I sought friends, especially males, to whom I could relate and form a fraternal bond.

One of my earliest and best friends was Curtis Bates Bonds, who attended the same church as I did. Our mothers were friends. My relationship with Curtis goes back to the first grade and the first day of school. Curtis and I cooked us a scheme to go to Walker and Mississippi

13

to Johnson's Sundry Shop to get a hamburger. Curtis suggested that he would tell Ms. Raines he had to use the restroom. After he left the room, I should say the same. And we would meet outside on Lauderdale and proceed to Johnson's Sundry to get our delicious hamburger that only Johnson Sundry could make.

Remember, I was only six years old, and I discovered the art of lying, an original sin I had heard preached about; and it must have been true, because it was not difficult to lie.

As we proceeded toward Johnson's Sundry, we turned on Edith Avenue, which was a shortcut. As soon as we turned on Edith Avenue, I heard a very familiar voice ring out. "Carlton!" It was unmistakably my father's voice. This caused instant paralysis and loss of voice, which I regained when I heard him call a second time with the authority that only his voice had.

Of course I answered, "Yes, sir."

"Where are you going?" he asked in a menacing tone.

That day, I learned a lesson many had not learned before. When you tell a lie, be prepared to have another one handy. My reply was preposterous, "Miss Raines sent us up to Johnson's to get her a hamburger."

Daddy did not even reply but simply put his US Mail bag down right there and said, "Let's go back to school and see what Miss Raines has to say about that."

That was the longest walk I had ever had, and Curtis made it worse laughing, not realizing that my daddy would give his father a report that day, which would not be a laughing matter. When we arrived at old Larose, as it was called, and made our way to the second floor where our class was, my father opened the door with a flourish that shocked us.

Miss Raines immediately stood up and exclaimed, "Where have you two been?"

My father quickly responded, "They said, Miss Raines, that you had sent them up to Johnson's Sundry to get you a hamburger."

This caused immediate embarrassment and fear when Miss Raines looked at us. Of course, she did not have to explain to my father that she had done no such thing. Before leaving the class, Daddy had to inform everybody that I would get punishment when I got home.

For the rest of the day, our classmates described what kind of whooping we would get when we got home. Although I tried to remain calm and uninterested, their description of the whooping seemed as if they had been at my house before. However, they did not really know my father, who always tried to make the punishment fit the offense. He always sought to use infractions as a "teachable moment." He did so that evening. He told me what I'd done was wrong, but more than that, I'd involved someone else who had not done anything. He also used the opportunity to remind me that one lie leads to another.

This relationship with my best friend Curtis lasted for more than sixty years. I miss him to this day and remember other escapades that happened but did not end as tragically as our first day in elementary school.

Since that first day of school, I made many friends in high school who remain in my life until today. High school friendships were different from those in grade school. These friendships were more serious because we now had developed more knowledge about life and especially girls. All the boys seem to be an expert on girls which made me feel a little uneasy; I thought I was the only one without this kind of knowledge. To my surprise, they did not know any more than I did but had overactive imaginations.

I would soon learn that, although my classmates and I were alike in many ways, there were areas of serious differences, especially when it came to home life. Many times, I would discover that their lives at home were not like mine. When I look back, I realize that my exposure was different from theirs in many ways. This is not to disparage any of my classmates but simply to say that, growing up, I recognized some of us had advantages that others did not. Some of us had both a mother and father in the home with our siblings, while others had one parent, with a man living with them who they related to as a father. Sometimes that man would change every few months or year. This did not affect my relationships with my friends, because we only looked at our friends for the values they had. Also, my parents never made judgments about our friends, although they may have known the circumstances under which they lived.

My greatest growth came at 623 Alston where I spent most of my life since Bethlehem Center kindergarten. We were truly a community in every sense of the word. We knew all of our neighbors, and I mean all. On my street, there was Dr. John Jackson who was what I now know as a podiatrist; we called him "foot doctor." Next door was my adopted godfather, Mr. Marion, which I will explain later. There was also Mrs. Bessie Holt, a housewife whose husband was a gambler, but nobody made any judgments. There was also Mrs. Jackson, who worked at one of the largest hotels in Memphis as a maid and whose son Jim, gassed in World War I, never recovered. Jim was protected by all of us because he had a serious nerve problem, which caused him to shake uncontrollably and also affected his speech and reasoning. Mrs. Jackson was a "saint," who cared for Jim for the rest of his life. There was also Dr. and Mrs. Elmore, who lived a very middle class lifestyle that did not alienate them from the community. They gave us jobs around their house for various chores and showed concern and interest in our development. There was Mrs. Clay who had the only beauty parlor on the street. Then there was Mr. Jackson, the local coal and woodman, who made a good living for his wife and six children. His son, Junior, and I became good friends, and his father employed me to deliver coal and wood in our community. One of the families that stand out in our community is the Newborn family who lived several doors from me. Mr. and Mrs. Phineas Newborn had two sons, Calvin and Phineas Jr.

This entire Newborn family was musically gifted, with Mr. Newborn playing drums for the Tuft Green Orchestra, a locally famous band known throughout the south. His wife was director of the Mount Vernon Baptist Church choir, and the boys played in the band at BTW. Calvin and Junior were gifted in flute and guitar, and Junior was gifted in piano. Calvin was far more sociable than Junior. Calvin would play football in the street with us, but Junior would play piano chords for what seem like hours. Although we did not know it at the time, we were looking at two of the most outstanding musicians of the twentieth century. Calvin ended up playing with and developing music for Elvis Presley and other artists of that time. Phineas became acclaimed as one of the most prolific and innovative pianists of the twentieth century, rivaling such greats as Oscar Peterson, Art Tatum, and Earl Garner.

Phineas would have hailed as the most outstanding pianist of the twentieth century if drugs had not cut his life short. I am honored to call Calvin and Phineas friends of mine. And although we went into different callings, I respect them and hold them in high esteem for their accomplishments. I will speak later on the influence they had on my brief music career.

High school was a challenge not only socially but also academically, in that we were introduced to many subjects such as algebra, Latin, chemistry, and American and world history. There were many extracurricular activities that were of interest to us—sports, cheerleading, band, and book clubs, to name a few.

I had been rejected by Mr. Charles Tarpley, who judged me to be too small to play football, although my brother Weldon was not any larger than I was when he played in the 1940s. I think it had something to do with my having defeated his son, Augustus White, in the tristate boxing tournament. I won in our weight class and received the tristate tournament champion jacket, of which I was very proud.

Although Tarpley's rejection was disappointing and all my friends knew I could play and would make the team if given a chance, I recognized that I would not become an all-American quarterback and turned my interest to music, which proved to be a wise and rewarding decision. After attending band orientation by Mr. W. T. McDaniel, the historic band director of the south, I decided that trombone would be my instrument. I had the same enthusiasm for my new interest that I had for football in my short football career.

Arriving home that evening, my father asked me how high school was going. I told him about football and how disappointing it was to not be given a chance. Then I told him about joining the Booker T. Washington marching band, which was as popular in Memphis as the football team. My dad was always supportive of me in every endeavor and promised to take me to the store to buy me a new trombone. At the time, I did not know the difference in the quality of musical instruments, including horns. We went to the local Sears and Roebuck store, where we purchased a brand-new silver tone trombone made especially for Sears and Roebuck. I was very proud of my horn, and I promised myself I would become an outstanding trombonist.

Every serious endeavor requires dedication and discipline. These qualities, I like to think, were watchwords in anything I endeavored to do. Through hours of practice and sacrificing certain other things, I made the band in my first year, playing second trombone to Daniel Harvey, whom I greatly admired.

Only a few of us made the marching band the first year. This was one of the best decisions I could have made. My playing in the band again brought new friends who also shared the love of music. I learned much from Daniel Harvey, who was graduating and helped me become the lead trombonist in the marching band. Next to sports, it was the most popular endeavor for gaining girls' interest. This only made me want to get better and become a member of the former Booker Teasers, the high school orchestra, which played for such functions as local dances and other social activities.

My interest in the band did not make me forget about football, and I still played sandlot ball in my neighborhood and other local communities. One of the local coaches at Booker T., who lived in our neighborhood, watched as I passed a football forty yards and inquired why I had not come out for football. I told him I had come out, but Coach Tarpley had refused to let me have a tryout. Coach Fowlkes assured me that he was interested and thought I could help the team. This was really flattering to me, and part of me wanted to accept. I thought the solution would be to do both. But I had reached the level I'd been toward working to join the orchestra and did not want to forfeit this opportunity. I informed Coach Fowlkes, and he understood. At least I had been confirmed as a legitimate candidate for the team.

The second year in high school was very exciting, in that we were comfortable with our studies, and my music career was taking off in many ways. I enjoyed all my studies, but some subjects had more appeal than others. My favorite subjects were chemistry, history, and English. I did not apply myself as I should have, as many of the classes came easy to me. I was particularly interested in chemistry because Mr. Lowe (Poppa Lowe) encouraged me and told me I had potential to go into the sciences, perhaps medicine. This was very encouraging, and I continued to do well in chemistry, although I was not sure about that field; I was brought up in the church, and my grandfather had been a minister in

Mississippi for forty years. Although I felt drawn to work in the church, I had not decided on what my life's work would be. But I was sensitive to Poppa Lowe's suggestion about medicine.

Although I could have done better in my studies, I was involved in several areas of school life. I had joined the glee club, which fit in well with my love for music. My second year ended very well, even though I was not entirely satisfied with my grades.

Mr. W. T. McDaniel, Booker T.'s band director, was also very sought after by city officials. He had dominated music in the city, providing leadership for all high school bands in Memphis, especially during the spring Cotton Carnival. People would come from every section of the south. There were many parades down Main Street and the famous Beale Street. Because of his popularity, Mr. McDaniel was chosen by the city to direct the summer youth programs throughout the city. I was honored to be chosen by "Mr. Mac," as he was lovingly called, to be one of the recreational directors for the city and assigned to one of the city's several recreational centers. The assignment allowed me to deal with young people and exposed me to other parts of the city that we didn't frequent much during the school year. This led to new experiences and new friendships. As I look back on these years, I now recall how easy it was for me to make friends, both male and female. I don't know what special qualities I possessed.

I served two years as the recreational director for the Orange Mound Community Recreation Center. I can't say I was sorry to see the summer come to an end, even though I enjoyed the young people I worked with. They reminded me of when I was their age and the many questions they must have had about life.

As the summer came to a close, I looked forward to my junior year. I anticipated it with much excitement, since I had become very sure of myself and my abilities. Also, I looked forward to advancing my musical skills and hoped to be considered for the jazz ensemble and rock and roll group.

Classes began on September 3, and we all arrived at school early to compare our summers. Everybody had something very unusual to tell about what had happened to him or her or what hadn't happened.

Junior year proved to be the pivotal year for my growth and development. Classes we anticipated and the teachers made us become very interested in academics. Chemistry and history would become very important, arousing my curiosity. Mr. Lowe and Mr. Williams were my favorite teachers. I had great interest in civics, because the way government was supposed to operate was not what I had experienced during my seventeen years.

Not only was Memphis was a segregated city; in addition, Negroes had no say in how the government was run. Boss Crump, the self-appointed dictator of city affairs, had the cover of a sham government that did his bidding. Although his influence had dwindled over the years, his minions had learned the art of control and carried on within their small group of city leaders. Positions such as mayor, police chief and municipal judgeships were passed around at will. You only became a city official after you had paid your dues in loyalty and followed the orders of the city fathers. This was always perplexing to those of us who were civic-minded. We read that America was a democracy ruled by fair elections. Although there were two political parties, Democratic and Republican, Negroes were not represented in either in significant numbers and were not a factor in the nomination process. This made it difficult to have any major impact on city affairs, including budgetary decisions, therefore ensuring that Negroes received what white people wanted them to have.

We received tokens from the Democratic Party. One of the prize rewards was to allow Negroes to become policemen—a decision hailed by many Negroes but recognized by others as another means of controlling the Negroes in Memphis. Many of my friends were disgusted to learn that the eleven black policemen, appointed by the police chief, had limited powers. First, they were not allowed to carry guns, only batons to be used on Negroes. To many in my class, this was the biggest joke, except to later learn that they could only arrest Negroes. They could only "request" white people to remain until they could secure a white policeman. These officers became the laughing stock of the young people. Our elders reminded us that it takes time for things to change. In addition, we were still reminded to excel in all of our endeavors because we would have to be twice as good as our white counterparts to compete with them.

During this period of so-called progress, I was extremely proud of my father, who had almost single-handedly integrated the Memphis post office. I had always admired my father because he had an excellent vocabulary and spoke with authority. Several years before, my father challenged the Memphis post office and Mr. McKellar, the postmaster, to appoint black clerks in the main post office. My father was president of the Postal Alliance of Letter Carriers, a group formed to protect their rights as Negro postmen, as well as argue for better rights. When this challenge reached the postmaster, my father was called to answer. My father met with the postmaster and told him to his face that he would file a charge with the Fair Labor Practices Committee and the United States postmaster general to correct this practice. This sent shock waves through the Negro community in general and Negro postmen in particular. Although I was young, I could hear my uncle Hubert and Daddy arguing about the merits of his position. My uncle was one of those Negroes who thought that any progress Negroes made was "moving too fast" and we needed to "cool off." I remember Dr. Martin Luther King say, if Negroes cooled off any more, we would be in a "deep freeze."

My father proceeded with the mission; he defied his brothers in the National Association of Letter Carriers (NALC) and carried his challenge to Washington, DC, where he met with the deputy postmaster general. Having heard my father's case, the deputy postmaster sent an investigator, attorney John Risher, to Memphis to determine the merits of the charge. The interesting thing about this investigation was that Mr. Risher was a very "fair"-looking person who could not be distinguished from a white person, and he checked into the segregated Hotel Peabody. This is significant because the postmaster and other officials thought Mr. Risher was white and would be sympathetic to the segregated policies of the south. This would be especially true since the postmaster's brother was Senator Kenneth McKellar.

Files and records were made available to Mr. Risher, and news was carried by the local newspapers, *The Commercial Appeal* and the *Evening*

News Scimitar. There was excitement in the air because never before had anyone challenged segregation in the post office.

After several weeks, Mr. Risher returned to Washington to make his report. Within two weeks, the news came from Washington that the "Memphis post office is found in violation of the fair employment standard." This news was unbelievable. Never before had we won any challenge to segregation and discrimination.

My father was hailed a hero by many. But this acclaim did not seem to faze him. He went about his work the same way he always had and did not seek any publicity for what had been accomplished. To everybody's amazement, the members of Daddy's organization congratulated themselves about what they had achieved.

My father's standing in the community and my popularity at school gave me a new confidence that would carry over to my relationships with friends at Booker T. Washington and at other high schools. During my junior year, we began to organize as a class in preparation for our final year. Although I thought I possessed leadership potential, I had never thought much about running for any class office. However, others saw something that I had not seen, and that was my ability to bring friends together. When the time came to elect class officers, I was nominated for president, which came as a shock because I had other people in mind. To my surprise, I was elected by a significant majority. My recognition as a leader made me very proud. I would later look back on this event as important to my future decisions and life choices.

The remainder of my year was uneventful, in that I gave more attention to my studies with the knowledge that, in two years, I would continue my education at some college or university.

Most of my free time was spent playing for dances and weddings as part of the Melody Makers, the jazz ensemble that was popular throughout the city, as well as parts of Mississippi and Tennessee. The legendary Rufus Thomas, for whom we had occasionally played, began to use us more for engagements where he needed a small backup group. This was not only exciting but also very lucrative. Sometimes we would get paid as much as one hundred dollars a night. This may not seem like a large sum, but in 1953, this was exceptional. Some men with families did not make that in a week. Needless to say I was financially independent in my last years in high school, which was reflected in my unusually good dress for a high school student. The only boys who dressed as well were those who worked at Hotel Peabody as waiters and busboys in the restaurants.

Our junior year seemed to go by quickly, as we were fast approaching the end of our high school career. Some who were fortunate enough were being interviewed for scholarships for football, track, academics, and music. Besides Southern, historically black colleges and universities, many were being sought by large universities, such as Michigan and Ohio State. Because I had excelled in music, especially in the band and the glee club, I was eligible for scholarships in band and choral music. Although representatives came to the school for early commitments to their various schools, we had another year to decide which areas we wanted to pursue.

My attention again became centered on the religious and spiritual side of my life. I began to ask the questions all pilgrims have been asking through the ages. Who are we? Why are we here? Where do we go from here? This may sound like fairly deep questions for a sixteen or seventeen-year-old boy, whose only religious knowledge came from the Central Baptist Church Sunday school where my father served as an assistant pastor to Reverend Roy D. Morrison, whom I thought was one of the most intelligent and thoughtful pastors I had ever heard. Reverend Morrison was a graduate of Bishop College in Dallas, Texas, known for producing some of the most outstanding preachers in the south. I also became an avid listener of Reverend Billy Graham and the Crusades every Sunday afternoon at five. I was awed by Reverend Graham's ability to speak without notes for almost an hour, as well as by his extensive knowledge of the Bible. He could tell biblical stories like no one I'd ever heard. His preaching was different from most preachers in the Negro community. Most preachers, with few exceptions, depended on their voice and volume to arouse the crowd.

One day, when my cousin was visiting from the north, we went to a church. The minister was limited in content but had a strong voice, or should I say throat. When he reached the close of his sermon, which was called "coming home," he became almost entranced and would do what we called whooping (an intonation through the throat). This became the standard way for Baptist preachers to excite a crowd, and they were able to do so effectively.

As you can see, I was exposed to a wide range of theological thought and homiletical practices. Although I questioned how this would be helpful to anyone on a search for eternal truth, it helped me immensely to understand that religious thought takes on many forms and practices. My ability to synthesize these different approaches to religion was very helpful. I never looked down on any manifestation of religion.

In fact, I found one expression very fascinating and exciting. There was one denomination in our community, which most people frowned upon, called the Church of God in Christ. This church was known as the sanctified church. Its practitioners believed in the power of the Holy Spirit and its gifts, especially the gift of tongues, a requisite since in the book of Acts. The people, who were there on the day of Pentecost, spoke in unknown tongues, evidence of the Holy Ghost and a requisite for becoming a saint as they called themselves. They lived simple lives, reflected in their plain appearance—no makeup, no jewelry—and an obvious piety that was always evident.

One of my best friends was J. O. Patterson Jr. ("Teeter," as we called him). Teeter's grandfather, Presiding Bishop Charles Harrison Mason, was founder of the Church of God in Christ, which made him very interesting to me. Because of my relationship with his grandson, I would see him in their house in his big chair. He had an unbelievable countenance that reminded you of the bearded prophets of old. Although members of the church lived very simply, the Mason and Patterson families lived very well, as their members would have them live. Teeter's father, J. O. Patterson, was a bishop in the church, having been named by Bishop Mason. Needless to say, he was the heir apparent to his father-in-law's church. My relationship with his grandson would have a profound impact on my future work.

Teeter's father owned a funeral home, and in order to use one his father's Cadillacs, we would have to play on Sunday nights between eight and nine during the radio broadcast at the Pentecostal Temple. Teeter played saxophone, and I played my trombone. We also had another friend, Sam Fletcher, who had the most melodious voice I had ever heard. Although the service would last beyond nine, the three of us were allowed to leave, along with Alonzo Mayfield, who was also a good friend and member of the Pentecostal temple. We would head directly to the liquor store before going to a local nightclub, where the music started at nine.

It was against the rule of the club to bring in liquor, but since our funds were low, we could not pay for the cover charge and have something for our young ladies to drink. This was the highlight of the week—meeting our girlfriends at the Flamingo Club. One of the outstanding artists of the evening was Calvin Newborn, outstanding guitarist and brother of Phineas Newborn, who was being hailed as the equal to Errol Garner, Oscar Peterson, and George Shearing. These were some of the best days of my high school career. Everything was going great. My studies were going well, and my music career was expanding, in that I had engagements with my friend Al Jackson's father's band. I did not have a steady girlfriend because I did not like the commitment that would carry. A steady girlfriend would mean visitations, going out weekly, and other things that would interfere with my music engagements and studies.

My father gave much privilege to me when it came to my time, and I did not want him to know what I was really doing. One Sunday night, after following our usual Sunday schedule, I arrived home after twelve. My father asked me where I had been. Instead of telling him what I'd been doing, I just told him that Teeter, Mayfield, and I had been driving around the city visiting girls. He asked me what else I had been doing, to which I answered, "Nothing."

He said in a solemn voice, "Son, don't lie to me. I know where you have been."

My mind ran through the possibilities of how he would know, and I could not figure it out.

Finally he said, "You were at the Pentecostal Temple at eight thirty when Bishop Patterson said he had his son there tonight, with friend Carl Veazey on trombone."

I hadn't mentioned that I'd been playing at Pentecostal Temple because I didn't know how my father felt about playing that kind of music in church. I should not have been surprised that it did not faze him at all because, as I knew, he was a very liberal and progressive man, even in religion.

The rest of the school year passed very smoothly, and my classmates and I began to think about the summer before our final year. In April 1953, I wrote my brother Erwin and his wife Marie to ask them if I could come to Chicago to work doing the summer. Although I had not been around my big brother much, he always supported me in everything I did. Erwin and Marie said it would be fine but added that I should make sure Mother and Dad knew of my plans.

I needed to get approval from my father, because Mother would always ask me if I had spoken to my father about my plans. Sundays were when Daddy and I spent time together. Every Sunday, he would listen to the famous commentators like Gabriel Heatter and Drew Pearson for up-to-date news on what was happening in the country and the world. It was May, a month before school would be over for the year, so I thought this would be the time to tell him. I sat on the floor beside his big chair and calmly said to him, "Daddy, I think I will go to Chicago this summer to live with Erwin and Marie and work."

He replied calmly, "If you start walking now, you may get there by June."

I broke out in the loudest laughter because I found his response so very funny. I hadn't asked him because I needed money; I had money from my music engagements during the year.

Of course his real answer was yes. He thought it was a good idea, as I needed to be exposed to a large city. He also thought it would be good for me to spend time with my big brother, since I hadn't really been around him much since the end of World War II in 1942.

The rest of the school year was spent preparing for final exams and making plans for my independent life in Chicago. I was very excited because I had many aunts, uncles, and cousins in Chicago who'd followed the great migration of the 1930s to the north for a better life and jobs that paid far more than they were being paid on farms in Mississippi, Alabama, Louisiana, and Arkansas. Many of the migrators relocated to Chicago, Saint Louis, Milwaukee, Detroit, and even New York City.

My final year was spent taking finals and socializing with friend at parties over the weekends. Our prom was the highlight of the school year. We dressed formally and escorted our girlfriends to the dance of the year. I had a very serious problem during this period, since I had been friendly with several girls during the school year. I did not want to hurt any of their feelings. So I somehow came down with a late spring flu, which lasted until prom was over. This was not a big problem because there were guys who did not have anyone to take, which meant there were girls available.

The final day of school, on June 3, was a time of rejoicing. Now we were officially seniors at Booker T. Washington High. We said our goodbyes and promised to stay in touch with each other during the summer. I would miss my summer job at the recreation center. However, it would not compare with what I had ahead going to Chicago on my own and having a real job in the big city.

On June 7, 1953, my uncle Hubert arrived at the house to take me to Central Station, where I would board the City of New Orleans train that would take me to Chicago. I was familiar with this train, as several years before my mother had taken me there to visit her sister and my siblings. It was different this time, though. I was going alone with a big mission, my first job in the big city.

Many people don't know there was a ritual around traveling during the days of segregation. Everybody had to prepare food for at least twelve hours on the train, as you were not allowed in the dining car, not even to carry out. Therefore we had to prepare food, water, and any other items we might need for overnight travel to Chicago. My mother prepared for me the best food one could desire. My menu consisted of fried chicken, cured ham, green beans, potato salad in an insulated container, and biscuits.

The City of New Orleans left Memphis at 7:05 p.m. and arrived in Chicago at 8:30 a.m. the next day. As you may suspect, leaving home alone for the first time was a momentous event, which required saying goodbye to everyone on the street, with details of my trip. Uncle Hubert arrived at promptly 5:00 p.m., and my parents were prepared to go with their youngest child to the station at 5:30. When we arrived at the station, my father secured a redcap to take my suitcase to the waiting room. Uncle Hubert parked the car and joined us in the waiting room, where I received advice about the do and don'ts on the train and in the city. Daddy had arranged for the redcap to come back at 6:15 p.m. to take us to the track for boarding. He arrived at the exact time and took us to the track to board.

Even then, segregation was evident in boarding the train, since whites had to board first. This required the services of all the redcaps. We waited patiently on the track for the redcap to return. Nervously, I kept looking at my watch to see what time it was and wondering whether we would make it.

Finally, the redcap returned to board me. My father had to board with me, per my mother's instructions, to make sure I was seated properly. This may sound like being overprotective. But in those days, parents wanted to make sure that their children were safe, even though I had celebrated my seventeenth birthday and had traveled with the bands under much direr circumstances. However, it does not matter how old you are; it is a good feeling to know that your parents care about you.

I had been seated about ten minutes when the conductor called out, "All aboard." It was kind of funny to me, because if you were not aboard, you would not be getting aboard. Just an observation!

Seconds later, the train moved slowly, allowing my parents and uncle to wave goodbye a final time, which was comforting and loving.

As I looked at my surroundings, I saw several teenagers on the train who I could tell were riding for the first time. I looked at the overhead luggage rack and could see evidence of the tradition I described—food had been prepared and put in shoeboxes. Mother told me to wait until we crossed the Ohio River before eating food, since I had already eaten before leaving home.

As the train pulled out of the station and headed to Millington, Tennessee, our first and the last stop we made in Tennessee, I knew we were on our way. I tried reading the newspaper, but my curiosity kept me watching people and their reactions to the trip. I knew most of the early stops since my mother had taken me to Chicago several years before. After leaving Millington, we would head toward Alabama and then toward Ohio. As soon as we left the first stop in Alabama, people in our car started reaching for their shoeboxes. This happened with such military precision that I wondered whether this had been planned. Later, I would learn it was a tradition to start eating as soon as we reached Alabama.

I thought in a humorous way that maybe the others had been told not to eat in Tennessee and that only when they reached Alabama were they allowed to eat. I instantly followed my elders on the train and took my shoebox down. A thought occurred to me. *If I eat now, I may not have food when we reach Ohio.* This thought was instantly replaced by another thought. *Maybe I would not live to get to Ohio.* I was just hungry!

However, I did not have to worry because my mother had packed enough for two people. She'd always taught me to share. Someone on the train may not have anything to eat, and I should share with them. However, as I looked around, I could see there was no one without food. And no one would starve, given the excess fat my fellow passengers carried. Although this thought was funny, it occurred to me because I was a slender 127 pounds; I might be able to use some extra fat on me, just in case. We all opened our boxes, and there was silence in the car, except for the smacking of lips enjoying our food.

My mother was the best cook ever until this day. She could fry chicken and fix potato salad like no one in the whole wide world. I could only eat half of what she'd packed, so I closed my shoebox until I got to the Ohio River. Although I disobeyed her original instructions, I did wait until we reached the Ohio River crossing to open my box again.

At about ten o'clock, the train lights were turned off, except for the emergency lights used to go to the toilet. Though most of the people in the car were asleep—with exception of the few having quiet conversations and babies waking up to be fed—I tried reading the papers and one of the books I'd brought about the world war. The subject had always fascinated me because I thought about my brothers fighting in the war. I was disappointed as well as relieved to find out that neither brother saw combat. Erwin was stationed in Camp Shanks, New York, for the duration of the war, and Weldon was drafted near the end of the war and spent most of his time in the Philippines.

Even so, I was intrigued by how one man, Adolph Hitler, could cause such destruction in the world and cause a whole world to be engaged in a war. I learned a lot about how the Jewish people were persecuted by the German people and their leader Adolph Hitler, who sent millions to the gas chambers in order to eradicate them from his country and the world. I was also saddened to find out that the Western world had stood by during this awful tragedy, thinking that the business of Germany was not their business, until the attack on our own country, when the Japanese bombed Pearl Harbor on December 7, 1941. Franklin Delano Roosevelt was president when war was declared on Japan, which was long overdue from my perspective many years later.

Needless to say, I never went to sleep, partly because I was too curious and too scared; we would be crossing the Ohio River with only a single rail each way without any supporting guards on either side. Around two o'clock in the morning, the conductor came through, announcing that we were about to cross the mighty Ohio River.

My appetite came back as soon as we finished the treacherous journey across the river. Those who were awake called the name of Jesus so many times it began to make me nervous. The danger of crossing the Ohio River and what could happen if God did not protect the train and it passengers became legendary.

Shortly, we were in Kankakee, Illinois. Everybody knew where the Kankakee State Hospital for the insane was located. The place had its own curiosity. I also thought it a strange name for a mental institution and wondered if the people who named it also had mental problems.

After leaving Kankakee we arrived in Champaign, Illinois, home to the University of Illinois, about which I had heard so much. Although it was still dark, I imagined how wonderful it would be to go to college there.

After leaving Champaign, I finally fell asleep and awoke to the lights in our car around six in the morning, the conductor announcing that we would arrive in Chicago in one hour. People in our car began to repack suitcases they had gone into during the night. As we approached the suburbs of Chicago, the train began to slow down, and I was amazed at how many houses there were, not having even reached Chicago.

Finally, the conductor announced our approach to the Chicago Twelfth Street station, where our trip would end. Instructions on safely leaving the train and directions on how to reach the main stations to meet our friends and relatives were given.

As we left the train, I followed the crowd, assuming that my fellow passengers evidently knew where to go.

Finally, we reached the entrance to the station, where relatives and friends had gathered to greet us. Before I knew it, Marie and Erwin were welcoming me to Chicago with hugs and kisses and words about how good it was to see me. Words cannot express how good I felt to see them and feel the love that was evident in their presence. Erwin instructed Marie to bring me to the Twelfth Street side of the station, where he would be waiting. Although I had not been around my sister-in-law much, she was so warm and caring that I instantly became attached to her. When we reached Twelfth Street, Erwin was there with his car.

The route to his house is indelibly printed in my mind. Years later, I would always find my way home by going to Roosevelt Road or Twelfth Street. We arrived shortly at 1242 Albany Avenue and Erwin and Marie's second-floor apartment. My uncle Thurman owned the building and rented the apartment to my brother. For the first time, I had my own spacious room. Growing up, I'd shared a bedroom with Melvin. This was wonderful; I could stretch out across the bed without interfering with anyone.

The next morning, my sister-in law prepared a wonderful breakfast. This was not unusual; most women from the south could cook and cook well. After breakfast, we talked about what I wanted to do during the summer and how to conduct myself in Chicago, since this was a big city, unlike Memphis in many ways. Although my mother had brought me to Chicago many years ago when I was young, Erwin and Marie realized that I needed to understand that I was much older and had to take on new responsibilities in the big city. They asked me what I wanted to do during the summer.

I immediately replied, "I want to work," which pleased them very much.

My brother asked me what I wanted to do for work, to which I replied, "Anything to make money."

He admonished me not to say that to anybody, as there were many ways to make money in Chicago that might not be the best way for me to work. After further explanation, I understood that some work was different in Chicago. We finally agreed that, the next day, he would drive me around the neighborhood to familiarize me with my surroundings. We lived on the West Side of Chicago at 1242 Albany, right off Roosevelt Road and across from Douglas Park, one of the largest parks in Chicago.

Uncle Thurman was one of my mother's younger brothers. My mother was the oldest of thirteen children, and all of her siblings gave her great respect. Uncle Thurman came to Chicago right after he got out of the army. He had a very good job driving delegated trains, which everyone called the elevated train.

The next day, Erwin woke me up early and drove me around the community to show me where to catch the bus to go downtown and how to get on the elevated train, which was a fascinating adventure. We also went to Douglas Park. There, he showed me the tennis courts, since he knew I was an avid tennis player. His brother-in-law was a semipro tennis player. I was very happy to know I knew someone who was an excellent tennis player and who taught young people in the park.

We drove down Roosevelt Road and turned on Keddie Avenue. Erwin explained this was a business district that was purportedly owned by Jews who had many pawnshops; the Negroes, often short on funds before their next paycheck, would pawn their radios, watches, or other valuables to make it to the next payday. He also told me my brother Weldon lived on the South Side of Chicago and that he would take me over there during the weekend.

When we returned home, Erwin gave me a list of businesses, grocery stores, restaurants, and the Woolworth on Roosevelt Road where I could possibly get employment.

The next morning, after eating Marie's deliciously prepared breakfast, I started out on my new adventure in the big city of Chicago. One of the first things I had to adjust to was not speaking to everybody. As I walked down the street and passed people, I would say good morning, and they would give me puzzled expressions, looking at other people I may have been speaking to. Perhaps they had reason to suspect me, because I'm sure I had that confused country boy look on my face.

After inquiring at several stores and restaurants with no success, I came across a restaurant called Carl's Hot Corn Beef. Since it had my name on it, I thought that might be a good sign. As I entered, the store the manager almost ran to meet me and inform me that they did not serve Negroes. Although Chicago was the North and I'd heard there was no segregation there, this was not true of Carl's restaurant on Roosevelt Road.

After several more hours of unsuccessful job searches, I decided I would try one more store, the Woolworth five-and-dime store, since I was familiar with that one in Memphis. I must have been inspired because, sure enough, there was a help wanted sign in the window. The sign did not say what kind of help was needed, but I was definitely going to find out.

As I walked in the door, I asked security the location of the manager's office. I was directed to the second floor, in the back. After finding the office, I walked in with confidence, head held high and speaking clearly, like my father had taught me. The gentleman sitting at the desk did not immediately look up, so I said very matter-of-factly, "Sir, I saw your sign in the window, and I am here to apply for the job."

After a few questions like, "What's your name?" and, "Where do you live?" I told him I was from Memphis, Tennessee; that I was living with my brother for the summer; and that I was here to work and make money before returning to school this fall.

He immediately asked the question that my dad had prepared me for: "What kind of work do you want to do and are you willing to work overtime?"

My answer was, "I am prepared to do anything that is honest work, and I'm definitely willing to work overtime, since my time is limited until August 30."

He seemed impressed with my response and asked me to follow him back to the first floor in the rear where the dish room was. When he opened the door, I saw dishes stacked almost to the ceiling. He looked at me expecting a negative reaction, which I did not give him.

His next question was very direct. "Do you want the job?"

To this, I answered an emphatic yes!

He did not realize my father had already lectured me about work. He'd advised me that, when you go on a job, regardless of how difficult it may seem, you should remember that you can only work eight hours or overtime. In other words, don't look at how difficult the work may be. Just give your very best during the time you are working.

The manager explained that several persons had quit because it was too much work, and they seem never to catch up.

We returned to his office, where he spelled out the details of the job and had me fill out an application. He explained my days would be Monday through Friday from eight to five daily, with one hour for lunch, and my pay would be $1.25 an hour. We would be paid every two weeks, and taxes would be taken out of my check. This did not bother me. I had read that the Internal Revenue Service did not charge taxes unless you made over $2,500 during the year, so I would have a refund at the end of my summer job.

I could hardly wait to get back to tell my brother and Marie how my day had gone and how I had found a job not far from the house. When I returned to Erwin's house, people were out front talking, eating, and having fun. On seeing Aunt Minnie and other relatives, I simply spoke and headed to the second floor to tell my brother and Marie I had found a job and would be starting tomorrow at eight o'clock sharp. For those who are not acquainted with the word sharp as it relates to time, it means not one minute after eight o'clock.

My brother was very proud of my independence and my ability to find a job the first day. After I'd told them the story of how I'd found the job and the conversation I'd had with the manager, my brother teased me, asking whether I'd acted like an "Uncle Tom" to get the job. I explained that the dish room was filled with dishes, seemingly from days of not being washed, which was a challenge. Mr. Swartz, the manager, had explained that three people had quit because of the amount of work required to catch up.

After a few more minutes, Marie called me to a dinner that was absolutely delicious. After dinner, we talked about what we would do on the weekend. First we had to visit our relatives, who were scattered around Chicago—Aunt Fannie and Uncle Roosevelt; my cousins Velma, Gwendolyn, Scope, Warner, and Donald; and their children. It would take a few weeks to visit them all.

The next morning, I got up at six o'clock to shower and was on my way at seven. Erwin had to retrieve mail for his route from his post office substation and offered me a ride, since he was going my direction. I declined the offer. I wanted to familiarize myself with the area and observe places and stores as I walked the five blocks to the F. W. Woolworth five-and-dime. Roosevelt Road was the longest road in Chicago, running from the western suburbs all the way to downtown Chicago, where Union Station was located. The West Side of Chicago had everything imaginable, including many restaurants with every culture represented—Italian, Greek, Jewish, Polish, Chinese, Japanese, and countless others I couldn't recognize.

People walked very rapidly and with purpose in Chicago. Southerners were known to stroll along, maybe because, when we got to our jobs, we knew there was a lot of work waiting, and we needed to take our time getting there.

I was also impressed with how the Chicagoans spoke—their proper tones suggesting sophistication and intelligence. When relatives came home for visits, we would notice that they spoke differently than they had before they'd left Memphis or Mississippi. We called "putting on." What was really fun was that though they talked "proper," their grammar betrayed their sophistication.

As I approached Woolworth, people were rushing to get into the store and not be late for work. Our store opened promptly at nine in the morning, and anyone late would be docked an hour's pay, which I did not understand. On my arrival, I reported directly to Mr. Swartz and received a Woolworth badge that I wore with pride; it showed my achievement of having secured my first job in Chicago.

Mr. Swartz walked me to the dish room and asked if I had any questions. He had already told me how to work the commercial dishwasher, which I thought was an absolutely marvelous invention. I had to clean each piece of food from a dish before placing it on the rack to be washed. The timing of the dishwasher was set so I could send the dishes through and had to go to the other end to remove them from the dryer.

After about an hour, I realized that some before me had quit because you really needed two people to do this job. Rushing to the other side was challenging, and keeping up with the cycle required physical skills.

Shortly thereafter, I mastered the timing, and dishes were washed and dried at a very fast clip.

My responsibilities also included keeping the concession stands supplied with staples. At the close of the day, I could see the progress I had made in reducing the number of unwashed dishes, which gave me satisfaction.

Mr. Swartz came by around four o'clock to check on my work and was very pleased with my progress. At the end of the first day, I felt tired but satisfied with what I had accomplished and with Mr. Swartz's approval. I left the store a little after five to walk the five blocks to my brother's house. This time, I did not saunter but walked like the Chicagoans, fast and with purpose; I was tired and hungry, and I knew that Marie would have a good and tasty dinner prepared. I was always surprised at her energy because she taught elementary school.

After dinner, we sat in the living room and reflected on our day. This would become common practice during my stay with Erwin and Marie during the summer. We all retired to bed at a decent hour because our day began at six in the morning in order to get to work on time.

The week past uneventfully, and by Friday, the battle of the dishes had been won. What a relief it was to be all caught up and know that I could breathe a little easier, although I had to work just as hard to keep up.

My relationship with my coworkers was very good. After conversations, we found that we had a lot in common. We all came from the Deep South, Alabama, Mississippi, Arkansas, and Tennessee. We talked about how things were back home and how much freedom and money we had now, which was a fortune to some of us. In the South, we could chop cotton for four dollars a day; or we could pick cotton all day for as little as three dollars and as much as twelve dollars a day. In Chicago, on the average job, we could make from ten dollars to as much as thirty dollars a day with overtime. This is difficult to understand, but considering the times, that was considered fair wages by a segregated, prejudiced, and repressive South.

If you're familiar with the Civil War, you know that one of the reasons it occurred was economics. The South had the advantage of free labor that the North did not have, and this fueled the Civil War.

Let me say that President Abraham Lincoln stated that his decision to free the slaves was also a decision to save the Union due to the enmity that had developed between the North and the South. One would be naive to think that the North was the Promised Land for Negroes. There was still subtle prejudice and, sometimes, open discrimination in many parts of Chicago (like that described in my job search). Potential employers discriminated with impunity because many of the city laws were not enforced.

At the end of the week, Mr. Swartz informed me I would not have to come in on Saturday, since I had the dish room caught up. The next week would be exciting; on Friday, I would receive my first check. Although I was grateful for the job and the pay, it was not just the money I appreciated. This was the first job I'd worked in a large city, an experience in itself. The money at the entry level was commensurate with what I'd made in Memphis at the recreational department during the summer. The independence and work experience in Chicago was invaluable.

My weekends were filled with endless visits to my many cousins and their families. They lived all over Chicago but mainly on the South Side, where Negroes lived in abundance. The Negroes who lived on the West Side were thought to be more affluent because the flats, or apartments as they were called, were much nicer than those on the South Side. However, I liked the South Side better and felt much more at home. Elsewhere, I was around many white people and the South Side reminded me of the South in general and Memphis in particular.

All of my relatives were doing well, with good-paying jobs. Although they lived in apartments, for the most part, they all aspired to own a flat or apartment building like my uncle Thurman and aunt Fannie, the most affluent relatives we had in Chicago. My relatives were loving and warm, and took me around Chicago to see such sites as the State and Madison intersection, which was the busiest corner in the loop. On the South Side, my brother took me to Sixty-Third and Cottage Grove. If you were looking for someone from the South, you would go there and wait. They would either appear or someone who knew them would tell you where they lived.

I spent many Saturdays and Sundays going to the great Chicago Theater, the first integrated movie theater I had ever attended. I could hardly watch the movie for watching some black and white young people kissing right in the open theater. This was just the beginning of my discoveries about race relations. We also visited Navy Pier, a landmark in Chicago. Riverview, in Chicago, was one of the largest amusement parks in the country and served Chicago and all surrounding suburban towns. I was more than happy when Weldon and his wife, Eddie Lee, asked me to go with them to Riverview. These were things that remain with me after over sixty-four years.

The best ride in the park was called the Parachute. While we were seated and belted, we ascended 150 feet in the air and, after reaching the maximum height, were dropped into a free fall for about 50 feet, when some gadget locked in, allowing us to descend slowly to the ground.

I was grateful for my brother spending time with me and for getting away from my neighborhood on the weekend. On Sundays, we would have a sumptuous dinner of baked chicken, corn bread dressing, green peas, mashed potatoes, and pound cake and ice cream. After dinner, I would go outside to Douglas Park's tennis courts to play or just watch my sister-in-law's brother, Arthur Jr., beat all the white guys he played. Arthur, now the best player in Memphis, had played tennis since he was an adolescent living next door to Lemoyne College's tennis court. Much of my better tennis playing was due to Arthur's tutoring.

We retired early on Sunday, with me looking forward to the coming week because, on Friday, I would get my first check. I was anxious to get it. In the meantime, I had tried to keep up with my hours and how much I would receive.

I woke well rested. I was ready to meet my coworkers, find out what they had done on the weekend, and report back on my activities with my brother and how many guys I had beaten on the tennis court. My coworkers also taught me a lot about Chicago life and where I should go on the South Side.

The week passed very quickly, as I had mastered the art of dishwashing and stacking dishes. I also was able to take a break, with Mr. Swartz's approval since he knew I would get my work done.

Friday finally arrived, and I was told that a person would deliver our checks. Around four o'clock, a slender man came to the dish room and asked if I was Carlton W. Veazey. His inclusion of my middle initial amused me.

I answered, "Yes," and he handed me a white envelope.

I opened the envelope quickly to a check that read, "Pay to Carlton W. Veazey." The amount of $146.50 was for two weeks work, including ten hours of overtime after taxes. My regular pay was $95, unless Mr. Swartz asked me to work overtime.

After leaving work, I followed some of my coworkers to the currency exchange to cash my big check. I had decided I would send my mother $15 and give Marie $15, even though both had insisted I not give them anything; my father had instructed me to do so before I'd left home. I did not mind sending the money home or giving some to my sister-in-law. I still had $116 to last me for the next two weeks.

I was amazed how excited I was about this check because, when I played with Rufus or our jazz group, we made almost this much in one night and without taxes (I don't know whether it was legal). The difference was I was in Chicago, working for an established corporation and drawing an official check. However, it did remind me that many men and women were raising families on this amount of money, when I did not have any fixed expenses and my cousins; aunts and uncles; and, of course, brothers paid for everything when we went out.

Although Marie and Erwin took the money reluctantly, knowing I was contributing something to the household made me feel good. Also, my sister-in-law had been so kind and encouraging; I wanted to do something tangible to let her know how much I appreciated her concern and help.

The days and weeks passed with many family reunions and outings. This was great because I had not seen some of my relatives since I was a child. They reminded me of that fact by telling me how bad I was a child; of course, much of this was exaggeration, as some of them were no older than me.

My social life was not that great. The girls I met were older, which made getting to know them difficult. Despite this, the girls thought I was an extrovert since I had so many friends. I always pushed myself to be outgoing because my father was so gregarious and open to people, and I wanted to be like him. This shows you that a child is greatly influenced by his or her parents, even by things that aren't verbally communicated.

However, there was one girl who lived next door to us on Albany named Sarah Lawhorn who was so beautiful and outgoing that I wanted to talk to her and take her to the movies or somewhere. I enjoyed talking to her, and she would get to tennis with me sometimes. It became obvious to me that her interest in me was not there when I found out that she was interested my cousin Donald Lenoir, my aunt Fannie's son who was a star football player at Crane High School in Chicago. After learning this, I made up my mind; I would just wait until I returned to Memphis, where the girls I knew would appreciate me. Although I knew Sarah was not attracted to me, to this day, I daydream about what would have happened if we had connected. As I look back over my eighty years, I know now this will not be the only disappointment I would have in relationships or in life.

The summer had passed so quickly that I suddenly realized I had only two weeks to work before I returned to Memphis, with much knowledge about the world through Chicago. I had learned that Negroes had really done well and were much more prosperous and happy up North than they were in the segregated and depressing South. They had far better living conditions than they ever had in the South. The difference between pay in the North and the South was like night and day, although the Northern employers took advantage of Negroes, knowing they would work harder for less, considering how little they were paid in the South.

During my last two weeks, I had mixed emotions. I had really become a Chicagoan, with all that came with it—good jobs, places to go, and things to do besides church and dances. One does not fully recognize what he or she does not have until exposure to greater things.

Although these feelings were prevalent, there was something to be said for the comfort of the familiar. The reason many people do not progress is because of the need to remain with what is familiar. Nonetheless, I was simply homesick and missing my friends, especially my girlfriends. At the seasoned age of seventeen, I suppose this was natural.

Before I knew it, the final week of work arrived. Friday, my last day, Mr. Swartz called me into his office to give me my last paycheck, along with a letter he wanted me to have. I knew what was in the pay envelope but was inquisitive about the contents of the other envelope. I asked him if I could open it, and he responded, "Yes."

I immediately tore the envelope open and began to read the most beautiful letter I had ever received. It was the first time I'd had someone compliment me on the work I had done and the way I had carried myself. This is hard for an eighty-year-old man to say, but it came from a white man. This is important because, growing up in the South and seeing so much racial discrimination and outright hatred by white people, I found it very encouraging—a white man had taken the time to encourage a young black boy who had his first job in the big city not only about his work but also about his character. I counted my summer in Chicago a success not only because I had found a job but also because I had bonded with so many of my relatives and gained a greater sense of what family meant.

On Sunday, August 27, I was scheduled to leave Chicago for Memphis at eight in the evening. There, I would to resume my old life but with a Chicago perspective. Marie fixed the best breakfast that morning, and I fortified myself with food, even knowing that I would have a shoebox to take with me.

During the day, I hung out with my cousin Donald, who was always a lot of fun. He was older and spoke of the gang he belonged to, the things they did, and fighting other gangs in Chicago. There was embellishment in his story.

After we returned that afternoon, my sister was busy preparing my shoebox, which smelled so good I did not want to wait for the Ohio River crossing. We left home around five thirty because Negroes were frightened to miss their train. It was like the world would come to an end. Of course, it never did!

When we arrived at the Twelfth Street station, also known as Roosevelt Road, my brother took charge of the suitcases, and Marie and I proceeded to the waiting room. I knew I had only brought two bags to

Chicago, but while the the my bags were being loaded, I noticed there were three, the third a beautiful leather bag. When I enquired why there were three, Marie told me it contained some things I could use during the school year, and the luggage was a gift from them. That was the first time I had owned any luggage, which I thought was for people with lots of money. Maybe my sister-in-law and brother also had lots of money.

I discovered later in the luggage all types of clothes—pants, sweaters, shirts, underwear, socks, and even a cap with Chicago engraved on it. During the few minutes left of my time with Erwin and Marie, I thanked them profusely for their kindness and caring, especially Marie, who had been just like a big sister to me during the summer. Of course, Erwin, my big brother, knew how much I loved and respected him; he had always made sure I had everything any another kid in the neighborhood had.

Finally, just before they left the train, after the conductor called out that we would be leaving in two minutes, Marie handed me an envelope, kissed me, and said to open it after the train left. As you may guess, the train had not reached cruising speed before I opened Marie's letter to find the most unexpected gift, along with a one-hundred-dollar bill and a beautiful letter telling me how much they'd enjoyed having me during the summer and hoped I would return next year. In her letter she said she had saved all the money I had given her during the summer and an extra ten dollars to give me a new hundred-dollar-bill. I will always remember Erwin and my sister-in-law who was really my sister for the many kindnesses they showed me the summer of 1957.

I focused on the outside, as it was late summer and still light. The scenery was beautiful as we passed through the suburbs of Chicago, which looked like the towns I had seen on television. While traveling by train, I always imagined what kind of people lived in the houses we passed, what kind of lives they led, and what their children were like. This was my way of passing the time and also a way of exercising my imagination, which I used often. This was before television was introduced, and we relied solely on radio, which required us to create the images of what we were hearing about in our minds.

After a period of time, I decided to return to earth and do what earthlings do—eat some good Southern cooking prepared by my sister

Marie that was in my shoebox above my seat. I don't know whose shoes had previously been in that box, but I was glad whoever it was had big feet, because there was so much food in it. Marie had packed the best fried chicken, which looked like a whole chicken; baked ham; and even a fried pork chop, which was her specialty, plus some delicious bread pudding. Needless to say, I gained at least five pounds during my twelve-hour odyssey.

I dropped off to sleep after dinner and remained in slumber land until the conductor and porter announced we would be crossing the great Ohio River in twenty minutes. I did not realize I had slept for almost five hours. It was almost one o'clock in the morning. I knew this because the conductor announced it was one forty-five in the morning. The river crossing also meant we were halfway to Memphis, which meant I would see my mother, father, Melvin, and Gerry. My sister had recently married and was living in Memphis with her husband, George.

Seemingly, the train travelled slower than ever for the next six hours. Erwin had purchased the *Chicago Tribune* for me to read, to encourage my reading habits. However, he did had no knowledge that I had begun reading *Varieties of Religious Experiences* by William James, given my serious interest in religion and theology.

After an hour or so, I again fell asleep and did not awake until the conductor announced we were nearing Millington, Tennessee, the last stop before the great Memphis, Tennessee, on the bluff of the Mississippi River, the second longest river in the United States.

Everybody on the train seemed to have an alarm clock. You could hear people stretch and moan as they awakened to a new day and almost home. When we pulled into union station in Memphis, there went up a cheer, celebrating our return from the North and Chicago, Illinois.

When we got off the train to the waiting crowds of people, it was the most remarkable scene I had ever witnessed. People were hugging and kissing each other and slapping one another on the back with excitement and obvious love and affection. You would have thought we had returned from Europe or some other foreign lands. Naturally, my parents and family were there to meet me.

I was so happy to see my mother and father and Melvin, but I was especially glad to see my mother. Uncle Hubert was there to take my luggage and me to the car and to our home on Alston Street. It was beginning to get dark by the time I arrived home, which meant not too many people were outside.

One person out on the front porch was Mr. Marion, whom I had adopted as my godfather since I was four or five years old. I always liked to go his house next door and sit on his porch with him. My father was kept busy trying to help Negroes who were being discriminated against and could not afford a lawyer. He would write letters for them defending their rights and attempting to get justice for them. Mr. Marion was not a formally educated man, but he was one of the most loving and caring persons I had ever known. My mother would allow him, when I was only four years old, to take me walking around the neighborhood, during which time he would talk with me and explain to me what was right and what was wrong. This may sound very elementary to some, but my days with Mr. Marion were some of the best days I remember in my childhood.

After a good night's sleep in my own bed and waking up in my house with the smell of bacon, sausage, grits, and coffee, I knew I was home and so glad to be home.

When I got up Monday morning, my father had left for his postal route. Mother had my plate set at the table and looked as beautiful to me as ever as I walked in the kitchen smiling and reaching out to hug and kiss her. Melvin was already at the table waiting for me to come.

Melvin, my older brother, was what we today call a special person, in that he required special attention because, when he was born, during delivery, the doctor used forceps to deliver him, causing brain damage. The injury to his brain manifested itself in my brother having limited brain function that did not allow him to attend regular public schools. My parents tried valiantly to find a school where he could progress. This was in the late 1920s, when special education was almost unheard of and nonexistent for Negroes. However, my parents were very progressive. They made a decision that we would educate Melvin, and I mean all of us. Melvin would be considered "challenged" today; back then was referred to as "retarded." It is such a blessing that the word *retarded* has been eliminated from the current lexicon. Melvin was a blessing to all of us in the love he always exhibited to everybody, especially his family.

Because of his condition, I grew up with a special feeling for people who were physically or mentally challenged.

One of the best things Mother and Daddy taught us was that we were not to treat our brother any differently than anybody else. The reason was that he was not any different from anyone else. This lesson has gone with me throughout my life, and it has been a blessing. Treating those who are challenged the same as you treat everyone else shows respect for them, rather than giving them the feeling that they are different and not like us.

Melvin stayed around me all day, asking me questions about Chicago and telling me what had happened on Alston Street since I left. Melvin was well liked by all my friends, and I did not have to worry about anybody mistreating him or making fun of him. Everybody on Alston Street had adopted him as a big brother or as part of the family.

I had only one week before I would go back to school, which I was looking forward to. I had something very special to tell my classmates about my experiences in the North. During the week, I visited my friends, especially my girlfriends, to find out who had broken up since I'd left.

When my father returned from work that evening, he wanted to know how I liked Chicago and what I had done. He was especially interested to hear about my job and how I'd liked it. Instead of telling him how I had made out in Chicago, I gave him the letter from Mr. Swartz. As he read the letter, he kept moving his head in an affirmative way, letting me know he was pleased with what I had accomplished besides making money. I told him I thought the letter was wonderful, but I had never heard someone be commended for being a dishwasher. He initiated another conversation on the value of work and the importance of doing the best job you can, regardless of what the job may be. He had instilled this value in me for many years, but maybe he thought he needed to remind me, since I was puzzled at the letter commending me for being a super dishwasher.

Monday, September 4, the first day of school, was a historical day for me—one I had looked forward to for four years. I was beginning my senior year at the BTW, the greatest high school in the South and maybe in the country. Forgive me for possible exaggeration, but after sixty-eight years, everything seems bigger and better. There was so much excitement among my classmates, because we realized that this would be the last year many of us would be together or even see each other. Our courses had been selected for us. My classes were geometry, Latin, American history, Spanish, English composition, and music, which included my participation in the glee club and the band.

Our homeroom teacher, Mrs. Mary Moore had died during the summer, which made all of us sad. But we remained grateful for her gentleness and the interest she demonstrated in each of us. Miss Anna J. Polk became our new homeroom teacher. I admired her very much; we attended the same church, and she was very strict but very fair.

During the year, I was very busy between trying to raise my grade average and participating in the band. Plus, on the weekends, I played music with Rufus Thomas and our group or with the Al Jackson Orchestra, the band of my friend's father.

My time was very limited and didn't allow time for much social life, with the exception of my girlfriends, Jean Gray and Doris Sims, who were both very attractive and very smart. Doris was one year ahead of me, and Jean was in my class. I am sure you must realize that this situation kept me busy trying to arrange time. They were very principled girls with high standards, and I am sure some of my friends today would ask why they were with me.

The first half of the year was spent on parties; football and basketball games; and preparations for the major event in our school year, the senior class prom. Everybody was excited—except me. My problem was I had to make a difficult decision regarding which girlfriend to take to the prom. Doris had finished the year before and was attending Lemoyne College, and Jean was in my class, which made the dilemma even more difficult. Well, that decision will come later in the narrative.

Our senior class election came early in the year, so we could plan the senior year, along with the senior yearbook, the historical document outlining what had happened to us during our four years at BTW. Although I was elected junior class president, I had not sought the honor of being elected senior class president. A group of my classmates campaigned for me anyway, and I was elected senior class president without opposition. This was an awesome responsibility. I was expected to represent the class in every way during the year, which put pressure on me to be the ideal person and student I was not. I would not be honest if I told you I did not enjoy the honor and popularity that went with it. However, I tried to make sure I conducted myself in a respectful way that would be consistent with my leadership role. Teachers were especially watchful and critical of any infractions, real or imagined.

I adjusted to this new role and scrutiny by simply being me, which I found was really enough. Other officers included Joseph Terry, vice president; Georgia English, secretary; Nellie Peoples, financial secretary; Saul Holmes, business manager; Betty Coe, assistant business manager; Ann Sraggins, treasurer; George Bake, parliamentarian; and Betty Neal, chaplain. At this writing, all of them are still living, which is remarkable. As I look back and remember all of these classmates, who have since become distinguished in their various fields of endeavor, it was an honor to have been a part of their formative years.

The year was passing so quickly because of distractions like football and basketball games and dances and parties on the weekends; our time as high school students was nearing an end. The senior class officers were busy planning our various activities for the close of the year, including the senior prom, the highlight of the year, and the design of our class ring. We also worked with the yearbook, which would enable us all to look back and see what we were about during this period of our lives. Now, eighty years later, looking at this book—seeing what we were then and how we have not only changed but also, in some ways, remained the same—is such a wonderful experience.

After the Christmas holidays of 1954, everything seemed to take on a fast but exciting pace, with college entrance exams and recruiters visiting the school for students who excelled academically or in some other area, such as sports, music, or fine arts. After the exam period, we all wondered how we had done and what our prospects for college or other schools were.

During this season, I had two interviews with Arkansas Agricultural, Mechanical & Normal College (Arkansas AM&N). Both of were for music, one for the marching band. Mr. Strong interviewed me for the trombone, and Mr. Ariell Lovelace interviewed me for vocal music. Although instrumental music was my first love, I was impressed with

Mr. Lovelace, then director of the Arkansas AM&N choir known throughout the South and Midwest as one of the best black college choirs in the country. It rivaled the Fisk University choir, which was nationally and internationally known and respected. Mr. Strong told me how much he had heard about my development on the trombone and said he thought I could be an asset to his band. Similarly, Mr. Lovelace told me I had a good baritone voice, which would also be an asset to the baritone section.

My mentor, Walter Martin, was a member of Central Baptist Church, where I had been baptized. I admired and tried to emulate him in many ways. Walter, who had also played in the BTW band, suggested I should accept the choir scholarship because it would give me more time for my studies. The band followed the football team on the road, which would mean sometimes missing a week of study. The choir scholarship would mainly require only overnight travel and not nearly as often as the band. Both scholarships provided four years tuition, room, and board.

One of the most exciting days of my life was when I received a letter from Mr. Lovelace officially offering me a scholarship to Arkansas AM&N. I decided to take the choir scholarship. It meant the end of my career as a budding musician, which I thought could help me join one of the big bands such as Count Basie and Duke Ellington. You must admit I had a vivid imagination to think I could ever do that. The deciding factor was the time for study; after all, that was the real reason for college or higher education. Since I had already discussed it with my mentor, I was satisfied with my decision. The letter indicated that I should report to the school on August 25 for orientation and choir rehearsal.

After I have received my acceptance letter to Arkansas AM&N, the school year seemed to pass even faster. The Cotton Carnival would be coming in May, during which the bands of Memphis played an important part and the Negro king and queen of the carnival, a distinct honor, were part of celebratory events held in their honor. These included a week of celebratory parades and dances and other activities like rides and food stands in the Beale Street park. The black Cotton Carnival was far more exciting than the white Cotton Carnival. In retrospect, it should have been, since Negroes picked all the cotton, and they sold it, and we had to excel somehow in this very unfair culture of prejudice and discrimination.

Beale Street was one of the most famous streets in Memphis, because it was where W. C. Handy had started the blues when he'd written the famous "Memphis Blues" and "Saint Louis Blues," both classics to this day. Memphis's Beale Street was like New Orleans's Bourbon Street, where blues and jazz were supreme. Beale Street and Bourbon Street were where you could get a job playing with a group you never met before. Guys who had a band and needed a horn player could come on either street and find someone who could play either horn or reed instruments, along with bass and drums. Beale Street was where the famous B. B. King got his start. I remember when B. B., as we called him, got his real break.

The year 1950 marked the year of the first black radio station, which was managed by one of my best high school teachers, Mr. Nat D. Williams, an outstanding United States History teacher. Nat D., as we called him, had developed a jingle for Pepticon, "a blood builder" to give you more energy and vitality. Nat D. asked B. B. if he wanted to sing the jingle on the radio. He immediately accepted, given and he was hardly known and in need of work. I was amazed how B. B. adapted to radio in singing this jingle. It went like this: "Pepticon sho is good. Pepticon sho is good. You can get it anywhere in your neighborhood." The jingle played every hour on the hour, and Pepticon became a best seller, and B. B. became a celebrity. Bookings for his group came from all over Tennessee, Arkansas, and Mississippi. I even played with him one time at the Plantation Inn in West Memphis Arkansas.

B. B. King, the "Beale Street Blues Boy, became more popular not for his guitar playing but for his ability to sing the blues with such authenticity. He, along with Muddy Waters and others made the blues a national and international idiom of music. Bobby "Blue" Bland was a contemporary of B. B., and he was also an outstanding vocalist and blues singer. During the Cotton Carnival these and other outstanding vocalist and musicians performed, making our version of the carnival an outstanding event, attended by many whites though we could not attend theirs.

May was almost gone, and the final days of our high school years were near. Excitement was high by the time the senior prom was within two weeks, along with the baccalaureate sermon, a worship service where one of the outstanding ministers would deliver a sermon on our responsibilities as Christians. At this time, the prohibition against prayer and religious practices in schools didn't exist.

I am proud to say that attorney Benjamin Hooks, an outstanding preacher and civil rights leader, delivered our baccalaureate sermon. Benjamin Hooks was a graduate of Booker T. Washington, with my sister Audrey. As you know, Hooks went on to become the first Negro judge in Memphis. Later, he became the first Negro to chair the powerful Federal Communications Commission (FCC) and also the president of the National Association for the Advancement of Colored People (NAACP), an honor he truly deserved. His message was so inspiring, not only because of what he said but also through his demonstration of his character in his fight for equality during a time when it was not popular.

Soon, the senior prom was only a week away, and everybody was talking about what they would be wearing and with whom they were going. Because I had two girlfriends, both of whom I liked very much, I conveniently had a serious cold, which would last at least through prom night. Both found very nice dates to take them to the prom, which saved me from a truly embarrassing situation. I understand it was a very festive and exciting affair. I really did not mind not attending, because I had played at so many functions and dances, although I did feel guilty about not taking either of my girlfriends. When I think about it, I quickly understand the reason; I wanted to live.

The last week of school was about saying goodbyes to some classmates we had known since the first grade and maybe would never see again. The next event would be the grand finale, which was the commencement exercise, as it was called. Miss Lucie Campbell, the famous songwriter of gospel music, rehearsed us every day for this momentous occasion that would change our lives forever.

The week before commencement, *The Commercial Appeal* morning newspaper ran an article about the Booker T. Washington graduation in which it named the three outstanding students in the class of

1954

1958—Carlton Veazey, president of the largest class in the school's history with over five hundred students; Betty Coe, valedictorian; and Camille Latimer, salutatorian. The caption was "Booker T's Best." My mother was so proud but when neighbors would compliment her, in her modesty, she would simply say thank you. The three of us gave graduation speeches at commencement. I was very proud of my parents, who had raised me with basic values and had always allowed me to explore life on my own terms, which I did vigorously.

We had much to talk about. Just two weeks earlier, in May 1954, the Supreme Court had ruled that the doctrine of "separate but equal" was unconstitutional and ordered that schools be integrated. This meant that justice was about to come to the South. Ours was, therefore, a historic graduation, which our eloquent principal, Rev. Hunt spoke about. My speech was centered on our parents and guardians who had sacrificed so much to give us the opportunity that many of them had never had. I thanked them for protecting us in such a racially violent time and encouraging us like Booker T. Washington would have if he were alive. Betty Coe spoke about the need to be excellent in whatever field we chose. Camille Larimer spoke on our relationships and what it should mean to each of us, since we would carry a part of each of us with us through our lives. The commencement was attended by many city officials, including Mr. E. C. Ball, superintendent for almost forty years. The leaders of the black community were well represented in the religious community, as well as in the civic sector.

The worst part was presenting diplomas to 535 students. Although the ceremony was long, our parents and relatives did not mind, because they had prayed for and looked forward to this day for what it would mean to us and to our children.

After the ceremony, we all went to different parties and celebrations throughout the city.

The next day, we began making plans for the summer and fall, when we would go our different ways to work or to college. My plans were already fixed. I planned to return to Chicago to work until it was time to leave for Arkansas AM&N, where I was to report for orientation and choir rehearsal.

In June 1958, I left for Chicago, Illinois, with confidence and great expectations. My previous trip to Chicago had been quite successful, and I anticipated an even greater summer since my brother had indicated that Hines Hospital, a Veterans Administration hospital, was hiring. The trip was uneventful, since I had done this before and was not nearly as excited as I was last year. Of course, the highlight of the trip was taking down my shoebox as we crossed the Ohio River to eat my food that my mother had so lovingly prepared for her baby boy.

After dinner, I decided to read about Arkansas AM&N, a land grant college that evolved in late 1920 to provide education for the citizens of the state. These colleges for Negroes rose all over the South, including places like Alabama State University (ASU), founded in 1867 in Montgomery, Alabama; Kentucky State University (KSU), a public university in Frankfort, Kentucky, founded in 1886 as the State Normal School for Colored Persons; Missouri State University (MSU), formerly Southwest Missouri State University, a public university in Springfield, Missouri, that was founded in 1905 as the Fourth District Normal School; and Tennessee State University (TSU), a public land grant university in Nashville, Tennessee, that was founded in 1912 and is the largest and only state-funded historically black university in Tennessee.

This was a giant step forward for Negroes and education. Thousands of young people attended, preparing to become teachers, agricultural agents, doctors, and lawyers, along with other vocations. Dr. Lawrence Davis was the youngest president of the college, having been a graduate of the college. He was young; innovative; an excellent administrator; and, above all, a splendid politician, which was requisite of leaders in dealing with the racist legislators and governors on whom they depended for college funding. Many times these presidents were called "Uncle Toms" because they were thought to be jesters for white people in order to get support. This was not so. They appealed to the better nature of those white people who may have supported segregation but had a humane view of people and supported the education of Negroes.

Much progress was made by people like President Davis and other black college presidents, although black colleges were not funded like other colleges in Arkansas. Despite the handicaps, the teachers and administrators were able to give their students a quality education for that day. One of the most impressive students who had finished State, as we called it, Dr. Samuel L. Kountz Jr., graduated with distinction from the University of Arkansas Medical School. He went on to become one of the most outstanding kidney surgeons in the world and was credited with the first kidney transplant in the United States. His commitment led him to South Africa to help his brothers and sisters who were dying of kidney failure. He performed many operations there, saving thousands of lives. As providence would have it, he contracted a serious brain infection that sent him into a coma. He remained in a comatose state for five months before he succumbed to his illness. After reading this story about a man who had come from a rural town in Arkansas, from a family of abject poverty, and had attended this college, I was convinced beyond a shadow of a doubt that I had selected the right college, and I was proud of it. I was anxious to see the college and environment in which this medical icon had studied.

The conductor announced our arrival at the Roosevelt Road Union Station in thirty minutes. I was prepared to get off the train because I had already taken my luggage, of which I was most proud, down to leave the train. The train slowed as it entered the train station, and my excitement began to take over. It had been a year since I had been to the Windy City.

As we passengers left the train, I walked toward the exit to Twelfth Street, where my brother asked me to meet him. Like clockwork, as soon as I passed through the gate leading to Roosevelt Road, Erwin and Marie ran toward me. I hugged them both. Erwin took the luggage they had given to me, and Marie took my hand and asked me about my trip. As we walked toward the parking lot on Roosevelt Road, I tried to tell them how thankful I was for their support and about the graduation exercises in Ellis Auditorium where 535 of us had received our diplomas. Of course they had heard that, as president of the class, I had given the first address. They also inquired what college I would be attending in the fall. I informed them I had received a four-year scholarship to Arkansas AM&N. They were very proud of my achievements, although they had wanted me to stay with them and attend Wright Junior College, which was near their home. This was very kind, but I had already decided that my choice was the right choice. I needed to become totally independent in order to grow and develop.

During the previous year, Erwin and Marie had bought a new house on Conran Street, which was still on the West Side but farther up Roosevelt Road, though not too far from the apartment on Albany. It was a beautiful single-family home, where they had rented the top floor to a family of four. Also, since last year, Marie had given birth to a beautiful little girl name Chrystal Veazey. Of course she was the apple of her father's eye, and time would prove just how proud he was of their daughter and my niece. Both Chrystal and I had our own rooms, with Chrystal sleeping in the room next to her parents' room. My room was across the hall, which would prove helpful when she would wake up during the night.

That night, I dropped off to sleep thinking about exploring the jobs at the Hines Veterans Administration Hospital in Hines, Illinois, about an hour and a half away by bus.

I made my way to Hines Hospital and found the employment office to make inquiries about the summer jobs my brother had told me about. The staff was very helpful and had me fill out an application, which asked for my basic information, including my highest education level. I proudly put down that I had received my diploma on June 7 from Booker T. Washington High School in Memphis, Tennessee. The application did not request all this information, but I thought they should know the name of the high school, since we were very proud.

After nearly an hour, a gentleman appeared. I followed him to his office, where he asked me if I would prefer a position as an orderly assistant, a maintenance assistant, or a kitchen support assistant. I thought to myself that everybody here must have an assistant. After a minute, I told him I would like to have an orderly assistant job, which meant that I would be assisting the nurses on the floor. This position paid $2.25 an hour, though the minimum wage was only $1 an hour. I was excited to have found a job for the second year in a row. Although this one did not pay more than my job at Woolworth the prior year, I thought it would be good for me, in that I would have experience besides washing dishes. I thought orderly or nurses' assistant sounded more important than dishwasher, so I called this advancement. I was told to report to work at nine in the morning and proceed to the fourth floor to meet Nurse Nicken, who would be my supervisor.

Upon my return home, I gave Erwin and Marie the news about the job. They were pleased but reminded me that it would cost 5¢ to ride to Oak Park, Illinois. After reaching Oak Park, I had to transfer to go to Hines, Illinois, where the veteran's hospital was located, which cost me another dime. So the cost to go back and forth to work was 30¢ a day.

One of my best friends, Saul Holmes, whose family had moved to Chicago two years earlier, had also applied for a job at Hines and was assigned to food services. I did not apply for food services because I did not want to be around dishes anywhere, for any reason. Saul's assignment turned out to be providential. My budget included lunch, which I estimated at 75¢ a day. However, Saul arranged for me to eat lunch free every day, saving me approximately $7.50 every two weeks. I budgeted at least $1 a day for snacks or other items. My expenses amounted to approximately $13 every two weeks, with $20 for weekend social expenses, totaling $33. I also gave Marie $10 for room and board, which she accepted. In addition, I sent my mother $10 for her use and enjoyment. After taxes and social security, my take-home pay was $160 every two weeks, leaving me with $107 free money to use as I've please after expenses.

I mainly bought something every two weeks for the fall when I would be attending college. This proved helpful because I would not have an opportunity to earn any money because of my studies and choir rehearsals twice a day—which, to say the least, was daunting. This was why we received scholarships for four years.

Hines Hospital was a great experience. I met new people and learned to carry out assignments given to me by Nurse Nicken. She was a very kind person, but she was serious about her job and expected all of us who worked under her supervision to be serious and responsible. My task was to assist the nurses in their duties, which included cleaning patient rooms, assisting patients with their hygiene, and taking patients for tests in other parts of the hospital, as well as other duties. I enjoyed these duties very much, especially since I was still considering medicine as a profession. I found going to work every day an exciting time. I had made new friends and was learning new things about the hospital.

The veterans were very informative about World War II and Korea, and they were also amazing with physical skills. Some of the workers challenged the veterans to a basketball game. Since they had to play in wheelchairs, it seemed impossible for them to beat us. We were amazed during our first game to see how skillful they were with their wheelchairs—maneuvering around us and passing to one another and then, unbelievably, shooting and making the basket. When we lost the game, we could only scratch our heads and wonder how it had happened. It taught me much about the capabilities of someone considered to be handicapped. These men were not handicapped by any means and actually made us feel we were handicapped.

This was the best working experience I had ever had. It allowed me the opportunity to learn many things and make contacts that would prove helpful to me in later years.

One of the most telling experiences I had was when I met a young white girl named Beverly, who also worked at Hines Hospital. We began to talk about our experiences, since we both were recent high school graduates. She was very interesting and knowledgeable, which made our conversation very stimulating and challenging to both of us. After several weeks, she asked me if I would like to go to a movie downtown at the Chicago Theater. I was surprised that she had asked me, rather than me asking her, but I accepted this as the culture of the North. We agreed on the Wednesday after work. It would take me an extra hour after work to go home, change clothes, and pick her up in time.

When the day of our first date arrived, I was very excited. I had never dated a white girl and did not know how to deal with white culture. I rushed home to get dressed for my first date with a white girl, which was a challenge for me. I got home around six o'clock and immediately showered and put on my best outfit. After getting dressed, I told my brother I would be a little late because I was taking a young lady to the movie and she was white. He asked me what her name was, and I told him Beverly. He asked me where she lived, to which I responded, "She lives in Cicero."

His whole demeanor changed. The look on his face told me something was just wrong. He simply said, with his big brother authority, "You are not going anywhere tonight."

I was astonished at his reaction and asked in an angry way, "Why?"

He told me to sit down and then told me that Cicero was one of the most segregated, prejudiced, and violent places in or around Chicago, especially against Negroes.

This was proven when Martin Luther King marched through the streets of Cicero and had eggs and other objects thrown at him and other marchers, with some of the whites threatening violence. I was confused and also wondering why Beverly had not told me the story of Cicero.

That night I called and told her that I would not be able to pick her up for our movie date because my brother had explained to me that Cicero was not safe for me.

The next day was somewhat awkward. I wondered if Beverly harbored some of those feelings that bubbled into violence in Cicero, although she showed no racism. When we met for lunch, she explained her total lack of awareness regarding the reputation of her city. She'd had asked her father about what my brother had told me, and he'd admitted there were strong feelings not welcoming Negroes in their community because some held anti-Negro views, with all the stereotypical but false views prevalent. I really believed she was not prejudiced and was ashamed of the white people who held those views.

We never went on a date but continued to talk and learned a lot about each other's culture. I came away from this experience realizing that many whites are not racist but simply ignorant to the issues around race. When I left the Hines Hospital, Beverly cried and said how she wished we could continue our platonic relationship that was very important in my development. I realized how many young people with prejudiced parents were at such a disadvantage because of the ignorance passed on by their parents. This would prove to be true as I became more aware of, and more involved in, the civil rights movement later in life.

Saul and I finished our summer with a wonderful experience and looked forward to a new chapter in our lives. On August 10, I resigned from my prestigious position as nurse's assistant to Nurse Nicken. On August 15, I left Saul in Chicago, headed for Memphis to begin preparation for matriculation at Arkansas AM&N, where I would spend the next four years.

Chapter 4

COLLEGE YEARS *1956* *1954*

August 23 arrived, and I was packed and ready to go off to the greatest adventure in my life, imagining all kinds of things awaiting me. The only mode of transportation was the Greyhound bus, which left twice a day for Pine Bluff, Arkansas, where the college was located. I had only been west of Memphis when my band attended a workshop at Dunbar High School in Little Rock, Arkansas. I had mentally mapped out my travel route, which I estimated would take just over two hours. Before my college education was over, I could name all the stops from Memphis to Pine Bluff—West Memphis, Forest City, Brinkley, Helena, Stuttgart, Wabaseka, Altheimer, and Pine Bluff. We left Memphis at noon and arrived in Pine Bluff half past two.

When we disembarked, the bus station was the smallest one I had ever seen. I was met at the station by a man who was driving a bus with Arkansas State College emblazoned on each side, making it official that I was now in college. The other students at the station were in the band. When we drove up to the campus, we passed through the most beautiful brick arch with a sign that read, "Arkansas Agricultural Mechanical and Normal" over it. After passing through the arch, we saw the beautiful campus, which was laid out as a quadrangle with buildings on all four sides. Women's dormitories were on the north side, men's dormitories were on the south side, the administration building was on the east side, and the vocational building was on the west side.

We were escorted to our preassigned dorm rooms, which raised anxieties resulting from questions as to who my roommate would be and whether we would relate to one another. I was assigned to Cook Hall and, on his arrival, met a guy who introduced himself. I in turn introduced myself as Carlton Veazey from Memphis, Tennessee, to sing in the college choir. He smiled and said he was also there on scholarship to sing in the choir. We immediately bonded, since we already had something in common. After unpacking and selecting which beds we wanted, Cook and I headed to the dining hall for a late lunch and orientation.

In the dining hall we met other new choir members from all over of the country. Students came from Memphis; Saint Louis, Missouri; Kansas City, Missouri; Chicago, Illinois; Milwaukee, Wisconsin; Baton Rouge and Acadia, Louisiana; and cities Arkansas, including Little Rock, Malvern, Forest City, Stuttgart, Hot Springs, and other parts of the state.

After lunch and orientation, we left for our dormitories to unpack and meet with our housemother, who would be with us for two years, after which we would move to the upper classmen dormitories for juniors and seniors. Notice was posted in our dormitory reminding us that our first choir rehearsal would be held at the college chapel at six o'clock in the Watson administration building. We were reminded of Professor Ariel Lovelace's expectation that we be on time.

When we arrived, Mr. Lovelace walked in with his pianist and his assistant, Mr. Hitchcock, who was also the choir's violinist. Having met Mr. Lovelace when he interviewed me during my last year of high school, I found him to be a tall, rod-straight, handsome man with a charismatic bearing that demanded respect. He was also one of the most compassionate people I had met. There was something very humble about him even though he was considered one of the most outstanding choir directors in the country. We also found out that he had been caring for his bedridden wife for years, with very little outside support. He was very businesslike in his rehearsals.

He organized us quickly according to our voices—altos in the first row, sopranos in the second row, tenors in the third row and baritones and basses in the fourth and fifth rows. We had a choir of over a hundred voices with more than half being returning members. Mr. Lovelace asked us to listen to the returning members sing the hymn,

"We Thank You, Lord," which opened each choir rehearsal. The lyrics were, "For all the blessings of the year / for all the friends we hold so dear / for peace on earth, both far and near / we thank thee Lord, Amen."

All of us were in awe at the lyrics, the unbelievable blend of harmonic voices, and the ease with which Mr. Lovelace directed the simple but powerful prayer. I had grown up listening every Sunday morning to the powerful Wing over Jordan Choir, heralded as the most powerful Negro choir in the country, and the Jubilee Singers, a very famous choir at Fisk University in Nashville, Tennessee. Writing about this opening prayer brings tears to my eyes as I hear heavenly tones and words that blended so well together. We all sat down with tears in our eyes, realizing we had become a part of a powerful expression of our school spirit. Our choir was known throughout the country as one of the most outstanding choirs in the country. Our college did have its beginnings as a church school, founded by the religious community with John T. Watson as its first president.

Mr. Lovelace welcomed all of us to join the Arkansas AM&N concert choir. Our introductions to each other included where we were from and the high school we'd attended. After this informal opening, we relaxed and old choir members sat by the new ones as we practiced the old music and the new music introduced by Mr. Lovelace for the new school year. Among those of us who were new, there was naturally some apprehension about our ability to fit in, as well as read music like the upper classmen. We also had to adjust to new languages since some of the music was written in Latin and Italian.

Our rehearsals were twice a day, at noon and six o'clock in the evening, which we had to arrange with our classes since we were on scholarship. The rehearsals lasted an hour, and we were also expected to sing for vespers, the mandatory church service for the student body, every Sunday at five o'clock. I suppose this was a carryover from the early days when the founders had insisted that religion be an integral part of our education.

Our early arrival to college granted us early class registration. Most of us were given the same basic schedule, which consisted of English, math, history, humanities, and music education. Since we were on the quarter system, these courses would basically continue, with minor variation. All of our classes were arranged to adjust to our choir obligation of twice a day rehearsals. Although it was a rigorous schedule, it was a blessing to have free room and board and fees paid for four years if we kept our grades above a C average and maintained our choir status. Since school did not officially open until September 4, which was when we would officially begin our college education as freshmen, this interlude gave us the chance to know and bond with one another. I was from Memphis, the largest city in the South, which had most of my classmates thinking I was more advanced in many ways because I was not from a rural area. Those who were from places in the north like Saint Louis, Chicago, and Kansas City were looked upon as city slickers who were more advanced in worldly ways.

Our early arrival also gave us time to explore the area around us. One of the first things I noticed when we arrived was the extreme foul odor emanating from somewhere near the campus. One of the students, who lived in Pine Bluff, explained that it was a paper factory not far from campus. My question to Wayne Weddington was, How does one live with that smell? He assured me that, in a few days, I would not smell it. He was right. It wasn't long before I had become acclimated to the smell and was not bothered anymore.

Although the student union building housed many activities, such as recreational facilities, along with the main dining room, we were anxious to see what was off campus. Pine Bluff was a small town with a significant black population, by my estimation was 20 percent, which was not unusual for a college town. It also had a significant middle class, with many people remaining and raising families after coming to teach. The school's teachers and college professors commanded sizeable incomes. And near the school was a black-owned grocery store that had been in one family for over fifty years. The city had black-owned cleaners and shoe shops and a barbershop and beauty shop as well.

There were two restaurants near the college. One, the Lion's Den, so-called high class, was where faculty and visitors to the campus ate. It was named after the mascot of our football team, the lion. The other, Elites, was a very pedestrian eatery with an upscale name. I can assure you that those of us who patronized Elites did not have influence, privilege, or even a little wealth. Mr. Elite, the owner, provided some good cheap food and was a very interesting character with a rather gruff personality, which he put on to keep you from asking him for credit. In retrospect, I see that Mr. Elite was responsible for many of us not starving between allowances. He had a phenomenal memory, in that, at the first of the month, he would ask you to pay up, since he knew that's when your parents sent you allowance. Besides the hot dogs, cheeseburgers and hamburgers, and spaghetti and meatballs, Mr. Elite's cheap specialty was what he called "chili-mac," a delicious combination of chili and macaroni. We really loved Mr. Elite, even though we were so careless not to know his real name. It was the only place you could satisfy your hunger with a chili-mac for twenty-five cents, and for a dollar and twenty-five cents, you could buy a full dinner of chicken, mashed potatoes, and peas with corn bread and lemonade. These places around the campus would become a part of our daily lives for the next four years.

When school opened on September 4, our population grew to almost fifteen hundred, which changed the atmosphere of the entire campus. Monday morning, the campus was bustling with students going various ways. The breakfast was held in the student union building from 7:00 a.m. to 11:00 a.m., which gave everyone time to make breakfast, especially those who had early classes. Those who were not going to breakfast were going to the administration building to complete their registration or to apply for student aid, which all of us needed, including those of us who were on scholarships, also a form of student aid. I was greatly impressed to see everybody moving with purpose.

My first class at nine o'clock was humanities, of which I had not heard before or since. It was taught by Dr. Alexander. This class dealt with interpersonal relationships and also touched on race relations. I was impressed with Dr. Alexander's grasp of this subject, although he was born and educated in India and also did some studies in the United States. He was very good at teaching, as he was able to convey, and we were able to understand, the relationship between what was going on in this country and what was going on in his own country. In India, Mahatma Gandhi was instrumental in gaining the country's independence from the British. This class was also interesting because Dr. Alexander was able to relate his experiences to our struggles.

My other classes were mainly subject introductions and receiving our first assignment to write a one-page paper on what we expected to get from the course. My classes were divided during the week. I had three classes on Monday, Wednesday, and Friday and two classes on Tuesday and Thursday, which gave me time to read and complete assignments. The first week went very well. I learned that college would require far more discipline than high school. My scholarship depended upon me making acceptable grades, along with fulfilling my responsibilities to the choir. We were also required to tour with the choir during the spring in order to recruit students from the North, as well as raise money for our scholarship program. This commitment meant we had to rehearse relentlessly in order to develop a new repertoire for the spring. And it would take us on tour to Saint Louis, Chicago, Milwaukee, and other cities in Wisconsin that were all white like Mukwonago and Delevan Lake. I realized the need for extensive rehearsal in order to adequately represent the college.

After several weeks, my schedule became routine. I tried to keep it so as not to fall back in my studies and to keep my commitment to the choir. After several weeks, it felt like I had been at Arkansas AM&N for months, as I got to know more of my classmates and the upperclassmen who had welcomed us to the campus and helped us make adjustments as freshman.

I received a scholarship to Arkansas AM&N, a college is knew something about because my god-brother, Walter Martin, had attended the college many years prior and encouraged me to attend and, especially, to select the choir. Walter was my mentor for many ways. Since my older brothers had left home, he provided the support I never had from an older brother. Part of the reason I chose to play the trombone was because he played the trombone so well that he was selected to be a part of the army band when he was drafted into the armed services. Walter and his mother, Mrs. Martin, had a great influence on me that was very important, since we all belonged to Central Baptist Church for many years.

My comfort level at Arkansas AM&N had grown tremendously after two months. Classes were going well, and our choir had begun to blend. The activities on campus increased, with some young men were being recruited for various fraternities, such as Alphas, Omegas, Kappas and others. You had to be at least a sophomore to pledge, and the selection process was very difficult. Not only did you have to be an upperclassman; you also had to have at least a C average in order to be considered. You were selected by a brother, who vouched for you character and ability to contribute to the mission of the fraternity.

Quarterly examinations had come before we knew it. Many of the students planned to go home for the Thanksgiving holiday. We had to prepare for our exams before we left, since exams would begin the day after Thanksgiving. Our choir director determined that we needed to continue our practice routine because we would be presenting the annual Christmas music featuring Handel's *Messiah*, a difficult piece that some of us had not sung. This proved to be a blessing, in that we would be able to study for our quarterly exams without the distraction of Thanksgiving. Half of the students had gone the day before Thanksgiving. The campus always seemed empty when students left for Thanksgiving holidays. Those who remained at "State", which we affectionately called our college, especially those who had yet to meet and know each other's background, now had the chance. Since we only had choir rehearsals, we began to talk to one another after choir rehearsals.

I really admired a young lady from Hot Springs, Arkansas, although we had never spoken except to say hello. She sang alto in the choir. Hot Springs was one of the largest cities in Arkansas, the other being Little Rock, the capital. The young lady's name was Callie Canion, and she had the most beautiful face and hair, and her complexion was the most beautiful ebony I had ever seen. I asked if we could have lunch together after choir rehearsal, and she responded yes with a beautiful smile that made me wish for choir rehearsal to end quickly. Callie was not vain or arrogant and confident in her own way.

We had lunch together, and it was like we had known each other for many years. She told me about her life at Ho Springs and that she would like for me to visit. After that lunch, it was breakfast, lunch, and dinner for a while. We were really compatible, as she was very sensitive to people and the way they responded to her, especially other girls. She was not only beautiful; she also had a walk like she had attended modeling school, although I was sure she hadn't.

Since coming to State, I had become involved in the Watson Sunday School class, named after the first president. Although my father was a minister and I had been in church all my life, I did not know I would continue my religious education when I went to college. Somehow, it seemed such a part of my life I automatically became part of the religious community and became known as religious, although I did not make any effort to create that image. I became irritated when others had judgments about my relationship with Callie, seeing the two of us as incompatible. She was a very confident person who was born with certain gifts, including beauty, in fact a black beauty. Many also looked at her as worldly according to their standards. Yes, she openly smoked and wore very nice clothes and carried herself in a confident way, which some thought was arrogant. I did not like people making judgments about people for superficial reasons. My only criticism of Callie was that she did not apply herself to her studies. She was capable of excelling, and because of her lack of academic background and study habits, college would not work out for her.

After Thanksgiving, we had to face our quarter finals, which in some cases would determine whether some of us would remain or be terminated from the school. This school policy, in retrospect, was good because, for those who failed, other educational options that may be more compatible with their skills could be explored. This was a difficult time for many of our fellow students, but some were resigned to the inevitable—that they would not continue after the Christmas holidays.

With the Christmas holidays fast approaching, we worked hard to prepare for our Christmas concert, one of the highlights of the university and the college choir. The concert drew students and great fans who'd seen the choir perform superbly for many years. Mr. Lovelace had scrupulously prepared us for this event, which was held a week before the holidays began. The anxiety around this performance was immense, especially for the new choir members. The reputation of the choir was so outstanding that the new members did not want this performance to be any less than outstanding.

The concert was held in the student union building, which was our newest building and had the greatest capacity. Those of us who had sung in glee clubs and small church choirs had not seen such a production—with violins, horns, and timpani drums. Although I had played with an orchestra during my high school days, this was the first time I had experienced singing with a strong orchestral background. Our last rehearsal included a group of musicians that produced the most incredible and beautiful sound I had ever heard. The rehearsal, held on the Saturday before the Sunday concert, featured the world-renowned George Frederic Handel's *Messiah*. This concert, held for many years, was one of the outstanding contributions to the college community.

The concert was held on Sunday at five o'clock, which accommodated the black community that attended their local churches in the morning. The converted student union building, seating approximately five hundred people, was filling fast well before the performance. The choir had arrived at two o'clock to do vocals, simply a practice to warm up our vocal chords. During that time, we had been given a delicious lunch prepared by the cafeteria staff like we were celebrities.

At four thirty, the choir met in one of the auxiliary rooms for our final meeting and to sing our hymn, which preceded every appearance. Something always came over us as we sang the hymn—"for all the blessings of the year, for all the friends we hold so dear, for peace on earth, both far and near, we thank you, Lord." This hymn always created a certain spiritual solidarity, which provided a powerful connection with our singing.

Mr. Lovelace was an ordained musical director or conductor. He had the persona and the presence that commanded respect because you could feel something special was about to happen when he came to the stage with an erect and purposeful walk. The audience responded to his arrival with a standing ovation before a single note was sung. There was always something magical about the way he raised his baton and came down with such a strong stroke and authority it brought out all the sounds of perfection that we had practiced for months.

Once we had opened our mouths to sing, something seemed to take over us and put us together as one voice even with different parts to sing. After a few Christmas songs, we went into the featured composition, Handel's *Messiah*, one of the most popular Christmas compositions in modern history. The supporting orchestra created the powerful music and sounds, whose music could only be compared to that of a New York concert orchestra. These sounds amplified our voices in such a way that we were amazed at how our choir sounded in a live concert.

As Handel's *Messiah* came to an end with the "Hallelujah" finale, the audience stood and began to sing with us, creating the feeling of a religious revival. At the final "Hallelujah" chorus, the orchestra, the choir, and the audience were one spiritually—a phenomenon I had never seen or experienced during my years of religious worship. Following the chorus, there was sustained applause like I had never heard before. There was electricity in the air, and the applause must have lasted over two or three minutes. It was not only for our singing but also in recognition of God's presence. During the applause, the choir filed out with a standing ovation and more applause. After we had filed out, the applause continued until Mr. Lovelace returned to take a final bow.

The next day, we started packing to go home for our vacation or some other destination. I had not been home since I'd left in September and was anxious to see my parents and Melvin (Gerry had married and moved to Louisville, Kentucky). Our concert was on the last Sunday before Christmas, and we would leave the next day.

Monday morning we all ate breakfast in the student union building before scurrying to our dorms to get our bags. Some would be going as far as Chicago and Wisconsin; those in Arkansas could be home within two hours. My bus was leaving Pine Bluff for Memphis at noon and would arrive in two hours at the Greyhound bus station at Third and Union Streets, which would become a major experience for me during the civil rights movement when we integrated the waiting room of that bus station.

I had not been home since leaving in September. Coming home for Christmas was very special. I would see my parents and friends whom, I realized I had missed very much, and the neighbors at 1610 Arkansas Street, where we had lived since I attended high school. When the cab finally arrived, I felt like I had been in a foreign country for a year. I had travelled to Chicago twice, so it wasn't like I hadn't been away from home. However, this was different for many reasons. it was not just leaving home; I was leaving so many other things and becoming independent and starting a new life. Although I had not realized it at the time, I would never live at home on a permanent basis again. This was a frightening and exhilarating thought that I could not understand.

When I finally arrived after what seemed like hours from the Greyhound bus station, my mother was standing on the porch with the biggest smile on her face. That smile told me how much she loved and had missed me and how happy she was to have me home again.

After paying the cab driver and getting my luggage out of the trunk, I placed my bag on the sidewalk and ran to meet her and gave her the biggest hug I could. Although I was eighteen years old, I felt like I was the ten-year-old returning from my grandfather's farm after my summer visit. I retrieved my luggage and entered the house, where the aroma of liver and onions made home even more special. Mother knew that I loved liver and onions with rice. She had the table set.

Melvin came into the kitchen, and I embraced him. I worried about him—this was the first time in his life that no sibling was home with him—even though I knew others in the neighborhood would look after him. Melvin loved to eat, and whatever Mother cooked, he was ready to eat it. Mother had set the table for all three of us since Daddy had not arrived from work yet. One of the blessings in my life was that I had never known a hungry day. When we sat down to the table, Mother asked me to say the blessing offering thanksgiving for the food, after which she passed me the liver, rice, and gravy, along with butter beans and biscuits, all of which we enjoyed with lemonade.

There was silence for almost five minutes as I concentrated on the delicious food the best mother in the world had prepared. After my second helping, I got up from the table and went to give the biggest kiss on her cheek that I could. She smiled and said how glad she was I had enjoyed it. She then asked me how I had been eating, which I think is the first question any mother would ask. I assured her that the food at school was ample but did not come close to her cooking. She reminded me I had to eat and remember to eat plenty vegetables.

Shortly after we finished, my father arrived and was met with my strong hug. This tradition of men embracing was not common practice during this time, although I had seen my father greet other men with an embrace. I later learned that this practice was commonplace during my grandfather's time. He was born in 1860 before emancipation, became a minister in 1890, and founded the Mount Enon Baptist Church in Arkabutla, Mississippi. The tradition was lost until much later, when I first saw my father embrace another deacon after a church service. This greatly impressed me; I realized embracing was not just for the opposite sex. This observation was profound in my openness to both sexes, even though I was heterosexual. It is amazing how many lessons and truths we learn at an early age that never leave us. My father was a tall, strong, impressive-looking man, who some may call extremely handsome. I had great respect for my father; I had witnessed how he stood up against the power structure during the time when he challenged the discriminatory practices of the US Post Office and won. His courage and convictions left such a strong impression on me that I would never fail to stand up for issues that were right and just.

After we greeted each other, he told me how much he had missed me and prayed for my success in college. Although he did not attend college, he was extremely well read, largely due to his father, who was born in slavery but was taught to read because he was favored by his slave master. My father's mastery of the English language was phenomenal. He used words I had not heard in school or any other place. He taught Gerry and me to look up words we did not know and learn how to use them. Although my father did not have a regular time to talk with me, he taught me by example, which meant treating people with respect and always trying to help other people. I can recall how often people would come to our house just to get Daddy to write a letter on their behalf because they did not know how to write. This impressed me so that, to this day, I try to help people, especially those who need my assistance.

After our brief conversation, he sat down at the table to eat his dinner. He was a large man with a large appetite, and he always complimented my mother on how well she cooked.

The next day, I scheduled to see my friends, including Albert Jackson; William Hawkins, who played tenor sax; Gene Miller, the best musician in the group; and another childhood friend, Robert Wesley McGee, who'd mastered the upright bass. These guys were special. We had spent much time traveling to gigs all over the mid-South. Although our playing days had ended for most of us, we still kept up with Memphis musicians. Among them were Isaac Hayes, Charles Young, Phineas Newborn, Calvin Newborn, Hank Crawford, and many others who had excelled during our high school days.

Christmas was always special in our house, as was the case with most of our neighbors. Decorations had been up since after Thanksgiving, with trees and window wreaths in every house on our street. There was a joyful spirit among all of us as we anticipated the coming of our Lord and Savior Jesus Christ. Downtown Memphis was a sight to behold, with all the department stores and other businesses competing to have the best window decorations. The largest department store there was Goldsmith, which always had beautiful decorations, though it was a Jewish business. That hardly mattered, because it was business to them, as they celebrated their Jewish holidays with the same fervor. One of the things I noticed as a child and young man is that people were different during the Christmas holidays. They treated each other with a special kind of love and cordiality, and that included the salespersons. People had a certain spirit of care for one another, especially those who were less fortunate. It has always puzzled me why people were so nice during the Christmas season and not during the other part of the year. That question has not been answered after eighty-one years of living.

Christmas morning was the same since I could remember. We would get up at four in the morning and prepare to go to the five o'clock sunrise service at church, whether the sun had risen or not. Although I was much older, it was amazing to me that the church would be packed at five o'clock in the morning, with not an empty seat and with people standing. As I recalled from earlier days, there was always something mystical about the Christmas service. There was a certain joy in the church and in the spirits of the people that made the service special. Seemingly, the ministers prayed better and read the scriptures of Jesus's birth better, and the choir of one hundred voices, under the direction of renowned composer and director Miss Lucie Campbell, sang even better. The preacher, Reverend Morrison, was outstanding in his sermonic delivery. Although the service lasted almost three hours, nobody seemed to mind and was still in a joyful mood when the minister pronounced the benediction.

After the service, we returned home, where Mother was busy preparing breakfast since she had left a little before the benediction to get a head start on us getting home. The Christmas tree was beautifully decorated and surrounded by presents for all of us—Melvin; Mother and Daddy; Gerry and George, who lived in Louisville, Kentucky, and would arrive in time for dinner; and my uncles Hubert and Judson.

The breakfast was outstanding. Mother had prepared all of our favorite dishes. Bacon; sausage; liver and onions; scrapple; rice; grits, scrambled eggs; biscuits and jelly; and molasses, which my father sometime used, filled our table. This was only breakfast, and it seemed like a lot to eat. But dinner would not be served until around six o'clock that evening when my sister and her husband, along with my uncles and their girlfriends, would arrive.

After breakfast, Daddy and I, along with Melvin, began a conversation about my college experiences and what I thought I wanted to do with my life. Although we had talked about this before, it seemed more serious since I was now in college and was on a career path to something. When I explained that I was thinking about medicine, I did not get a lot of encouragement, which I will explain later in my book. For some reason, I did not take it as a negative response, although it was spurring that he did not comment except to say that medicine was a very honorable profession.

Our conversation went to my anticipated travels with the choir. I told him we would be leaving in the spring around May for such places as Saint Louis, Missouri; East Saint Louis, Illinois; Chicago, Illinois; Milwaukee, Wisconsin; and several all-white towns such as Mukwonago and Delavan Lake, Wisconsin. On our way back, we would have a concert in Memphis, which I hoped he, Mother, and Melvin would be able to attend.

After we talked, I talked to Melvin like I always did to determine how he was doing. Melvin was the most positive person I had ever met. Regardless when you saw him and asked him how he was doing, he would answer "just fine," which was common among adults, although, after saying that, they would give you a laundry list of things that were wrong, such arthritis, rheumatism, and varied other ailments.

Christmas dinner was an event beyond description. It followed a pattern I remember to this day. Daddy would be in the living room reading the paper or the Bible and listening to the radio. Melvin would be in his room waiting anxiously for dinner and our uncles to arrive with their girlfriends, along with Gerry and George. When my uncles finally arrived, we all gathered in the dining room, where seats were assigned, with my father always at the head of the table. My uncles' girlfriends always assisted my mother in bringing out the sumptuous and plentiful food. The first thing they would bring out would be the twenty-two-pound turkey that had cooked most of the night, along with a large baked ham, giblet gravy, corn bread dressing, collard green, turnip greens, mashed potatoes, sweet potato casserole, and the rolls from Snyder's bakery that I had picked up after church. Of course we had cranberry sauce, lemonade, coffee, and iced tea. The dessert was on the buffet, where cakes and pies had been lined up for two days and covered by my mother to prevent them being eaten before Christmas.

After dinner, the women assisted my mother with the kitchen and dishes, while my uncles and other male guests went into the living room, where Uncle Hubert would attempt to engage my father in debate. My uncle was not nearly as smart as my father, though he could make his point even if it was weak. My father was always reluctant to debate Uncle Hubert because he did not think my uncle was capable of debating him. However, he would humor my uncle and allow him to engage him, which delighted my uncle. The most memorable thing about their debates would be how angry they would get. I would always think the debate was going to end in a fight but found out later it was all show. Even so, it was great entertainment. And I learned a lot from my father's way of making his points, plus many new words, which helped me to build a fairly broad vocabulary.

The evening ended with a visit to my girlfriends' places, which was always a challenge, having been invited to a late dinner by both girlfriends and their families. This required eating sparingly at home in order to eat two more meals that day. This was the best reason for praying that I could return to college early—a prayer that was answered by Mr. Lovelace, who expected us to return the day after Christmas.

The next day, I left for college. It seemed like I had been away for a long time, though we'd had only two days before Christmas to celebrate. The student body was not expected before January 3. We choir members returned early to prepare for the mid-western tour, about which all of us freshman had heard so much, including the wonderful time not being in classes. However, we were told we would be responsible for our class work and our reading assignments. Even so, it was with great expectation that we looked forward to spring and our mid-western tour.

I arrived back at State the next day to what seemed almost a ghost town. There was very little activity, with only the few who had remained on campus and the faculty, who lived in housing adjacent to the college, around.

Mr. Lovelace called rehearsals for the next day at nine o'clock in the morning and at six o'clock in the evening. This was necessary for us to prepare for the January engagements, usually at churches, throughout the state. One of our stops was a church in Fort Smith, Arkansas, where the pastor was the father of a choir member. Our music went beyond Negro spirituals, which everyone enjoyed, to very difficult music sung in Latin and German.

We also prepared to sing at the opening, shortly after the New Year, of the Arkansas state legislature. This was very special. We represented the president Dr. Lawrence Davis and the college. The event was always interesting, because this all-white legislature would get so excited to hear Negroes sing. I always thought this dated back to the minstrel shows, where we danced and sang for their pleasure. However, I was astute enough to know that our appropriation from the state depended on our president's ability to persuade this group of white men to give us enough money to educate Negro young people.

One of the most outstanding voices in the choir was a tenor named Samuel Fletcher from Memphis, Tennessee. His voice box had to have been made in heaven; he was so blessed with the gift of timing and phrasing that you could hear him telling a story through his voice. We always opened the legislature with "God Bless America," with Samuel Fletcher as soloist. The prelude to the hymn brought men and women to their feet as Sam sang, "While the storm clouds gather far across the sea, / let us pledge allegiance to a land that's free / let us all be grateful for a land so fair / as we raise our voices with a silent prayer." Then the choir would open with almost a whisper, "God bless America / land that I love. / Stand beside her and guide her / through the night with a light from above." By this time, you could see and hear weeping in the audience as they listened to this great American hymn. This happened every year during the four years I attended State, and I can report the legislature gave us the total appropriation that President Davis had requested, although it was not nearly comparable to that given the white state colleges in Arkansas.

Our first trip was to Fort Smith, Arkansas, where we sang at the church of our choir mate. We sang at churches mainly because of financing associated with travel and lodging. Churches provided housing and meals and made sizeable donations to the school. On Friday, the last day in September, we left on school buses for Fort Smith. The buses were used Greyhound buses purchased by the school for travel by the football and basketball teams. We arrived at the church that day, greeted by many church members, who picked us up and took us to their homes, where we would stay from Friday until Monday morning to return to State and resume our studies.

Our concert on Sunday was a resounding success, with the church filled to capacity. The congregation received the music with such positivity that we were called back for two encores. Mr. Lovelace was so pleased with the effort of the new choir members in their first concert away and with the performance overall that he gave us Tuesday rehearsal off.

After returning to the campus late Monday, we had to report to our classes on the following day. This became a common occurrence during my years at state college. After many concerts in Arkansas, we would prepare in April for the mid-western tour—a trip many of us had looked forward to since coming to State. Mr. Lovelace announced the tour, which would commence on the Monday following Easter, would start with East Saint Louis, Illinois, for a concert at a prominent church that Wednesday night. The following cities would be Saint Louis, Missouri;

Chicago, Illinois; Milwaukee Wisconsin; and two all-white cities in Wisconsin, Mukwonago and Delavan Lake.

On our way home, we would perform in Memphis, Tennessee, my hometown, where my relatives, friends, and church members could hear us. This performance was at the Pentecostal Temple, where my high school friend's father, Bishop Patterson, was pastor. This was significant because this was the church home of Samuel Fletcher, lead soloist. During our tour, we wore tuxedos and tails depending on the taste of our director. Family members and friends of Memphis choir members turned out en masse, creating a packed house, which was not exceptional in that this was the last concert we performed before returning to State the following day.

It was a happy day when we returned to State. It seemed like we had been on tour for a month, when it had only been fourteen days. We returned in early evening, just in time for dinner in the student union building. We rushed to take our bags to our dormitories and rushed to the student union for dinner. Although we had enjoyed our time away from campus, we were eager to return to the reality of getting up at six o'clock for breakfast and preparing for our first class at eight o'clock. The return to classes required an adjustment. While on tour, we had been able to sleep late and relax during the day before preparing for rehearsals in the evening. After the first day back on campus, we were already back to the routine of college life.

We were studying hard for final exams, which would be held in a month—not a long time if you've been away for the past two weeks. The senior members of the choir were preparing for graduation and preparing résumés to send to prospective employers. Most of the employment opportunities were in education. Others were preparing for graduate schools to pursue such fields as medicine, architecture, business, and law. Those of us who were freshmen were proud of being able to complete our freshmen year. Although the year was almost over, we had to make some important decisions related to our life's work, which meant selecting a major that would best prepare us to achieve our goals.

I had been thinking about this challenge and decision throughout my freshman year but could not decide which major I would select. I knew if I selected medicine, I would have to major in the sciences, such as biology or chemistry. Alternatively, if I were to select something from the field of law or theology, I should major in sociology and history. This decision was critically important, in that it would set me on the course toward my future life's work.

Fortunately, I had the summer to think about it. This decision would be shaped by the events that would occur during the summer of 1956. This would be the beginning of my recognition that I was on a pilgrimage of clay feet.

After the graduation exercises, for which we sang, the choir left for summer vacation, with anticipation of new experiences. This summer, however, I would experience the most traumatic, emotionally shattering, and fearful events I could ever bear. My dear mother, whom I loved with all my heart, was diagnosed with cancer! Words are inadequate to express how I felt when I arrived home on June 1, 1956, to learn the news of my mother's condition. The diagnosis came as a result of an annual examination by Dr. Slutsky, her primary physician. It was confirmed by Dr. Lloyd of the University of Tennessee Medical School oncology department, one of the finest oncologists in the state of Tennessee.

Dr. Slutsky explained that the cancer had not metastasized, but time was of the essence and we needed to start treatment as soon as possible. During this time, a diagnosis of cancer was a death sentence, with few exceptions. Dr. Lloyd explained that the only possible treatment would be with cobalt and radium, two powerful chemical elements in their early trial stages and at a stage only allowed in certain situations, where the subject was diagnosed not to survive without some experimental treatments. After consultation with the doctors and my father, it was agreed to try cobalt and radium as a treatment for her cancer. We were all hopeful that this would save our mother. After several treatments of cobalt and radium, the good news we had waited for was the cancer was shrinking and possibly disappearing. This was very good news for all of us, and we were relieved that she would live.

However, in the midst of our joy, within a month, we received some devastating news. Although the cobalt and radium had eradicated the cancer, the dosage was so high that it had left serious burns on my mother's buttocks the size of a quarter in diameter and about a half inch deep with serious infection that was poisoning my mother's system and causing serious problems in her organs. If the condition persisted, it could cause her demise. The doctors worked feverishly to contain the infection, but it continued. My mother went from 140 pounds to approximately 85 pounds within weeks, which made her recovery problematic.

Although I had planned to return to Chicago for the summer and work at Hines Hospital, I could not leave my mother. I decided to get a job in Memphis so I could be near Mother, who was at John Gaston General Hospital, and visit often.

I found employment at the Cotton Boll restaurant, a few blocks from the hospital, which allowed me to visit before and after work. Mother remained in the hospital throughout the summer.

Finally Dr. Lloyd called us together and told us that they could not get the skin to graft in those places on my mother's buttocks, which meant that the infection was a serious issue and could be fatal in time. He thought, because of the dire prognosis, it would be better for her to be home and kept as comfortable as possible. Needless to say, this was devastating news that brought sadness to my heart that I had never known. I tried not to think of my mother dying, but each day brought no change. Time was of the essence. We all knew she could not live with this fatal infections, which was made worse because the skin would not graft around the deep burns that constantly seeped pus as fast as we cleaned them.

My heart broke every time I went into her room to see her and heard her groan when the pain medicine wore off. The hardest decision for me was whether I should return to school or stay to be with my mother and of assistance to my father and sister. Both Gerry and my dad encouraged me to return to school, saying they would keep me informed of any developments.

August 15 arrived. It was time to return to state college for choir rehearsals before September 5, the beginning of the school year, which would be when students would return for registration and classes. After returning to State, most of my time was spent thinking about my mother and what else could be done. Our family was very religious, with my father being a minister and my grandfather whom I never knew, having been a minister and pastor in Arkabutla, Mississippi, for forty years at the Mount. Enon Baptist Church. I was born a year before he died. Although I never really talked about it, somehow I always thought my father was hoping and praying I would follow him and my grandfather in the ministry. In my high school annual book I had even said my ambition was to study theology. This did not mean ministry as much as my fascination with religion and God, which had so dominated people's lives as I was growing up. Perhaps all of this was a way of getting me to realize that God speaks through circumstances, as well as through the prophets.

After returning to State I selected sociology and history as my major, since I knew I wanted to be in some area of social services. Although I previously attended church fairly regularly, I now made it a point to go every Sunday and hear the most dynamic preacher I had ever heard, Rev. A. Edward Davis, pastor of the St. Paul Baptist Church, the oldest church in Pine Bluff, Arkansas. His preaching inspired me to become more active in my prayer life. Talking to my father, after returning to school, he assured me that everything was being done that could be done for my mother. This was not comforting at all. It was not the answer I wanted.

One Sunday, after several weeks in school, I decided not to go to church and told others in my dorm to go on without me. After everyone had left the building, I got down on my knees and bowed my head and cried profusely. In the middle of my tears, I talked to the Lord as though he was right there in the room with me. It was not a formal prayer, but a conversation with God. First, I thanked him for my mother's life and what a good mother he had given me. I also pointed out the many virtues she possessed, including kindness, forgiveness, and empathy for others. I even recounted the time when a "'hobo," as we called them in that day, had come to the back door of our home and asked if my mother or father was home, and if so, would I ask them if he could have something to eat. When I went inside and told Mother, she had to come to the door and invited him in to sit down while she prepared him some food. She also took out the best dishes we had, which we only used on Thanksgiving and Christmas and prepared his plate. She gave him a sumptuous breakfast of eggs, sausage, grits, and biscuits, which he ate with great relish and enjoyment. After he finished and thanked my mother profusely, she gave him a bag with additional food in it.

After reciting all the virtues of my mother, I then proceeded to make my petition to God. First, I acknowledged that I could not bargain with God because he was sovereign. I had no power to make any kind of deal. However, I proceeded to make my request known to him. I promised God that, if he would heal my mother, I would forever know that he was God, who had power and answered prayer. The most important promise I made was that I knew he had called me to preach the gospel, and I was ready to surrender the rest of my life serving him and preaching his Word. Although I made this promise with utmost sincerity, I had no idea what the promise meant until much later in life. After my prayer—it seemed like an eternity that I had been on my knees—there was a strange sense of relief and peace that I had never felt before. After about an hour of reflecting on the past hour I'd spent talking with God and what I had promised, I called my father.

When he answered the phone without much greeting, I blurted out, "Daddy, Mother is going to be healed."

To this, he replied, "Yes, son, we hope so. But we will have to wait for the tests from Dr. Lloyd."

I responded, "Daddy, I talked with God this morning and promised him I would preach the gospel for the rest of my life if he would heal Mother."

For what seemed like five minutes, Daddy did not respond but simply said, "Son, I am glad you surrendered your life to God."

Somehow, I knew that God had answered my prayer, and Mother would be healed. How and when, I did not give any thought, because I had the evidence of things not seen, which was the promise of God. After this epiphany, everything seemed different. I had the most joyful feelings of spiritual freedom that I had ever known.

Weeks passed without any change in my mother's condition, but I did not fret or become discouraged. I knew what God had promised, and I knew what I had promised. Around the first of November, when we were thinking about Thanksgiving and returning home, my father called me to say Dr. Hose, the family doctor, had stopped by the house to check on mother, although he was not her doctor. After briefly examining her, he'd called my father aside and told him to clean the pus out of the burns on my mother's buttocks each day and pack them with Vaseline petroleum jelly. This sounded strange to me for a medical doctor, but my father followed his instructions each and every day. After several weeks, my mother was taken to Dr. Lloyd for her monthly visit. Dr. Lloyd announced that the infection that was killing my mother had subsided and the skin had begun to graft. When I heard this news, I cried out, "Thank you Lord! Thank you Lord!" I did not realize there were people in the hall where I used the pay phone, but it did not matter. God had kept his promise, and my mother was on her way to total recovery and healing.

Just prior to my return home for Thanksgiving, I sent a two-page letter to Rev. W. 1. Taylor, who had become our pastor since moving to South Memphis. He knew me because I had been active in the Sunday school and youth programs. My letter expressed my desire to be licensed as a minister of the gospel of Jesus Christ to preach.

When I arrived home for Thanksgiving, my heart was so full I could only hold my mother but silently thanked God for saving her and returning her to me.

As God would have it, Rev. Taylor came by the house to announce to my mother and father that I had accepted the call to the gospel ministry of Jesus Christ and how happy he and the church was that one of our young people had responded to the call. The strange thing is he did not know I was home for Thanksgiving.

When my parents called me to come to the living room and say hello to Rev. Taylor, I was so excited I could hardly speak. He told me that the church had accepted my request, and, if I desired, I could preach my first sermon before returning to school on the following Monday. He set the time and date for the coming Sunday at seven o'clock in the evening. This may seem like a short period of time to prepare for such a momentous occasion. But in the reasoning of my father and Rev. Taylor, if God called you to preach, you should be prepared to preach. All of this was before I'd attended the Howard University School of Religion, which had a completely different view of preparation. Needless to say, I was excited. And believe it or not, I had a sermon prepared, just in case the church approved my request.

Sunday evening after Thanksgiving came quickly. I was facing the most spiritual moment of my young life—a moment when I would speak for my Lord and Savior Jesus Christ. The little church was filled to capacity with many members of the church, my friends and friends of the family, and some people from the Central Baptist Church where I had been baptized and received my early religious education. The service was incredibly spirit-filled, with testimonies and prayers for my success in the ministry. The final hymn was my favorite, "O' How I Love Jesus," which I had known since I could remember singing. Rev. Taylor's presentation was short but heartfelt—which I could understand (in case I did not do well, he would not be held responsible).

After he had presented me, I walked to the pulpit and began by thanking God for allowing me to preach His Word. I also thanked my pastor and church for having the faith in me to allow me to proclaim the "Good News" about the gospel. My text was the last verse of 1 Corinthians chapter 13, which read, "Now abideth faith, hope, and love, but the greatest of these is love." The theme of my sermon was that God loved us so much that he sent his only son to save us from our sins. Because he loved us, we should love our brothers and sisters, not only those in our church but all people regardless of their race or station in life. If love could have changed the world that night, we would have had peace all over the world. I had people loving each other everywhere.

When I look back over the feeble presentation, I believe that my church was generous to give me any amens. After Rev. Taylor and the church voted to license me as a minister of the gospel of Jesus Christ, the church broke out in shouts of praise and the old "Amen" hymn, which meant "may God approve."

I will never forget that night. It was the first formal acknowledgement of my "pilgrimage in clay feet," which I would acknowledge many times during the sixty-one years I would commit my life to the ministry. There would be many times when I could not walk and he carried me because of my weaknesses, which would remind me of my total dependence on God.

My return to State was very exciting. I had made up my mind as to what would be my life's work. Although many of my friends and some classmates attended my initial sermon, my choice of ministry would be news to many on campus and especially my fellow choir members. Also, since I had assumed the presidency of the John B. Watson memorial Sunday school, I knew many of my friends and classmates would support me in my call to the ministry. I could not wait to talk with my mentor and friend Rev. A. Edward Davis, my pastor in college and one who had counseled me during my mother's illness.

The first days of my return were joyous ones. It seemed that a burden had been lifted, and I was spiritually free. This changed my outlook on life, including my college studies and my seriousness in preparing my life for future studies in seminary, at least three years away. After a flurry of congratulations and some calling me "Rev" in a teasing manner, I settled down to a regimen of study and attending choir rehearsals, where Mr. Lovelace announced my call to the ministry and congratulated me. He also informed me that his father was a minister, as was his brother in Milwaukee, who we had met at our concert at his church.

The weeks passed quickly. We were almost at the Christmas holidays, which meant examinations and additional choir rehearsals in preparation for our annual Christmas concert. The concert drew people throughout Arkansas, in addition to our state college family. I was anxious to return home for Christmas to see my dear mother, who Dr. Lloyd had pronounced free of cancer and infections; and the sores had completely healed. This news made every day at school exciting. Now, all I needed to do was study and continue to thank God for the beautiful, magnificent healing of my sainted mother.

The week before our concert, the campus had an air of excitement that I had not experienced the first year. I think it was due to the fact that we were freshman and not as appreciative of college life as we had become during our sophomore year. The campus was beautifully decorated and the student union was busy with activities as we prepared to leave for the long Christmas holidays. The annual concert was coming up on the Sunday before Christmas, and many of us would have the next day to spend Christmas with our families and friends.

Mr. Lovelace was a perfectionist and did not accept mediocrity in any of the compositions we sang. The concert was attended by the president of the college, along with presidents of Baptist College and Philander Smith College in Little Rock. The religious community would attend in record numbers. Our concert would be accompanied not only by Arthur Porter, Arkansas's best pianist, along with trumpets and timpani drums, but also by our own Mr. Hitchcock and the string section. This, our biggest event of the year, again featured Handel's *Messiah*, including the finale, the "Hallelujah" chorus, when the audience always stood in respect. Mr. Lovelace's charisma, dignity, and air of confidence seemed to transfer to every member of the choir.

After the extensive applause subsided, Mr. Lovelace seemingly looked at all fifty-three members of the choir. With his strong downstroke, the pianist hit the introductory chord. The choir responded with power, clarity, and unbelievable spiritual energy. The accompanying instruments transformed the student union building into a concert hall. The leading soloists that evening were Irene Griffin, Eugene Holmes, Myrtis Jones, and Samuel Fletcher. Several of these soloists went on to become nationally acclaimed singers.

The most powerful part of the *Messiah* was the finale. As soon as Mr. Lovelace gave the cue to the pianist and the celebrated child protégé, Mr. Porter, the down stroke we were on our way to the most exhilarating and powerful part of this renowned composition.

When we reached the final contrapuntal part, where Handel repeats the words, "King of Kings and Lord of Lords," an astonishing thing happened. The audience joined in. All of our combined voices could only be described as the celestial choir singing before the King and Lord of heaven and earth.

After the finale, the audience remained standing and excitedly applauded for what seemed like fifteen minutes. There was no encore because the praise of God was the encore, and it continued until people began to mingle with each other, giving one another genuine embraces of love and joy.

The morning came quickly since most of us did not sleep in the dorms that night. We would be leaving the next day for our home destinations until January 3, 1956, a long vacation for us since choir rehearsal would not resume until January 4.

The holidays would have special meaning for me this time. I would not only celebrate the birth of Jesus Christ as Savior of the world; it would also be the new birth of my life as a servant of Jesus Christ to preach the gospel the rest of my life.

The next morning, we all rushed to make our bus connections. My bus left for Memphis from Pine Bluff, Arkansas, at one o'clock in the afternoon and would arrive in Memphis at three thirty in the afternoon. This trip was so familiar I could call all the stops between Pine Bluff and Memphis. Although segregation in interstate travel had been ruled unconstitutional, many places were reluctant to serve us; we had begun to challenge these bus stops, which served food.

Since it was a short trip and I had not slept much the night before, I decided to remain on the bus until we reached Forest City, Arkansas, and I was halfway home. I left the bus to get a sandwich and cola, which would last me for the duration of the trip.

The most beautiful sight in the world is when we reached West Memphis, Arkansas, and could see the skyline and soon would cross the Memphis-Arkansas Bridge and the mighty Mississippi River, also a sight to behold. On my arrival at the bus station, Gerry would meet me with open arms like I had been away for years. The bonds you develop as a family, the full strength of which you only realize after you have been separated, are amazing.

The trip to 1610 Arkansas was only be twenty minutes but seemed like an hour. Arriving at home, I saw my dear mother standing on the small porch with her apron on, waiting for her baby boy to come home. I could hardly wait to hug and kiss her and hold her for a prolonged time. When we went into the house, I could smell the calf's liver she had prepared, along with the rice and butter beans, my favorite dishes. My father had not arrived home because, after his duty as a postman, he would stop by the office of National Alliance of Postal Employees, where he once served as president. Melvin was just as excited to have me there as I was to be home, because he knew Mother would be cooking extra food for me, as well as getting ready for the Christmas holidays.

Daddy arrived home just as Mother had completed setting the table. He was glad to see me. And before we could finish our greetings, he told me he had arranged for me to preach at two churches while I was home. I was not disappointed or reluctant to accept this challenge, although this would be my first sermon since my initial trial sermon during the Thanksgiving holiday.

Mother soon called us to the most beautiful dinner table she had ever prepared. Thanksgiving was a sumptuous dinner, but this was one that celebrated the birth of Jesus the Christ and the rebirth and recovery of my mother from cancer. My father asked me to say the blessing for the food, which was a first. I immediately accepted and asked everyone to bow their heads and join me in thanking God for this blessing and the healing of our mother. The prayer, as I recall, went something like this, "Our Father which art in heaven, hallowed be thy name, thy kingdom come on earth as it is in heaven. Thank you for this blessed day that thou has made and allowed us to meet and have this wonderful meal, which mother has prepared. Thank you for her life and the healing power, which thou sent to deliver her from the bonds of sickness and death. Thank you for our father, who has been strong and faithful in supporting her with prayer and love. Thank you for my brothers and sisters who are here or far away. Keep them in your love and grace through all the days to come. Now, we thank you for this food, which thou have given and our mother has prepared, in the name of Jesus, Amen."

I don't know why, but this was the best late lunch I had ever had. I called it lunch because of the time of day, but it was actually dinner (though we would eat more of the same later if we could).

After dinner, Mother would start cleaning up the kitchen as usual. This time I told her I wanted to help her, but she insisted that I go into the living room and talk with my father. She was always so selfless, which made me think of her in angelic terms. Another reason I thought of her in angelic terms was because she never gave me a whipping. She left that to my father, who also never whipped me. They were before their time, because I surely deserved whippings.

Christmas Day 1956 was a beautiful day in Memphis. Snow had fallen the day before, and the temperature was in the low thirties, which gave the snow a beautiful glow with the sun shining on it. Mother was busy in the kitchen preparing breakfast after we returned from Christmas service at Bethlehem Baptist Church, where I had preached my first sermon. Our mother tried to please everyone at mealtime. She knew I loved liver and onions, Melvin loved ham, and Daddy love all of it. Our plates were full of our favorite meats and eggs, fried potatoes, fried apples, grits, and biscuits, and our mugs were filled with coffee. This was just breakfast, which should carry us to Christmas dinner at four o'clock in the afternoon when my uncles Hubert and Judson would arrive with their girlfriends.

I went to visit friends after breakfast to catch up on what had been happening in college life and exaggerate as much as I could. I did not feel guilty, because they exaggerated more about what had been happening in Memphis since I'd left, making it sound as though I had been holding back progress. All of us knew how ridiculous it sounded and had a bit of a laugh about all of it. It was a joy seeing my orchestra friends, like William Hawkins, our tenor saxophone player; Gene "Hot Lips" Miller; Al Jackson, the drummer whose father gave me the opportunity to play with some of this groups; Robert Wesley McGee, our bass player whose father taught us Latin in high school; and especially our band director and orchestra leader, the legendary W. T. McDaniel, who played the piano and made all the busboy arrangements for us. He had the best position in the group, and I mean the best. Seeing these guys again made all of us feel old. It seemed so long since we had traveled all over Tennessee playing gigs in dance halls, whiskey and beer joints, and other unsavory but beautiful places. I say beautiful because, despite the oppression we faced as a race, somehow we managed to survive through religion and entertainment. This may sound like a strange combination to some people, but both brought the things we needed, which were hope and joy.

The Christmas holidays were the best. Our family was again intact with our mother back to her old self. My preaching engagements were great, and I was well received at both Central Baptist Church, where I was baptized by Rev. Morrison and Mississippi Boulevard Christian Church, where my former principal was pastor. It was not only an opportunity but also an honor to be asked to preach at both churches,

1957

considering these two were the most learned ministers in the city of Memphis. My acceptance by these ministers meant that I was worthy to enter the ministry, notwithstanding I had yet to finish college and receive any formal theological education. This was the highlight of my Christmas vacation. On January 3, I returned to State with a new spirit of determination to be the best minister I could be.

On our return, Mr. Lovelace informed us that we would again be going on our Midwest tour to publicize the school and raise money from our alumni. This meant two rehearsals a day until April.

Again the grades for the second quarter had come out, and other classmates did not return, which was always difficult in some ways. This second year was more intense, since we had declared our major. Everything took on a new emphasis; this was preparation for the graduate or professional schools we had selected.

I was very pleased with my major in sociology and my minor in history. Rev. A. E. Davis, my mentor, had suggested this major because it was general but also gave me a background for social service as well as ministry. The head of my department, Dr. Tillman, was one of the smartest professors on campus, a fact about which all of us in his department took great pride. He was respected by faculty, having received his doctorate from the University of Chicago, and noted for having the best department of sociology in the nation. He was not sparing in his demand that we read and retain the knowledge of what we read. His lectures were always informative and entertaining. I was amazed that he could speak for an hour without notes, quoting many authors, chapter and verse.

One of my best friends in my class was future attorney John W. Walker, now the renowned esquire in the Arkansas. John made me work hard to keep up with him and also debated points of disagreement. Some of the brightest and most articulate students in the college were sociology majors. They were also some of the most popular students on campus.

Dr. Cochran, after finding out that I was preparing for the ministry, took a special interest in me and suggested a special reading list for me to introduce me to some new ideas in religion and theology. He suggested *Varieties of Religious Experiences* by William James, a classic in the fields of religion and sociology. To this date, I quote him in my argument for world religions.

The year was passing fast, and our rehearsals were becoming more intense. Our choir would be leaving on our annual mid-western tour, for the second year. Although sometimes we would complain about the many rehearsals, we were proud to be learning new music, sometimes in German or Italian.

This year would be one I would never forget for many reasons. I *1957* would become attracted to one of the most beautiful and intelligent girls on campus, Joyce Alvia McClinton of Little Rock, Arkansas. She was a music major but also attended sociology class with me and was a member of the choir. It's amazing how you could be around someone for so long and never have an interest, and then, all of a sudden, you see something in him or, in this case her, that really makes you wonder where this person has been. This was such a ridiculous question; we had known each other since we'd entered as freshmen members of the choir. Joyce was multitalented, in that she could sing and also play the marimba, which she'd mastered before coming to State. Our relationship grew slowly through conversations about life's issues and questions that intrigued me, as I was drawn to her intellect and determination to win the argument. During the year she received many honors, such as Alpha Phi Alpha fraternity's queen and would later become queen of the Cotton Carnival. I was greatly impressed with how all of these honors and accomplishments did not cause her to become arrogant. Our relationship became stronger and our conversations more intimate as a result of our realization of how much we had in common in family values and mutual attraction, which was also physical.

Our friendship had become a serious relationship, and we could not see enough of each other. We shared lunch with each other as much as possible. She became a part of the college Sunday school I taught. And our choir rehearsals were no longer an obligation but an opportunity to see Joyce. The relationship continued to grow, which also motivated me in my studies and especially in my work in preparation for the ministry.

Our choir's mid-western tour of was only a month away, which meant we would be away from the campus over two weeks and also that Joyce and I would spend more time together. Needless to say, the time went slowly. But April would soon come to be, and only a few weeks remained before the tour.

In the meantime, things were going well at school and home. My dear mother was still thriving and gaining more energy every day. She would write me and inquire how I was doing and always asked if I had preached lately. When I would tell her I had preached, she would insist that I give her a short version of my sermon with the text, including the chapter and verse. Although I did not want to do it, whatever Mother asked me to do I did. Ever since God gave her back to me, I did not take the blessing of her in my life for granted and tried to please her in every way I could.

The days went by faster because my teachers had intensified our reading list, which would be part of our quarterly examinations and determine much of our grades.

During our last rehearsal before leaving for Saint Louis and the tour, Mr. Lovelace spoke to all of us, including the new members, about what he expected on tour. We were to be on time for all functions, including breakfast, lunch, and dinner; our schedule for leaving from one city and getting to the next city on time was very tight. We were also told we were going to all-white cities, which meant we had to make sure we conducted ourselves in such a way that we would be a credit to our race and college. This may seem a strange talk to young people, but there was a time when our teachers and elders drilled into our minds that we had to be better than whites in order to advance, which seemed unfair but was true in practice. "Pops" Lovelace was our father away from home, and we loved him as a father.

Before we knew it, April had arrived and we were scheduled to leave on tour on Friday, first to East Saint Louis, Illinois. We left early that morning from the student union building, after having a breakfast specially prepared for the choir, since we would make very few stops on our way. The morning of our departure was relatively smooth. We brought our bags to the student union building, where the bus was waiting to take us on our ten-day tour to the Midwest. Joyce had gotten there early to secure our seats for the trip. Several other couples had claimed seats on the bus that were not close to the front, where the chaperones were seated, since we planned to do a lot of smooching and kissing on our way to the Midwest. The freshmen, because they had yet to develop relationships with other choir members, were assigned to the front of the bus with Mr. Lovelace and the chaperones. The first few hours were spent sleeping, since most of us had not slept much the night before. Some were leaving girlfriends or boyfriends who they would not see for almost two weeks.

From State, we <u>road</u> about nine hours, arriving in East Saint Louis around five o'clock in the afternoon at the Bethel Baptist Church, which was hosting us for the concert to be held that Sunday afternoon. The church served as the meeting place for the families who were picking us up to spend the next two nights before leaving for Chicago. The church had prepared a sumptuous and plentiful dinner for us. The menu, as I remember almost sixty years later, was fried chicken, mashed potatoes with chicken gravy, turnip greens, and corn pudding, with either corn bread or biscuits. The beverage was always lemonade, and the dessert was apple pie. After dinner, we were taken to our respective assigned homes. One may wonder why we did not stay in hotels. The truth is that segregation in hotels was forbidden by the Interstate Commerce Commission (ICC). Moreover, our choir was on a very tight budget, which made that option impossible. Also, there was something about the church members that made them proud to have us in their homes as guests and aspiring young Negroes.

After dinner, Mr. Lovelace spoke to us about the schedule for Sunday. Our hosts would get us to the church no later than five o'clock in the evening. Our concert was set for eight o'clock. We were to come to the church with our formal dress, consisting of tuxedo tails for the men and beautiful long formal dresses for the ladies. The church graciously provided us with areas in which to dress before the concert.

Mr. Lovelace was a very detailed person who demanded that we look, act, and be professional in our conduct. This meant no loud boisterous talk in the church and careful observation of all church rules. We always rehearsed at least an hour before we performed, and he wanted us there by five o'clock to go over how we would enter and leave the stage or pulpit area. After rehearsal, we would relax and socialize until seven o'clock, when we dressed and waited for Pops Lovelace to give our last-minute instructions. One may think this is quite a detailed preparation for a concert, but Mr. Lovelace left nothing to chance, and all of us were confident because we had prepared extremely well. Our choir was quite famous due to the history of its performances well before many of us got to State. We all felt an obligation to keep the tradition of excellence that our former choir members had left us.

People began arriving at the church as early as six thirty. The choir met in the large assembly room in the basement dressed and ready to perform. At seven thirty, Sam Fletcher began to sing the prayer we offered before every meal and every performance. After singing the blessing, there was silence in the room until Mr. Lovelace directed us to line up and prepare to enter the sanctuary. As I looked around the room, I saw that everyone looked great; the men looked elegant in their tuxedoes and tails, and the ladies were stunningly beautiful in their evening dresses.

At the signal, the door was opened and the choir entered in the order of sopranos, altos, tenors, baritones, and basses. We had done this so many times it was second nature. Mr. Lovelace even taught us how to walk with dignity—heads and shoulders erect with a pleasant look or smile as we entered. After we were in place, the pianist, our violinist, and then our leader followed. Mr. Lovelace, the one and only, the elegant and eminent director of the Arkansas AM&N of Pine Bluff, Arkansas, entered with thunderous applause and a standing ovation before the concert had even begun.

He looked toward the pianist, and with his down-stroke, the concert began. The first set was in Latin and German. Although the audience may not have understood, the sound was perfect, our voices blending along with the soloists—soprano Irene Griffin from Chicago, tenor Sam Fletcher, and baritone Eugene Holmes from Saint Louis, Missouri. All of fellow choir members went on to fame in New York; Los Angeles, California; and Europe.

Our concerts followed the same pattern throughout our tour in the Midwest. When we left East Saint Louis, we went to Chicago, where we presented in a large church. From there, we went to Milwaukee, Wisconsin, where we sang in the church pastored by the Reverend Lovelace, brother of our director.

While we were in Milwaukee, someone suggested we tour the Schlitz Beer Company. The reason for this tour of the plant was to get a chance to sample their beer as long as we liked, which was not a good idea.

The concert in Milwaukee was received with great acclaim.

From there we went on to Delevan Lake and Mukwonago, Northern towns located in the farm areas of Wisconsin. What was unique about this town was that some of the children had not seen Negroes in person, only on television. Seeing us was not only fascinating to them; it was also very interesting for us to watch them as they looked at us like we were from some other planet. Because they were so young, I also found it humorous. Our concerts were received with great enthusiasm and praise in both towns, with invitations to come back every year.

After leaving the last town, we headed home, stopping only in Memphis for our last concert before returning to State.

The trip to Memphis from Wisconsin would take ten hours, with several stops for food and rest. We left Delavan Lake late on Friday night, arriving in Memphis at noon on Saturday at the Pentecostal Temple, where we were met by members of the church who had prepared lunch for us before taking us to their homes for the night. Of course, several of us who were from Memphis went to our homes and, in some instances, brought our roommates for the night. Our instructions from Pops Lovelace were to arrive at the church no later than six thirty in the evening for rehearsal and other last-minute instructions before the concert.

My roommate Ashton Wilkerson, also called Jerry, came home with me to spend the night and meet my family. During our time together, we had become like brothers. He had been raised by his aunt since the death of his mother when he was very young. She was loving and kind to him and to me. His aunt would come up from Acadia, Louisiana to bring us home-cooked food such as fried chicken, butter beans, and mustard greens with corn bread and when she brought him back to school, she would bring food for a week, including many canned goods. My mother was like his aunt, offering him a home-cooked meal of baked chicken, corn bread dressing with giblet gravy, mashed potatoes, and corn bread, along with lemonade and apple cobbler. Of course, she prepared enough for us to take back to State the following day.

Sunday morning, Mother prepared a late breakfast since we were tired and did not have to be at the church until six thirty in the evening for rehearsal. Jerry was made to feel at home with my family, and we spent time watching television and sleeping, since we never slept too much on our bus rides. Some friends came over in the afternoon to see me and catch me up on what had been happening since I had been gone.

Some of my friends had played with me in the orchestra while I was in high school. Jerry did not know about this, and it surprised him, since I had not mentioned it. William Hawkins, the saxophone player, lived around the corner from me and told us about the other members of the orchestra. I was very interested to know how other members of the orchestra were doing. One of the most talented members, Alvin Jackson, whose father had given me an opportunity to play with his orchestra, had become a staff member of Stax Records. He was playing with many big-time artists, including Elvis Presley and many up-and-coming black artists.

My brother-in-law George Greene took us to the church around six o'clock. People had begun arriving for our eight o'clock concert. This was the church of the father of my childhood friend, J. O. Patterson Jr. Bishop J. O. Patterson Sr. was pastor, and Bishop Charles Mason was founder of the Church of God in Christ, which today is the fastest-growing evangelical church in America. This was also the church of our celebrated tenor Samuel Fletcher, who sang in the choir for many years at Pentecostal Temple.

During rehearsal Mr. Lovelace asked whether we wished to remain in Memphis overnight or leave for State following the concert. We unanimously agreed to leave from the church and return to State, only three hours away. This decision made all of us anxious to get the concert done. But we also wanted to make this concert special for the Memphian classmates' families who had come to hear their children sing. We also wanted it to be special for Sam Fletcher. Our celebrated tenor was in his last year and would be leaving to further his bright career.

Mr. Lovelace gave instructions for us to move into the sanctuary and take our places. Although we had been told our first musical presentation would be a Latin aria, to our surprise, Sam Fletcher took the mike and began to sing the beautiful hymn, "America." This was one of the many songs he could sing like no other, his emotion unmatched. His sweet, melodious voice almost whispered the first lines: "While *Refrain* the storm clouds gather far across the sea / let us all be grateful for a land that's free / let us pledge allegiance for a land so fair / as we raise our voices with a solemn prayer." The choir, with perfect harmony and grace, joined in with, "God bless America / land that I love. / Stand beside her, and guide her / through the night with the light from above."

This hymn may sound strange for a people who had endured untold and harsh treatment from the founders of this land and their children. However, in 1954 when the Supreme Court ruled in the case of Brown v. Board of Education of Topeka that segregation was unconstitutional, all black people had new hope and felt that this could and would it be our county, despite hundreds of years of slavery and oppression.

This concert was the highlight of our tour, with every offering having special meaning. This was especially true of the lyrics of one of the founders, Thomas Jefferson, who wrote, "The same God who gave us life gave us liberty." These words also gave meaning to the evening, with all the discussion of civil rights that was taking place throughout the South.

Although we had been touring for almost two weeks, we had no feeling of tiredness but, rather, a feeling of accomplishment. Following the concert, the church gave us prepared boxes with dinner for us to eat on our way back to State. After boarding the bus, we shared a sense of excitement—our destination was Pine Bluff, Arkansas.

We arrived around midnight. Except for the security officers who patrolled all night (which many of us realized after being caught smooching in private areas of the campus) the campus was shut down. All of us were very glad to be home from the tour, to which we always looked forward each year. As we left the bus, we were dragging from our all-day ordeal and concert in Memphis. The word *ordeal* is not the correct description, since the congregation had given us Royal treatment, and everyone had been so encouraging to us—young Negroes who would change the world.

The next day, we were required to be in class. That had been negotiated between our director and our teachers as part of our agreement to go on the Midwest tour. Although I was tired from our travels, there was something welcoming about being back in the academic setting.

The remainder of the year seemed to pass quickly, and we were soon almost at the end of our second year of college. My sociology major had proven to be right for me, in light of the fact that I would be going to seminary and preparing for the Christian ministry.

Returning to Dr. Cochran's class was a joy, as he challenged our thinking, introducing new thoughts and ideas that made our study captivating. The class assignments I kept up with while on tour were sociology because I wanted to be prepared to demonstrate to Dr. Cochran that I really wanted to be a sociologist, although I would use it in my Christian ministry. I looked forward to my junior year because Dr. Cochran's alma mater, University of Chicago, produced many of the renowned sociology professors in the nation.

The last six weeks of the term would end, and many of our choir members would be leaving to pursue other areas of education or music careers, among them Samuel Fletcher, Eugene Holmes, and Irene Griffin. Some of the others in our choir would be offered jobs in Arkansas as music teachers, band directors, or teachers in the educational system. There were rumors that Central High School in Little Rock would be integrated in the fall, and tension was palpable, as we realized the stakes of racial violence that could occur. This was the world as we ended our sophomore year and prepared to enter our junior year at State. Time had passed so quickly since the first year we arrived on the campus of this historic land grant college, which we would come to love and I would long cherish as the beginning of my "journey in clay feet."

My relationship with Joyce had developed to a serious stage as we said goodbye for the summer, although we would see each other at some point during the summer. The next few days were spent with the seniors in celebratory events and commencement activities. After saying goodbye to Joyce and promising to see her during the summer, I boarded a bus for Memphis to spend my summer with family and friends and pursue my chosen field of Christian ministry.

Summer 1957

96

My father knew so many ministers that I could preach every Sunday if I chose to, but I wanted to have some time for myself and my friends. I did attend some church every Sunday with my friend Alexander Sykes, who had also accepted the call to the ministry. His father pastored the Person Avenue Baptist Church only a few blocks from our house. Sykes, as I called him, was a very sincere young man, for whom I had great respect, even though he was far more pious than me. He ate and breathed preaching, which was strange to me, since I still had a social life that was very different from my religious life. Our relationship continued through the summer, even as I left for my summer job in Chicago at Hines Hospital in Oak Park, Illinois, while he worked in the service industry in Memphis.

This was my second year working at the hospital with my good friend Saul Holmes. Saul and I had shared many experiences during our high school days. We both made the band in our freshman year, with Saul playing clarinet and me playing trombone. This was a signal honor for us, since not many were selected for the band in their freshman year. We bonded for the next three years, sharing many experiences. Saul was an excellent student and well-liked by all the students in our class. He was also a good student who took seriously his studies, which challenged me. This was why our relationship continued when his family moved to Chicago. Our sharing the summers will never be forgotten. To this day, Saul and I remain close friends, along with his wife, Lou.

The summer went well, both in terms of my job and my social life in Chicago, the latter of which consisted mainly of visiting relatives, going downtown to the Chicago Theater, and eating at some fancy restaurants that we could only find "up North," as we called it.

Although I loved Chicago, I was anxious to get back to Arkansas AM&N to start my junior year and return to my sociology classes which were exciting because of Dr. Cochran. To this day, he has had a great influence on my life, although he was not particularly religious. His legacy to me was his ability to convey ideas and challenge your ideas in a way that made you think more deeply about things, rather than just accepting the surface or the obvious.

I left Chicago to return to Memphis, saying goodbye to Saul and Lou. Arriving in Memphis the morning of August 25 meant I had about a week before I would leave for State for early choir rehearsals and to reunite with my classmates and choir members. The junior year promised to be an exciting one, since I would be eligible for membership in the Alpha Phi Alpha fraternity, the oldest black fraternity in the country. I had been impressed with the fraternity since first coming State.

I left to return to State on September 2. Leaving was, in some ways, a bittersweet experience. My mother was doing great, for which I will always be thankful to God. My father was enjoying life and preaching at various churches throughout Memphis. I realized that I would never again spend as much time with them as I had in the past. This is a reality that children must come to grips with as they mature. Your parents will always think of you as their child and in some ways want to protect you. But they realize, as you must also understand, that life moves on, and we all must make our way. This is not to say that we young people will ever forget our parents, which is impossible, but it does mean that our lives await us, like theirs awaited them when they were our age.

As the bus left Memphis, heading toward the Arkansas-Memphis Bridge, I looked back at the landscape of my beloved city and realized that I was about to witness something about which my parents and grandparents has only dreamed. Integration! There were rumors that this would be the year when Little Rock Central High School would be integrated, and the city and state had braced for this historic event. Governor Orval Eugene Faubus had vowed to prevent the integration of public schools at all cost.

Incidentally, the ICC had entered an order stating that there could be no segregation on interstate carriers, so I was seated on the first seat of the Greyhound bus, which I had ridden for two years segregated. This time, I was exercising my constitutional right to sit where I wanted to without interference. This was not the most comfortable ride I had ever had returning to State. Some blacks still went to the back, and some of us took the position that Negroes would have to exercise their rights if we were ever to be free. Rosa Parks had already demonstrated this courage with her refusal to move when ordered, thereby exercising rights that led to the historic Montgomery, Alabama, boycott. One of the most honored and historic figures in black and American history, the Reverend Dr. Martin Luther King Jr., pastor of the Dexter Avenue Baptist Church, emerged from this boycott.

As I arrived at State, many things were running through my mind. I had been thinking for the past two hours about what this year would hold for me personally—in my studies and in my relationship with the young lady who I knew was the one I would love to marry. However, the most important issues for our school and the state of Arkansas and the nation was how would this idea of integration in schools and public accommodations were issues that would usher in the best and worst of America.

My arrival was met with the talk of other students about what had happened during the summer, especially the possibility of the integration of Central High School and the nine brave and courageous students who had already been selected to attend. The Supreme Court had ruled that these nine and students be enrolled, and we waited with great anticipation the date of September 25, though we tried to keep things at school as normal as possible by attending classes, choir rehearsals, football games, and other activities. Although all of these historic issues were permeating the conversation on campus, we were remarkably calm in our wait.

Classes resumed on September 5, and my first sociology class was one of the best lectures Dr. Cochran had ever delivered in my estimation. He associated his lecture with issues that were about to occur in our state and how this would test whether or not we were a nation of laws. The amazing thing was that, although this ominous cloud hung over our state and college, it was remarkable how we went about our studies and activities without interruption.

When the date finally arrived for the integration of Central High School, the entire college was tuned to radio or television to find out what was going on. Governor Faubus had called out the Arkansas National Guard to prevent the Negro students from entering the school. This pleased many segregationists who had resolved that their children would not attend school with the Negro students.

After a confrontation at the school, the attorneys for the government advised the attorneys and civil rights activists to retreat until the court could issue another order or President Eisenhower could direct the Department of Justice to take other actions. The leaders of the movement on behalf of the students were Daisy Bates and attorney Wiley Branton, who had advocated for equal rights for many years in Arkansas.

The order from the president of the United States came quickly. Eisenhower federalized the Arkansas National Guard and activated the 101st Army Division to go to Little Rock to enforce the order of the court. This confrontation between Governor Faubus and President Eisenhower would create tension unlike anything the people had ever experienced.

When the students returned to Central High under the protection of federal troops, it was a beautiful scene to see these students with their heads held high and their mentors walking with them into the front doors of the school. Our pride soared and our self-esteem was raised to a level we had never before known. Governor Faubus did not interfere, and the registration and other activities went out as planned. Although this was trying for these students, they had been adequately prepared by their mentors, which minimized the negative impact of their new educational experience.

After several weeks of taunts and insults by students and outsiders, the tensions began to subside. Life began to return to normal at State, although we were well aware that the violence we had seen in Little Rock was just under the surface throughout Arkansas.

Our choir rehearsals took on a new meaning. We were not just preparing for concerts throughout Arkansas; in a subtle way, we were trying to encourage our elders who were fearful that integration would lead to violence and retrenchment in race relations. Our repertoire included Thomas Jefferson's words, "The same God who gave us life gave us liberty." The words resonated with our audiences and encouraged them to know that, although the founding fathers did not mean to include Negroes, these words emanated from a source that could only be called God. Our attitude toward studying and preparation took on new meaning as we recognized that civil rights movement had taken on a life of its own and could not be stopped. There was a sense of purpose in everything we did, and the teachers seemed energized, too, by our eagerness to learn and prepare for the future.

The time seemed to pass quickly. Before we knew it, Thanksgiving was again upon us, and all of us were looking forward to going home or visiting with relatives and friends.

My relationship with Joyce had developed beautifully or had become full. I was sure she would be my life mate. I was shocked but pleasantly surprised when she asked me to come to Little Rock and have Thanksgiving dinner with her family. I was elated for the invitation but unsure how her parents would accept me (or any young man) spending time in my girlfriend's home. After talking with her mother, I was assured that both she and Mr. McClinton were in agreement with Joyce's invitation. Of course, this had not been cleared by my parents, who also had a sense of propriety when it came to young men staying over at their girlfriends' homes. Mother and Daddy were in agreement that, if the McClinton's had invited me to share Thanksgiving with them and their daughter, it would be fine with them.

Although I had met Mrs. McClinton on several occasions, I was astonished how independent she was, having been declared legally blind at a young age. She had finished Philander Smith College in Little Rock and was employed by the state of Arkansas as a social worker assisting the blind. She was remarkable, in that she never emanated any feelings of pity but, to the contrary, was one of the most positive persons I had ever met.

Mr. McClinton was also a person I admired. His community involvement in the political issues of Little Rock and the state impressed me. He formed a separate Negro caucus to the Democratic Party, which helped the group to have a voice in the decisions about that part of Arkansas. He also served as a deacon at the Mount Pleasant Baptist Church, where the family had belonged for many years. I was greatly impressed with the family, including Charles, who was an upperclassman at State and Joyce's older sister, Verna, who was classy and very aware of people. That part made me nervous, even though I did not have anything to hide that I knew about. I really liked the affection Verna showed toward her little sister, Joyce.

Thanksgiving dinner was everything you could ask for, including a very interesting and informative conversation with Joyce's father. At the dinner table with all of us gathered, Mr. McClinton offered a beautiful

Thanksgiving prayer, which included me as Joyce's friend. The dinner was just like my dinner at home over the years. We had a beautiful baked turkey, which must have weighed at least twenty pounds, with corn bread dressing, green peas, mashed potatoes, giblet gravy, sweet potato casserole, turnip greens, cranberry sauce, and hot homemade rolls, with lemonade and sweet tea. This was just like home, and Joyce made me feel special. Sitting beside her, I found it difficult to eat, as I was trying to make sure I exhibited the right manners.

After dinner, we took a walk, which was just what I needed for many reasons. I had not really been alone with her since coming home with her. We stopped at a park, where I was able to give her that kiss I had been saving for almost two days. After sitting in the park and talking about how long will we'd wait before making the decision to get married, we returned to the house, where her family had just finished serving dessert. Joyce fixed me an ample piece of apple pie à la mode, which was delicious.

The next day, we returned to State, since Mr. Lovelace had called for a rehearsal in preparation for a concert in Fort Smith, Arkansas, that following Sunday. My visit to Joyce's home was not only enjoyable; I also really liked her family, especially her mother, whom I admired so much for what she had accomplished despite her blindness.

Things in Little Rock had settled down quite a bit since Central High had been integrated. And the Negro students were adjusting, despite the difficulties they were experiencing as Negroes in a white environment. We went about our classes and rehearsals without interruption, even though the news carried reports of daily indignities against the Negro students. The students comported themselves with so much dignity that the country realized that the decision to integrate was the right decision, despite the upheaval it had caused.

Joyce and I had become even closer after my visit to her home in Little Rock during the Thanksgiving holidays. She did not know it, but I had planned to propose to her during the Christmas holidays, when I would invite her to come to Memphis after Christmas to spend the weekend with my family. Once I'd made this decision, the days seemed to pass quickly, and our annual Christmas concert was soon upon us.

Our rehearsals increased, with Mr. Lovelace planning our last rehearsal with the full regalia of horns, violins, and timpani drums, which required extreme coordination.

The Sunday before Christmas was the date for our annual concert, which would feature the entire Handel's *Messiah*. Mr. Lovelace had prepared us for perfection, and we were so prepared that rehearsals became boring. For those of us who had met three years before as freshmen with anxieties and uncertainties, this would be the third Christmas concert. Now, we were on the verge of becoming seniors in a few months, a prospect that was both exhilarating and the cause for some anxiety.

My thoughts were not on anything but waiting to have Joyce visit me and to propose to her and give her the ring I had borrowed money from my father to purchase from Mednikow Jewelers, with a firm promise to repay him. Dad was very elated to learn I had found someone with whom I wanted to spend my life and share my ministry. My mother was equally excited about Joyce. The two had spoken many times, and she had become very fond of my future bride.

The Sunday of our concert was a beautiful day. Negroes came from far and near to join in solidarity, remembering the long struggle for equality and celebrating the birth of Jesus the Christ and the hope he would bring to the world. This was especially appropriate in light of what had happened in Little Rock during the integration of Central High. This concert was different in many ways, especially as we contemplated the future of our state and country with this new and powerful social change.

Mr. Lovelace directed us to take the stage in the formation we had always followed. Then the supporting cast of violins, trumpets, and timpani drums followed. After the applause, Mr. Lovelace came forward, once again with thunderous applause greeting him not only for the day's offering but also for the many years he had labored to keep the school in the public eye and forward the pathway to progress for us as a race. This had been made possible thanks to his excellent representation of the possibilities through music, not unlike the Jubilee Singers of Fisk University.

This time, Handel's *Messiah*, without exaggeration, we knew to be the most powerful presentation since we had been at State. It is almost impossible to describe how the electricity in the audience was palpable throughout the concert. Although this may sound redundant, the historic social change that had taken place in September made everyone realize this Christmas would not be like any other in our lifetimes. The "Hallelujah" chorus finale was the most powerful I had ever heard. I took in the audience singing "King of Kings and Lord of Lords, King of Kings and Lord of Lords" in between wiping tears from my eyes. I noticed other choir members also overcome with emotion, and many in the audience were weeping openly, without shame or restraint. I had never witnessed such a powerful display of emotion taking over an entire crowd, nor have since in my long years of attending services or celebrations. After the final note of the *Messiah*, there was not a formal closing, only people embracing each other with the joy and peace this Christmas had brought to us as a race.

The next day, all of us left for home to celebrate with friends and relatives during the Christmas season. My Christmas would be special. Joyce would be coming on Friday to spend the weekend with my family. To her surprise, I would propose and present her with an engagement ring.

Christmas came on Wednesday, heightening my anticipation not only for the holiday and all the festivities it brought but also because, after Christmas Day, I would only have two days to wait before my present arrived—which would be Joyce, my soon-to-be fiancée.

Christmas morning arrived with our usual arising at four o'clock in the morning to prepare for Christmas sunrise services at our church, the Bethlehem Baptist Church, where I was licensed to preach. Preparing for church was a real work in logistics having only one bathroom. But we always managed to be on time and arrive before the procession of the choir

Our choir came down the aisles singing "Hark the Herald Angels Sing, Jesus the Light of the World," which put everybody on his or her feet, rejoicing that the Savior had come. When the choir reached the chorus, everybody was singing, "We'll walk in the light, beautiful light / Come where dewdrops of mercy shone bright. / Shine all around us by day and by night / Jesus the light of the world." By this time, shouting had broken out all over the church, and ushers were busy trying to comfort those who had been stricken by the Holy Ghost. This was a beautiful sight, which may not have been understood by the uninitiated, but these people found hope and joy in their lives, realizing that their living was not in vain. The service lasted no less than two hours; the pastor's sermon would take at least one hour. Although this may seem like a long time to worship, life was much simpler then than it is now, which meant the most important time in our lives next to worship was education. This was a carryover from Reconstruction, when slaves realized the value of education and the need for a deep spiritual life.

After Christmas service, we returned home for a light breakfast. We had to prepare for a Christmas feast that afternoon when my uncles and their girlfriends would be coming. Mother was amazing, even with the help of my sister Gerry, who was married but always helped mother during the preparation of the Christmas meal.

My father and I had our yearly conversation about my plans for the New Year and how my studies were going at State. I told him that, since I had been licensed to preach, I had inquired about seminaries and schools of religion. He was very happy to hear this, as he was supportive of ministers being prepared for their work. Although his father had been born into slavery and had never received a formal education, my grandfather had implored the slave masters to help him read and write, which was unheard of during the time of slavery.

Daddy asked me if I had searched for a good school of religion in the area. I told him I had found a very good school in Louisville, Kentucky. The Southern Baptist Seminary was rated among the best Baptist seminaries in the South. I also told him that my sociology professor had mentioned that I should look at Howard University School of Religion, which was the oldest accredited school of religion in the country. Daddy was impressed with the fact that I was thinking about further preparation, rather than attending some local religious school that did not have the scope of knowledge that seminaries and schools of religion offered.

Christmas Day went well, with a very delicious dinner prepared by my saintly mother and my dear sister. After dinner, I met with some of my high school friends, who took me around Memphis to the many classmate parties. Since it had been a long day, I asked to be taken home to be with my parents before they retired for the evening.

When I arrived home, my dear mother still had her apron on, although the kitchen had been cleaned by my sister Gerry and my uncle's girlfriends, Miss Lizzy and Miss Arlene. I talked briefly to my mother and went to bed in our only additional bedroom, to which Melvin had already retired. I loved him dearly, but he would sleep all over the bed, causing me find a spot on the edge and to fall out of bed several times.

The next day was Thursday. I called Joyce to see how things were going and how Christmas Day had gone at her house. She told me that Verna and Charles were well and her mother had prepared a wonderful dinner for all of them, including Charles's girlfriend. Verna, along with Joyce, always helped her mother with dinner. I told her how much I loved her and wanted to see her on Friday. She expressed her excitement about coming to visit and meet my parents and Melvin, about whom she had heard so much. She had talked with Gerry over the phone but had never met her in person. I knew they would be great together, though, because of their compatible personalities.

Friday morning came. And I was excited. Joyce would be arriving at one thirty in the afternoon by Greyhound bus at the Third Street and Union Avenue station. My brother-in-law agreed to take me to the station. I was greatly appreciative of this, since my dad did not have a car and my uncle's car was unbelievably unreliable. The last time I'd used his car to take my date for a high school dance at a club in West Memphis, Arkansas, it had broken down on the Harridan Bridge that connected Memphis with West Memphis.

When George and I arrived, we were told that the bus was running behind and would arrive almost an hour late. George was not just my brother-in-law; he was also a good friend to whom I divulged a lot of personal things since I did not have a brother with whom I could share my concerns around.

When the bus arrived, Joyce was one of the first to disembark. When she stepped off, I embraced her as if we had not seen each other in many months. Our kiss lasted so long that other riders went around us.

Joyce's introduction to George was easy, as she had spoken to him many times since we had been dating. George stopped at a liquor store to get some scotch whiskey because, even though Joyce did not drink, he knew I would need a drink, and he would also.

When we arrived at 1610 Arkansas Street, my mother was on the porch to welcome Joyce, giving her a very warm embrace. After we'd entered the house, my father greeted her and also embraced and welcomed her to our home. My father was always the ultimate gentleman that he taught me to be, and I have tried to emulate him since my childhood.

Mother had prepared lunch for us that seemed more like dinner, with friend chicken and mashed potatoes and green peas. After lunch, Joyce, George, and I left to go to his house, where Gerry had prepared to receive Joyce for the weekend. When we arrived, Gerry was in the yard near the driveway, waiting for her with open arms. After their greeting, we went into the house, and Gerry showed Joyce to her room and helped her to unpack and get comfortable.

After staying a few hours and listening to jazz music, of which George was an ardent fan, I went back to the room where Joyce was spending the night and gave her a passionate kiss, being careful not to get carried away. After assuring her that I would call later that evening, I left for home, knowing that Gerry and George would entertain Joyce during the evening and allow me time to spend with my parents. The next day I would be busy taking her around to meet my friends.

Saturday was the day when we would tie our lives and destinies together by accepting each other as partners for life. I picked up Joyce around noon and took her to lunch at Tony's, one of the nicest lunch and dinner places in Memphis (the place all of the high school prom attendees selected for their after-hours dinner and dancing). At Tony's, we would share lunch, and I would propose and have the waiters bring candles and cake to us to celebrate this special day.

We arrived at Tony's around twelve thirty. People were already there for lunch. Since I had made reservations, we were escorted to our table located at a window that looked out on Bellevue Boulevard. I had already selected a waiter I had known since high school, who one of the best in the business. I ordered a bottle of Kendall Jackson chardonnay for the table, and even though Joyce was not much of a drinker she accepted a glass of wine and a toast to our long and loving relationship.

Rather than wait until after dinner, I wanted to propose as soon as possible and then enjoy dinner without the pressure of thinking about it. After the wine arrived and the waiter had opened the bottle and poured two glasses, we prepared for the toast. Instead of the toast, I raised my glass and said, "Joyce, will you marry me?"

After a pause for her to recover, she said, "Yes, I will."

I placed the most beautiful ring on her finger, which had cost the unheard of sum of $300. (I had promised my father I would repay him when I went to work in Chicago.)

Without a doubt, this was the happiest day of my life. The woman of my dreams had accepted my proposal and ring.

After dinner, we went directly to my parents' home, where Gerry had invited some of my closest friends to share with Joyce and me a light lunch, which my mother had prepared. Most of them were former band members, among them Al Jackson, William Hawkins, Gene Miller, and John Wesley McGee. This was a fitting climax to a day that held much promise and happiness.

Sunday, we all attended the Bethlehem Baptist Church, where members congratulated me on my engagement to such a beautiful and elegant lady. The service was spiritually uplifting and inspiring to us both. Since church service was so long, we both were ready for dinner, which my mother had left church early to prepare. We had the typical Sunday dinner—fried chicken that only my mother could fry, mashed potatoes and gravy, green pea, biscuits, and ice tea. As usual, my mother had prepared a beautiful dinner.

After dinner, William Hawkins and J. O. Patterson picked Joyce and me up to visit with them and have drinks. Later, we would do what we had done so many Sunday evenings—go downtown to Beale Street and the Flamingo Club, where J. O. Patterson and I would once go every Sunday night with our girlfriends for the week. There, we would find Calvin Newborn, an outstanding guitarist with whom I had grown up on Alston Street, along with his brother Phineas, who became one of the most outstanding jazz pianists in the country.

At the Flamingo, we met many old friends I had not seen in many years. I was proud to introduce my fiancée to them. They congratulated us and wished us a happy life together. The music was great, and Calvin was outstanding and even acknowledged Joyce and me from the stage, asking the audience to give us a hand of applause.

We left after the first set because the bus going back to Little Rock was leaving at noon so that she could be with her family for the New Year. My friends dropped Joyce off at my sister's home and took me home, where we wished each other well until another time during the summer.

The nest day, George brought Joyce over to see my mother and father before she returned to Little Rock. After a short time, we left for the bus station, about a twenty-minute drive. My mother and father warmly embraced her and wished us well on our future life together, even though we had not yet set the date of our marriage. Gerry was very fond of Joyce and was satisfied with my choice of life partner. After arriving at the station, Gerry and George waited for me in the car.

Joyce and I waited for the bus to Little Rock to be announced. Our talk was mainly small talk about what would be happening during the new year. I told her about having received a letter from Alpha Phi Alpha inviting me to become a pledge during the next quarter. This was quite an honor, as Alpha Phi Alpha, the most prestigious fraternity on campus, was very selective about who they invited to become members. Joyce's brother was the president, and I wondered whether my relationship with his sister or my own character was the reason for my invite.

Joyce was very happy to hear the news. She had also been invited to become a pledge—to the Alpha Kappa Alpha sorority, the sister organization to our fraternity. We agreed this could not come at a better time. This was another area we would have in common, which was important during this time where we are trying to share as much as we could before marriage.

The announcement was finally made for passengers to board the bus to Little Rock. We kissed each other as if we would not meet again, and I reluctantly left the bus and returned to the car, where George and Gerry were patiently waiting.

After being dropped off at my parents' house, I went in and greeted my parents and told them that Joyce hi asked me to again express her thanks and appreciation for the hospitality they had shown her doing her stay.

Joyce arrived at home around three o'clock and called me to let me know that she had arrived safely and that her parents had been there to pick her up. I was glad to hear from her and told her I would call later that night, realizing her family wanted to share the joy of her new status as a newly engaged woman. During the evening, I also thought about my decision to marry Joyce and how our lives would change after our wedding the following year.

New Year's Eve came, and we all went to the church service, traditionally called "watch night," where we prayed until the New Year, at nine o'clock that evening. The deacons would lead the services that would consist of three hours of testimonials, praying, singing, and preaching. After praying in the New Year on our knees, we all would rise, singing the old Negro spiritual "Amen," which recognized the power of God in our lives.

This time, I could not abide three hours of service. So, after going with my parents and greeting all of the people, I decided to visit some friends near the church for a couple of hours, realizing that the last hour of service would be the most important. After visiting with William Hawkins around the corner on Person Street for an hour or so, I persuaded him to come back to the church for the closing of the old year and greeting of the New Year with my family. He accepted my invitation, and we walked over to the church. It was full, but we managed to get two seats in the back, although the ushers tried to get me sit up front with the other ministers. I declined and remained with my friend William. Together, we joined in the singing of hymns and the gospel songs that were common to both of us, even though he was a member of the Disciples Church, also known as the "Christian" church founded by the Disciples of Christ denomination.

When Rev. Taylor finished his sermon at exactly 11:52, he invited members to kneel at the altar as we closed out the old year and prepared to thank God on our knees and receive the New Year. During his prayer of thanksgiving and blessings of the old year, he prayed for God to protect us during the new year of 1957.

After the prayer the choir began to sing the old spiritual, "Amen," which meant God was sovereign and in charge of our lives. The slaves would sing this hymn as a way of understanding their plight and that God would deliver them. "Amen" gave them strength and courage.

After we returned home, Daddy delivered a special prayer for our family.

I spent New Year's Day hanging around home, talking to my mother, and thanking God for her life. She was full of questions about my education and wanted to know what I would do after my graduation, even though I had a full year before graduation. I explained to her that I wanted to study theology in preparation for my ministry. I wanted to be as prepared as I could to make a real contribution to the world.

I spent the evening with George and Gerry and my niece and nephew, Patricia and Rodney Greene. I also visited my uncle Hubert and uncle Judson, who were always encouraging me in my educational endeavors. The day ended with my mother preparing liver and onions with rice and green peas and corn bread and ice tea.

On January 2, I prepared to catch my bus to Pine Bluff at noon. After arriving at the Greyhound bus station, I purchased my ticket and also exercised my right on interstate transportation to sit wherever I wanted without interference by the police. This time, I had no problem, except that, after I had taken my seat next to the window, a young white girl boarded and decided to sit next to me, directly behind the driver. This made me very nervous. I had never anticipated that a white person would want to sit next to me, especially a white woman. I tried to relax and occupy myself by reading or pretending to read, which would give the appearance that I had not noticed who was sitting next to me. My integrating the bus was one thing; but trying to start interracial mixing was not on my mind.

Pine Bluff was a two-hour trip, with two bus stops in Forest City and Marianna, Arkansas. After we had left Forest City, the young lady fell asleep on my shoulders, which caused me to feel panic. I thought that anyone boarding in Marianna would think we were a couple, which would definitely cause an incident at that stop. My problem was complicated. If I suddenly awakened her, she may be shocked and make a noise like she was being attacked. That would definitely cause real problems for me, even though I had nothing to do with her sitting there in the first place. Fortunately, she awakened and spoke to me politely, which was a relief.

For young people today, this may seem like an unimaginable situation. But it was part of the culture in which I had grown up, although I knew—as did many others—the things would have to change. What that young lady did that day would become common practice. But that day was not now, and it would be some time in the future before it arrived.

The rest of the trip was uneventful, and we arrived in Pine Bluff at one o'clock in the afternoon. I took a ride with a black gentleman, who hired himself out to transport people from the bus station to State or other places throughout Pine Bluff.

I arrived on campus and went directly to the new dorm to which I had been elevated and which had opened for the first time. All the choir members arrived on January 2 to resume rehearsals, as we had a concert in Texarkana, Arkansas, the next week, and Mr. Lovelace wanted us to learn some new material for the concert. The next day, the other students would arrive to begin the third quarter of our school year. I was excited about joining the Alpha Phi Alpha fraternity and becoming a pledge. I also learned that Herbert Nunn, one of my friends from Memphis and high school, had also received an invitation. It was nice to know someone who would be initiated from the same class.

Everything seemed to be working well, and I must say, I was very satisfied that Joyce had accepted my ring and I was about to become "a frat brother" as they called the men in fraternities in that day.

Ashton, my roommate, was really not interested in fraternities, which seemed kind of odd to me. But it was understandable, given that, even though Ashton and I got along well, he was really a loner.

Everybody was busy telling each other what had happened the holidays, which was interesting in light of some of the small towns my classmates came from. Many of them made me envious when they talked about visiting friends and family and the many things they'd had to eat and the parties they attended.

One of the things that circulated on campus was the engagement of Joyce and me. Everybody was happy for us, even though it was no surprise to many people. We had been a couple for the past year. Mr. Lovelace congratulated us and took credit for bringing us together as members of the choir.

Soon, the excitement of our engagement faded, and we all resumed our regular schedules, including Joyce and me.

My junior year seemed to pass quickly, maybe because we had become acclimated to the routine of college life and to other interests. The dominant thing in my life, other than Joyce, was the invitation to join the fraternity. The first meeting was scheduled to determine our interest and to interview us personally to determine whether we were worthy of such an honor. We met in the student union building housing facilities used by all the Greek fraternities and sororities. Walking into the meeting was very disarming because of the mystique surrounding the Greek organizations.

The president of the fraternity happened to be my fiancée's brother. I didn't know whether this would be an advantage or a disadvantage. It did not take long to find out, because Charles McClinton was very respectful, and you could tell that my relationship with his sister would not matter. What the fraternity members wanted to determine was what kind of Alpha man you would become, not your relations with girls. During the meeting, we would discuss what was important in life to us. Who were some of the black people we admired? How did we see becoming an Alpha man helping us to reach our personal and professional goals? These and many other questions were posed to us without any previous notice, which made each of us think deeply and quickly. I probably had the advantage, since I had already determined what my life's work would be.

All of us were glad when this session was over, and we were informed that we were now formally Alpha Phi Alpha pledges, who would be inducted if we passed the rigorous and physical tests we would have to endure. This sounded ominous, especially since we had heard from others that the hazing week would be unbelievable.

The second week in March would be Greek week, when all the fraternities and sororities would induct new members. During the week, we had been given several arduous tasks beside charitable work in the community. We had such assignments as going to Atheimer Bridge five miles from campus and looking under the middle of the bridge for further instructions and staying up all night to carry out other assignments given by any Alpha big brother. These assignments were to be done without missing any classes, which could easily be verified and would also make the week difficult. We found ways to meet the requirements of each assignment by dividing the tasks between the twelve of us.

Sleep deprivation was one of the issues that caused much difficulty. I remember sleeping sitting on the commode, which I must confess, under the circumstances, was some of the best sleep I had ever had.

Other fraternities and sororities would have assignments and would also have to perform drills around the quadrangle during lunch hour for the entertainment of the student body. The week would start on Sunday and would end on Friday. I had never wanted a week to pass as fast as I did this week, except I had heard that the hazing on the last night would include some things I am not allowed to reveal even today.

The closing of the initiation week was most exciting, since the brothers had planned an elaborate banquet in the student union for us, with invitations to bring a lady guest. After the initiation was completed, we were allowed to escort our guests to the Lion's Den.

Joyce looked glamorous and elegant when I picked her up. What made this evening especially special was that she had been initiated the day before into the Alpha Kappa Alpha sorority. The Lion's Den had closed for the evening to accommodate our affair. The tables were elegantly laid, and our brother Alphas were dressed immaculately in formal wear, serving as waiters that night. Even this was to give us a lesson—that even though we had accomplished a very high and sought-after position, we were to always remember we were servants of all.

Our president, brother McClinton, opened the evening with a welcome to our sisters as well as the other guests. After the welcome and introduction, the president called on me to give the invocation and blessing of the food, since everybody knew I was aspiring to be a minister. Our fraternity brothers then served us—quite a turnaround from the last few days. Their serving us was more than a gesture; it was the manifestation of our Alpha philosophy, which was to be "servants of all." The evening was festive and enjoyable, with some of the Alpha Kappa Alpha sorority members speaking and congratulating us on our elevation to Alpha brothers. The evening ended with us singing the Alpha hymn and our Alpha Kappa Alpha sisters singing their hymn.

The annual Midwest choir tour was only four weeks away. We would leave on April 15 for East Saint Louis, Illinois, always our first stop. As the date of departure neared, rehearsals increased to two a day for new music that had been selected for this year's tour. This was rather difficult, as we had to make arrangements with our teachers to make up the work. This was not as difficult for us upperclassmen, since we had been through the drill before and knew how to arrange our study schedules.

Finally, the day arrived for our third tour for those of us who had come to State three years ago as freshmen, wild-eyed and totally unaware of what was ahead. We upperclassmen could detect the nervousness and anxiety on the faces of the freshmen, who did not know what to expect on this venture (though they had been given exaggerated information as to the excitement and fun we would have at each stop). Although we did enjoy each city, it was not a vacation by any means. You could stay out all night, but remember the choir bus left at nine o'clock, and we were expected at the church by ten o'clock.

On the morning of April 10, we boarded the junior class buses for our third Midwest tour. It was an exciting time, since we would have a vacation from attending classes. But we still had the responsibility of keeping up with our class work.

We arrived in East Saint Louis, Illinois, at six thirty that evening at the First Baptist Church. The church housing committee met us to give us the names of the families with whom we would be staying, and then we were taken to their homes, where dinner was prepared, always the highlight of our tour. The families always went beyond our expectations, maybe because we were young Negro people endeavoring to prepare ourselves for the challenges that our race faced. This was their way of demonstrating their support and encouragement to us and motivating us to do well in our chosen fields. The dinner was the typical Negro dinner of fried chicken, mashed potatoes, sweet peas, turnip greens, corn bread, and ice tea.

We were told to eat as much as we desired, as there was more in the kitchen. We did not disappoint our host. The four of us who would be staying with the family to whom I had been assigned continued to eat, requiring our host to bring more food out of the kitchen, which we welcomed with glee. All forty choir members were housed and enjoyed similar experiences, which we would be repeated throughout our tour.

The next morning, the host family had put out towels and soap for us to bathe before coming downstairs for breakfast. We dressed and gathered in the dining room for the best breakfast we'd had in months. Our dining at State was great, but it couldn't compare with a family dinner or breakfast.

After we had finished breakfast, we had to prepare to leave for Chicago immediately following the Saturday concert and church dinner. When we arrived at the First Baptist Church at ten o'clock, Mr. Lovelace was in the sanctuary, ready to start the rehearsal. Mr. Lovelace taught us by example. During the three years I had been in the choir, I had never known him to be late for rehearsals.

All of our concerts were held at eight o'clock in the evening, which allowed people to complete daily tasks and prepare for the concert. After our ten o'clock rehearsal, which lasted for three hours, we were free to sightsee or remain at the church in the lounges, where there were television and snacks.

Many of us elected to explore the city and visit some of the places of interest, including the Saint Louis Cardinals stadium and the local breweries for which Saint Louis was noted. We were also interested in seeing how blacks lived and what life was like in a large city. After several hours, we returned to the church for rehearsal, although it was an hour and a half before it was scheduled.

After an hour rehearsal, we could again relax in the church lounges but could not leave the premises and had to be in the choir room at seven o'clock dressed in our formal wear. Mr. Lovelace did not abide any of the members not following his instructions, which were meant for everybody. In our choir, there were no stars, regardless of how talented you were or how vital your voice was to the choir. His consistency made us follow his instructions exactly.

At seven o'clock, we were all in the choir room, dressed and receiving instructions. Mr. Lovelace, after conferring with the support musicians, instructed us to line up as we had practiced. And at the stroke of eight, the assigned ushers opened the sanctuary doors, where our choir was met with thunderous applause as the sopranos led, exuding confidence and dignity as we had been taught to walk. The altos, tenors, baritones, and basses followed with sustained applause.

After we had remained in place and the applause had subsided, the doors in the rear were opened, and the director, Mr. Ariel Lovelace, entered, coming down the aisle with such dignity that it almost seemed like majesty had entered. The congregation gave him a standing ovation even before the concert had begun. The concert was a resounding success in every way. We sang music from Beethoven and Bach, along with contemporary composers. The performance consisted of two parts, with a fifteen-minute intermission.

The second half always featured the Negro spirituals, was always the most popular of the concert and included the popular work from Thomas Jefferson's writings, which said, "The same God that gave us life gave us liberty." This fitted perfectly with the wave of civil rights that was storming through the country, as witnessed by the Montgomery bus boycott and school integrations. Central High in Little Rock, Arkansas, in particular, had become a nationwide symbol of how far Negroes had come in this country. After the finale, always a musical work that showcased not only the choir's amazing voices but also Mr. Hitchcock, our violinist, along with the virtuoso performance by Arthur Porter, who was recognized as one of the outstanding pianists in the country.

After several encores, Mr. Lovelace directed the lead soprano to lead the recessional, bringing an end to another very successful concert.

After receiving congratulations from church members, we were all given box dinners to eat on the bus. We needed to be in Chicago by morning to prepare for another concert scheduled for Monday night at the Monumental Baptist Church, one of the largest and most prominent churches in Chicago. This stop would have special meaning for me because of my years of work in Chicago and having family there; the city was really my second home. Also, I was anxious for my family members, especially my brothers and their wives, to meet Joyce. Though they had not met her, they had heard much about her from my sister and mother.

We arrived in Chicago at six o'clock on Sunday morning and were scheduled to stay at Hotel Theresa, which was arranged by our host church, the Monumental Baptist Church. Staying at a hotel was a treat for us to, though it was only for two nights.

Our concert was scheduled for Monday at eight o'clock in the evening. This church was far larger than the one in Saint Louis and with a larger congregation. Many of us had relatives living in Chicago because of the great migration from the South that had begun in 1920. I called Erwin. I also called my younger brother Weldon, who had inspired me to play sports while I was in high school and also was more active than Erwin because of his age. There were also aunts and uncles in Chicago who found out that I would be singing with the State choir at Monumental Baptist on Monday night. Other choir members had relatives in Chicago who would also attend the concert, which meant we would have a capacity crowd.

After arriving in the early hours of Sunday morning, we slept until noon, when we went to the restaurant at the hotel. The church had made arrangements for our food as well as our lodging until we left on Tuesday for Milwaukee, Wisconsin. Mr. Lovelace allowed us to have Tuesday for free time and sightseeing for those who did not have relatives in Chicago. This was welcome news; many of us wanted to visit with our relatives after the concert. I was especially elated to hear this, since I wanted my family members to meet my fiancée. I was sure Mother, Daddy, and Gerry had told the family about this happy development in the family.

After a late breakfast at the hotel, we were told we could have free time until five o'clock, when we would gather for our daily rehearsal at the church. Since I knew I would be seeing my relatives on Monday, I wanted to show Joyce around Chicago. I had spent summers there and had become familiar with the city.

We caught the elevated train (a contrast to the subways in New York and other cities) for downtown, stopping at State and Madison, the busiest intersection in the country. I was narrating as we left for the Loop, the downtown area of Chicago. I also told her about my first time riding the el—how I had purchased my ticket and was attempting to go through the turnstiles to reach the trains when I got caught in the turnstiles with a rather fat woman. Neither of us could move, and I'd had to get down and crawl to the other side. This was one of my most embarrassing experiences. I'd learned to wait until the turnstiles were clear before attempting to go through, no matter how rushed I was.

After arriving downtown, I showed Joyce all the fancy stores, like Marshall Fields and Carson's, where my sister-in-law and brother had bought all my summer clothes. We walked down Michigan Avenue, later named the "Magnificent Mile" because of its high-end stores and fancy restaurants. We passed the legendary Palmer House, famous for housing the Democratic and Republican Conventions. We passed the legendary Grant Park and visited the Navy Pier, also one of Chicago's famous landmarks.

After getting something to eat, we started back to the hotel. We were scheduled to leave for the church from there. The trip back was fast, since the elevated train would take us back to the South Side, only blocks away from the hotel.

Arriving at the hotel at four o'clock, we decided to go into the bar area, where I ordered a glass of red wine and, since Joyce did not drink, a coke. We talked about our engagement and the plans she had for our pending marriage in the fall. Everything seemed to fall in place for us, with our parents giving their blessings and friends celebrating with us on our engagement.

On our free day, we visited my brothers, aunts, uncles, and cousins before leaving that evening for Milwaukee, Wisconsin.

Back at the hotel we were teased by our classmates because they thought we had slipped away to have some "intimate" time together. We both thought was funny, since we had spent our time walking and exploring downtown Chicago.

Our choir bus left at exactly five o'clock for the church, which was only twenty minutes away from the hotel. The church was a large Gothic-looking edifice. It had a commanding presence, especially for me because of my ministry and interest in the churches of Europe, after which most of our older churches were patterned. Upon entering the sanctuary, you could feel a sacred presence come over as you took in the stained glass windows and beautiful chandeliers. I learned later that the church was built during the early part of the twentieth century, around 1905. I could understand this. During the great migration of Negroes from Mississippi, Alabama, and Arkansas, those who had migrated had arrived in a city that was both North and liberal, bringing their own culture with them. This included strong religious beliefs, and thus, churches were established throughout the city. Because of the increase in wages in the North, these new arrivals were able to build great churches in Chicago, many of which stand today. Along with Monumental, there was the great Pilgrim Baptist Church. There, the great gospel writer Thomas Dorsey wrote, "Precious Lord," along with many other hymns. Therefore, it was not surprising that Chicago had some of the most historic churches in the country.

Everyone was on time for the rehearsal—as always a review of those songs that had certain problems during our concerts. Mr. Lovelace was a perfectionist. He made us proud to sing arias in Latin and German, a feat for all of us.

After rehearsal, he gave us last-minute instructions for the next day when we would perform. When the bus returned us to the hotel, we all planned to hang out in the neighborhood on the South Side of Chicago, where most of the blacks lived. Joyce and I, with some other choir members, found a jazz club nearby. Jazz and blues were big in Chicago. Most of the musicians had come from Mississippi and Memphis, among them Muddy Waters, Bobby "Blue" Bland, B. B. King, and many others. After listening to some good music and having some wine and beer, we all agreed the next day would be busy. Although we had the morning and afternoon off, we would be leaving for the church for a special dinner at six o'clock, which was unusual. Mr. Lovelace did not like for us to eat before a concert, as doing so could affect our singing. The food could make you sluggish, which could also affect your attentiveness.

The night of the concert people began to come in right after our rehearsal, which ended at six o'clock sharp. During the next two hours, we relaxed and dressed around seven. Getting ready required time for both the guys and the ladies, as additional attention was paid to hair and makeup. We were asked to meet in the choir room for last-minute instructions. At the stroke of eight o'clock, the doors of the sanctuary were opened, and the processional began. We were greeted with thunderous applause that continued until we'd all taken our places.

After a short pause, the church was eerily quiet. The concert followed the regular pattern with the same compositions and arias. Mr. Lovelace always taught us to sing like this was the first time we had sung any composition, as this would be the first time that *this* audience had heard it. Although this may sound fun and easy, doing so required concentration and focus, which was reiterated each time we rehearsed. This was the largest audience for which we'd performed on our tour, and they responded enthusiastically to our presentations.

Just before the second half of our concert, the pastor asked Mr. Lovelace to come before the congregation of over a thousand to receive a special citation for his untiring service to young people, not only training them in the musical field but also helping them to develop into the kind of men and women who would be a credit to our race. The congregation stood in admiration for him and his work over the years he'd brought choirs to Chicago to inspire the young and old with the message that the future would belong to those who prepare for it. Mr. Lovelace thanked the church and pastor for this honor and assured them he would continue as long as the Lord allowed.

After returning to the podium, without a glance at the audience, he raised his baton, and we were again into the inspirational Negro spiritual, "Go Down Moses":

> Go down, Moses
> Way down in Egypt land
> And tell old pharaoh
> Let my people go.

With the civil rights movement sweeping the country, the congregation rose and gave the most powerful ovation not only to us but also to the affirmation of these words.

The evening ended with what would become the anthem of the civil rights movement, "We Shall Overcome":

> We shall overcome
> If in my heart I do believe
> We shall overcome someday.

Again, there was no formal closing. But while still singing what would become our freedom hymn, we embraced each other for several minutes, with choir members embracing the members. Finally the pastor announced the benediction, and our choir responded with a threefold "Amen," which was beautiful because the congregation joined in.

We returned to the Dunbar Hotel, which had been paid by the church for the evening, after having sung for over 1,500 people, the largest attendance in our concert history. The hotel had granted a four o'clock late checkout, which gave us time to visit friends and relatives before leaving for Milwaukee immediately thereafter. We returned to the hotel late, so we rested. The next day, we spent most of the time visiting relatives if we had them there, sightseeing, and exploring the great city of Chicago.

Some of us went to the bar and had a beer or drink and talked about various things. Among the topics of discussion was how this would be next to last tour before we would graduate from State, a topic that always led to a discussion of what we would do after graduation. We also talked about the civil rights movement and the safety of our leader, Dr. Martin Luther King, who was supporting Rosa Parks and the Montgomery bus boycott. Because of his bold and brazen attitude, the Negroes' plight in the United States was being brought to light, and he had been receiving many personal threats, which alarmed all of us. After several hours, we all agreed it was time to go to bed, as some of us had early commitments.

The next day, I got up early and called Joyce to see you when she would be ready to visit my brothers and other relatives. We agreed on eleven o'clock, since my family was expecting us around one o'clock at my Erwin's home on the West Side of Chicago. We left early, after having a continental breakfast in the hotel's restaurant; we didn't want to be late. I was familiar with the elevated train going to the West

Side, which required taking the el to Twelfth Street station, where we transferred to ground transportation, taking Roosevelt Road to Albany Avenue.

My brother and his wife had bought an unusual house that was detached, with two separate living areas, called a duplex, allowing another family to live upstairs. When Joyce and I arrived, we were also met by Uncle Thurman and Aunt Fannie, my mother's younger sister and brother. Mother had told them I was engaged to a very nice young lady of whom she and my father were very proud. My aunt and uncle embarrassed me by telling Joyce what a fine young man I had always been. I changed the subject, telling them that, along with having an excellent voice, Joyce was a very talented player of the marimba, an unusual instrument for blacks to master, with the exception of Lionel Hampton.

After a very delicious lunch, we excused ourselves to go to Weldon's home on the South Side of Chicago, driven by Uncle Thurman. We arrived two hours before we were to return to the Dunbar Hotel to leave for Milwaukee, Wisconsin, for our concert scheduled for Friday at Mr. Lovelace's brother's church.

In Milwaukee, we arrived at a large Gothic Methodist church, where we were greeted by the church welcoming committee and their pastor, Rev. Dr. Lovelace, who was as funny as Pops Lovelace was serious. Again, the committee assigned us to various families for our three-day stay. This was planned to be the longest stay at Rev. Lovelace's church, because he wanted his brother's choir to enjoy a full day of recreation in Milwaukee before leaving for our last engagements Wisconsin.

Jerry Wilkerson and I were taken to the Taylor family's home, where a delicious and sumptuous dinner had been prepared. After dinner and some conversation, we excused ourselves and were escorted to rooms that were tastefully furnished and very comfortable. Our hosts had hung towels in the bathroom, with color designations for us to identify which were ours.

Jerry and I slept very well, after a busy and tiring schedule in Chicago. We were awakened at eight o'clock as we'd requested, so we could be ready to leave for the church and rehearsal at eleven o'clock.

Mrs. Taylor had a delicious breakfast prepared, after which we returned to our rooms for some last minute details.

When we arrived at the church, Mr. Lovelace was prepared for rehearsal as usual, with the music having already been distributed by monitors, a position in which we all served periodically. Before rehearsal began, Pops told us that we would have a free day after rehearsal. This was welcome news, s we had been on a tight schedule since Chicago. When the very lengthy rehearsal finished, we called our host families to let them know we would be sightseeing and visiting friends until the evening and would call them when we were ready to be picked up.

Some of us agreed to get some lunch and visit the Schlitz Brewery, where we would be given a tour and receive a courtesy happy hour with unlimited beer. This sounded like heaven to the beer drinkers in our choir. I was not among them. My favorite drink was rum and coke that some of us were able to get on our tour of the Schlitz Brewery. This free-time adventure lasted for several hours, with some of us stopping at eateries for corn beef sandwiches and other foods. After several hours, Jerry and I phoned our hosts for pick up and we told them we would wait for dinner after resting and sleeping for a couple of hours.

We had a wonderful host family, the mother being from Alabama, which meant she was an outstanding cook. She had prepared beef stew like we had never had before. My mother had prepared this dish before, and I must confess she was a runner up to my mother in beef stew. It was a meal in itself, which included diced beef, onions, potatoes, and carrots, served with white rice. After dinner, we watched television and talked with our host family and thanked them, as we would be leaving after the concert the next day to go to Mukwonago and Delavan Lake for our final concerts in the Midwest.

The day of our concert arrived. We slept late, since we were not scheduled to be at the church until six o'clock in the evening to prepare for our eight o'clock performance. This also allowed Jerry and me to catch up on the reading for our classes, which we tried to do whenever we had some real free time.

After the very intense rehearsal, we were dismissed and told to report to the choir room at seven o'clock dressed in our formal wear and prepared to enter the church for our final major concert of our Midwest tour. Pops did something he'd never done, which was to tell us to be especially good because his older brother had been so supportive after their parents had died. Rev. Dr. Lovelace had supported Pops through college and made it possible for him to get his education, allowing him to become one of the premier college choir directors in the country.

Our concert was received with great enthusiasm and appreciation, especially those selections that dealt with freedom and liberty, in light of the leadership of Dr. Martin Luther King and the young people who were sacrificing both their safety and their education by integrating public facilities throughout the country. "We Shall Overcome," the civil rights anthem, had been selected as the closing song and was sung with fervor and power that I had never before heard. Rev. Dr. Lovelace gave the benediction, and again the congregation joined in singing the closing "Amen."

We thanked the members of our host family for their hospitality and left almost immediately for Wisconsin to perform our final two concerts. They would be held on Sunday at eleven o'clock in the morning in Delavan Lake and at seven o'clock in the evening in Mukwonago. Because this was so tiring and difficult, Pops wanted us to rest in the hotel, for which their congregations had paid and which was only twenty minutes between the two churches. We were grateful to Pops for this. We were really tired, and he knew we would have to rest in order to do two concerts with only an hour between the two towns. We were also looking forward to these concerts because, after we left Wisconsin, we would leave for State, only stopping in Memphis for a concert, which was always the tradition.

The concerts in Delavan Lake and Mukwonago were well attended. At both, the audience was totally white; still, they were kind and accommodating of all our needs.

After the concert in Mukwonago, we returned to the hotel for the night in preparation for our long trip to Memphis. Since we were tired, many of us would rather have left Wisconsin for Memphis that night and then rested in Memphis for two days before our final concert. However, Mr. Lovelace said the bus drivers were required to rest that night before leaving on Monday for the ten-hour drive to Memphis. After breakfast the next morning and goodbyes to our hosts, we left for Memphis and

State after almost two weeks away, which seemed like two months. I had made the trip from Chicago to Memphis several times. I had never made it by car or bus. Although we were tired from our two-week odyssey in the Midwest, we were anxious to get to Memphis—home for some of us and then State in a day or two for all of us.

The trip from Wisconsin to Memphis was uneventful, with several stops for personal needs, lunch, and snacks. After we'd arrived in Memphis around eight thirty that evening, the members of the Church of God in Christ Pentecostal Temple met us at the church to take us to our host homes for the next two days before the final concert of our celebrated soloist Samuel Fletcher, whom we all knew was headed for fame and fortune. Since I was from Memphis, as were several other members, we were met at the church by relatives, who would take us home for the next two days. I invited my roommate Ashton Wilkerson to spend the time with me at my parents' home where he was warmly welcomed.

We spent our free time visiting with my friends from high school. Ashton had been to Memphis but not to Beale Street, famed for having blues and jazz. We visited several nightspots, along with going to some beer joints as they called such places when I was growing up. Memphis, along with being known as the home of the blues, was also the barbeque capitol. People far and near would come to Memphis to eat barbeque and listen to B. B. King, Muddy Waters, and Bobby "Blue" Bland. We also had great jazz at the Flamingo Club, with the most outstanding young pianist named Phineas Newborn and his brother, Calvin Newborn, an excellent guitar player. Ashton was impressed by the food, even though he came from Louisiana, also known for outstanding food like gumbo.

Thursday, the day of our final concert of the tour, we met at the Pentecostal Temple at six thirty in the evening for our final meeting. Mr. Lovelace knew we would perform well, since for two weeks, we had been singing at different places. Memphis was home for some of us and a second home for the rest. Since our school was only 150 miles from Memphis, many students would come to Memphis over the weekend to enjoy the music, the barbeque, and the nightlife.

The night of the concert, Bishop Patterson, my childhood friend's father, had requested that we sing "The Lord's Prayer" for the concert

126

opening. Usually we did not sing this, except at vespers at our college worship services. At the stroke of eight o'clock, the processional began, this time with risers to give us greater visibility to the director and the pianist.

After the applause had ended, Mr. Lovelace opened "The Lord's Prayer" with almost a whisper of, "Our Father," which became a crash as we went into the prayer, "who art in heaven." As we continued, we could hear the saints, as they were called, cry out, "Yes, Lord," which was the response of the sanctified church, rather than "amen." Although we were singing, the prayer affected us and created in us a spirit of worship that lasted throughout the concert.

After "The Lord's Prayer," Mr. Lovelace called on the favorite son of Pentecostal Temple, Samuel Fletcher to sing the opening of "God Bless America," which was appropriate considering the turmoil integration had brought throughout the South. Sam had a voice you could only say came from God. Without effort and with his spirit, he made every word meaningful. He opened with the beautiful introductory words, "While the storm clouds gather far across the sea, / let us all be grateful for a land that's free / let us pledge allegiance for a land so fair / as we raise our voices with a silent prayer." Then the choir joined him with a powerful response: "God bless America / land that I love. / Stand beside her and guide her / through the night with the light from above."

Some may think this selection inappropriate in light of the prejudice and segregation that we as Negroes suffered. However, many of us thought this song aspirational, in that the white people would live up to the promises of the US Constitution.

After this emotional opening, we sang songs from compositions of Mozart, Beethoven, and other composers of that time. The concert went well and was received with overwhelming response, which called for an encore.

Mr. Lovelace immediately selected James Weldon Johnson's "Lift Every Voice and Sing," also known as the "Negro National Anthem." Every child and adult knew the words to this most powerful hymn of our race. As soon as the audience heard the introduction, they all stood in respect for our national anthem. The words still resonate in my spirit: "God of our weary years / God of our silent tears / Thou who brought us thus far on the way / Thou who has by thy might / led us into the light / keep us forever in the path, we pray." The congregation joined in with us, and it seems more like a religious revival than a college choir concert.

Again there was no formal closing as the people embraced each other and all of us in the choir with words of thanks and encouragement. Finally, Bishop Patterson asked that, before we leave the sanctuary, we ask God's blessing on our choir for traveling mercies and that we may continue to inspire our people until God would bring us to the Promised Land.

After the concert, we were given boxes of food for our travels back to State that night. Somehow, none of us seemed tired as we arrived back at state college around midnight to a mostly dark campus, lit only by the bright lights in the dormitories, since final examinations were in two weeks. We would have to cram to catch up, although we had been reading in preparation for exams alongside our other classmates when we started the tour. The bus pulled up to the student union building, and we all got our belongings and headed toward our dorms. That night, I could not really sleep for thinking about our tour and how next year would be our last one—something I'm sure we all looked forward to.

The following two weeks were crucial and intense because of finals, the outcome of which would determine whether or not we would become seniors. The weeks passed swiftly, and all of my friends and fraternity brothers were confident that we had passed our respective exams and would be returning for senior year.

After the exams, although the school year was not officially over, most of us assumed that, for all practical purposes, we could leave— with the exception of those seniors who would be graduating in another week. However, president Lawrence Davis requested that the choir sing. He was proud to listen to the choir because of our fame throughout the state of Arkansas. On commencement day, all of us had packed and were prepared to leave for home as soon as the benediction was given by the minister.

Commencement was held on May 7, and we assembled in the risers strategically placed on the quadrangle where commencement was always held, with the exception of rain. The commencement speaker was the Reverend William Holmes Borders of Atlanta, Georgia, a spectacular speaker who, by his delivery, made me proud to be going into the ministry, though I would never be able to speak like him. The choir was excellent as usual, and we were proud of our choir members who were graduating and would pursue other educational opportunities at other institutions of higher learning. The commencement was long but very moving and emotional, since many of us those graduating would not see their classmates again.

We were not required to attend the reception that followed in the student union building for relatives and friends of the graduates. After saying goodbye to my choir members and other friends, I went to Joyce's dormitory to say goodbye, even though I knew I would see her several times during summer vacation.

I was given a ride to the Greyhound bus station. After I'd purchased something to eat in the lunchroom that we students had integrated last year, the call for boarding was announced. I tried to be first in line because I always liked to sit in the first seats in order to get off first. It seemed like a long time since I'd first broken the segregation law on interstate travel the year before, when I was challenged by the police for sitting in the "white section."

Our trip to Memphis was uneventful. We made the regular stops before seeing the skyline of Memphis sitting on a bluff overlooking the Mississippi. Arriving in Memphis, I was met by my Gerry and George, who told me that Mother had insisted that we be there on time to meet her "baby boy," because she wanted to keep the food hot for his dinner. Arriving at home, I found my mother, as she had always done, standing on the porch in her apron waiting. I immediately got out of the car and rushed to embrace her and tell her how much I loved her. She just smiled and kissed me on the cheek.

After I'd gone inside, Melvin came up to me and greeted me in a way he had never done before saying, "Welcome home, college boy," and smiling broadly, which really made me feel good.

Mother had prepared my favorite dinner, and everybody had sat down at the table, with the exception of my father, who had to attend one of his many meetings. After saying a blessing, we all began to pass around the delicious and plentiful food Mother had prepared. I didn't worry about running out of food, because Mother had put aside an extra plate in case I wanted some more later. Of course, she saved my father's dinner for him to eat later in the evening.

After dinner, we went into the living room, where everyone wanted to know how school was and what courses I would take my next and final year.

First, I told them that Joyce sent her love to all of them and hoped to see them during the summer. They inquired when we would be married, which I could not answer. I was sure, though, that it would be sometime next summer after graduation. George suggested we go out to one of the clubs to have drinks and meet with some of our friends. We went downtown to Beale, where we had drinks and met some of the regulars who always stopped for drinks after work. This was very enjoyable, as they brought me up on the latest jazz artists, like Charles Lloyd, an outstanding saxophonist, and Phineas Newborn, who had lived on Alston Street with me before I moved to Arkansas.

This summer, I decided not to go to Chicago. Rather, I would work in Memphis where it would be more convenient to visit Joyce. I was able to get a waiter's job at the Cotton Boll restaurant in the most affluent area of East Memphis, where the white folks lived. I had worked there before and had found it a very lucrative job. Although I had not done this for a long time, I was confident I could make substantial money during the summer that would help me buy clothes for the next school year.

I also was invited to play with the Al Jackson Orchestra, with which I had played during my high school years. Between the two jobs, I was able to set aside a handsome sum for my schoolbooks and other college expenses.

During the summer, I preached at several churches, which gave me the opportunity to develop my homiletical skills even though I had not attended any seminary. I also talked with other ministers about my desire to attend seminary and the seminaries they would recommend. Some of the outstanding ministers who encouraged me were Dr. C. M. Lee of Pilgrim Baptist Church; Dr. R. W. Taylor of Bethlehem Baptist Church; Dr. R. D. Morrison of Central Baptist Church; and Dr. W. W. Ragsdale, a longtime friend of my father.

During July, I received a letter from Joyce's father inviting me to come to Little Rock, Arkansas, to preach at his church, the Mount Pleasant Baptist Church, one of the prominent churches in Little Rock. I was asked to come the third Sunday in July and plan to stay at the McClinton home during my visit. I was elated to have been invited by the father of my fiancée, which suggested his confidence in me. I arrived the Saturday before the Sunday I was scheduled to preach at Mount Pleasant. The McClinton family was the essence of graciousness, which I will always remember. Mrs. McClinton, whom I had admired from the first day, was not only a gracious host but also an excellent cook. It amazed me to witness the things she could do that sighted people could not do. I will always remember that she gave me my first lesson in typing, although she was blind.

When Sunday morning arrived, we attended Sunday school, taught by Deacon McClinton. After Sunday school, Deacon McClinton escorted me to the pastor's office, where I was warmly greeted. He made me comfortable and assured me that the congregation was anxious to hear me on this Men's Day.

After my introduction by Deacon McClinton, the choir sang the hymn of preparation before the sermon. I proceeded to the pulpit and began by thanking the pastor and Deacon McClinton and his family for their hospitality. After a few other preliminary remarks, I took my text from the book of Psalms, which read, "What shall I render unto the Lord for all his benefits to me." The theme was "From Gratitude to Service," and it encouraged us to recognize the blessings in our lives and the responsibility to be blessings to others.

The sermon was well received, and the pastor encouraged me in my seminary endeavors.

After the service, we returned to Joyce's home for dinner and to keep my schedule to catch the bus for Memphis at five o'clock. Joyce's sister drove us to the bus station, where I said goodbye to them and kissed Joyce before boarding the bus for Memphis. When I arrived in Memphis, I was met by my brother-in-law, who took me home. My parents were anxious to know how Joyce's parents were and how the church service had gone.

After speaking with my parents, I called some of my friends to see what was going on this evening. I had only a month before I would return to State as a senior.

On July 15, I received a call from Joyce asking me if I could come to Pine Bluff on July 18 to see her for an important conversation. I inquired what the urgency was and why it could not wait until school began on September 4. Her reply was very disturbing—there was something I should know before school began. Although I was concerned, because of our engagement, I decided to meet her on July 18 at the Lion's Den. A friend allowed me to use his car, since I assured him I would be back the same day so he could go to work.

We met at one o'clock at the Lion's Den, where we embraced and kissed quickly. After the server took our coffee order, she asked me how my drive had gone and how my parents were doing. I also asked about her parents, and she said they were well.

After a few minutes of small talk about mutual friends, she said, "Carl, I cannot marry you, and I have to give you your ring back. I am sorry."

I sat there stunned, trying to process what I had heard, many questions going through my mind. Finally, after what I thought was several minutes of silence and pain, I mustered up enough courage to ask the question, which was one word, "Why?"

After a prolonged silence, she finally said words that were more confusing. "I just can't marry you." There were no words of explanation, just those five words, which would haunt me for years.

After a cordial parting, I started on my way back to Memphis with a heavy heart and a very confused mind. I went through my mind to see if there were issues where we had differences, searching for things she did not like about me that she had not disclosed. Had she met someone else to whom she was drawn and wanted to be free to pursue the relationship? She provided none of these reasons, which would have brought some pained comfort. After some other small talk about our senior year, we said goodbye until school began on September 4.

My drive back to Memphis was the longest ride I had ever had by car or bus. All I could do was mentally rehearse our conversation and try to make some sense of it. I could only hear during the entire 150-mile

132

trip to Memphis were the words that had become indelibly etched in my mind and heart and spirit" "I cannot marry you, and I have to give your ring back to you."

After I'd arrived in Memphis, returned the car, and gone back to my parents' house, my parents asked me how Joyce was and whether we had set the wedding date. I told Mother and Daddy I would talk with them the next day, which I am sure left them worried. But I couldn't bring myself to tell them about what had happened and how I felt.

A sleepless night—during which I woke several times believing that the previous day had been a dream or, rather, a nightmare—ensued. I finally got up and went to a special breakfast my mother had prepared, having sensed that I was very upset and disturbed upon returning from visiting with Joyce.

After breakfast, she said very softly and sweetly, "Son, do you want to talk to me?"

Although I really did not want to talk, I could not deny my mother knowing how her baby boy felt. I told her what had transpired.

She simply said in her saintly voice, "God knows best."

I received but did not accept her words. My heart was hurting and my mind was confused beyond belief.

After several hours, I decided on a course of action to deal with this serious disappointment and personal failure. I asked my mother if she thought I could visit Aunt Bessie, who lived in Como, Mississippi, and had boys my age. I thought this would give me time to clear my head and adjust to my new status—"not engaged."

I am sure that mother had not explained to Aunt Bessie why I was coming there for a week. Aunt Bessie was as welcoming as were my cousins John, Byron, and Kermit, who were also glad to see me since I was a city boy.

My time with Aunt Bessie was definitely what I needed. She prepared breakfast like my mother and had the same kind of spirit during my time in Como. I enjoyed horseback riding and other things, like horseshoes, that my cousins enjoyed for recreation.

Uncle J. D. Taylor was a deacon in the local Baptist church and took special interest in me since I had dedicated my life to the Christian ministry. During my visit, he wanted me to go with him to the meeting of the Baptist Conference, which met every August to raise money for the local Negro high school. He also wanted to present me to the Baptist Conference as his nephew who was a minister and would be going to seminary for further training after graduating from Arkansas AM&N.

Aunt Bessie, after talking to my mother on a daily basis about my broken engagement, decided to take action. I deduced that my mother had told her how heartbroken I was so Aunt Bessie hoped my time there with the boys would help me to get over it and return to school in September. Aunt Bessie was a very well-known teacher in Como who was responsible for training new teachers. One day, she suggested that I might want to go out with one of the new teachers in her first year at her school, Jackie Smith. I accepted her invitation, and she immediately gave me Jackie's number. She had already informed Jackie that I would be calling. I am sure she told her I was free and single since my engagement had been broken.

Jackie and I agreed to go out to one of the local restaurants for dinner and dancing. She picked me up in her car, as I didn't have transportation and didn't want to ask Uncle J. D. to use his car. Dinner was great, and at nine o'clock, the music started. Playing over the loudspeaker, it was, of course, blues by B. B. King and Bobby "Blue" Bland. We danced several dances, which were very suggestive but did not affect me because I was still in a recovery state from my relationship with Joyce. Jackie was very nice and thanked me for inviting her out to dinner and dancing. I much appreciated her understanding, even though she did not let on to the fact that my aunt Bessie had told her I was recovering from a broken engagement.

Time passed quickly. I could not believe I'd been in Como for a week. I returned to Memphis to prepare to go back to State for my final and senior year. As I contemplated my return with my friends, and especially realizing that Joyce and I were no longer engaged, I tried to imagine what it would be like meeting them and having to explain what happened.

When I returned to State on September 4 to register, along with the rest of the student body, many choir members greeted me as if nothing had happened. This was startling and very difficult to accept. After reflection and conversation with my roommate, I understood at least a little better. He explained that the choir did not want to speak about the breakout because Joyce and I were both choir members. Commenting on it would be awkward, especially since they, like me, did not know why our engagement had ended.

Mr. Lovelace called for a rehearsal later that day to begin our new schedule for the year. We had many engagements throughout Arkansas. Although Pops must have heard about our broken engagement, he was quite sensitive and never even alluded to it in choir rehearsals or at any other time. Sometimes, silence really is golden.

After about a week and people on campus expressing their regrets, things began to settle down. And our broken engagement became old news, except to those ladies who had interest in me even before our engagement. This was interesting. Some who I had not imagined were attached to me began to make subtle overtures: "Carl, could we talk sometimes?" To this, I would respond, "Yes," even though I knew it would not happen.

After a few weeks, everything settled down, and even Joyce and I were able to communicate without talking about our failed engagement.

The school year began on a very positive note, in that I was elected vice president of the Alpha Phi Alpha fraternity, was an honored position on the campus. I also became a contributor to the college newspaper. The editor was my roommate John Walker, a fraternity brother and close friend.

My interest in the ministry had never wavered, even through my engagement and disengagement. Dr. Cochran, chairman of the sociology department, took a special interest in me during my senior year. My fellow majors elected me the president of the sociology club, which was an honor, since our department had some of the most knowledgeable students on campus.

After attending my classes for the first month, I found that my new relationship with Joyce would not be as difficult as I had anticipated. We remained cordial and shared conversations from time to time. Although neither of us had a steady girl or boyfriend respectively, we never dated each other during the year.

My plans for theological education increased as I enquired about various schools and what the requirements were for each school. I requested information from several schools, including Gammon Theological Seminary, Southern Baptist Seminary, and Howard University School of Religion. All of the schools were accredited by the Association of Theological Seminaries, which meant I would receive an excellent theological education at any one of them. I was leaning toward the Southern Baptist Seminary, since the campus was integrating next fall and was looking for Negro students and prepared to offer substantial scholarships to qualified students for the fall semester.

Although it was early in the year, I expressed my interest in attending and asked for an application for financial assistance. I also sent the same request to the other two seminaries, in case one didn't offer assistance.

The school year was moving quickly. My duties as president of the sociology club, vice president of Alpha Phi Alpha fraternity, and at the John Watson College Sunday school kept me busy.

Dr. Edward Davis, my pastor and mentor, was especially helpful in making the adjustment after Joyce and I severed our relationship. His advice to me was to keep my focus on my calling to the ministry, since I had promised God I would serve him for the rest of my life as a minister of the gospel of Jesus Christ. Because of my faith and admiration for his ministry, I was motivated to make this my best year, anticipating my new life after graduating from college and entering a new phase of my life and purpose in my seminary education.

Thanksgiving was approaching. I made plans to go home. It would be my last time to visit and be with my parents for a while, depending on what my studies and time at my new school would allow. I also wanted to make this visit very special because of my plans for the next year.

After our quarterly exams, all of us prepared to go home in just two days. I told my parents I would arrive on Thanksgiving Day, because our fraternity had prepared baskets of food for those in need. My parents were satisfied as long as I would be there for Thanksgiving dinner at four o'clock. On Wednesday, many people claimed baskets, which made all of our frat brothers very happy and fulfilled. After distributing the baskets, we prepared to leave for our homes the next day.

Thanksgiving was a bright and sunny day. I left State for Memphis at two o'clock in the afternoon and arrived at the Greyhound bus station at four o'clock, where my brother-in-law and sister were patiently awaiting my arrival. When we arrived at 1610 Arkansas Street, my mother was waiting on the porch as usual with her apron on, ready to welcome her baby boy home. I am sure she realized that this could be my last Thanksgiving dinner at home for a few years, since she knew I would be attending some seminary next year, though we knew not where. This was always my welcome, and it seemed to suggest my mother was always cooking for her last son. I embraced and kissed my mother, which I did every time I returned and many times during my stay. It may seem like I was a mama's boy, and I readily admit that I was, especially since the Lord had answered my prayers and had given my mother back to me.

My mother's dinner was superb as usual, with the traditional twenty-pound turkey, corn bread dressing with gravy, sweet potatoes, turnip greens, mashed potatoes, cranberry sauce, and homemade rolls, along with iced tea and several kinds of pies and cakes.

I had phoned my friends to announce that I was home and wanted see them after our Thanksgiving dinner. William Hawkins and Carl Johnson agreed that we should go to the Gray Hawk drive-in, where our friends held a daily class reunion.

It was almost nine o'clock, not late since we all had to attend our Thanksgiving dinners with our families and friends, and I had to stay and answer questions from my uncles Judson and Hubert Veazey. After I met up with our former classmates, we agreed to go downtown to Beale Street and to the Flamingo Club. They were excited to know that, after my graduation from State, I would be attending theological seminary to prepare myself for the Christian ministry.

Our evening was incredible. We saw classmates we had not seen since graduating in 1954, almost four years earlier. After spending an hour or so at the Gray Hawk, we headed to the Flamingo Club where the real action would be for the evening. Calvin Newborn and his brother, Phineas, would be featured and would surely rock the club. This was a great day to end a beautiful Thanksgiving with my family and friends.

I knew that I had to return to State for a special rehearsal in preparation for our concert in Hot Springs. The location, of course, reminded me of my first college girlfriend Callie Canion, and I couldn't help but wonder what would have happened had she remained at State and not gone to Chicago. These thoughts could not have come at a more inopportune time, since I was still recovering from the breakup with Joyce. However, I allowed myself the luxury of playing the "what-if" game.

The following day, Mother had prepared a wonderful breakfast of sausage, eggs, grits, and biscuits—the quality of which only she could make. Since my father was not working that day, he joined me for breakfast. We talked about the seminaries to which I had applied and my prospects for getting financial assistance. I told him that it seemed like Southern Baptist Seminary was the most promising and provided the most financial assistance. We also discussed which seminary provided the best theological education. Gammon was a Methodist seminary, which I thought would not conform to my beliefs. Howard University School of Religion was nondenominational, which also was confusing, given that I had been raised, licensed, and ordained a Baptist. I told my father I was going to pray on it. I was sure God would direct my path, as he had healed Mother.

George and Gerry picked me up at eleven o'clock in the morning. My bus was scheduled to leave for Pine Bluff at twelve fifteen in the afternoon. They dropped me off. I went into the passenger waiting room and sat at the counter that some of us had integrated the year before— an integration the city had accepted. After I had ordered coffee and a sweet roll while reading the morning paper, *The Commercial Appeal*, the dispatcher called for all passengers going to Pine Bluff to board.

I was able to get my favorite seat right behind the driver, allowing me to get off first at our rest stops and board last after our stops. Leaving Memphis, we stopped briefly in West Memphis to pick up passengers but were not allowed to get off the bus. The next stop, Forrest City, was the only stop where we were allowed a fifteen-minute rest stop. Leaving Forrest City, our next stop would be Marianna, which was only to pick up. Then the final stop would be Pine Bluff, only one hour away. Since this was my senior year, I was rather nostalgic about the trip. I knew that the next time I made the trip from State to Memphis, it would be my final one. The next year I would be in seminary somewhere. When we pulled into the bus station, other buses were arriving with students from other parts of Arkansas, which made for a festive time and a reunion of sorts.

I returned to the campus, unpacked, and headed to the dining hall, where dinner would be served. I wanted to be at the head of the line. Many students complained about the food, but I found it rather good for preparation for such a large number of students. After eating meatloaf, mashed potatoes with gravy, and spinach, I met with some choir members and talked about my Thanksgiving and inquired about theirs. We went to our dorms to finish unpacking, shower, and dress for our six o'clock rehearsal.

This concert in Hot Springs was important for State. We would be singing for the Baptist Convention, which drew pastors from cities in Arkansas, Memphis and other Tennessee cities, giving us great exposure and perhaps leading to pastors recommending other young people to attend State.

After rehearsal, Mr. Lovelace spent time asking about our Thanksgiving. He also informed us that his wife, of whom he had taken care since we'd arrived at State, was now growing weak and asked us to remember her in prayer. There was not a dry eye in the choir. We had become so close to our director and knew how dedicated he was to his wife and how he had cared for her while still heading up the music department and directing one of the premier choirs in the country. Since he had not spoken about her condition often, we all knew it must have deteriorated and that her death was imminent. We all gave our beloved Pops a hug and held him tight, which made him shed tears.

Pops Lovelace had been so strong since I'd first met him after coming to state college in 1954. He demonstrated his faith and strength through his love and care for his dear wife.

After Sunday vespers and we'd returned to our dorm, the word came. Mrs. Lovelace had died. Those of us who lived in our dorm met in my room and offered prayers for Mr. Lovelace and his family, asking the Lord to provide comfort and strength during this time of bereavement. Because of her lengthy illness and his desire for privacy, the memorial service was held was held off campus in a private graveside service.

Pops returned to his daily routine and rehearsals two days later and seemed at peace; his wife had been sick for several years. During the period of bereavement, we were not sure what we should say to him, if anything. His poise allowed us to get back to normal and return to our daily lives. Pops also returned to his usual self, and we were all grateful to know that he was all right.

The days quickly passed. Soon the Christmas holidays, with all their demands on our time (the preparation for our annual Christmas concert top among them), were upon us. Also, we seniors were only a few months from our graduation from State, which meant that we were about to enter a new chapter in our lives. Mr. Lovelace seemed to be intent on making this Christmas concert the best ever. I wondered whether it was because this would be the first Christmas without his beloved wife or because this would be the way of closing a chapter in his life.

The Christmas concert, which took place the Sunday before Christmas, was a resounding success. It was well attended, and the presentations chosen by Mr. Lovelace made those of us who were seniors very proud; this would, after all, be our last Christmas concert at State. This time, when the concert closed with Handel's *Messiah*, the "Hallelujah" chorus it felt like closing one life and entering another, given the realization that this would be the last time some of us would ever sing with or see each other.

The Christmas holidays at home were a very happy and joyous occasion. But in some ways, it was rather sad, in that I would most likely be away in some seminary this time next year and didn't know if I would be able to come home for Christmas as I had done every year since I had been in college. After returning to State on January 3, I found that everything seemed to move very swiftly. Registration and selection of classes for third quarter, especially my major subjects in sociology, flew by. Also, my activities in the Alpha Phi Alpha became more intense. As vice president, I would have to assist our fraternity president, Roosevelt Brown, with administrative duties and preparations for bringing our new pledges into the fraternity. My choir responsibilities were increased too. I had been selected, along with three other choir members, to perform on Saturdays on the local television station to promote the school and the choir. Although this seemed like a heavy responsibility, in some ways I welcomed it. Stay busy with constructive things helped me not dwell on my failed engagement.

On top of it all, our two-week Midwest tour would start in April. And graduation would follow shortly after we had returned.

It had been rumored that the young civil rights leader and pastor of Dexter Avenue Baptist Church, the Reverend Martin Luther King Jr., would be our commencement speaker, which meant that Mr. Lovelace would definitely have us present new music for the occasion.

Rev. King had just launched the civil rights movement that had energized the entire Negro community, especially the young Negroes who were integrating lunch counters and restaurants throughout the South. The Student Nonviolent Coordinating Committee had mobilized students throughout the country to do sit-ins and other acts of civil disobedience. Other students and I were doing our part in Pine Bluff and Memphis by integrating the interstate bus system and the stores in the Pine Bluff area. As a prelude to Dr. King coming, our fraternity decided to organize a march throughout downtown Pine Bluff, which consisted of seven blocks of stores and other business establishments. On the day of the march, over five hundred students showed up to march from State to downtown to protest the segregation and prejudice of our city. Since we did not have or seek a permit to demonstrate, the police department warned us that we would be arrested and jailed if we violated the directive not to march.

The day of the march, we went to downtown Pine Bluff, where a contingency of fifty uniformed police officers were lined up on the main street to intimidate us. We marched, sang, and chanted the slogans of the civil rights movement. The chief of police warned us over a bullhorn that, if we did not disperse, we would be arrested. This only seemed to motivate the crowd, which grew stronger as we passed through downtown. Attorney Wiley Branton, the prominent and famous Arkansas lawyer, told us to go forward, and he would represent us.

The ending of this march was comical. After the order was given to arrest us, the fifty or so police officers seemed stunned when faced with over five hundred students and members of the community. We later learned that Branton had negotiated with the chief of police, who'd asked us to go to the local Negro high school to be processed. To this, Branton replied that the police department would have to provide transportation. When this was announced, the marchers began to cheer. We knew it was impossible for fifty policemen to arrest over five hundred marchers and then ask us to turn ourselves in to be processed. Branton advised us that we had won the day, and the city had promised to comply with our demands of ending all segregation policies immediately. We all laughed and joked about the stupid decision of the police chief to have us arrest ourselves and go to the Negro high school station to be processed.

Our fraternity was praised for organizing the march and winning all of the demands from the city. We considered this a total victory and a way of welcoming our fraternity brother Rev. Dr. Martin Luther King Jr. to our campus and the city of Pine Bluff, Arkansas. The march seemed to bring a new spirit to the campus and made us feel like we were in solidarity with Negro college students all over the country. It also motivated those in Little Rock at Philander Smith and Baptist College to join in national protests.

The next few months were spent preparing for quarterly examinations, which would really determine whether we would graduate from State. Our teachers were more than intense when it came to imparting knowledge to us, especially those of us who were going on to graduate schools such as medicine; law; and, in my case, theological seminary.

Mr. Lovelace had intense rehearsals, preparing us for our Midwest tour and the commencement, which would bring thousands from across the state of Arkansas. Many would could to hear this young preacher and civil rights leader tell us that a new day was dawning in America and in the Negro community.

March was a busy time for our choir. We had to prepare music not just for Sunday vespers but also for several concerts in Hot Springs, Texarkana, and Malvern, Arkansas. Additionally, we also had to sing for the Arkansas legislature, as we had every year around the time they made their appropriation for our college, which was always at the whim of the governor and legislature.

The first week of April was very busy. I had to give much of my time to the fraternity, in preparation for the induction of new pledges. This was exciting; I knew they felt, as I once head, that a new milestone had been reached in their college education. Our twelve pledges had gone through hazing week, which tested their endurance and their bond of brotherhood, a key part of our fraternal relationships. After their induction into the fraternity, we held a sumptuous banquet for them and their guests, which was a festive and happy affair. My favorite little brother, John W. Walker, later a prominent lawyer and member of the Arkansas legislature, thought I was a very strict big brother; I was determined to make our relationship a lifetime partnership. I succeeded, and that partnership has lasted over sixty years. We are both now in our eighties.

When we returned from concerts in Arkansas, it was time to prepare for our annual Midwest tour, the last for some of us. Mr. Lovelace had us prepare to leave in five days. On April 14, we left for our first stop, always East Saint Louis, Illinois. Although Joyce and I were friendly, we did not spend much time together during this tour. This year's tour was shorter, since Memphis had been omitted due to commencement being only a month away. We were anxious to return for our historic commencement, where we would witness the Reverend Dr. Martin Luther King give his message to our class and also to Negroes throughout the nation about their struggle for the fairness and equality guaranteed by the Constitution of the United States.

We had concerts in East Saint Louis, Illinois; Saint Louis, Missouri; Chicago, Illinois; Milwaukee, Wisconsin; and Mukwonago and Delevan Lake, Wisconsin. The tour became a nostalgic one for us seniors as we visited each of these places with our choir for a final time. Each concert was overwhelmingly successful, with record numbers attending, probably due to the fact that the civil rights movement had commanded everybody's attention, causing new feelings of racial pride.

At each stop, we closed with the theme song of the movement, "We Shall Overcome." We also sang a composition with lyrics based on words spoken by President Thomas Jefferson: "The same God who gave us life gave us liberty." This always resonated with the audience, as the line described what our civil rights movement was all about and motivated us to demand our rights accordingly. Those who were seniors were amused by the excitement and joy of the freshmen, who had not had the experience and only reminded us of what we had experienced three years prior.

Even though Memphis is my hometown, I did not mind not stopping there. I was excited about our graduation and the opportunity to hear Dr. King. As we traveled back to State, some of us reminisced about how fast the four years had passed and all the things we accomplished. One of the things that passed through my mind was my relationship with Callie Canion, who was my first love and my girlfriend my freshman year.

We arrived in Pine Bluff on Saturday, April 26, just four weeks before some of us would become alumni of the college that was founded in 1873, nine years after emancipation.

The campus was quiet, with only security evident, when we returned. All of us were tired and anxious to rest before returning to classes on Monday. Fortunately, the Sunday vespers service had been canceled, allowing us additional rest.

The commencement was set for May 21 at noon on the campus quadrangle. Now, four weeks before commencement, everything was in high gear. Final exams would be held the next week. The choir rehearsed twice a day for the commencement and Rev. Dr. Martin Luther King Jr. All of the seniors were busy sending invitations to family and friends—even those we knew would be unable to attend, just to let them know what we had accomplished.

Of course, my parents were coming. I had asked the coordinator of services to reserve housing for them that would allow them to stay in one of the guesthouses near the campus. My father had retired, and he was not that steady on his feet. So I worried about his balance and the danger of him falling.

Mother and Daddy arrived from Memphis on May 19, two days before commencement. I met them, along with a friend of mine, at the bus terminal and took them to the guesthouse where they would live for the next three days. The school had provided for parents to have breakfast, lunch, and dinner at a modest cost in the cafeteria. However, because of my father's mobility, I purchased groceries for the next two days, and several of my Alpha Kappa Alpha sisters agreed to come every day and check on them and provide needed assistance. This was very much appreciated, since my parents had reached the age where they did need support and assistance.

On the morning of the twenty-first, my young fraternity brothers picked my parents up and escorted them to the main campus, where they were comfortably seated, waiting for the processional to start at exactly noon. The band struck up "Pomp and Circumstance." I, along with those around me, felt a strong feeling of pride and excitement as we prepared to march into the quadrangle to take our seats before the impressive and charismatic Dr. King, our guest speaker. The quad was filled with thousands of people, including those watching from the gymnasium over closed-circuit television. Those in the choir were strategically seated so as to join our classmates on the risers directly in front of the guest platform. Traditional preliminaries and the welcome were given by President Davis, our beloved "proxy" who had skillfully led our college during these turbulent times and had been able to maintain funding from the Arkansas legislature.

Our presentation of "God Bless America," originally sung by Samuel Fletcher, who had graduated the year before, was sung by another outstanding tenor, Anthony Wiggins. The choir quietly joined in the refrain, with a prayerful "God bless America / land that I love. / Stand beside her and guide her / through the night with a light from above." Our commencement was carried over Pine Bluff and Little Rock television throughout most of Arkansas. Friends reported that, during the singing of this touching hymn, the cameras caught many in the audience openly crying.

Following remarks by the chairman of the board of trustees, President Davis proceeded to introduce the commencement speaker, the brilliant and charismatic leader of the Montgomery bus boycott and the powerful growing civil rights movement that was spreading throughout the South and would eventually speed throughout the nation. Watching our young dynamic president introduce another dynamic and prophetic leader was a sight to behold—a sight that made many of us realize a new day had arrived in the South and, indeed, in the United States.

Our choir was called to sing just before Dr. King would speak. Professor Lovelace directed the singing of "This Is My Heritage"—the composition with Jefferson's powerful words, "The same God who gave us life gave us liberty." from Thomas Jefferson, founding father and third president of the United States.

After we had sung this very potent hymn, the audience rose almost in unison not only acknowledge the prophetic words of this hymn but also to acknowledge the Reverend Dr. Martin Luther King Jr. as he strode to the lectern with dignity and purpose.

After acknowledging the president and trustee board, Rev. King spoke directly to the choir, especially to Dr. Lovelace, telling us that the words of your powerful hymn were words that had motivated him through these difficult days.

Rev. King immediately went into his speech, outlining his experiences of the past years—experiences that were pivotal to a new era progress for Negroes and this nation. Although we would go through some difficult days fraught with violence and frustration, the walls of segregation were coming down, and the nation had awakened to a new day of reality that we as Negroes would never turn back, regardless of the costs. He also admonished us to use our privilege of education to further the cause for which our fore parents had fought, bled, and died.

He was the greatest orator I had ever heard, and I felt proud to be following in the tradition of ministers of the gospel who had brought us thus far on the way.

Dr. King's closing words—which I will never forget—were a poem by John Oxenham "The Ways." When he spoke these words, I knew that my calling was completely validated:

> To every man there opened a way, ways, and a way;
> The high soul takes the highway
> And the low soul takes the low.
> And in between on the misty flats, the rest drift to
> and fro.
> But to each man there openeth a way, ways, and
> a way.
> But each man must decide the way his soul shall go.

After speaking these words, Dr. King strode back to his seat, like a prophet who had delivered the word of the Lord. To this day, I use those words to motivate myself and to challenge those who remain on the sidelines while they should be soldiers on the right side of history.

The commencement moved to the next milestone of conferring degrees to the graduates of the class of 1958. President Davis called on Dean Johnson to present the graduates. This was done efficiently, with each graduate's name being called to receive his or her degree and the audience being asked to hold applause until the entire class had been served. Even though there was no applause, there was a certain pride and excitement in hearing your name called and your discipline announced. When I received my degree, I whispered a prayer of thanksgiving for my parents, who, through God, had brought me to this day.

After commencement, which had lasted well over two hours, our families and friends were invited to a special reception in the student union building. However, after seeing my parents after the commencement, I thought it best for them to return to the guesthouse and rest before leaving the next morning. I arrived at their guesthouse to find them packed and ready to return home to Memphis. My mother had cleaned the place and left it immaculate, consistent with her habits.

My fraternity brother loaded their luggage in the car, and we left for the bus station. My parents were scheduled to leave at noon. Arriving at eleven forty-five, we were able to chat a few minutes before they boarded the bus for their departure. They said how proud they were of me and what I had accomplished and also expressed how much they looked forward to my going to theological seminary in preparation for the Christian ministry. I expressed my gratitude for them being such wonderful parents and raising me with Christian values. Once the dispatcher announced that their bus was ready for boarding, we walked out to the bus, where I embraced my dear mother and also my strong father as they left for home. I assured them I would be home in a few days, and we would have a wonderful summer before I left for school.

When my frat brother and I returned to the campus, it seemed like a ghost town, with the exception of the security and maintenance staff driving around the campus carrying out their daily assignments. We went directly to our dorm to begin the task of cleaning out our rooms and throwing away things that had been acquired over four years. As I went through the items, they brought back memories, which made it more difficult to part with them. I also had to get my deposit back from the dean of students before leaving the next day.

Choir members met to say goodbye to our classmates and our dear and beloved director, Professor Lovelace, who had taught us so much more than music.

The following day, some of us, who had come to State together, met in the student union building to share a few final minutes together and promises to stay in touch. Joyce and I spent a few private minutes together and wished each other well in our future endeavors. I asked her to give my best regards to her family and thank them for the hospitality they had always extended to me during my visits.

My bus was scheduled to leave for Memphis at one o'clock, and I had arranged for a fraternity brother to give me a ride. We arrived at the station with only five minutes to spare. The bus was already loading, so I would not be able to get my coveted front seat behind the driver, a feat I had managed to achieve on most of my trips.

It seemed like I had not slept in several days, and I felt very sleepy after getting on the bus and relaxing. Shortly after leaving Pine Bluff, I did not awaken until we reached Forest City, only an hour from Memphis, my home sweet home.

When we reached West Memphis, Arkansas, I could see the skyline of Memphis. My mind returned to the first time I'd returned home and had seen that skyline, which seemed so beautiful to me. Gerry and her husband George met me at the station. And after they'd helped me load my trunk and other items in the car, we headed toward home on Riverside Drive, a most beautiful drive along the powerful and majestic Mississippi River, the longest river, which started in Minnesota and ended in the Gulf of Mexico.

When we arrived at 1610 Arkansas, my mother was there standing on the porch with her traditional apron on, like she had done every time I'd returned home from college. She had my special dinner of calf's liver with onions and gravy and rice and turnip greens ready to be served.

Since this was a special homecoming for me, my father had canceled all of his meetings to join in this special dinner. After he offered the prayer of thanksgiving and all of us had repeated a favorite verse, we began to enjoy my favorite dinner.

Melvin was ready to start and asked mother to pass the liver. She asked him to let me go first. His reply was, "Carl can have them after I finish."

We all laughed because, although Melvin was proud of me, we all knew he was serious about his food.

This was absolutely the best dinner Mother had fixed, although all of them were delicious.

Rev. Dr. A. Edward Davis
College Pastor—St. Paul Baptist Church, Pine Buff, Arkansas
Spiritual Mentor and Friend

Pastoral Installation—Zion Baptist Church
December 1960

Rev. Carlton W. Veazey and

Dr. Earl Harrison, Pastor, Shiloh Baptist Church,
on of the oldest churches in Washington, D.C.

Pastoral Installation—Zion Baptist Church
December 1960

Rev. Dr. Daniel G. Hill— Dean of the School of Religion, Howard University and former Dean of the Rankin Chapel at Howard University.

Pastoral Installation—Zion Baptist Church
December 1960

Rev. Dr. Evans Crawford, Dean of Andrew
Rankin Chapel, Howard University

Graduation from Howard University School of Religion
1961

Graduation from Howard University School of Religion
1961

Dr. Mordecai Johnson, Mrs. Johnson, Geraldine
Greene, George Greene, E. Earlene Veazey, Rev.
Veazey, Mrs. Dolly Veazey, Rev. M.G.F. Veazey,
Patricia Greene and Rodney Greene (front)

Rev. M.G.F. Veazey, Rev. Carlton Veazey and **Dr.
Mordecai Johnson**, former president of Howard
University

Council of the District of Columbia
Rev. Veazey speaking at his swearing-in ceremony

Council of the District of Columbia
Rev. Veazey, Councilmember during Activist days.

Pastoral Installation—Zion Baptist Church
December 1960

Rev. Veazey and **Rev. Dr. Jerry Moore,** Pastor of Nineteenth Street Baptist Church, the oldest church in Washington D.C.

Pastoral Installation—Zion Baptist Church
December 1960

Dr. Gladys T. Peterson—Zion Baptist Church Chair of the Finance Committee and also Deputy Superintendent of the Public Schools of the District of Columbia under Dr. Carl Hansen

Pastoral Installation—Zion Baptist Church
December 1960

Keturah Barnes—Superintendent of Zion Baptist Sunday School and Church Clerk

Pastoral Installation—Zion Baptist Church
December 1960

Rev. Veazey and Genevieve Johnson, President of the Auxiliary Planning Committee

Mrs. Dolly C. Veazey and Rev. M.G.F. Veazey

Parents

Erwin Veazey and Marie Veazey

Melvin Veazey

Audrey and Madison Shockley

Geraldine (Gerry) and George Greene

Eddie Veazey and Weldon Veazey

Gayle

Michael

Katea

Caron

The Veazey Family

Parent's 50th Wedding Anniversary
(Front) Maid of Honor, **Rev. and Mrs. M.G.F. Veazey**
Minnie M. Jolley (My Grandmother)
Audrey, Gerry, Weldon, Melvin
Back—Erwin, Carlton

(rear) — **Melvin, Erwin, Audrey,Weldon**
(front) — **Carlton, M.G.F. Veazey, Dolly Veazey, Gerry**

Rev. Veazey officiating his first wedding after becoming pastor of Zion Baptist Church

February 25, 1961

Tyrone and **Oceola Briscoe**

Pastoral Installation—Zion Baptist Church

December 1960

Rev. Carlton W. Veazey

The Latture Family

Rev. Veazey and daughter Caron

Robert Earl—Cousin and the Father of James Earl
Jones, the acclaimed actor

Gina Latture — Jean's God-daughter

Chapter 5

SEMINARY YEARS AND EARLY PASTORATE

The next six weeks would be very important to me. I had to decide which seminary I would attend and what kind of scholarship would be offered. I also decided to stay home and work, rather than going to Chicago for employment. I called my old band director and asked if he had an opening for a recreational director at one of the parks. Shortly thereafter, he offered me a job as supervisor of several recreation centers. I was very appreciative. Not only did the job pay well; I would also not have to spend a week or so searching for employment. It was also helpful that I had done this work when I was a senior in high school.

While I was home, my routine was spending time with my parents and friends, sharing experiences and anxiety as I prepared to enter a new phase of my educational life and prepare for the Christian ministry. Two weeks later, I received a letter from the Southern Baptist Theological Seminary in Louisville, Kentucky, offering me a three-year scholarship, with all expenses covered. This was great news, and I thanked God for this blessing, especially since Southern was a Baptist seminary, unlike Gammon Theological Seminary in Atlanta and Howard University in Washington, DC, which offered only modest financial assistance. I thought at the time that my theological education should be Baptist oriented. (This has since proven not to be the case, fortunately, as you will see as our journey continues.) The letters from these schools helped me make my decision: I would attend Southern Baptist Theological Seminary in Louisville, Kentucky.

After a successful summer of work and fun, I settled down to the idea of leaving for the next phase of my life as a seminarian. On the Saturday before I was to leave for Louisville and my new future, my father was visited by Dr. Dearing King, an in-law and pastor of Zion Baptist Church of Louisville. The visit was a casual one. His nephew Hillary Lewis was married to my sister Audrey, and his sister was a member of my childhood church Central Baptist Church.

When he arrived on the Saturday before the Monday I was scheduled to leave, he asked my father where I would be attending seminary.

My father replied, "Carl will be going to Louisville to attend the Southern Baptist Theological Seminary, where he has been given a full three-year scholarship."

After listening to my father's proud announcement, he said something stunning. I remember the stark surprise I felt at his words. "Rev. Veazey, Carlton will not be going to Southern Baptist, because I want him to attend the Howard University School of Religion in Washington, DC." I was shocked, especially given that I had received such a lucrative scholarship to Southern Baptist.

My father listened as Dr. King outlined why I should go to Howard. Among them, he pointed out that he did not want me to attend a denominational seminary like Southern Baptist, as it would not provide the worldview of theology that Howard would provide. He also argued that I should be prepared to speak across denominational doctrines to ecumenical issues, which Howard would prepare me to do. He then reminded Daddy that the president of Howard University was Dr. Mordecai Johnson, a Baptist minister and an outstanding leader on the world stage. Finally, after several logistical questions about Howard and Washington, DC, he asked my father if he could use the phone to call Washington.

When he reached Washington that Saturday, he asked to speak to Dr. Daniel G. Hill, Howard's dean of the School of Religion. I could only hear Dr. King explain to Dean Hill that he was a friend of the Veazey family, whose son was about to go to Southern Baptist. He explained to Dean Hill how bright I was, what great potential I had, and what an asset I would be to the School of Religion. Hearing someone express such confidence in me was embarrassing for me.

When Dr. King hung up the phone, he announced to my father I would be going to Howard University in Washington, DC, on a full scholarship, which would cover room and board, as well as tuition and books.

Although I was somewhat confused by these radical changes in my plans and future, I somehow felt that this was a decision that was not unlike the message I had gotten from God about my mother's healing several years ago. Dr. King gave me the address to which I was to report and the name of the person I should contact when I got there. The amazing thing was, instead of leaving for Louisville, Kentucky, on Monday, I would be leaving for Washington, DC, to attend the Howard University's School of Religion.

I wrote a letter to Dr. McCall, president of Southern Baptist, to inform him I would not be attending. I thanked him for the generous scholarship and asked him to pray for my future in the Christian ministry.

Monday morning, I rose early to pack and make sure I had all of the things I needed, because I was going to Washington, DC, eleven hours from Memphis by train on Southern Railroad. My train was scheduled to leave Union Station at three o'clock in the afternoon, which gave me a few hours to say goodbye to family and friends. My mother was busy preparing breakfast for all of us. My father was sitting in the living room and I joined him for some last-minute conversation. He told me to remember all the things I had been taught and not to forget to pray without ceasing.

I asked him if he was pleased that I would be attending Howard, even though it was not a denominational seminary like Southern Baptist. His response was surprising but very instructive. "God is not a Baptist, Methodist, Presbyterian or Catholic," he told. "Therefore, you need to know all religions." He was always profound. His father, Reverend George Veazey, who was born in 1860 and began preaching in 1890, had established the Mount Enno Baptist Church in Arkubutla, Mississippi, where the site of the church and the church cemetery exist to this day.

After our conversation, my mother called us to the breakfast table, filled with everything you could desire for breakfast—sausage, eggs, grits, hash brown potatoes, and biscuits with an assortment of jelly and jams. Of course, juice and coffee was available. The conversation at the table was limited, as we all enjoyed mother's delicious breakfast.

After breakfast, I returned to my room to double check that I had all the things I needed before leaving for Washington, DC. I had traveled extensively in the mid-western states of Missouri, Chicago, Wisconsin, and Michigan. But I had never traveled east, even to Nashville the capital of Tennessee. This would be my first time going east to places like Knoxville, Chattanooga, and other cities about which I had only read.

At one o'clock in the afternoon Gerry and George arrived. He helped to load my bags into his 1956 Cadillac, and we left for the train station, where I would leave for the nation's capital—a place I had only read about and seen on television. This was, indeed, an exciting trip for me. It would prove to be my pilgrimage in clay feet.

As we walked toward the waiting room, Gerry wished me well and told me to write and let her know if I needed anything. She had always been very protective of her baby brother, which sometimes embarrassed me. At two fifteen, the red cap came to take us to the track where my train was leaving. After kissing my sister goodbye and giving my brother-in-law a firm handshake, I followed the redcap onto the train and selected a seat, near the door as usual. The train pulled out and passed by my sister and brother, who were furiously waving as I waved back with the same enthusiasm.

I still, like all Southern people of the time, never traveled without a "shoebox," and mine contained the best food in the world, which my mother had prepared. There was fried chicken—I think half a chicken—with biscuits and pound cake. The shoeboxes were never opened until we'd left the station and reached the first stop, in this case, Millington, Tennessee. Although many of my fellow travelers opened their boxes at the Millington stop, I decided to wait until we'd reached at least Nashville or Knoxville, which would be at least another four or five hours.

When we arrived in Nashville, it was still light enough for me to see the city. It wasn't as impressive as Memphis, except for the replica of the Parthenon and the Hermitage, home of Andrew Jackson. Nashville was not nearly as large as Memphis, and where Memphis was known for the blues, Nashville was known for country music with Grand Ole Opry, a famous site for many television viewers. After leaving Nashville, we were on our way to Knoxville, Tennessee, home of the University of Tennessee, which had an outstanding football team and had just admitted its first Negro students. Since it was dusk, we could still see beautiful mountains and valleys, which we didn't have in Memphis, Mississippi, and Arkansas.

Our trip would take at least eighteen hours, and we were scheduled to arrive in Washington at nine o'clock next day. I planned to stay at the local Young Men's Christian Association, or YMCA, for the night before going to 2617 Georgia Avenue NW, the place designated for me to come for my housing assignment and orientation.

This was the longest train ride I had ever had. But it proved to be historic. It took me to the capital of the United States of America, where the business of the nation took place and the president of the nation resided. This fact stood out in my mind as I realized I would be here for the next three years, studying for the ministry at one of the outstanding Negro universities. Howard University was founded by Oliver Otis Howard, a former general in the Union Army, to provide education for the freedman seeking a better life. Although I knew I would be busy with my studies, Washington would always be a place of inexhaustible wonder and discovery.

The train arrived in Washington, DC, as scheduled, and I proceeded to the YMCA, where I was assigned a room for fifteen dollars for one night. As a courtesy, the YMCA provided doughnuts and coffee each morning for guests, especially those who were members of the "Y." I had joined the YMCA in high school, which allowed us to use the gym and other facilities.

That night, sleep came with difficulty. I was thinking about all the days before me and what they would bring. I had many questions related to the School of Religion. What would the professors be like? Would they be interesting and probative? Would their liberalism make me uncomfortable? What would the student body look like as far as male and female, although females were mainly majoring in Christian education? And would my college preparation support me in my study of theology? These and other questions came to mind as I drifted off to sleep my first night in the nation's capital.

I woke to a beautiful August morning, and after using the breakfast the YMCA staff had prepared, I left for the dormitory at 2617 Georgia Avenue NW. The Capitol Cab pulled up at a very stately apartment building that bore no resemblance to the dormitories at State. I made sure that I had the right address, paid the cab driver, and retrieved my bags from the trunk.

Standing in front of the building was a distinguished gentleman who I asked whether the building was the dormitory for the School of Religion. His reply was yes, and he asked if he could help me. I also asked him whether there was an office where I could register, to which he replied that he did not think so. But I could go to apartment one, where Dr. Evans Crawford and his wife lived, and they could direct me from there.

Leaving this gentleman, I was impressed with his commanding voice, which sounded like those of the preachers I had grown up hearing. I thought to myself that maybe he was a professor, since he had such poise and gravitas.

I knocked on the door of apartment one, and a very kind and gentle man with a great smile came to the door and asked if he could help me. I replied with a firm, "Yes, thank you," and proceeded to tell him that I was a new student from Memphis, Tennessee, here to attend the Howard University School of Religion. He responded that the office would be open tomorrow, and I could spend the night with him and his wife, Betty.

I accepted his hospitality and proceeded to the living room. Betty came into the room. I immediately stood up and greeted her with an open handshake. They asked where I was from and how I'd selected Howard, and I gave them a verbal résumé I had practiced for meeting new people. I was from Memphis, Tennessee, and my father and grandfather were Baptist ministers and had graduated in May from Arkansas AM&N College in Pine Bluff, Arkansas, where our president was Dr. Lawrence A. Davis. I also told them that our commencement speaker was Rev. Dr. Martin Luther King Jr. and that we all were very honored and proud to have him as our speaker. I told them how inspired we'd all been to hear him talk about the work he and others were doing in the civil rights movement.

Several minutes after I had finished, Dr. Crawford informed me that he and Dr. King had been classmates at Boston University. He also said how proud he was of the work for equality and justice that Dr. King and other ministers were doing throughout the South. Dr. Crawford informed me that he and Betty were also new at Howard University, where he would serve as dean of the Andrew Rankin Memorial Chapel and professor of homiletics and Christian ethics.

Mrs. Crawford also welcomed me to Howard and told me she was sure I would enjoy the experience. I would learn later that she was a teacher for the District of Columbia public school system and an excellent musician and pianist.

I was shown to my room, where I unpacked the items I would need for the night. I asked the Crawfords if it would be all right for me to explore the campus and the neighborhood. They encouraged me to do so and invited me to have dinner with them that evening at six o'clock. I thanked them again for their hospitality and kindness and left for my tour of the campus and the neighborhood.

I arrived at the corner a block from our building and proceeded to climb a very high hill off Georgia Avenue. I continued through gates that led to the main campus, where the first buildings reached were the Schools of Law and Engineering. I entered a security checkpoint for cars and saw a very imposing Gothic-looking structure, which I found out was one of the oldest buildings and a landmark on the campus, the well-known Andrew Rankin Chapel. The chapel was named after the brother of the first president, Jeremiah Rankin, whose life we celebrate today.

On reaching the Howard quadrangle, I saw the Carnegie building that had been built and donated by the great philanthropist and had housed the School of Religion for decades. It was not by any means the largest building on campus, but it had a certain grace and beauty that we seminarians learned to love and appreciate. Walking a little farther, I came to the historic building called Douglass Hall to honor Fredrick Douglass, who escaped from slavery in St. Michaels and fled to Massachusetts to become one of the great abolitionists. He was also one of the great orators of his time. Today, his house in southeast Washington is a national historic site under the care of the United States Department of the Interior.

There were many other buildings, but another one we must acknowledge is the Freedmen's Hospital, where many Washingtonians were born and many medical students interned during their term at the Howard Medical School. Freedmen's had some of the most outstanding doctors in America. Among those who practiced at Freedmen's was the famous Dr. Charles R. Drew, who discovered blood plasma, a discovery that saved millions of people around the world. How ironic it is that, when he was involved in a serious automobile accident in the South, his death was partially attributed to lack of blood plasma, which was denied him because the hospitals were segregated.

I toured for several hours before I became exhausted trying to read about all the building on the campus. After leaving Howard, I turned north on Georgia Avenue and discovered Griffith Stadium several blocks away. It was a huge stadium, where the Washington Senators played. This was definitely a plus, being only four blocks from the university.

Further down Georgia, I discovered another famous start, Florida Avenue and the famous Howard Theater, where all the great stars and bands played and offered floor shows.

After three hours I headed back up Georgia Avenue to 2617 and the Crawfords, hello so graciously housed me for the night, as well as providing me dinner. During dinner, I told them about my campus tour and how impressed I was with Rankin Chapel.

When we finally turned in for the night, I was unable to sleep because of all the excitement I had experienced during my first day on Howard's campus and in the community. Betty Crawford had made everything comfortable for me and assured me that they were glad to have me.

The following day, I awoke at six o'clock and turned on the television to watch the local news, which was very interesting in that the reports addressed a decision made by the commissioners of the district in a meeting the day before. This was puzzling to me, as I thought every city was run by a mayor and a city council. Washington, I would learn, was unique in that the citizens of the District of Columbia were not allowed to vote. This was startling, as one of the major grievances in the South was the denial of the vote in many places. We were allowed to vote in Memphis, although no Negros had ever been on the ballot. But in Washington, the Congress of the United States appointed three commissioners, who would run the city with the oversight of the congressional district committee.

After watching the local news, I prepared to dress and found towels that were neatly arranged in my room. After showering and dressing, I ate the breakfast Mrs. Crawford had prepared for me, which was delicious. Dean Crawford told me where to go to register after going to the School of Religion building to receive the classes I would take this semester.

We were all told to go to the chapel, where Dean Daniel G. Hill would speak to us and his assistant would give us classes. Then we would go to the administration building, where we would be given our registration forms and cafeteria cards for our daily meals. When Dean Hill walked into the room, he immediately projected charisma in his carriage and persona. His kind and empathetic face reassured us that we were in good hands for the most important phase of our lives as we prepared for the Christian ministry. There were only 125 of us in the freshman class.

Mr. Herbert Eaton, the administrative assistant to the dean, then told us the rules regarding our class attendance and hours when we could use the seminary library, even though the university's library, Founder's Library, was always open. Mr. Eaton next told us who our professors were by calling out the subject and then the teacher's name and room number. He reminded us to take this information down in our notes.

The following were the classes and professors he named: Dr. Gilbert, Church History; Dr. Gene Rice, Old Testament Literature; Dr. Leon Wright, New Testament Literature; Dr. Deotis Roberts, Systematic Theology; Dr. Evans E. Crawford, Christian Social Ethics and Homiletics; and Dr. Mark Fax, Church Music. It has been sixty years since that Thursday morning when I was introduced to seminary education. We were also given the room numbers, which were all on the second floor of the Carnegie Building.

Following this meeting, we left for the administration building, where we were given forms that detailed our classes, dormitory fees, cafeteria cards, and other fees for the first semester. After finishing the registration process, some of us decided to go over to Baldwin Hall for lunch before going to our various dorms or apartments. Some of my first friends in seminary were Soloman Phiffer, Samuel Turner, Rafe Taylor, Lawrence Henry, and Wendell Beane. Over lunch, we discussed what we expected to get from seminary and whether this new knowledge would diminish our faith or beliefs. All of us came from different denominations, which was what Howard was about; it was a nondenominational school that did not teach from any single denomination's polity. After a very enjoyable lunch, which assured us the food was not going to be bad, we returned to the Carnegie Building to pick up our bags and go to our rooms or apartments that had been assigned to us. Although some class members were assigned to Slowe Hall, Wendell Beane and I were given an apartment at 2617 Georgia Avenue, where Dr. Crawford lived.

After retrieving our bags, Wendell and I went to our apartment, where we began to put our things away in the simple but ample apartment. There were twin beds, two chests of drawers, and two desks with chairs. We went to the local Sears to purchase towels, bathroom mats, sheets, and pillowcases, which the university did not provide. After setting up our room, we engaged in conversation about our backgrounds and how we had come to the ministry.

Wendell didn't know much about the South, and I knew very little about Bermuda, Wendell's home. He knew about the violence against Negroes and the segregation we had experience but was unaware of the denial of the right to vote. He was aware of the young black leader Rev. Dr. Martin Luther King Jr. who was leading a civil rights movement that had captivated the South and the nation and had heard of Dr. King's courage and ability to motivate through his oratory and marches throughout the South. Wendell was extremely bright. Having someone with whom I could dialogue challenged and inspired me. And he could also teach me because of the British influence on his education.

Before Bermuda won its independence, the nation was a part of the British Empire, as were so many of the other islands. The British educational system was far more rigorous than that of the American educational system and required students to take an examination covering the four years of high school, a very difficult task. This meant that everything learned in the last four years could be called for you to remember. We, in this country, would be fortunate to remember what we'd learned during the current year. This is just to give you an indication of the kind of student Wendell was and how well read he was. He had studied at Howard University during his undergraduate education, majoring in history under Dr. Logan, a renowned history professor.

Wendell, with all his gifts, was a very sociable person, with a very sensitive spirit and a reluctance to make judgments about anybody, except theologians with whom he did not agree and whose views he thought were misleading to Christians. He also was very tolerant of me being a smoker, which I realize now was a great sacrifice, since antismoking laws have been enacted. I never realized that I was putting his health jeopardy through secondhand smoke. In many ways, I had the perfect roommate for seminary.

We did not have to report to class until Monday morning so Wendell decided to guide me on a tour of Washington to become familiar with the city that would be our home for the next three years. On Saturday morning, we took the streetcar, still part of the Washington transportation culture, downtown to catch the tour bus. I also remember the street cars from my childhood days in Memphis and moving up to trolley buses, far more convenient—something I could brag coming from my hometown, Memphis +. We caught the tour bus at Seventh Street and Pennsylvania Avenue and were given an allotted number of minutes to see each monument or historic site.

We went directly to the United States Capitol, where the narrator gave us all the pertinent facts about the building, including the date it was built and the divide between the House of Representatives and the Senate. He also spoke briefly about the function of each body. We learned that the House of Representatives was where the appropriations for bills originated, and the Senate was the body that reviewed the bill and determined whether or not it was acceptable. The Senate also was responsible for confirmation of all Supreme Court justices nominated by the president of the United States, which was called the act of advice and consent. There were many other responsibilities, but these were the major issues with which these congressional bodies dealt.

Leaving the capitol, we were toured the National Mall, stopping at the Smithsonian Institution, where many of our nation's treasures are housed and on display. The next stop was the National Archives Building, where such documents as the Declaration of Independence and the Constitution of the United States of America are displayed. Many of the writings and correspondences of the presidents can be viewed here as well. The building also houses the original writings of historical value to our country's history.

From there, we went directly to the Lincoln Memorial, which celebrates President Lincoln, who was responsible for freeing the slaves through the Emancipation Proclamation. This was particularly important to us, being Negroes and still suffering from oppression and discrimination. Next, we visited the Jefferson Memorial near the Potomac River and majestically located between Virginia and Washington. Thomas Jefferson was a founding father, responsible for writing the Declaration of Independence. He became the third president of the United States. Finally, we were taken to the sacred and honored Arlington Cemetery, where heroes from our wars were interred with honor.

On return to our starting point, the driver intentionally saved for our last stop the White House, which at that time was home to Dwight D. Eisenhower, the thirty-fourth president of the United States. It was the most beautiful house and has been the home of US presidents since 1800, beginning with John Adams. Although we did not tour the White House, the narrator named all the rooms, some of which I can recall, such as the East Room and the Blue Room.

When we had returned to our starting point at Seventh Street and Pennsylvania Avenue, Wendell and I both agreed that this tour of US history was one we would never forget. It had made us proud not only to be in the nation's capital but also to be attending the premier Negro university in America.

After arriving back at school, we prepared for our first day of seminary education. This included making sure we had notebooks for each course and adequate pencils, pens, and other needed items.

The conversation then turned to which church we would attend the next day, since Sunday chapel would not open until the following Sunday. Wendell decided on Asbury United Methodist Church, a historic black Methodist church in Washington. Since I had taken the tour up Georgia Avenue before registration, a little storefront church called Carron Baptist Church attracted my attention. I had not ever heard of the name Carron in the Bible, which was fascinating to me. Also, I had always been fascinated by small churches and storefronts.

Somehow, I felt these churches related more to the early Christian churches, which said that they held their meetings from house to house. Although I did not want to criticize the larger churches, I felt these smaller congregations were more sincere and closer to each other in sharing their experiences in the Lord Jesus Christ.

The following day, we got up early and went across the street for a quick breakfast before going to our chosen churches. Asbury United Methodist Church was downtown, which meant Wendell had to take a bus. My church, Carron Baptist Church, was at the corner of Kenyon Street and Georgia Avenue. I was interested in what the services would be like, since I had been brought up in a large church, where there were many rituals and traditions.

Carron was a very small church about six blocks from the university and very convenient for me. When I arrived around ten thirty in the morning, Sunday school had just ended. The classes were divided by different pews. The first front pews were for the adults, the middle pews were set aside for the teenagers, and the last three pews were for the rest of the children. The church was in the basement of a building that was not completed; the goal was to build the upper structure someday.

After I had introduced myself to the teacher of the Sunday school class, he introduced me to the class of seven men and five women. They asked me to say a word before class ended. It was close to eleven o'clock and formal church services would be starting. In my brief remarks I shared that I was from Memphis, Tennessee, and a member of the Bethlehem Baptist Church and that my pastor was Rev. R. W. Taylor.

I intentionally did not mention to the class that I was in Washington to attend the Howard University School of Religion.

The teacher of the class, Mr. Watson, immediately asked me to follow him to the pastor's study located behind the pulpit and the choir loft to meet the pastor. Rev. Rodgers was a very tall man with a preacher's bearing, which meant he had a big stomach and a commanding voice. He welcomed me to Carron, asked me to come again, and said he'd like to talk with me after I began my studies in the School of Religion.

The services reminded me of the services at my friend J.O. Patterson's father's church, with the swinging gospel music and the dancing down the aisle to the choir loft singing, "Step by step, we are nearing the kingdom." This song began to electrify the congregation as the processional proceeded to the choir loft. After reaching the choir loft Rev. Rodgers went to the pulpit and began to intone the Lord's Prayer, which the choir picked up. The congregation joined in to ask for the Lord's presence in the service. After the singing of "The Lord's Prayer," the minister offered the prayer of invocation, which led the congregation to sing the morning hymn, "O How I Love Jesus," which was very spirited, causing some members to shout. Following the morning hymn, the assistants offered the New and Old Testament scriptures, followed by the doxology. The choir sang another hymn, which was also familiar, "What a Fellowship," universally sung in Baptist churches across the country. After the announcements and remarks by the pastor, the choir sang the hymn before the pastor preached.

Rev. Rodgers was an informally trained minister, meaning he had not had training at a seminary. Notwithstanding this, he gave a very effective sermon entitled "Where Is Your Faith?" It implored all of us to search within and find our faith in times of difficulty and hardship. He had many good examples of faith, starting with the prophet Job, who endured many hardships and tragedies but never gave up on God. This sermon meant a lot to me, since I was entering a new phase of my life and did not know what hardships I would experience. The sermon would remind me to always reach for my faith in God, and he would bring me through.

After the service, I congratulated the pastor on a very helpful sermon. He thanked me for coming and asked me whether I had been licensed to preach. I told him I had been licensed three years ago and also ordained in Memphis by Dr. J. 1. Campbell, nationally known through the National Baptist Convention as an outstanding preacher. Upon hearing about my ministerial background, he asked me to come early in the future, because he wanted me to participate in the service. After talking with Rev. Rogers, I knew I had found the right church, which would help me to grow.

I returned to 2617 Georgia Avenue, where Wendell was already waiting for me so we could go to Baldwin Hall for dinner and talk. The distance from the apartment to the Baldwin was a short ten-minute walk, during which we compared our worship experiences.

Although I had never seen Asbury United Methodist Church, I thought it was a rather large church, which Wendell confirmed. He also said the service was terrific and the choir was spectacular. Since Wendell was from Bermuda and had a British accent, he made the church sound like the St. Patrick's Cathedral in New York. He told me the pastor, Rev. Williams, had delivered a fantastic sermon. I quickly learned that Wendell was very fond of the English language, since he spoke so well.

After he had exhausted everything about Asbury, he asked me about the church I'd attended. I told him that I had attended a storefront church, to which he exclaimed, "What's the name?!"

I repeated the name, Carron, and told him that I would try to find out its origins next Sunday, as I did not remember a reference to that name in the Bible.

We shared our first lunch of fried chicken, mashed potatoes, and green beans, which was the best thing we had eaten since we'd received our meal tickets. Following our dinner, we sat there and talked about what we expected Monday morning, which would be the first day of our seminary experience. Although the School of Religion was new to Wendell, he had attended Howard over the past four years, majoring in history. On our way back to our apartment, I thought how blessed I was to have such a smart and religious person to share an apartment.

The evening was spent mainly reading and watching the little television I had managed to buy with money I received from family for my graduation gift. I watched the Sunday television shows that were part of our Sunday ritual was when I was home and even when I was at State. Wendell would watch some television, but he was an avid reader, which evidently had been a part of his enjoyment. We were supposed to report to the library of the school at nine o'clock for an orientation on the library by Mrs. Williams, who had been with the school nearly twenty years.

When I turned the television off at ten o'clock and got into bed, I asked Wendell to make sure we did not oversleep, since we had to be at the school at nine o'clock. We agreed to set the alarm clock for seven thirty, which would give us adequate time to shower and dress for the day.

Neither one of us slept well that night anticipating the next day's experiences for which both us had waited so long. Wendell fell asleep before I did, but shortly afterward, I felt very sleepy. When I could not resist any longer, I finally fell off to sleep.

The alarm clock went off at exactly seven thirty. I immediately shut it off. I asked Wendell if he wanted to go to the bathroom first, and he answered that I could go first so he could sleep longer. After showering and dressing, I awakened Wendell and told him it was eight o'clock, and we had to be at school at nine. We left for school at eight thirty, stopping at the corner deli for coffee that we drank on our way to the School of Religion.

Just before getting to the school, we stopped and sat on one of the benches lining the quadrangle, since we had at least fifteen minutes to get to the library, only five minutes away. During that time, we watched the undergraduates go to class, especially the beautiful, expensively dressed girls. The interesting thing was, although I was surrounded by some beautiful young ladies, it was like sitting at a sumptuous table of food with no appetite. Although I had not come to grips with this reality, I had lost my appetite or should I say "my heart" at State with the broken relationship with Joyce. I did not realize at the time that this feeling would last most of my seminary years.

We arrived at the library at exactly nine o'clock, where we were joined by almost a hundred other students who would be our classmates the first year. After Mrs. Williams's orientation, we all headed to our very first classes as seminarians.

Wendell and I headed upstairs for Dr. Roberts's Systematic Theology class. Dr. Roberts entered the room looking like the theology professor he was. The school had passed out brief curriculum vitae on all of our professors, so we knew that Dr. Roberts had received his PhD from the University of Edinburgh in Scotland, which made him eminently qualified according to the Association of Seminary and Theological Schools. We would find out later that all of our professors were exceptionally qualified in their areas.

Dr. Roberts began his lecture by welcoming us to the school and informing us that we would be much better equipped to have an effective ministry as a result of understanding the nature and character of God. As he went forward in his lecture, I realized why seminary was important for an informed ministry. Discussing the nature and character of God gave us a basic understanding of why religion was important to us as human beings. When I was in college, Dr. Cochran had given me a book by William James, *Varieties of Religious Experiences*, which helped me differentiate religion from theology. We went to our next class, New Testament literature, which would be taught by Dr. Leon Wright, who would prove to be one of the most influential professors in my seminary life.

Dr. Wright was a Phi Beta Kappa from Harvard University in Sacred Literature, which meant he was versed not only in the biblical literature of Christianity but also in all of the world's religious literature. He was a very studious looking man who entered the room speaking to us and informing us that we would have a very strenuous study in his class. He explained that he had been away in Burma, where the religion was Buddhism, which would be a major part of his lectures, as he would compare the major religions with Christianity. He also told us reading would be a major part of his class, rather than a daily lecture on the New Testament. After receiving the reading list for the semester, we all realized this would not be like Bible study, which was an understatement. Dr. Wright was also proficient in Greek, which he taught and which was the language in which the New Testament was written.

The final class, History of Christianity, was after lunch on Mondays. At State, a class after lunch was always difficult for me because food would make me sluggish and sleepy. This class was taught by Dr. Gilbert, who was also recognized as an outstanding church historian. Although he was one of the few white professors, none of us thought that would make a difference, especially in a theological seminary. Dr. Gilbert was a kind, soft-spoken man, but we quickly realized that his demeanor did not mean that this would be an easy class. He informed us that our text for this class would be, *A History of Christianity* by Kenneth Scott Latourette. He also warned us not to be intimidated by the size of the book, as we would be studying it for the next two years—which was intimidation enough. He simply gave us a brief outline of the course, telling us we would trace the beginnings of Jesus's preparation for his ministry from the years he spent with the Essenes, a Jewish sect who gave themselves to studying the hidden documents that later would be called the Dead Sea scrolls. While he was talking, I was thinking back to my early days when everything started with the birth of Jesus, not realizing that Jesus's study with the Essenes influenced his ministry when he returned to Nazareth at the age of thirty. The intervening years were called the hidden years of the life of Jesus Christ. This knowledge made me wonder why others in my church did not know these things. Dr. Gilbert was also a believer in supplemental reading assignments, which he gave us before the class ended.

After purchasing the required books, I returned to the apartment to read the introductions to each, which made me understand that seminary would be challenging if I remained.

Dinner was served each day beginning at five o'clock and ending at eight o'clock. I always tried to get there early so that I would not have to wait. Baldwin Hall, on Fourth Street, was about a ten-minute walk from the apartment. The ground floor housed the huge cafeteria where all on-campus students ate. I realized while having lunch that many of the students were younger, some in their freshman year and others in their senior year. You could always tell the freshman and sophomores from other students because they laughed a lot. I attributed that to their not realizing what lay ahead of them, which was serious study and challenges. Although I loved humor, I did not find much humor in the books and assignments ahead.

Returning to my apartment on Georgia Avenue, I found Wendell already reading one of the assigned books. This level of study would remain throughout our time together.

Shortly afterward, Wendell left to go to dinner before the cafeteria closed. I decided to read from one of the books, *A History of Christianity.* Its more than nine hundred pages made it seem overwhelming. I remembered what Dr. Gilbert had said about this book remaining with us for two years in order for us to cover the voluminous material contained therein.

After watching a few hours of television and arranging my clothes for the next day, I decided to turn in early for the second day in seminary, when we would meet the teachers of our other classes.

That night, both Wendell and I slept much better, since we had a full day of activity and we were adjusting more to our community, giving us a sense of comfort in our new surroundings. Wendell was more familiar than I, since he had attended Howard as an undergraduate. However, this was a new experience for him; this was graduate school and a new challenge.

The next morning, we followed our usual pattern of stopping at the corner deli for coffee and doughnuts on our way to classes on our second day at the School of Religion. We had meal cards that would allow us to eat in the cafeteria, but we chose to sleep an extra half hour and get coffee and doughnuts instead of going to Baldwin Hall for breakfast.

However, the weekends were different, since we had no classes and the dining hall was open for breakfast from seven to eleven o'clock.

Our second day of study, we had Old Testament, Christian Education, and Church Music. Our classed were divided into two segments, with Monday, Wednesday, and Friday for the major courses, with the exception of Old Testament, a major course that was ninety minutes long since it was only two days a week.

The first class at nine o'clock was taught by Dr. Gene Rice, who had the mildest manner of all our professors. No one would ever think that this quiet man was once a marine and had served in combat in the Korean War. Although he was mild mannered and very humble, he was serious about our preparation and the knowledge that was necessary for an informed ministry. He also gave us book assignments and reading lists. He informed us that his goal was to give us an in depth understanding of the Old Testament text and the people called Hebrews, who God would call to be his chosen people through whom his message to humankind would be revealed. His manner of teaching was very interesting and made the Old Testament literature come alive and be relative to our everyday lives. I knew this would be one of my favorite courses.

Dr. Tymns, one of the older faculty members, having taught at the school for over thirty years, taught Christian Education, essential to a well-rounded ministry. He was a very strong-looking man. Born in Mississippi, he had a wealth of experience on the cruelty and horrendous violence during the Jim Crow era. He had the best speaking voice of the entire faculty, in that his deep bass gave him a strong persona.

Following Dr. Tymns's class, we were required to attend chapel twice a week, where either faculty members or some noted minister from the Washington community would deliver the sermon. Although it was required, all of us were eager to attend in order to see how our faculty preached with all of their learning. Mr. Mark Fax, a professor in the School of Music provided the music and the soloists for our chapel. The first speaker was the honored and respected dean of the School of Religion, the Rev. Dr. Daniel G. Hill, to whom Dr. Dearing had spoken about a scholarship for me to Howard and to whom I will be eternally grateful. Dr. Hill was a very thoughtful and well-read minister in the Methodist church. In his welcome to us, he reminded us that our preparation was our witness to God, and we should take it seriously. This was a welcome spiritual interlude to our day of study.

After lunch, I returned to our final class of the day, which was Church Music taught by Mrs. Corbin from the School of Music. It was an interesting class that informed us of the origins of church music, an integral part of worship. I particularly liked this course, since my love of music had always been part of my development. There would not be any textbook for this class, but we would be given handouts outlining what Mrs. Corbin planned to cover in the course.

The second day was finally over, and we would repeat our schedules for the rest of the week. This was a major change from State in every respect. There would be no reminders of our academic obligations, especially for those of us on scholarships. After completion of the second day, the schedule would continue throughout the semester. I felt a sense of accomplishment having survived the first two days and an uncertainty as to whether I would be able to matriculate on this level.

Wendell's adjustments were not as difficult as mine.

The remainder of the week was spent preparing assignments and, most of all, keeping up with the unbelievable reading lists. Gradually, we were able to introduce ourselves to other classmates living at 2617 Georgia Avenue. We discussed where we were from and why we chose Howard, although some of this was done on our first day as a formality. Some of the classmates with whom I quickly bonded were Gus Roman, Soloman Phiffer, Samuel Turner, and Cameron Byrd. I gradually began to know other classmates, some of whom were from DC. Our conversations with our Washington classmates were very informative in helping us understand the Washington culture. This became very important as I became involved with other friends outside of the school.

One of the things those from DC pointed out was that Washington had many freedmen who were emancipated before the proclamation by President Abraham Lincoln. This, in a subtle way, gave them a certain sense of not being like other Negroes, who were only emancipated in 1864. Other information they provided was about major churches and pastors in the area. The ones I remember were Shiloh Baptist, pastored by Dr. Earl Harrison; Zion Baptist Church, pastored by Dr. A. Joseph Edwards; Metropolitan Baptist Church, pastored by Dr. E. C. Smith; Florida Avenue Baptist, pastored by Dr. Rollins; and First Baptist Church, pastored by R. Lavelle Tucker. These were some of the Northwest churches about which our classmates had spoken. Washington was a class-conscious city as far as the Negroes were concerned. The churches would indicate the social status of the members, which, I would find out later, was a myth.

Wendell and I set aside Saturday to do chores around the apartment, such as cleaning the bathroom and going to the wash-and-dry facilities close by. We also found a barbershop where we could get a haircut at a reasonable cost. In addition, I set aside time to study the Sunday school lesson in case I was called upon to teach, which I was eager to do.

Sunday morning I got up before Wendell because I wanted to attend Sunday school at Carron Baptist Church, where I had attended the week before and where the pastor seemed to have taken an interest in me. After breakfast in Baldwin Hall, I headed to Carron Baptist Church. I arrived fifteen minutes before the class was to begin and was greeted with a hug and a warm Baptist kiss from the teacher, Mrs. Johnson. One thing about Baptist people, they are affectionate and warm when they meet you, even if they don't mean it. But most of the time, they do mean it.

When class began, I was introduced again to members who had not been present the previous Sunday, although I could tell I had been discussed. After the introduction, Mrs. Johnson asked if I would do the honor of teaching the lesson. I had known by instinct, informed by my many years in the Baptist church, this may happen. I graciously accepted and asked the class to join me in prayer for a successful lesson.

Paul, in writing his letter to the church at Corinth, reminded them that, of all the gifts Christians could possess, the gift of love was the greatest. Paul also reminded us that, even if we had the gift of prophecy or sacrifice or martyrdom, the highest gift was that of love. His letter closes with the admonition that "now abided faith, hope, and love. But the greatest of these is love."

At the end of the morning lesson, the class responded that they prayed I would become a member of the church.

Following Sunday school, I went immediately to the pastor's study, since he'd invited us to share the service by participating in the morning service. When I reached the study, Rev. Rodgers met me with a strong handshake and a heartfelt, "God bless you." Dr. Rodgers had several assistants, who looked at me with curiosity, behind which I detected a sense of fear that I was there to take their places. Before going out to the congregation, Pastor Rodgers introduced me and welcomed me to Carron Baptist and asked me to offer the Morning Prayer in the service.

I was honored that he'd asked me to be a part of the morning worship. In the pulpit, Pastor Rodgers took the large chair in the center and asked me to take the one beside him. When he rose to open the service with a call to worship, the pianist began the processional with "O How I Love Jesus." The song was executed with enthusiasm and great spirit as the choir came down the aisle, breaking into a semi-dance that was what we in college called the "two-step." Before the choir members had reached the choir stand, the church was electric with the spirit and shouting.

Rev. Rodgers asked that we pray with our young minister, who was a student at the Howard University School of Religion, Rev. Carlton Veazey. I opened my prayer as I always did, with thanksgiving for a day and the blessings of this day. I also prayed for the pastor of the church and the wonderful members who had so graciously received me as a child of God and the Holy Spirit, which met us in this house of the Lord. After asking God's blessings on the poor and those in need, I asked blessings on the nation and the president of the United States and finally to help us to live so that we might live again with Thee. At the close of the prayer, the church gave me the loudest amen that I had ever heard from any prayer I had rendered.

Rev Rodger's sermon that Sunday was taken from the Sunday school lesson on love. Growing up, I noticed many ministers would preach the Sunday school lesson. I did not know whether the Holy Spirit led them to do this or whether it was because they had not prepared. However, Rev. Rodgers brought out some good points in his message on love. One that I remember until this day was, "It is not enough to do good you must do well for the right reason." He emphasized that many people did good things but for the wrong reasons, such as for praise of others. Paul said, "Though I give all my goods to feed the poor, and have not love, it profited me nothing." Rev. Rodgers may not have had had the eloquence of other ministers I had heard, but I was fascinated with his ability to relate the scriptures to the daily lives of ordinary people.

After the benediction, Rev. Rodgers invited me to the study and thanked me for coming and offering the invocation. My response was that I had been prayerfully considering becoming a watch care member while in Washington, DC. I also told him how much I was helped by his sermon. He was very appreciative of my words and told me he would like to hear me preach sometime in the near future.

As I made my out of the church, several members invited me to their homes for dinner, including several young ladies whose mothers would love to have me come to dinner. I thanked them but declined due to the realization that it sounded like the beginning of a relationship for which I was not ready to begin. Others invited me to prayer service every Wednesday evening at seven o'clock, which I explained would be difficult because of my study load at the School of Religion.

I returned to the apartment to find Wendell waiting to go to dinner with me. As we walked to Baldwin Hall, he asked me about the little church up the street. I at first took exception, since he was going to a large, established church, and I had chosen a small church, which spoke to my spiritual needs. He explained that he was not disparaging the size but merely trying to describe it. I told him that I had attended one of the best services I'd experienced in a long time. Not only had I found it to be a very inspirational church; I also planned to join the following Sunday.

I then asked if he had joined Asbury Methodist. He said he wanted to wait awhile before making that commitment.

After our discussion about our reasons for our choices, we decided to go to dinner, which was served early on Sunday, and the lines would be shorter.

During lunch, Wendell asked if I had a girlfriend. I really did not want to discuss this topic for obvious reasons, but I told him no, adding that I wasn't interested in finding one soon. Naturally, he asked me why, since he said he'd heard the sound of resignation in my voice. Since he was going to be my roommate, I thought I would share with him my last experience, which was still painful to impart.

After about a half hour of allowing me to tell my story, Wendell interrupted to say that we were starting a new life at the seminary, and we should move on. Wendell was very versed in the Bible as far as scripture was concerned, and he quoted St. Paul's words from Romans: "Forgetting those things in the past, and looking forward to those things in future, I press toward the mark of the high calling God in Jesus Christ."

Hoping not to be sacrilegious, I told him with a very strong voice, "Wendell, I don't want to hear that."

He immediately apologized.

I knew he had not meant to cause me emotional pain after our talk about Joyce; he thought biblical words would help me recover. Our conversation did help me to know that I had not gotten over the pain of our relationship.

Walking back to the apartment, we discussed the coming week and our progress on our reading lists. When we arrived home, we both began to read and take notes with our radio tuned to jazz music. After several hours, we both turned in for the night, since our first class was at ten o'clock in the morning. Wendell always knelt beside his bed to pray before going to sleep. I did not kneel beside the bed but went into the bathroom and knelt because I wanted to pray aloud without disturbing him. My prayers were always short, since I prayed during the day whenever I felt the need.

The alarm blared at eight thirty, which gave us time to dress and get to class before ten o'clock. We arrived early and went to the library to check out some of the books on our reading lists before other students checked them out. The day went well, and we began to know the personalities of our teachers, which helped us to understand them better.

Dr. Wright, the New Testament teacher, reminded me of a mystic, since he always spoke with his eyes closed as he exposed us to Eastern religious thought. After about thirty minutes of this mysticism, he began to ask us questions about the books he had assigned and would contemplate our responses. After an open discussion about his favorite writer on the New Testament, William Cadbury, he returned to his lecture on Eastern religions and how they differed from or related to Christianity. Later, I would find this class to be the most interesting and spiritually fulfilling.

Our class in systematic theology would also be interesting and very informative. Dr. Roberts explained that the class would not teach what to preach but what not to preach, which I found a very interesting statement. He explained that we would study the nature of God, such as his three great qualities—God was omnipotent (he was all powerful); God was omnipresent (he was present everywhere); and God was omniscient (he was all knowing). These great principles would guide our thinking throughout the class. He explained that the reason the class was called Systematic Theology was that God was consistent and was the source of order in the universe. Thus, all we would learn in his class or other classes would be tested by these three great principles.

After lunch, we returned to our afternoon classes, Old Testament and Church History, taught by Dr. Rice, the youngest of the new professors, who had come to teach in 1958. All of us still could not believe he had been a marine and had served in Korea. He was soft-spoken and very humble and was proficient not only in the Old Testament but also in Hebrew. His first lecture was on the Hebrew people's relationship to God, from slavery in Egypt through the wilderness experience to the Promised Land, Palestine. He explained that each phase would shape the Hebrews relationship with God and would be finalized in the land of Palestine, where they would remain. I was very pleased with the content and the lecture of Dr. Rice. He dismissed us after finding out where we were on our reading assignments.

Our final class for the day was Church History with Dr. Gilbert, a scholarly looking man who seemed serious all the time. He was one of the outstanding church historians in the country. Knowing we had such a knowledgeable professor made us feel special. His teaching method was to lecture us on the various chapters of *A History of Christianity*, which was intimidating by its very size. His lectures were helpful because, as we read, many questions were raised, which he put in perspective through his lectures. There was nothing dull or boring about any of these classes because of the new knowledge. The forty-five minutes for this class went very quickly.

Since we had finished for the day, we had time to prepare for our Friday scheduled classes. I headed toward Founders Library to check if the books that had already been checked out at our school library were there. Founder's Library was a huge library and served the entire university, although all of the professional schools had their own libraries. However, there were some books only Founder's Library would have.

Leaving Founder's Library, I met some of my fellow seminarians, and we stopped a few minutes to evaluate the week so far; Friday would complete our first week. We agreed that the most difficult professor would be Dr. Wright given that he'd made it clear his lectures would be mainly information from his years spent in Burma studying other religions and how they intersected with Christianity. We also agreed that the best lecturer and traditional teacher would be Dr. Rice; he assumed that we had not read the Old Testament and would teach us with that assumption. This would give us a complete understanding of how Jewish literature and the Old Testament were written out of the experiences of the Jewish people.

When I returned to the apartment, I found Wendell reading and making notes as usual. I decided that my routine would be to read and write at night, unless there was an assignment for which I needed to prepare the next day. Around eleven o'clock, I began my study for the night, reading the first chapter of A *History of Christianity* as assigned by Dr. Gilbert. This chapter mainly explained that Christianity, along with other major religions, emerged or evolved around the same time throughout the known world. This was not a completely new concept, since I had read *Varieties of Religious Experiences* by William James, in which the evolution of religions throughout the world were traced. Nevertheless, Dr. Latourette taught that Christianity was an outgrowth of Judaism, which evolved along with other major religions. After reading some of my other assignments, I decided to try and get some sleep.

The next morning, as soon as Wendell came out of the bathroom, I had to get showered and prepared to leave for my nine o'clock class with Dr. Wright, although he was very seldom on time. Dr. Wright would enter the classroom and begin lecturing without any preliminary remarks, which amazed me. It was as if he was thinking up exactly where he'd left off the last time he'd lectured.

After about thirty minutes, I believed him when he said most of his presentations would be on his experiences in Burma. However, he expected us to read the books assigned, in order to demonstrate our understanding of the New Testament literature. He also told us that, the week before our examination, he would review the pertinent issues surrounding understanding the New Testament. This proved to be true, but this reinforced his directive to read the New Testament and the books assigned. He would supplement this reading with several lectures pertaining to the New Testament before the end of the semester.

As Dr. Wright continued his lecture on his experiences in Burma, he taught us about meditation, which the Buddhist practiced religiously. Meditation would help us to get into our higher power, which would enhance our understanding and ability to understand the essence of the New Testament. The more he talked about the Buddhist practices, the more I found what he said very intriguing, which would later have a powerful effect on my ministry.

The remaining classes on Friday followed the same pattern, which was to determine what progress we had made on our reading assignments and opportunities to ask questions about the reading materials. Drs. Gilbert, Roberts, and Rice all followed this pattern. And we were soon completing our first full week as seminarians in the Howard University School of Religion, which made us all extremely proud.

Nearing the end of the first semester and with Thanksgiving looming, my fellow seminarians and I discussed what we would do during the break. I had ruled out going home. I did not have the money, and we had to be back to classes on Monday. I wrote my parents and told them my decision not to come home for Thanksgiving. Mother wrote me a letter, telling me how proud she and my father were of me and the progress I was making in seminary. She also said not to worry about coming home for Thanksgiving, but they would have a special prayer for me and my success. She added that Mama Jolly, my grandmother, had asked about me and wanted me to preach at her church, Mount Carmel Baptist Church (Mount Calm as it was known) in Coldwater, Mississippi. This would not be the first Thanksgiving I had missed, but somehow I felt that this would be a lonely one. Although I had made new friends, the only one I felt close to had been invited to celebrate the day with members of Asbury.

The following Sunday, I had so many families inviting me to share Thanksgiving with them, including Pastor Rodgers, I declined, saying I had a previous invitation. Although it wasn't true at the time, it turned out to be true. During the first semester I had become very close to the dean of the Rankin Chapel, Dr. Crawford. One day, he'd called me into his office to say he had observed me and asked if I would be interested in becoming his student assistant for the chapel; his assistant, Arnold Walker, was resigning to accept another position on campus. I was absolutely stunned with disbelief but realized that he was very serious. Although I did not know what the position entailed, I accepted, trusting God that I could do the job. After our conversation, Dr. Crawford asked me to meet the next day with his secretary, Ms. Lucille Stubblefield, a very attractive and friendly woman admired by all of the middlers and seniors.

I met with Ms. Stubblefield, who was very kind and gracious, recognizing I was a freshman. She explained that the student assistant would be responsible for picking up our guests in the Baldwin Hall suite and escorting them to breakfast and to the chapel at ten thirty. I would also be responsible for making sure that the pulpit was prepared and the dean's robe was ready and, if our guest speaker did not have his or her robe, that a robe would be available to them. After chapel services, we would all go back to Baldwin Hall, where a private dining room would be set up for Dean Crawford and, sometimes, Howard's president, Dr. Mordecai Johnson. Following the luncheon, I would make sure the guest speaker would have transportation to the airport or train station. The money from the morning service was put into a safe for counting and banking the next day by Ms. Stubblefield.

This seemed like a lot to do, but I enjoyed every minute of it. I was very fortunate and blessed to meet some of the most renowned preachers and speakers in the world; those speakers from Africa were in great demand.

I immediately phoned my parents to tell them that I had been selected as the student assistant to the dean of the chapel, Dr. Evans E. Crawford. They were both very excited and congratulated me on such an accomplishment. I asked them to pray for me that I would not be a disappointment to Dean Crawford, who had shown so much faith in me.

During the week, I received congratulations from classmates and some instructors; this position was not normally given to a freshman.

Classes became routine, and we all developed our own study habits. Along with studying at home, I found the school's library a very good place to study and sometimes I would go to Founder's for a change.

My first Sunday as student assistant to Dean Crawford, I got up early Sunday morning to take the honored guest speaker to breakfast. I had called him at eight thirty Sunday morning and told him I would be at the Baldwin Hall to escort him to breakfast and the chapel service. The first guest speaker I had was Dr. Vernon Johns, one of the most brilliant preachers and scholars on the scene in the 1950s. Dr. Johns was also the pastor of the Dexter Avenue Baptist Church in Montgomery, Alabama, which would later be pastored by Rev. Dr. Martin Luther King Jr.

Dr. Johns, a very down-to-earth minister, told me to relax and suggested we have a good breakfast and talk together. I found him brilliant on very many subjects and able to communicate on any level, which was fortunate for me. After breakfast, I walked with him to the chapel only a block away. When we reached the chapel office, the dean greeted him, and then I was excused until ten forty-five, at which time I would return for robing and to make sure Dean Crawford had what he needed. These were my basic assignments as assistant.

The next day, I met Dean Crawford and Ms. Stubblefield in his office and was offered the job for fifty dollars a month, rather good pay for approximately six hours a month. Beyond the monetary benefit, I considered it an honor to be chosen by Dean Crawford to be his assistant and have the privilege and honor of escorting distinguished guests during their visits to the campus. As I look back over my days as dean's assistant, I feel blessed—just to think I had one-on-one interactions with such distinguished guests as Dr. Gardner Taylor, Dr. Benjamin Mays, and many others who are nationally known. Although I did not share breakfast with him, I had the honor of having private conversations with Dr. Mordecai Johnson at least three times.

My first Sunday assisting Dean Crawford was in October, with my assignment to Dr. Vernon Johns. In our private conversations, Dr. Johns was very humorous and self-deprecating. One of the stories he told me was about how, as pastor of the Dexter Avenue Baptist Church, he had taken a deacon to Birmingham for a Baptist meeting. After they had arrived in Birmingham, Dr. Johns had stopped with Deacon Harrison to get something to eat. When the waitress came, both ordered catfish with potatoes and turnip greens. When she asked what they would like to drink, Rev. Johns requested a cold beer. Deacon Harrison looked at him with one of those half smiles, as if to say, "People don't know pastor is a drinker." Dr. Johns said that he immediately asked Deacon Harrison if he would like a beer also, and he answered with a strong and unequivocal, "Yes, sir!"

After their meeting, they headed back to Montgomery for Sunday service the next day. During the Sunday services, Deacon Harrison was unusually happy, and Dr. John's could tell he was thinking to himself that the church didn't know their pastor was a drinker. When Dr. Johns rose to give the remarks for the morning, he mentioned that Deacon Harrison had been so kind to drive him to Birmingham for a special meeting with the ministers of that city. He also mentioned that he had suggested they stop and have a bite to eat at the local restaurant. "We both had a wonderful fish dinner, and the waitress asked if he would like something to drink," he said. He said he then looked at Deacon Harrison and noticed that he had his head down as if praying.

Dr. Johns continued and told the church they had both ordered two bottles of Budweiser beer. Dr. Johns had then stopped and asked, "Isn't that right, Deacon Harrison?"

He went on to say that, as Deacon Harrison tried to answer, he suffered one of the worst coughing spasms he had ever seen, which prevented him from answering. Dr. Johns then said to me, "Young man, remember to always share with your deacons beer or liquor when you have a drink, which I am sure they will not refuse. But also bring your report back to the church, because the report that the pastor drinks has already been made to members of the church."

Dr. Johns said that, from that day on, Deacon Harrison was never available to drive him.

Dr. Johns was as humorous as he was the most brilliant preacher I had ever heard.

Another benefit of serving as assistant to the dean of the chapel was that I would get a firsthand lesson on how to deliver a sermon from some of the most gifted Negro ministers in America.

During the last Sunday before Thanksgiving, Lucille Stubblefield asked me whether I had somewhere to eat on Thanksgiving. I answered no, although I had been asked by many Carron Baptist Church members to their homes. She asked me if I would like to join her for Thanksgiving dinner at her home. I was so flattered that she would desire my company for Thanksgiving, I immediately answered, "Yes. I would count it a blessing to share Thanksgiving with you."

She told me what time to arrive and gave me her address, adding that, if I did not have a ride, she would pick me up. I must admit that, not only was this a very generous invitation, but for a minute I also found myself thinking that I would love to get to know her better. This was not withstanding the facts that she was twelve years older than me and that she worked for the dean. I immediately dismissed the thought and just thought about how nice it would be to share Thanksgiving with such an attractive and engaging lady.

My schoolwork went very well, and I was very excited to be in a seminary, where I was exposed to many new ideas and knowledge about things I had never given much thought before. This was what made every seminary day very interesting.

During the week, I made a habit of speaking to Lucille every day and inquiring about her day. Dr. Crawford did not think this was unusual, since I had to work with her and him on our guest speakers. The day before Thanksgiving, Lucille said she would pick me up at four o'clock in the afternoon on Thanksgiving Day, which would work well, since I wanted to attend the Carron Baptist Thanksgiving service; I had so many blessings for which to be thankful.

Remembering my manners, which my mother had taught me, I purchased a bottle of Christian Brother's wine to give to her. Thanksgiving Day arrived, and Wendell inquired where I would be spending it. I simply said someone had invited me to Thanksgiving, for which I was most grateful. He also had been invited to her Thanksgiving dinner; he would be joining a family at Asbury.

After coming home from church at Carron Baptist, I changed into something casual, since I anticipated that it would be a very relaxed kind of afternoon. Lucille picked me up and drove to her home on Queen Street in northeast Washington. Entering her home, I found it to be very warm and inviting. She put some music on and asked me if I drank rum and coke. I was surprised; that was my drink of choice. While I listened to jazz music, she excused herself to finish preparing the dinner and, after a few minutes, returned with a drink and joined me.

We had already talked about my background, including my music background with Rufus Thomas and other artists in Memphis. I was surprised to find out that her ex-husband was also a musician in

Compton, California, which was her home. This subject dominated our conversation until she told me to come in the dining room for dinner.

After I had seated her as my mother had taught me, Lucille asked me to say the Thanksgiving prayer. I thanked her for asking me and offered thanksgiving for all the many blessings we have received. I also thanked the Lord for Lucille and her generous spirit and concern for me. Finally, I asked that we would not forget those who were less fortunate and for help to find opportunities to serve others.

Lucille was not only a very attractive lady; she was also an exceptional cook. The dinner was a traditional Thanksgiving dinner of turkey, mashed potatoes with giblet gravy, green peas, and hot porterhouse rolls.

As we ate, she inquired how I liked being the student assistant to Dr. Crawford. Although she had not known Dr. Crawford before he had come to Howard, she had nothing but praise for him and his lovely wife, Betty. She knew all about how I had spent my first night at Howard at their apartment and how impressed he was with me. This was very encouraging.

The food was very delicious and I told her that it reminded me of my mother's cooking. I knew that this was a much overused expression, but remembering that her mother was from the South, I knew it explained everything.

During dinner, we talked about our experiences at Howard. She had served as the secretary to Dr. Daniel G. Hill, the former dean of the chapel and currently the dean of the School of Religion. She was very fond of Dean Hill, who was like a father figure to her and many of us in the seminary.

Finally, we began to talk about our lives, which included relationships and marriages. She was quick to say that she'd had a very troubled marriage due partly to his being a musician and all that went with that profession. She finally said that she and her ex-husband had decided to divorce, since reconciliation was not possible. After the divorce, she had come to Washington and found work at Howard.

After an embarrassing pause, I finally spoke up and said I had no girlfriend here or at home. I decided to tell her about my tragic relationship with Joyce and that I had not had any kind of personal relationship since finishing Arkansas State. Although I did not want to go into detail about my relationship with Joyce, there was something about her that made me want to give her a more of a detailed explanation about my broken engagement. After I had recited this difficult account of my pain and how the experience had left me not wanting any personal relationship, she interrupted me and said we should just be friends.

After several drinks and more talk about our likes and dislikes, I asked her if she would call me a cab to take me back to school. She insisted that she could take me back, and it would not be any bother at all. I declined again, and she called Capitol Cab.

As we stood at the doorway, and I thanked her for such a wonderful evening and dinner, something in me felt a special feeling for her. She looked at me with the look that said, "What next?" I pulled her close to me and kissed her with all the pent-up passion that I had in my heart. Surprisingly, she returned my kiss with as much passion.

The cab arrived as if he had a cue to come as soon as we'd finished our goodbye kisses. I said goodnight and promised to call her as soon as I got home. The trip to the apartment was filled with thoughts about what had really happened.

Although Lucille was twelve years older me, there was nothing during the evening that suggested an age difference. I also thought about how we'd easily shared our most intimate details about our past lives with other partners.

When I arrived home, Wendell was finishing his reading for the night and preparing for bed. His first question was, "You must have had a great date tonight?"

I surprised him with, "You'd better believe it."

This made him give me the half smile and wave me off, something he'd learned in Bermuda.

After he was asleep and snoring, I called Lucille and told her I was home and thanked her for such a wonderful evening, which I would never be able to repay. She simply replied that I had already paid her by sharing Thanksgiving and being such good conversationalist. I also told her that I felt we would be very good platonic friends as we got to know each other, and she agreed. After a few more pleasantries, we both said we looked forward to seeing each other soon.

Since we had Friday following Thanksgiving off, I used the time to catch up on some assignments and reading that I'd neglected. Now as we were more than halfway through the first semester, I felt confident about the examinations that would be given in three weeks. My confidence rose when I was asked by other classmates to help them with term papers and essays. I enjoyed doing this because it helped me with my writing skills and the new subjects I had to research before writing. This also helped me to bond with my new classmates from various parts of the country.

December passed rapidly, and our examinations were two days before the end of the semester. I had my apprehensions about two of the courses, whose tests would require total recall of facts, New Testament and Old Testament. The other two exams would be comprised of essay questions. These were for History of Christianity and Systematic Theology. The other courses required term papers we had already submitted.

On December 15, 1959, the semester ended, and we were out of school for about three weeks until resumption of classes on January 3 and my chapel responsibilities on the second Sunday in January. During this period, I worked at the US Post Office, where many college students worked alongside the regular employees during the Christmas holidays. This was a great job, since we could work as much overtime as we could until Christmas Eve and remain on salary until January 1. Some of us worked sixteen hours on each shift, which allowed just enough time to go home, bathe, and get a few hours' sleep before returning to work. We, including the regular employees, were given Christmas Day off.

On Christmas Day, I was so tired I did not go to church and spent most of the day resting and missing my parents and the special Christmas dinner I knew they would have. Sunday afternoon around four o'clock, when I knew dinner would be served, if my uncle Hubert and uncle Judson were on time, I called my mother.

When she answered the phone, I said, "Hi, Muh," which I sometimes called her since I was a very young child.

"Hi, son," she said. "I was just thinking about you and wishing you could be here. How are you?"

I told her I missed home very much, but I had been working at the post office since school was out and will continue to do so until January 1. She told me they were about to serve dinner, and my father would like to speak to me.

He came on the phone with a booming voice, saying, "How are you, my son?"

I repeated what I'd told mother about working at the post office, which would help me financially when the new semester began. He inquired how my studies were going and said that he would pray for me at the Christmas dinner, which brought me much comfort.

Strangely though, I missed Lucille, who told me she would be going to California to spend the holidays with her family. Although I had only dated her once, I realized that I really enjoyed her company and missed at least talking to her in the dean's office.

The day after Christmas, I returned to my post office job to finish with the end of the year mail, after which we were let go on New Year's Eve. After leaving early from the job, I got a haircut and prepared to continue on to Carron Baptist Church for their watch night service, a part of my church life since a small child.

I had not attended Carron for several weeks, since I had become an assistant to the dean of the chapel. When I was given the appointment. I had called Rev. Rodgers and told him that I would not be able to attend due to my new responsibilities at school. He was very gracious and wished me well. I did not tell him I was coming for watch night and surprised him at ten thirty while the deacons were leading the praise service.

The church was almost full, which was typical; church members not in regular attendance at Sunday service always made the watch service, which they thought was mandatory to be blessed in the New Year.

When I went into Pastor Rodgers's study, he stood up and said, "My prodigal son has returned," and greeted me with a warm embrace and a strong handshake. He expressed how he had been praying for me to have good success. He offered to allow me to preach, but I declined. I had missed his preaching, which had sustained me during my first semester of difficult days.

After Rev. Rodgers told the church how long he had known me and then called me his son, the church burst out in sustained applause, which made me feel very welcome and encouraged.

Rev. Rodgers preached on the subject called "Go Back Another Way." He illustrated the topic beautifully using the biblical text in which the three wise men, after meeting with King Herod about the whereabouts of Jesus the Messiah, were asked by Herod to return to him and tell him where the child was born so that he could worship him. The real reason he wanted to know the Jesus's whereabouts was to kill him, since the prophecy of Jesus being the king of the Jews was a threat to him. After the wise men found Jesus and worshipped him, they were led to go "another way" and not return to Herod. Rev. Rodgers advised us that New Year's gives us the chance to change the direction of our lives by resolving tonight to go back another way during this new year.

This sermon was so powerful that I still preach it after sixty-one years of preaching.

After his sermon, Rev. Rodgers offered the New Year's prayer, where all of us, kneeling at the altar, joined in prayer and made our petitions to the Lord. I vowed to become a better person and try to witness for him in my daily life. We rose from the altar after the stirring prayer by Pastor Rodgers and wished each other happy New Year with warm embraces.

When I returned to our apartment, it seemed lonely. Wendell had gone to Bermuda for the holidays. This then became a time to enjoy the apartment alone and have a five-day mini-vacation. While Wendell was away, I could play jazz music as loudly as I wanted, which was wonderful.

I also used this time to think about Lucille and the relationship I wanted with her, which was quite presumptuous, since she had not indicated she wanted such a relationship. I decided that, if we had a relationship, it would have to remain platonic. This sounded good to me, but again, this was not anything to which Lucille had agreed. Anyway I decided to let fate take its course. But I was sure I did not want to enter into another romantic relationship after Joyce. One reason I thought a relationship with Lucille wouldn't work was our age difference, which we agreed would not lend itself to a marriage that we were definitely not considering. After all of my mental gymnastics, I rested my brain and thought about much more practical things that required my immediate attention, such as the several books to be read for next semester. I read for several hours and took notes until I fell asleep.

The final days of my mini-vacation were also a time to explore Washington more closely. During school days, we had no time to visit the many monuments and Smithsonian museums. After two days of this exploration, I felt I could do a mini-tour of Washington.

Wendell returned from Bermuda on Friday to prepare for our new semester. January 6, 1960 started the final semester of our freshman year. I considered making it to this point a real accomplishment, since several of our classmates were not allowed to return due to unacceptable grades.

Monday morning, Wendell and I followed our normal routine in preparation to leave for school at eight thirty. As we walked toward the School of Religion after getting our coffee and doughnut at the corner deli, we talked about our favorite professor. We both agreed Dr. Wright who was the most interesting one, because he talked about things other than the New Testament. Although we liked his extracurricular lecture, this absence of the New Testament would come back to haunt each of us.

The second semester followed the first semester as part two. By the second semester, we had become acclimated to our new routine and schedule.

At the end of the first day of the second semester, I took time to visit the dean of the chapel's office to obtain the schedule of our second semester speakers. Along with seeing the dean, I would have the opportunity to see Lucille and find out how she'd enjoyed her holidays in California.

When I walked into the office she was sitting at her desk busily typing. Since she was concentrating on her copy and did not see me come in, so I walked over to her desk and leaned down and gave her a soft kiss on her cheek. Surprised, she turned, and when she saw it was me, she gave me a very warm embrace. As we talked for a few minutes, she told me how much she'd enjoyed seeing her relatives and friends. I told her about my work at the post office and how it had helped me to purchase new clothes and put money away to possibly go home during the Easter holidays to visit my parents.

After a few minutes, I went in to see the dean and talk with him about the new guest list and any changes in our preparations for Sundays. Dean Crawford indicated there would be no changes and congratulated me on my first semester's work as his assistant.

The second semester was a complete change from the first because of an increase in my confidence. My ability to establish and maintain study hours and schedule my time wisely made a huge difference. My classes took on a completely new meaning, in that I could see the value of a theological education for a meaningful and effective Christian ministry. All of my subjects began to come together as we explored the relevance of each to our knowledge and understanding of our chosen work in ministry.

Returning to my work as student assistant to Dean Crawford took on new meaning, and I was newly appreciative of my opportunity to serve in such an honored position. The new schedule of guest speakers read as a "Who's Who" in the Negro community of preachers and orators. The list included such luminaries as Dr. William Holmes Borders, Dr. Gardner Taylor, Dr. Howard Thurman, and Dr. Roy Wilkins—president of the NAACP, the voice of Negro rights. Many others followed during my tenure. I learned as much listening to these great men as I did in the classroom.

After several weeks, I was summoned to the dean's office, where he surprised me, saying that the dean of student life would like to see me about accepting a position as a graduate fellow in his office, working with freshmen on their social activities during the first semester. Dean Crawford assured me he would not interfere with my accepting this position and would still allow me to maintain my position as assistant to the dean of the chapel if I so desired.

My meeting with Dean Carey went well, and he offered me the position, which paid the handsome sum of one hundred dollars a month. I immediately began working with another graduate fellow named Carl Anderson who was working on his PhD. Carl and I developed a close friendship, which led to a lifelong friendship that exists to this day. Dr.

Anderson would become a vice president of Howard University, which was an honor to him.

These added responsibilities, along with my study schedule, made the semester move swiftly, with Easter holidays fast approaching. Mother had called to ask me if I had money to come home for Easter. I called home and thanked her and my father for their offer but assured them that I was able to save money from the Christmas holidays to purchase a round-trip ticket. I told Mother and Daddy I could not wait to see them and tell them all about my experiences at Howard University. I asked them to have my sister Gerry pick me up from the airport at three thirty on Good Friday.

The Thursday before Easter, I awakened before Wendell to dress and leave for the airport. My Braniff Airways plane was scheduled to leave Washington National Airport at noon. I called Capitol Cab for transportation to the airport. We arrived at eleven fifteen, causing me to go directly to the gate with my bag. Boarding had already begun, so I proceeded directly onto the plane and put my small bag in the overhead compartment and got comfortable.

The flight to Memphis was rather short—only two and a half hours from takeoff to landing. We arrived at two thirty, and I went directly to the curbside pickup, where Gerry and George were waiting. After our greetings, we headed home to 1610 Arkansas, which I had not seen for almost a year.

When I arrived, I was greeted by Mother, with her apron around her waist, waiting, as she always did, on the small porch for her baby boy, whom she had not seen in nearly eight months. Gerry and George told me to go ahead. They would get my bags. This allowed me to run to my dear mother and give her the biggest hug and kiss I could. Her arms around me made me know how much she had missed me and loved me. This was the best feeling I had ever experienced; my months away from home were the longest I had ever been away from my family.

After sitting in the living room with my mother and father, talking with them about my life in Washington at Howard University, Mother asked the question I had been waiting to hear. "Are you hungry, son?"

"Yes, ma'am," I answered, which I sometimes said when teasing her.

After so long away from home, I thought the menu may have changed. But I could smell the liver and onions simmering in the kitchen. The rice and turnip greens were also waiting. I was eager to eat them, as well as the corn bread, which I had not had in almost a year.

After serving my plate with the liver and onions, the gravy, and the other side dishes, I asked my father if I could give the blessing for the food. He enthusiastically agreed. I offered thanksgiving for my parents and my sisters and brothers and my opportunity to join them at this Easter season. I always thanked God for my mother, who prepared the dinner, and for the opportunity to share this table again.

I cannot describe the feelings I experienced being at my home with my brother and sister and parents to share the family table once more.

I had to be back at Howard the day after Easter, which only gave me four days to visit with family and friends. On Good Friday, we all went to church to hear the Seven Last Words from the Cross.

After a moving service in which I did not participate, choosing to sit with my mother and father during the service, the minister recognized me and presented me to the congregation to say a few words. I spoke about the significance of the day and the great sacrifice of Jesus on the Cross, to give us new life. In addition, I thanked the congregation for their prayers during the months I had been away. After the service, I thanked Rev. Taylor and asked him to continue to pray for me that I would be strong and remain faithful to the ministry, which I'd promised God I would do since he had healed my mother from cancer and returned her to me. This would be my mantra for the rest of my life.

My time at home was the shortest four days I could ever remember. Since I had asked for and received permission from my instructors to be absent on Monday, I had to leave on Monday to be present for my Tuesday classes. Leaving home was very difficult. I now fully recognized that my life had changed so much that I would never live there again on a permanent basis.

Before leaving on Monday, I asked Mother and Daddy to have a moment of prayer with me and Melvin, who had always lived with them because of his disability. My father prayed the most fervent prayer I had ever heard him pray, which alarmed me, as I sensed that he may not be here when I returned.

I thanked God for him and left with Clair Jones, a friend who had been waiting to take me to the airport.

Arriving at the airport at two o'clock, we had a few moments to share about growing up together. His father was the Methodist minister across the street from Central Baptist Church.

Before Clair left, I assured him I would stay in touch and asked him to check on my parents and Melvin occasionally. He promised he would, and I retrieved my bag and headed for the gate. My plane left at three o'clock in the afternoon and arrived at National at four thirty.

I got a cab and headed to my apartment at 2617 Georgia Avenue, the place I now called home. When I arrived at the apartment, Wendell was there reading for a class he had the next day. After giving him a short version of my time at home during Easter, I told him I was a little depressed, realizing I would never again live at my parents' home on a permanent basis. He tried to comfort me by saying he had been away from Bermuda for almost five years and thought he would never return. This was somewhat comforting, as our shared experience pointed to the knowledge that leaving the home where you grew up was just part of maturing.

We had only a month before our final examinations. Our thoughts turned to what we would do during the summer and where we would work. I heard some of the middlers talking about working for the National Council of Churches in New York in the corporate office. My upper classmates told me the council was offering jobs to seminarians, working with migrants from Florida and those traveling throughout the East Coast harvesting crops. They were hiring seminary students to provide counseling and services to those who needed community services and also to assist the children with educational opportunities in Virginia, Maryland, Delaware, New Jersey, and upstate New York.

I wrote to the president of the National Council of Churches and received a letter from the council's migrant office, offering me an opportunity to work on the Eastern Shore of Maryland from June through August. I would be provided housing, meals, and a station wagon for transportation. I would also receive a stipend of two hundred dollars a month, plus a hundred dollars for gas and other incidentals.

This sounded great, and I immediately accepted. I wrote Rev. Snyder, my supervisor, asking when and where I should report. Mr. Snyder replied right away and asked me to prepare to come to Princess Anne, Maryland, on May 25 for a five-day orientation session that would be mandatory if I accepted the position of migrant minister. Since my finals and classes would be completed by May 15, this would work perfectly and give me a few days' vacation before reporting for my summer job.

Wendell planned to stay in Washington, DC, and work at Howard in the administration offices. I was happy for him. Since he was staying at the apartment for the summer and other seminarians were also remaining on campus, he was paired with another roommate. That meant I would need to get a new roommate when classes resumed in the fall. Although I was sorry to lose Wendell as a roommate, I also looked forward to having a new roommate from the School of Religion.

Lucille and I continued to see each other every weekend until my time to report to Maryland for my summer job. She was a great cook and a wonderful platonic partner, though our relationship would grow into something more serious that would continue over the summer months, even though I would be away on the Eastern Shore of Maryland. I reasoned that, since I would have transportation, I would be able to visit her during the summer.

We received our final grades on May 20, which gave me a few days to get ready to report to my new summer job in Maryland. After a semester of grueling study and part-time work, I was gratified to receive a B average. My best grades were in Systematic Theology, Church History, and Old Testament. My grade in New Testament was just average, which was not too disappointing given that Dr. Wright only gave us a reading list for New Testament, along with our overall assignment to read the Synoptic Gospels and be prepared to be examined on the contents.

In addition, I thought Dr. Wright would become more lecture oriented on the contents of the New Testament next year. Although I was concerned about my knowledge of the New Testament, I was fascinated with his lectures on the occult and parapsychology and other areas of spirituality he had learned about during his years studying

Buddhism in Burma. Little did I know that this book would be a result of his lectures.

All in all, I felt that my first year in seminary had been a success and that I was being prepared for my life's work by some of the most brilliant teachers in the country.

Before leaving for my summer work on the Eastern Shore of Maryland, I had lunch with Dean Crawford and thanked him for the interest he had taken in me. I told him I looked forward to next year, when I would take several classes from him, including Homiletics, because I and others thought he was a superb preacher. Homiletics, the study of the art of preaching, would be a major part of our work in the ministry. He wished me well and told me he and Betty had also done migrant ministry when he was at Boston University. He had also been an assistant to Dr. Howard Thurman, acclaimed as one of the most dynamic preachers and mystics in the country.

May 25 arrived, and I caught a bus to Princess Anne, Maryland, for orientation in preparation for my assignment as a migrant minister. I even liked the name, since Jesus implored us to give special attention to the poor and neglected. I had never traveled in Maryland, except for an occasional trip to Baltimore to hear some jazz and have some of the city's famed seafood.

As we traveled out New York Avenue headed toward Route 50, I began to think what this new adventure on the Eastern Shore of Maryland would be and to wonder if I would really make a difference in the lives of the migrants and their children. When we arrived in Princess Anne, I realized we at the University of Maryland, Eastern Shore, which was a predominantly black college before integration. We were assigned to dormitory rooms, with most of the students gone for the summer. We reported to the auditorium at two o'clock for our first orientation session after lunch in the cafeteria. The lunch was most delicious, consisting of meatloaf, mashed potatoes with gravy, green beans or turnip greens with the turnips still on them, and real corn bread and apple pie. There was also plenty of iced tea and lemonade. I am convinced that there are no better cooks than those in rural places in any state.

Reverend Snyder was a very short man with the same beautiful spirit I observed with my New Testament teacher, Dr. Rice. I could tell he was called to this work by the way he spoke to us about its importance. His references to the Bible were few, but he did admonish us to remember what Jesus said in the book of Matthew: "When I was hungry, you fed me, when I was thirsty, you gave me drink, when I was a stranger, you took me in, when I was a sick and in prison you visited me." After teaching that these persons would sit on the right hand of God, Jesus summarized by saying, "In as much as ye have done it to the least of these my brethren, ye have done it also to me."

Rev. Snyder spoke with a soft voice that had such a spiritual sweetness about it all of us were emotionally moved, and some of us, I among them, even had to shed tears.

There were other speakers, who would provide assistance to us and information about the difficulties and rewards of the migrant ministry.

The time came to announce our assignments. None of knew where we would be headed. We all waited for our names to be called and to learn the areas of Maryland and Virginia where we would work. When we heard our names, we were to report either to the Maryland or Virginia tables to receive further instruction.

When my name was called, I was told to report to the Maryland table. A very nice young lady told me I would be working in Preston, Maryland, fifty miles from Washington and about fifty miles from Princess Anne, where we were meeting. My package also contained the name of the person with whom I would be living for the next two months and where I would receive most of my meals, except when I was on overnight travels. The name of the gentleman was Mr. Dewey Townsend, a native of Preston, Maryland, and the Eastern Shore. The information she supplied also included the name of the person who would meet me at the bus station the next day at three o'clock and take me to Mr. Townsend's house.

After our final session, we were free to mingle and share past experiences. Not all of us were seminarians; there were other graduate students and undergraduates who would serve in other capacities. One young lady I met who was particularly interesting was from Spelman College, a historical college dating back to the turn of the nineteenth century, in Atlanta. I met her as we prepared to go to our dorms for the evening. Her name was Eva Earlene Marshall, and she was from Nashville, Tennessee. She was in her last year at Spelman and majoring in home economics and education. She would be in Virginia in a little town called Kiptopeke, which I could only surmise was at the tip of Virginia.

I told her I was from Memphis, Tennessee, and had graduated from Arkansas AM&N College in Pine Bluffs, Arkansas. I also told her I was a seminarian at the Howard School of Religion and would be entering my second and milder year. My assignment for the summer was in Preston, Maryland, and I had ten camps to serve in Caroline County.

She would be serving in the migrant day care center and working with migrant women on healthy food preparation and how to make clothing for their children. They were very poor and needed any assistance they could get to better their lives.

When we left each other, we promised to stay in touch. We had the names and addresses of all the migrant workers in Virginia and Maryland.

Each of us was fortunate enough to have our own private room, since the college was out for the summer. I thought about the day and how my life was being changed in so many ways. I had finished my first year in seminary and was about to experience my own ministry for the first time in my career. I also thought about Earlene and what a wonderful spirit she had. There was something of a strange attraction I felt for her, which was different from the usual feelings guys would have for the opposite sex. I then prepared for the night with thoughts about the next day, when I would take a Greyhound bus to Easton, Maryland, five miles from Preston. I decided to read one of the books I should have read for my New Testament class that put me to sleep like anesthesia.

The next morning I got up around seven o'clock to go to the cafeteria for breakfast. And what a breakfast it was. We had eggs; sausage, bacon, or ham; fried potatoes or grits; and homemade buttermilk biscuits with jam and jelly. Coffee or tea was also available. I wished my assignment had been near the college so I could visit from time to time.

The conversation at our table was mainly about what our assignments would be like and what we would do for socialization. We also wondered about the kind of migrant committees in which we would work, since every community had organized to assist us wherever they could. We finally turned to a discussion on the kind of vehicles the committee would provide us, since they were responsible for our transportation. Somebody quipped a query as to whether they had any used Cadillacs or Mercedes, and we all had a hearty laugh.

All of us left around the same time since the committees had a set time during the day to meet us. Wishing everybody well, especially Earlene, I rushed to enter the van leaving for the bus station, where I would then take an hour-and-a-half ride to Easton, Maryland. There, I would connect with Mr. Townsend, with whom I would be staying over the next two months.

Although it wasn't a long ride, I was already impressed with the Eastern Shore, which was divided by the beautiful Chesapeake Bay. Crossing the bridge was a breathtaking experience, as you looked down on the beautiful bay with all kinds of boats I had never seen before. Although this was only a two-lane bridge, it was seemingly the longest ride over a bridge, with the exception of the Ohio River Bridge I'd once crossed regularly en route to Chicago. The Ohio River was just like the Mississippi River, but this was a beautiful bay, with blue waters and sandy beaches.

I was impressed with the several towns we passed. One stood out more than any other—Cambridge, Maryland. I would later learn that Cambridge was one of the oldest towns on the Eastern Shore. I would visit Cambridge, one of the more progressive towns during the civil rights era and home to some outstanding civil rights leaders, many times.

As we neared Easton, one of the larger towns, for some reason, my heart began beating faster, and I became a little anxious. When we pulled into the bus station, there were six people standing near the parking area for our bus. I surmised this was my committee, since five of them where white and one was Negro.

As I stepped off the bus, there was a chant. "Welcome, Rev. Veazey, to Easton and Preston." The very kind and welcoming people who warmly greeted me introduced themselves and finally introduced Mr. Dewey, an elderly man who appeared to be in his sixties. He was a slender man with a classic Negro face, meaning he had chiseled black features and an elegance that went with his carriage.

Mr. Dewey, as everybody in Preston, both black and white, called him, took my bags as I thanked the committee for welcoming me. I would meet with them on Sunday after church at the First Methodist Church of Preston.

Mr. Dewey had an old Ford pickup truck that reminded me of pickups of my grandfather and uncles. As we rode to his home about five miles from Easton, he spoke about my family and asked if I was born in Washington. I responded that I was from the South and lived in the city of Memphis, Tennessee. I also shared that I had five sisters and brothers and I was youngest. I told him that this part of Maryland reminded me of my grandparents' home in Coldwater, Mississippi, except I knew there wasn't as much prejudice here as there was in Mississippi.

After I'd made that remark, he looked at me and said, "There are some Mississippi people here too." Although he did not mean they were from Mississippi, he was saying that the prejudice and racism I was referring to existed there also.

Mr. Dewey's home sat on a hill overlooking Preston Road. His house was a very typical country home, with a beautiful porch and two stories. The living room and kitchen were on the first floor, along with a bedroom. There were two bedrooms on the second floor, plus a bathroom.

Mr. Dewey had retired from a factory in Queenstown, which was about fifteen miles from Preston. His wife had died many years before. He had not remarried and was what I thought an eligible bachelor would look and be like. He asked me whether I was hungry.

I replied, "No, sir."

To this, he replied, "Just call me Dewey," which I knew I would not do.

I thanked him and said I was not hungry because we'd had a big breakfast at the Maryland State College in Princess Anne.

After we'd sat on his beautiful porch overlooking the road, he pointed to the house across the road and said, "My brother Mnason lives there with his wife and six children."

I told him how fortunate he was to have his brother and his family living so close.

He responded very dryly, "I guess so," without any further comment, which spoke volumes about their relationship.

We continued to talk about my work with the migrants. Mr. Dewey seemed to have a negative attitude toward the migrants in general but was very sympathetic when it came to the children. His general attitude was they could do better if they would work harder, not realizing it was a matter of education and opportunity. Although I did not argue my point with him, I wanted him to know my commitment to the migrants was based on the fact that they had not had the educational opportunity that some of us had.

After talking more about my life and family, including my seminary education, we finally went inside for dinner before turning in for the night.

While I waited in the living room, Mr. Dewey was busy in the kitchen preparing our evening meal. After about an hour, he called me into the dining room, which was also a part of the kitchen. A small table that seated four was covered with a waxed floral tablecloth like those I'd seen growing up in Memphis, in Mississippi at my grandmother's house, and at Aunt Winnie's house, who also lived in Mississippi. As soon as I saw the dinner table, I knew I had the right house and the right host. The table was laden with crab cakes and rockfish, along with mustard greens from his garden and sweet corn, which had been cooked in the skillet. He also had a dish I had not seen since leaving home—stewed tomatoes. Mr. Dewey even had corn bread, which I thought only women knew how to prepare.

After we had taken our seats at the table, Mr. Dewey asked me to offer the grace for our meal. I thanked God for Mr. Dewey, who had welcomed me into his home, and for the food that had been prepared and asked that God would bless the food for our use and use us for his service.

I can only say that the meal was the best I'd had since leaving home, with the exception of the meal prepared by the cooks at Maryland State College where we had our orientation. Mr. Dewey was a very plain and simple gentleman. He told me to relax and eat as much as wanted. I knew that my stay would be a very pleasant and enjoyable one, since we were compatible in personality, and most of all, he was an awesome cook.

When we'd finished dinner, I offered to wash the dishes, but Mr. Dewey insisted that I go either on the porch or to the modest bedroom upstairs. I decided to sit on the porch, since it was a beautiful summer evening. I would experience many before my summer work was over. Living out in the country reminded me of the days I had spent in Mississippi with my grandparents and the many nights we'd sat on the front porch looking at the beautiful stars and listening to the crickets, which always provided their cricket concert.

After about an hour, Mr. Dewey joined me on the porch to smoke his pipe and enjoy something in a glass that looked like wine. He did not offer me any. I suppose his thinking was that if I was preparing for the ministry, then I did not drink alcohol. I would disabuse him of that thought before summer was over.

We sat quietly for more than forty-five minutes, just enjoying the beautiful stars and the cool breeze that was unique to the country evening. The fact that Mr. Dewey did not have the need to talk, and instead just smoked his pipe and thought, made him that much more attractive to me, given that I would spend the next eight or nine weeks living with him.

I finally decided to turn in for the night. Saying good night to Mr. Dewey, I headed upstairs to my bedroom. After I'd prepared for bed and before I'd gone to sleep, it dawned on me that I had not written my parents since school had ended and I had started my new summer employment in Maryland. I decided to write them a letter that would bring them up to date on where I was and how much I thought I would enjoy my summer with the migrant program. Although I'd told them about the initial offer by the National Council of Churches, I had not told them about where I would be assigned.

After finishing a rather lengthy letter, in which I also inquired about family and friends, I decided to turn out the light and go to sleep. I had a special two o'clock meeting on Sunday with my migrant committee at the First Methodist Church of Preston, Maryland.

On Sunday morning, Mr. Dewey was up and preparing breakfast when I awoke at eight o'clock to read and prepare for my meeting at the church. Mr. Dewey had the house smelling like my mother's kitchen on Sunday morning. I could smell the ham and bacon, along with other breakfast foods, as I dressed.

Downstairs, Mr. Dewey greeted me with a hearty, "Good morning, Rev. Veazey."

I asked him to just call me Carlton. He said he appreciated that but would continue to call me Rev. Veazey, which I decided to let be.

He informed me that he, along with most of the Negroes, attend the First African Methodist Episcopal Church, which was founded in the late 1800s in Philadelphia, Pennsylvania, by Reverend Richard Allen. I told him I could not attend this Sunday but would like to attend when I had an opportunity and my schedule allowed. He thanked me and also informed me that Mr. Kenneth Horner would pick me up and take me to the church at one thirty.

Mr. Horner was a very dignified man, who was not very talkative but was very interested in the migrant program. He was originally from Philadelphia but had lived in Preston for many years and had opened a handyman's business, making repairs on all kinds of machinery and also doing carpentry and other needed work. As we drove to the church, which was less than a mile away, he told me that, although Preston was a separate community, when it came to Negroes and whites, they got along very well.

When we pulled in front of a beautiful Gothic-style church, its bell tower was ringing to announce the two o'clock hour, the time scheduled for the migrant committee meeting. Mr. Horner escorted me into the side entrance of the church and to a conference room where the meeting was to be held.

All six members were present, with Mr. Horner being the seventh. They all warmly greeted me and welcomed me to Preston and their church. After a brief prayer by the chair, the meeting began. The committee asked if I would like to say a few remarks about my work in Preston this summer, which I was prepared to do. First, I wanted to thank Mr. Kenneth Horner for bringing me to the church for this meeting and my host, Mr. Dewey Townsend, a longtime resident of

Preston and a supporter of the work of the migrant ministry. I also thanked the committee for their generous support of this ministry, an extension of their home mission ministry.

The committee was headed by the chair of the stewardess board, Mrs. Mary Houston of Preston. She was a very sincere person, to whom I knew I could relate in this work.

After a series of remarks by other members, the committee made a commitment to support the migrant work in every possible way. Along with providing Mr. Dewey with a monthly stipend for my room and board, before the meeting was over, the committee presented me with the keys to a 1956 Chevrolet station wagon for my transportation during my summer work. They also said that the local Sinclair gasoline station had promised to provide me with all the gas and oil required for my work during the summer. This was very generous financial support from the committee.

Before closing the meeting, the chair asked Mr. Kenneth Horner to serve as the liaison for the committee. He would make any decisions for the committee regarding any request I made between our monthly meetings. Mr. Horner agreed. We left the meeting with a commitment to ensure that, over the summer, the children would be helped, and their conditions would be improved.

Before I'd come to Maryland, Mr. Snyder, my supervisor, had briefed me on the conditions of the camps. He'd asked me to address the problems of inadequate living conditions, along with the lack of educational opportunities for the young children during their eight-week stay on Maryland's Eastern Shore. Mr. Snyder warned me this would not be easy, due to the powerful landowners who enjoyed the benefit of low wages and lack of housing during migrant stays.

The following day, Mr. Horner picked me up at seven thirty in the morning to take me to the camps where I would be working. There were six camps for which I was responsible—two in Preston, and one each Easton, St. Michaels, Benton, and Cambridge. These camps were at least twenty-five minutes apart, requiring me to divide my visits to different days of the week. Preston, Benton, and Easton would be served on Monday and Wednesday, while St. Michaels and Cambridge would be served on Tuesday and Thursday. Friday would be reserved to ferry those needing medical care to the public health office for treatment, especially those who were expecting and in need of prenatal care. Saturday would be my day off to plan and have some time for rest and relaxation. Sundays would be the most difficult day, since I had to provide worship services for all campsites. This meant I would have to start with Preston at ten o'clock and continue on to Easton at eleven thirty. St. Michaels and Cambridge would have services at one o'clock and three o'clock. This sounded great on paper, but implementation was a real challenge. This schedule would be difficult to maintain, but it would be a part of the overall schedule we would operate.

On Monday morning, Mr. Horner and I visited the camps, since he had been designated by the committee to make decisions between meetings. I drove my station wagon, with Mr. Horner navigating and me taking mental notes of his directions. The first camp was just outside Preston in a community called Hurlock. When we drove into the camp, I was shocked at the living conditions, which were deplorable to be generous. The migrants were living in converted chicken houses that were one-room houses with just two windows for ventilation. The furniture consisted of four bunk beds with a woodstove in the middle of the room for cooking. There was one pump in the middle of the camp for water and outhouses for men and women at each end of the camp. This was what landowners provided for workers in 1959. I had a torrent of questions for Mr. Horner concerning these conditions, and his response was that he had seen no other way. This is the way migrant workers had been treated since he had been in Preston.

Returning to where I was staying in Preston, I was disillusioned about the conditions—the likes of which I hadn't even seen in Mississippi on my grandfather's farm, where he had sharecroppers. Although this was my first summer as a migrant minister, I was determined to make conditions better for these migrants during my stay on the Eastern Shore.

Tuesday morning, I went out to the camps to meet with the migrants and, hopefully, the owners of the farms. Driving to each camp, I saw the people preparing to go to the field for the day. I introduced myself as a minister, who would be working with them and their children during their stay in Maryland, and saw their skepticism. They referred me to their crew leader, who had brought them from Florida and was responsible for their welfare. I inquired where I could find him and was directed to the rear of the camp, where I would see a 1959 Cadillac and in the modern trailer he lived in.

My knock on the trailer door was answered by a Negro gentleman who called himself Calvin Covington from Hollywood, Florida. He explained he was responsible for the seventy-five people he had brought with him using several large trucks to transport them. He also explained they had just left Chesapeake, Virginia, and would be in the area for the next three to four weeks to harvest the overdue cucumber crop. I asked him why he would allow his people to live in these deplorable conditions. He answered that they were accustomed to such conditions, as their housing in Florida was not much different. I pressed him again as to how he could allow his own people to be treated like this, to which he gave me the same answer. I then inquired whether their housing was free. He answered that they paid seven dollars a week. I was getting angry hearing him talk with a straight face—this black man who could transport families in less than safe trucks while he and his family drove in a Cadillac and had a trailer for their living arrangements.

Before I left, I told him I would like to talk to both him and the landowner about these conditions. His reply was that he did not want any trouble, and his people had not complained. I could hardly control myself, having just left the South, where we were fighting segregation, prejudice, and unfair treatment. It was beyond understanding to see a fairly intelligent Negro man taking advantage of his own people for the sake of profits.

Leaving the camp in Preston, I headed to Easton, thinking that the place I was leaving was just a bad camp, and I would find a different kind of situation when I went to a more progressive town like Easton.

I soon realized that Preston was not a single incident but, rather, was exemplary of the plight of the migrant labor workers. After going to St. Michaels and Cambridge, I returned in Preston, went directly to my room, and tried to reach Mr. Snyder. My supervisor at the National Council of Churches was not in his office. I left word for him to call me as soon as possible, because I had some real questions that had to be answered before I could proceed.

After an hour, Mr. Snyder returned my call. His voice was filled with concern when he inquired about what may have gone wrong. I told him in a very urgent voice that everything had gone wrong and that I could not believe the living conditions of the migrant workers.

His reply was not very sensitive, but I would later understand what he meant when he said, "Carlton, what you have discovered is that we hired you and other seminarians to change that culture." This reply was very challenging and reminded me of my father when he integrated the Memphis post office without the assistance of his fellow members of the Postal Alliance.

I immediately answered Mr. Snyder with assurance that what he'd said was all I needed to hear, and I would report on the progress of my work.

The first day of my official launch of my program assisting the migrant workers in my four camps was Wednesday. Since I had not been able to meet with the landowners or farm owners, I returned to speak with Mr. Covington, who had brought these workers from Florida on the journey of misery and poverty. This time, the crew leader explained that the migrants had agreed to his terms before they'd left Florida, so he did not see anything wrong with what he was doing. Rather than trying to get him to see the error of his ways, I asked additional questions, such as how much they made a day pickling cucumbers, the major crop on the Eastern Shore. His response was that the owner agreed to pay them twenty cents a bushel basket for their labor.

It did not take me long to figure out the number of baskets it would take to make ends meet. Picking ten bushels an hour (done by the best workers in the camp), at the end of a day, would amount to sixteen dollars tops. The average worker bringing in only half that number of bushels a day would receive only eight dollars. The crew leader, on a weekly basis, would collect the seven-dollar-a-week rent of from each laborer. After paying the rent for their chicken house, the workers would also have to settle with the crew leader for any food purchased from him during the week. The crew leader had brought many food staples for purchase during their stay. He would raise the cost of food items like bread, crackers, sardines, salmon, Vienna sausage, soups, and chili, along with sodas and cigarettes and other items by at least 50 percent, which was devastating to the average migrant worker.

The migrants could do much better if they had transportation to stores in the town, where they could purchase the items for half the price they paid to the crew leader. However, they were not allowed to go into town. The claim was that they would violate the rules they and the crew leader had agreed on before he had brought them north to work. The average migrant, after paying his rent plus the credit the crew leader had given him during the week, would be left in the red, with an outstanding balance that was a way of keeping these workers loyal. This was the problem with sharecropping, which many of our ancestors had to endure trying to get economic independence.

These issues would occupy much of my time, along with my other responsibilities, such as education for the children and health care including prenatal care for the women.

The first week of my ministry was completed with the Sunday worship services. I preached on the dignity of humankind and how we must honor that by insisting that we be treated as men and women with respect and given a living wage for the work we perform each day in the fields while laboring under unbelievable heat and humidity to make a living. I delivered this message in all six camps each Sunday and during our weekly meetings, which were not well attended. The sparse attendance was due to the crew leader threatening those who attended with not being able to get credit from his "trailer store."

Although the farm owners and the crew leaders were not supportive of any changes, the members of the committee supported me and challenged the community to speak out against such cruel treatment and the unfair labor standards the landowners were imposing on the migrants. This was encouraging, and I decided to go public with these deplorable conditions and set up press meetings with the *Baltimore Sun* newspaper and local television stations in Baltimore.

Although these conditions I vehemently opposed existed, I realized that these people had to survive. I knew to that my opposition would only be effective if people in the town and other major cities agreed with the need for reform in migrant labor standards. Not only did the Baltimore papers and television report these issues, but the *Washington*

Post also interviewed me about the spirit of the migrants who labored under these conditions. I expressed to the reporters that, although they knew that these conditions were wrong and unfair to them, the migrant workers did not have the luxury of not working, as they had children depending on them for their survival. This left me quite despondent, in that I knew these conditions would not improve unless they did what the Negroes in Montgomery, Alabama, and other cities had done, which was to boycott.

The press reports brought much publicity to this unjust and cruel practice of exploiting migrants and their children for profit, even though these practices were not new to me, coming from the Deep South, where they were common practice.

During the summer, I was encouraged greatly by a documentary by one of the greatest broadcasters of the twentieth century, who exposed this practice while I was still in Maryland. This newscaster was Edward R. Murrow, who gained fame during World War II, broadcasting from England when the nation was under siege by German Nazis. His courage made him a respected and honored member of the press, to whom Americans listened and whose views they respected. The release of his documentary during the height of the harvest season was a powerful boost to those of us who had been raising the issues of the migrant's plight throughout the country. Morrow's documentary was titled *They Follow the Sun*. It showed the plight of migrants trying to make a living harvesting crops from Florida to New York. When the season was over in Florida, they would begin their trek north to states like Virginia, Maryland, Delaware, New Jersey, and finally New York.

This was also true on the West Coast, where migrants from Mexico would cross the border to harvest crops throughout California and other states. Murrow vividly showed the living conditions of the migrants and the exploitation by the crew leaders, who had no care that the migrants were also Negroes like them. This was very painful, especially in light of the new attitude of black leaders, who were risking their lives to improve the status of Negroes throughout the country.

After Murrow's documentary, the local papers began to investigate and press the leaders in these communities for reform in the agriculture industry.

My major migrant camp was the one in Preston, Maryland, so I spent most of my time there, partly because it was the largest camp and also because it was where most of the deplorable conditions existed. In Preston, the cucumber crop grew plentiful in this area and was needed for the pickle factories. The typical day for a migrant worker began before dawn, during which the workers dressed in their work clothes—pants for both men and women. They wore heavy shirts, which protected them from the sun and provided a means of insulation against the heat and sun. Many people do not understand that, when you work in hot weather averaging about ninety degrees, it's important to dress appropriately—in heavy clothes with a very big sun hat. The theory behind dressing in a heavy shirt was that, although you became hot and perspired profusely, the perspiration would soak the shirt and would provide a degree of insulation from the heat. This may sound weird and unworkable, but I can testify to the efficacy of this method and how it allowed me to work eight to ten hours a day in the camps and the fields.

After a breakfast of grits and fried bologna with day-old biscuits, the workers would all head for the trucks that would take them to field. The best time to work was early morning, before the sun rose and while the morning breeze still circulated. The bushel baskets would be lined up at the end of each long row of cucumbers. Although one may think it not difficult to pick cucumbers, cucumbers grow low to the ground, and the bending and stooping for eight or ten hours was extremely difficult for the workers.

Cucumber picking was backbreaking work only the healthy and young could endure. This work paid twenty cents a basket, and very few could pick more than sixty baskets in a ten-hour day; thus, these people were paid approximately twelve dollars a day with one hour for lunch. As a whole, the average worker would make only six dollars a day or less. This approximated the cotton-picking work in my part of the country in Arkansas and Mississippi that paid four dollars for a hundred pounds of cotton, which very few could pick in an eight- to ten-hour day.

Migrant workers would also bring their elderly along. Even though they could not do much in the fields, the elders would help with children and other chores in the camp. Given the pay structure, even

215

the most productive migrant worker would, at best, only break even after feeding his family and buying cigarettes for the week. I have seen pregnant women working in the field and, many times, giving birth in the fields before being rushed to the nearest hospital. Although this seems inhumane by our standards, it was not unheard of throughout the South and in the migrant world.

After seeing the Murrow documentary, I became more dedicated to changing the condition of the migrant worker in the United States. One of the most influential persons to support me was Mr. Horner, who assisted me during my Sunday service and worked with the Preston migrant committee to get childcare for those with young children. Although I met with the committee several times during my tenure, my key contact was Mr. Horner.

Before the summer was over, Mr. Horner had acquired a pump organ to assist me in my Sunday and midweek services. This added much to our services and allowed me to provide a sense of spiritual inspiration to those who had very little, including hope.

I had the opportunity to have four days leave in mid-July to recharge my physical and spiritual batteries. I went to Kiptopeke, Virginia, to see the young lady I'd met in Princess Anne, Maryland, during orientation in May. I wrote Earlene and asked if it would be possible for me to visit during my leave. She responded quickly and said the lady with whom she was living had a spare bedroom and would not charge me for it, since Earlene and her roommate had been helpful to her during the summer with other chores. On July 17, after conferring with Mr. Dewey and Mr. Horner, I left for Kiptopeke. It was a straight drive down Route 50 until reaching the bridge connecting Maryland and Virginia. I found the house where Earlene and her roommate, Shirley, had been living using my map and the address. Since it was a Friday, they had completed their work at the day care center for the migrant children.

When I reached the house, Earlene and her roommate were waiting for me with dinner prepared. After I'd given her a very affectionate hug and kiss, we went into the living room, where her roommate, who was from Norfolk, Virginia, was waiting to be formally introduced. I told her I was from Washington, DC, and was attending the Howard University School of Religion in preparation for the Christian ministry.

She was a religious young lady, which made her very compatible with Earlene from what I could remembered from our conversation at the orientation in Princess Anne earlier.

After dinner, Earlene and I went to sit on the back porch while the lady of the house was in the living room and Shirley had gone to the bedroom. As we sat on the porch, we did a lot of small talk about how our summers had gone working in the migrant ministry. I told her how disappointed I was at the treatment of the migrants, not only by the farmers but also by the Negro crew leaders, who exploited the migrants in every way, along with the landowners, who paid intolerable wages for the hard work the migrants had been doing. Earlene was very upset with what she had seen in the day care nursery that she ran for the local committee. She talked about how the children were not being nourished, except by the food they received at the day care center. Also, the lack of health care was evident from sores on their bodies from insect bites and head lice. After talking about how depressing this was, we both agreed we would return because the work was so desperately needed and would allow us to make a difference. Although I had briefly talked with Earlene in Princess Anne, I realized more now what a sensitive and caring person she was.

After a while, our conversation got personal, when I asked her if she was dating someone special. It was an awkward way to put it—why would she date someone not special? After realizing how clumsy my inquiry was, I asked her directly whether she had a boyfriend at school or in Nashville, her home. After assuring me she was not in a committed relationship, she asked me about my love life and whether there was someone in my life at Howard University. I told her I had no time to seriously pursue a relationship, though I was in a platonic relationship with an older lady. Naturally, she inquired why I was dating an older lady, to which I responded that this was a safe way not to become too deeply involved in a serious relationship.

After an hour or so, we turned the radio on to some romantic music, and I kissed and held her close, telling her how much I had missed her since Princess Anne. After several hours, we agreed to call it a night, since we had planned to have a picnic in the local park with Shirley and her friend Ralph the next day.

The room that was prepared for me was very comfortable although it had no air-conditioning. The windows were open, and there was a cool breeze that made the room temperature very tolerable. I slept well, but I awakened several times to drink water and read some of the books I had brought with me in preparation for my next semester at Howard. *The History of Christianity* was a two-year course, and we were assigned to read at least four chapters during the summer. This book was one that nobody thought possible to read cover to cover. This exercise put me to sleep, and I did not awaken until Earlene knocked to inform me that it was eight thirty and breakfast would be ready a nine o'clock.

I rose immediately, showered and shaved, and went downstairs to the dining room, where I met Mrs. Johnson, a matronly lady whose husband had died. She was a member of the church committee that sponsored the migrant ministry in Kiptopeke, Virginia. Mrs. Johnson welcomed me and told me what fine young ladies Shirley and Earlene were and how delighted she was to have them. She also talked about how impressed she was with the work they were doing for the migrant workers. Mrs. Johnson had given Earlene and Shirley kitchen privileges, and they had prepared the most delicious breakfast of eggs, scrapple, and fried potatoes with wheat toast. After eating and finishing my coffee, we agreed to leave for the picnic around one o'clock after they returned from shopping at the local grocery store.

I decided to go back to my room and read while they were gone. This also gave me time to think about the relationship I was about to develop with Earlene and how I would explain my past, especially my engagement to Joyce and how it had ended. I thought that this was important. I had not really resolved my emotions around what had happened between Joyce and me. And I didn't want to enter into a relationship with Earlene without telling her I was still emotionally attached to Joyce and make her the victim of a rebound relationship. Thinking this through, I decided to wait until Sunday night to talk. I would be returning to Maryland on Monday. After this time of reflection and resolve, I decided to dress in more comfortable clothes for the picnic.

When Earlene and Shirley returned, I was sitting in the living room watching television with Mrs. Johnson, who I found very interesting and informative about news. Earlene and Shirley asked me to help with picnic preparations and help load the car as we prepared to leave. Shirley's friend Ralph would meet us at the park, since he had to work this Saturday.

Arriving at the picnic area of the park, we found that most of the tables had been taken, except in a very nice area under a large tree that would shield us from the sun and heat, now in the upper eighties. Shortly after we'd arrived, Ralph, who would become the grill master, joined us and helped set the grill up and prepare the charcoal for cooking. Shirley and Earlene had packed chicken, pork ribs, baked beans and corn on the cob, which they immediately put on the grill. While our food cooked, we had beer and wine.

Since it would take some time for the food to cook, Earlene and I excused ourselves to take a walk around the park for some privacy and to allow Shirley and Ralph to have the same.

As we walked, Earlene thanked me for coming to Kiptopeke to see her and said she hoped we could continue to see each other after our assignments ended in late August. I told her we could possibly see each other during the Thanksgiving holidays, when I could come to Atlanta where she was in school at Spelman College. We also agreed to spend the night together after the picnic at the local Holiday Inn, since I would be leaving early on Monday morning and she had to be at work early on Monday morning.

Upon our return to the picnic area, we found Shirley and Ralph sitting on the picnic seat kissing, which caused us to delay—waiting until they had finished their passionate kiss to join them. We talked loudly as we approached, and when we had joined them again, they said they were hoping we would get back soon so we could eat. The chicken and ribs and baked beans had the whole area filled with the aroma of good food.

After eating to our hearts' content, we cleaned up the area and informed Ralph and Shirley that we would not be going back to the house tonight and wondered if they could drop us off at the Holiday Inn. After a moment of awkward laughter, Ralph said he would be glad to take us there, as he and Shirley would also be staying there for the night. We all agreed that would be perfect, since we would all be going back to house in the morning.

During the evening alone, Earlene and I discussed how we would manage a long-distance relationship during the next year. Earlene would be in her last year at Spelman, while I would be entering my middler year in seminary, which meant I would have one more year after she had graduated. We agreed to write often and try to see each other during Thanksgiving and Christmas.

The night was a beautiful night of consummating our relationship and feeling the beginning of a new and wonderful future.

The next morning, we met Ralph and Shirley for breakfast and prepared to return to Earlene and Shirley's home that afternoon. Mrs. Johnson had gone to church, since it was Sunday and going to church is what Southern people do on Sundays, especially in Virginia.

After some small talk, I excused myself and retired to my room for the next few hours, while the girls prepared dinner for the evening, when Mrs. Johnson would return from a full day of church services. Ralph agreed to return after work for dinner and share the evening, since I would be leaving early on Monday morning.

I spent the afternoon reading my A *History of Christianity* book. It was the most pressing class I had, and I wanted to do well in it during the next semester. After falling asleep, as was my usual custom after reading a chapter or two of Latourette's tome, I heard a gentle knock on the door and found Earlene standing there and asking if she could come in for a minute.

After she came in, she immediately found my lips and gave me the most passionate kiss since last night at the Holiday Inn. It required all my willpower and prayer to not go to the next level of making love to her before leaving and returning to Preston, Maryland. After getting ourselves together, she said dinner was ready, and I should come downstairs in fifteen minutes. I was glad she gave me fifteen minutes, since I needed that time to get myself and my mind together after that brief love interlude.

When I got downstairs for dinner, Ralph was already there, and Shirley seemed to be enjoying the afterglow of their previous night's lovemaking. In fact, all of us were happy, including Mrs. Johnson, even though she was supposedly in church all day.

After all were seated, I was asked to give the blessing for dinner and immediately thanked God for the food and the hands that had prepared it, asking that may it strengthen our bodies for his service. Amen.

Earlene and Shirley had prepared a beautiful feast of baked chicken with corn bread dressing, green peas, mashed potatoes, and mustard greens. Mrs. Johnson's homemade rolls were the highlight, since she was known throughout Cape Charles and Kiptopeke for having the best rolls in town. Ralph and I did not hesitate to begin serving our plates, as it was Southern custom to have guests serve their plates first. When everyone had prepared his or her plate, we began to eat the most delicious food, which was even better than Mr. Dewey's in Preston. Of course, it was not as good as my mother's food. After finishing our dinner, we were surprised with a dessert of strawberry shortcake and whipped cream that was equally delicious. This reminded me of home on a Sunday afternoon after church.

Ralph excused himself. He had to report to his job at the local hospital where he worked as a nurse's assistant. I said goodbye to him and invited him and Shirley to Washington, DC, where I would show them around the capital. I also extended the invitation to Mrs. Johnson and told her how happy I would be to her escort her around the city.

After Ralph had gone, we all went to the front porch to enjoy a beautiful summer evening together. Mrs. Johnson gave us a history of Kiptopeke and Cape Charles and how much it had changed from a very small country town into a much larger town with many more people. The growth, as I later found out, was from 1,800 to 3,000.

After an hour or so of talking and reminiscing about our lives, we all agreed that we should turn in, since we had to get up early the next morning. Mrs. Johnson said good night to me. She would probably not be awake when I would leave at six thirty. I had to be back in Preston by ten o'clock for a meeting with Mr. Snyder regarding our final report and the closing out of our summer program in one month.

Earlene and I were left on the porch alone, so naturally we continued our kissing and holding each other while looking at the most beautiful moon. This, of course, made us even more passionate, and we continued to kiss and hold each other and snuggle.

Finally, we agreed that we should both get some rest, since Earlene had to be at the day care center at six thirty in the morning and I had to leave at that same time for Maryland. After a final good night kiss, we left for our rooms on the second floor. At the top of the stairs, I asked her to wake me up at five thirty so that I could get started on my drive to Preston. We then left each other for the night.

In my room, I prepared for bed and then prayed a long time for guidance and direction after meeting someone with whom I thought I could spend the rest of my life sharing my ministry. I also asked God to remove from my mind the vestiges of my love for Joyce and help me to love and appreciate Earlene. This may sound simple; after all, I had enjoyed a beautiful weekend with Earlene, who possessed all the qualities I wanted in a person to whom I would commit my life and love. The only nagging problem was the fact that I could not say that I had the love for Earlene that I'd had for Joyce, which was very troubling. I did not want to continue with Earlene if I was not certain that I loved her.

I finally fell asleep with beautiful memories of the wonderful weekend, which I hoped would be the beginning of a new life together.

The morning came quickly, as the previous day had been long, and I was physically exhausted. I looked at my watch and saw that it was five twenty-five. I decided to stay awake, since Earlene would be knocking on the door at five thirty. Before I could lie back down again, the knock on the door came, along with the calling of my name. "Carlton, it's five thirty."

I quickly opened the door and invited her to come in. She was reluctant at first but came inside, and I immediately kissed her with all my passion. To my surprise, she returned my kiss. We found ourselves continuing, and without any forethought, we made love, until Earlene heard Shirley calling to remind her they would have to leave in thirty minutes. We both seemed embarrassed but very satisfied.

I assured her I would call her when I got back to Preston, and she hurriedly left the room. I began to prepare to return to Maryland. Downstairs, Mrs. Johnson invited me to have juice and coffee, along with a sweet roll before I left. I thanked her and sat down with her, how grateful I was for her hospitality and kindness. I also reminded her of my offer for her to come to Washington and be personally escorted by me during her visit.

My two-hour drive to Preston was fraught with questions and doubts about my commitment to Earlene, realizing that I had not really emotionally divorced myself from Joyce. I rationalized that Earlene possessed all the qualities I desired. She had a very kind and compassionate spirit, evidenced by her work in the migrant ministry. She was also more than prepared to make a real contribution to my ministry, whatever and wherever it might be. Her background mirrored mine in many respects. She had come from a religious home and had been educated by her aunt, Mrs. Ivey Roddy of Memphis, whose husband was principal of Woodstock High School, the leading high school in Shelby County. She was very sophisticated and carried herself like a refined woman. All these things considered, I thought that, even though the emotional connection of what we call romantic love was absent, we could have a good life together. I decided to continue to pray about it like I had for my mother's healing when God provided the answer.

I was surprised how quickly the two hours passed given my preoccupation during the drive. Arriving back at Mr. Dewey's home, I found him across the road with his brother, Mnason, and Mnason's children. When I went across to greet them, they all ran to meet me and inquired where I had been, which left me speechless, except to say, "Away."

Somehow, all accepted my answer, except the oldest daughter, Greta, called "Butch." Butch was the oldest of five children and a great help to her wonderful mother, functioning as a surrogate mother to her brothers and sisters. She and I had met before, but due to my work we had not spent any private time together.

I asked her if she would like to attend a drive-in movie that evening, to which she responded, "Yes."

I then asked Mr. Dewey if it would be all right for me to call my friend Earlene in Kiptopeke, Virginia. He said that I could if I paid the charges at the end of the month.

I called Earlene and was stunned when she answered and immediately called my name, since I had not said hello. She told me that she had been watching the clock and somehow knew it was me—at least she was hoping it would be me. We talked for several minutes, during which I thanked her for the wonderful time I'd spent with her during the past several days. She also expressed how much she had enjoyed seeing me and how easy it was for her to connect with me. I agreed and added that it had something to do with our similar backgrounds. She agreed but added that it was also due to our compatible spirits. This comment caused me to pause and take in what she had said, since I had not heard her express anything spiritual during our time together. Although I was somewhat surprised, I agreed that our spirits were similar and made our time together very enjoyable.

When I picked Greta up at seven thirty, she was dressed in a very attractive dress. I told her parents we would be back before eleven o'clock, which they accepted. When we arrived at the outdoor movie and paid for our tickets, I went to get popcorn and drinks for us well we waited for the main feature. It was, of all things, *A Man Called Peter*, about Peter Marshall, a Scottish minister who was a very famous preacher. Marshall would later come to America to pastor the New York Avenue Presbyterian Church, where he would become one of the premier preachers in the country.

Although this was not a very romantic movie, it was one I found very interesting. It spoke about Marshall's struggles during his ministry, which he overcame, and was able to minister to many people for many years in Washington, DC. We headed home after the movie, since it was already ten thirty and our drive would take approximately twenty-five minutes. Fortunately, there was very little traffic, and I had her home exactly five minutes after eleven, ask we'd talked several minutes after arriving.

I walked Greta to the door, kissed her on the cheek, and thanked her for a wonderful evening. She thanked me for inviting her and said she hoped we could do it again. I drove across the road to Mr. Dewey's, unlocked the door, and had started up the stairs when I heard Mr. Dewey call out, "Reverend, is that you?"

"Yes, sir," I responded. "I will see you in the morning."

That night, I had no problem sleeping—after my long day driving back from Kiptopeke, Virginia, and having spent a busy three days visiting the girl I called "my girlfriend," although Earlene had not given me the right to say that. After listening to music for a while, I set the alarm clock for seven o'clock, since I wanted to be at the migrant camps at eight o'clock. This was late for the migrants, who had to be in the field by seven o'clock and would have to board the trucks no later than six thirty.

In the morning, I did not try to see the migrants before they left for the fields, which I had done many times before. I had planned to meet with the Negro crew leader to talk with him about improving the lot of the migrants. My purpose for this meeting was to understand why he would impose such harsh conditions upon these migrants, Negroes who were already poor.

The conversation turned out to be a very important one, allowing me to voice my frustration and even anger at how he was treating members of our race. One thing my father had taught me was, no matter how much you differed with a person, you should always hear him or her out and try to understand the other's point of view, even if you did not agree with it. After I had challenged the crew leader about his treatment of his own people, he asked me respectfully to listen to him, which I agreed to do. He spoke about his years of growing up with his father, a crew leader who had brought many migrants to the North for work. This he did because, after the harvest season in Florida, of oranges and other fruit, the year would be over by May—meaning no work until the next year. That was unthinkable, since the harvesters had children to feed and needed places to stay. After hearing these explanations of their plight and why they needed work, I wanted to know more about why the crew leaders still exploited the migrants in terms of rent and food and the living conditions that the landowners provided.

Although the crew leader's explanations were rationalizations for the situation of the migrants, what he said did not explain why the Negro crew leaders had to also exploit their own people. I tried to understand but concluded that it all led back to greed and lack of compassion on the part of the crew leader.

After he finished with his explanations of how his father had taught him, I posed a question: Was his father also a victim of trying to placate white people in order to get favorable treatment from them? This crew leader vehemently denied the suggestion and repeated what I had heard so many times from white people when I was growing up. "I treat my nigras well. You can ask them, and they will tell you how good I am to them."

Sadly, this was true in many situations. What the Negroes did not understand was they were supposed to be treated right, and their labor was separate from how the white man treated them as human beings. Somehow, I felt the conditions of these migrant camps and the treatment the harvesters and their families were the vestiges of slavery, which the white man had not forgotten and the Negroes had not yet rejected.

My spirits were raised, however, when I read that the civil rights movement was moving across the country, which meant that it would soon come to Maryland and Virginia and challenge the exploitation of the Negroes and also Latinos. Although Latinos were only in the country during the harvesting season, they were also exploited.

Following my meeting with the crew leader, the church committee had arranged a meeting with the congressman from their district so that I could voice concerns about the landowners' treatment of the migrants. After I had met the congressman and outlined my concerns, the congressman agreed to address the issues in his next meeting with the landowners. I was also encouraged by the interest the committee was showing in these issues, motivated by the work of Mr. Kenneth Horner, the only minority member of the committee.

I had just a little more than a month before I would return to Washington, DC, and the School of Religion, where I would enter the second year of my theological education. I was very appreciative of the experiences I'd gained through my summer work in Maryland. But I was anxious to get back to completing my seminary work so I could continue my work in the migrant ministry, which I had decided would be my career.

I thanked Mr. Dewey and the Townsends and members of the committee, especially Mr. Horner, who had been so invaluable to me during my migrant ministry before leaving Maryland. The following day, I drove to Easton, where I met Mr. Snyder, my supervisor from the National Council of Churches, to give him my final report and return the station wagon.

Mr. Snyder and I met at a luncheon counter in town, where we spent more than an hour going over my report and recommendations for whomever would succeed me the following year. He asked me if I would be interested in coming back next year to work in Preston. I was surprised and readily accepted the offer, since I was very interested in making this my life's work. When Mr. Snyder heard my response, he expressed how happy he would be to have me and how delighted the local church committee would be to hear the news. These sentiments were surprising given that I had condemned their friends and neighbors for creating the deplorable conditions in which the migrants lived, especially since they professed to be Christian. I had seriously consider making this my life's work, instead of my initial interest in becoming a college chaplain.

I arrived in DC for my second year in seminary to find I had a new roommate, Cameron Byrd, a senior in the School of Religion. I had met Cameron my first year and found him very personable and very smart. Cameron was a native of Buffalo, New York, which made him a big city guy. He was heavily involved with a beautiful young lady named Maxine. I would get to know her well during my year of rooming with Cameron.

Our classes began on September 4, which meant my duties as Dean Crawford's assistant and pass graduate fellow in the Office of Student Life would also begin. My first day of school was mainly a social session. We talked about our summer experiences and what we anticipated for our new year in seminary. Cameron told me it would be a recapitulation of the first year, just more intense, with some added classes. Our Old and New Testament classes would continue as we progressed through the literature. Church History would continue as we applied ourselves to reading Latourette's book, which I was only halfway through. I was not discouraged, since I was ahead of most, having read during the summer.

Two of the new classes included Religious Education with Dr. Tymns and Christian Social Ethics with Dr. Evans Crawford, who would also be our Homiletics teacher (teaching us the art of preaching).

This would also be the year when we would each be assigned to a local congregation for an internship. I was excited for the opportunity to apply what I'd learned during my theological education.

This would be a fateful and providential year, the details of which you will later learn. In the meantime, I pursued my studies with new vigor, recognizing the value of being as prepared as possible in every way in order to have an effective ministry.

This year would prove to be very challenging, considering my new work in the Office of Student Life and that I was continuing as the assistant to the dean of the chapel. But I appreciated the work with a new interest and a very inquiring mind about some of the theological concepts I was learning about. I was very proud of the discipline I'd incorporated into my routine—how I used my time between my studies and my work assignments. Something I noticed in all of us was our new sophistication about religion. We had learned new information about religion, which removed some of the mythology we all grew up believing.

One of the major stories in the Bible, about the Garden of Eden, which I had believed for many years, really existed in the book of Genesis as a way to explain the concept of "original sin" and how humankind has become estranged from God. This was a major adjustment from my previous Christian education classes growing up in the Central Baptist Church in Memphis. This was just one of the new theological and religious concepts I would have to consider as I developed into what church people called a "trained minister"—which was looked at with some skepticism and could raise questions about your calling. Although I knew this was a great departure from my religious views and theology, it was also exciting to explore new ideas and possibilities of new areas of truth.

Fall seemed to pass quickly, and our classes went smoothly with our reading and preparation of term papers and other assignments. Part of our second year would be fieldwork or internships, which would be assigned by Mr. Herbert Eaton, assistant to Dean Daniel G. Hill, dean of the School of Religion. These assignments had been approved by him and supposedly had something to do with our strengths and abilities. Mr. Eaton called a meeting of all middlers (second-year students), during which he called each name and gave the name of the church where the student would spend the next year, with the pastor assisting in any way that he thought would be helpful to the church and the student. Since my name was always last or near the end in any alphabetically ordered list, I waited to hear that I would be serving Zion Baptist Church, one of the historical churches in DC.

After the meeting, the dean passed out packets containing all the information about the church. The packet listed the pastor's details and résumé, as well as contact information for who to call to set up a meeting with the pastor.

Rev. Dr. A. Joseph Edward, who had pastored Zion for twenty-two years, was recognized as one of the best preachers in the city, with one of the most historical and prestigious churches in the city. I was anxious to get home to read thoroughly about the church where I would be serving for the next year. The history of Zion was interesting and exciting. Zion was founded in 1864 by seven freemen who came to Washington from King George, Virginia. Rev. Dr. Edwards was a native of Georgia and finished his theological studies at the Gammon Theological Seminary in Atlanta, where he also received an honorary doctorate of humane letters.

In 1950, the city had used the law of eminent domain, which allowed it to take property deemed necessary for the betterment of the city. Zion Baptist Church was located in Southwest, Washington, DC, in a Negro community that was very close and supportive of each other and prided themselves as a community that was family oriented. Zion and several other churches declared open to eminent domain included First Baptist Church, Rehoboth Baptist Church, and Berean Baptist Church. The only Negro churches not taken were Friendship Baptist Church, which the city declared was not in the path of development, and Second Baptist Church due to its location. The churches that were open to eminent domain fought for years to remain in Southwest, especially Zion Baptist Church where it had been for over ninety years.

The city's decision was patently unfair, in that the Catholic Church at Fourth and F Streets, though not taken, was situated in the path of development. After several years of litigation, Zion Baptist Church finally settled with the city for $600,000, which many felt totally inadequate, recognizing that this church was built by the children of slaves called freedmen. The four oldest churches in the District of Columbia were Nineteenth Street Baptist Church, Shiloh Baptist Church, Zion Baptist Church, and Metropolitan Baptist Church. Shiloh and Metropolitan were not affected, since they were not located in Southwest.

Rev. A. Joseph Edwards was the sixth pastor of Zion, who led the church through the most critical period of its history. He was succeeded by Rev. William Walker, founder and first pastor, who was also the founder of Shiloh Baptist Church; Rev. William Gibbons, second pastor; Rev. William James Howard, third pastor and to date the longest serving at thirty-nine years; Rev. William Washington, fourth pastor; and Dr. Ellison, fifth pastor, who served only a brief four years, having accepted the presidency of Virginia Union University.

Rev. Edwards was a preacher's preacher, which meant he was sought after by many ministers throughout the city and country because of his homiletical skills. Eminent domain was a traumatic time for many of the members who had been born in Southwest and had belonged to Zion since birth. Rev. Edwards was also an excellent administrator, which was demonstrated during this transition period. Zion had been blessed with many able and intellectual members who assisted Dr. Edwards in these very critical and historic times. The church decided to move temporarily to the Phillis Wheatley YWCA located at Ninth and Rhode Island Avenue in Northwest, Washington, DC. During this period the church would seek a new area for building a new edifice, negotiate for the land required, and hire architects who would plan the building of the edifice.

After reading this brief history and reading about this prominent pastor, Dr. Edwards, I was elated to be able to intern at this historic church and have a mentor of Rev. Edwards's stature to guide me in my ministry. I discussed my assignment with my Cameron, who had interned at another prominent church, the Plymouth Congregation

Church pastored by the outstanding Dr. Arthur Fletcher Emes, also sought throughout the city. Cameron agreed that this was an opportunity to learn a lot from a minister such as Dr. Edwards, as well as have the experience of a church in transition.

The internship paper also told me to report to Ms. Keturah Barnes, superintendent of the Zion church school. Her telephone number, as well as her address, was a part of the orientation paper. She would be my supervisor, and Rev. Edwards would have me assist him in the pulpit on Sunday. This could pose a serious problem for me if I could not reconcile this with my work at the chapel. I would have to discuss this with Dean Crawford in order to accept this internship.

I met with Dean Crawford the following day regarding the internship. He immediately told me to accept the internship, saying we would work out the details. I left the meeting with a feeling that Dean Crawford was proud of my assignment and wanted me to have the experience of interning at such a prominent church. I did not have to meet with Dean Carey, since most of freshmen activities were held on Fridays or Saturdays, which always freed me up on Sundays.

When I arrived back at the apartment, I had a letter from my mother, which made me very happy. In it, she told me how much she and my father missed me and hoped things were going well for me. She also said members of Bethlehem Baptist Church wanted to know when I would be coming home to preach again. Melvin told them to tell me he wanted me to come home for Thanksgiving, only three weeks away. Gerry had moved to Louisville, Kentucky, to be with her husband, who was stationed there in the army.

The news made me homesick, reminding me how much I missed being there to know what was going on. My mother's letter made me realize that it would probably be almost a year before I could go home. I had already committed to the internship that would require me to be available during the Christmas and Easter holidays, high days in the church.

After arranging a meeting with Mrs. Keturah Barnes to discuss my internship at Zion Baptist, I prepared my résumé to take with me. My other assignments at Howard with the dean of the chapel and the office of the dean of students would occupy much of my time during the week.

I arrived at Mrs. Barnes's home at 1242 Girard Street about three blocks from my apartment on Georgia Avenue. When she opened the door, I met a woman who was robust, with a contagious smile and a welcoming personality. She invited me into her sparse basement apartment, though she was the owner of the building who rented out the rest of the apartments. She was a very well-spoken woman, who told me the history of Zion Baptist church. She had been raised in the Southwest community, where the church was originally located. I could tell she was very proud of her church and considered it the most historic church in Washington, DC. She was also effusive about the diverse membership, which included some of the most prominent members of the Washington community and some of the most respected pastors, especially Rev. Howard, the church's longest-serving pastor. Finally, she asked me about my background and how had I decided to come to Howard University to attend the School of Religion.

I gave Mrs. Barnes my résumé and asked if I could also tell her my motivation for choosing the ministry and how I had been led to come to Washington. She was excited to hear my story and asked if she could get me some refreshment before we continued. I accepted her offer and enjoyed the most delicious lemonade I had ever had.

I began to tell her about my grandfather and father, both ministers. I mentioned that my grandfather had been born in 1860, five years before emancipation, and had founded the Mount Enon Baptist Church in Arkabutla, Mississippi, in 1890, where he remained until 1920. My father hadn't followed in his father's footsteps immediately and was over fifty years old when he'd accepted the call to the gospel ministry of Jesus Christ in 1948. I also told her how, through my mother's miraculous healing from cancer in 1956, I had accepted the call to the ministry at twenty years of age at the Bethlehem Baptist Church in Memphis. I also told her about being set to go to Southern Baptist Theological Seminary in Louisville, Kentucky, until a family friend had advised my father that the best school for me would be the Howard University School of Religion. I shared the story of how Mr. King had arranged with Dr. Daniel G. Hill to grant me a full scholarship.

After I had told Mrs. Barnes about my background, she expressed how fortunate Zion was to have me intern with the church. I would tend specifically the church school and the Christian Endeavor Society, a home mission organization serving many charitable organizations in the city. Mrs. Barnes wanted me to know that she would be my mother away from home. I was welcome to come anytime and have dinner or just visit to talk. I left Keturah's (she asked me to call her by her first name) excited and grateful for having met someone so encouraging. She would insist on calling me Rev. Veazey.

When I returned to my apartment, Cameron was busy studying but stopped to ask me how my intern interview with Zion had gone. I told him that my assignment had to be God sent, since I could not ask for a more welcoming and encouraging person than Mrs. Barnes. I told him about her service in the church and how she was born in Washington and had been a part of Zion since childhood. I was expected to attend and teach Sunday school class and speak on Youth Day and any other times that the pastor requested. Cameron was impressed and said his assignment at Peoples Congregational Church would lead to a paid assistant position after he graduated in May. His words of encouragement were very motivating for me. But my plan after graduation was to work with migrants or to seek a position as a college chaplain.

Sunday morning, I rose early to prepare for a long Sunday. Dean Crawford had asked me to continue to take guests to breakfast, and someone would escort them to the chapel later that morning. I was grateful to the dean for helping me carry out my intern responsibilities at Zion, where I was to teach a Sunday school class at nine thirty that morning. My special guest that morning was Dr. William Holmes Borders, one of the premier preachers from Atlanta, Georgia, and a close friend of Dr. Martin Luther King Sr. At breakfast, I reminded him that I had heard him when I'd attended Arkansas AM&N College in Pine Bluff, Arkansas. He was elated to know that I remembered him and congratulated me on my decision to become a minister and attend the Howard University School of Religion. When we finished our breakfast at Baldwin Hall, I escorted him to his suite and instructed Dr. Borders to go in twenty minutes to the Rankin Memorial Chapel for morning service. He thanked me for my hospitality, wished me well on my internship, and asked me to give Dr. Edwards his regards.

Before going to the YWCA to meet my Sunday school class, I went to the chapel to make sure the robes and altar were prepared, since I would not be there for the morning service. When I arrived at the chapel, Dr. Crawford was waiting for me with the most anxious and concerned look on his face.

He asked me to sit down a minute. After we had sat, he explained that Rev. Edwards had died of a massive heart attack at the drug store on the corner of Seventh and Rhode Island Avenues, five minutes away from the YWCA. Dean Crawford explained that the Sunday school and other church members who had arrived early were extremely distraught and quite depressed, especially since the fourth Sunday in September was supposed to be a great day in the church. Zion was to break ground on the new edifice that the church had waited for nearly seven years that very afternoon.

Keturah asked if I could come as soon as possible to pray and encourage the congregation to have faith in God's plan for them. I went immediately to the Y, where I found the auditorium filled with sobbing men, women, and children. Keturah asked me to have prayer and asked Mrs. Jennie Smith to have the choir prepared for the eleven o'clock service, where I would preside. Although I had led services many times before in Memphis and in Arkansas, this was the most difficult challenge I had ever faced. The members, after having their church in Southwest—their home for over eighty years—taken by eminent domain, now faced the possibility of another blow. Many feared this one may be fatal, and their church would not be built.

During the eleven o'clock service, the choir sang with great power and conviction when they led the church in the hymn, "The Church's One Foundation." The song brought a feeling of renewal and hope to us all.

Rev. Thomas C. Garnett, a wonderful minister and member of Zion, offered the morning invocation. His prayer would set the tone for the service. Rev. Wilbur Henry, another member, read from the book of Isaiah, which said, "They that wait upon the Lord shall renew their strength, they shall mount up with wings of eagles, they shall run and not be weary, and walk and not faint." Everything was leading the

234

church to come to grips with the untimely death of our beloved and sixth pastor of Zion Baptist Church.

Then the time came for me to deliver the message to the congregation. The tragic morning had left the congregation despondent and unsure about the future. I selected Psalm 46 as my text, which read, "God is our refuge and strength, a very present help in times of trouble." I also gave the admonition of the God—"Be still and know that I am God." My message was simple but hopefully encouraging, in that it reminded the congregation that the same God who had brought Zion Baptist Church along for over eighty years would not forsake us. I also reminded them of the seven founders who had difficult and adverse times but had continued to trust God and his grace. Finally, I said that the Word of God reminds us to not panic but to "be still and know that I am God."

After the sermon, Mrs. Smith, the choir director, led us in singing one of the most powerful and beloved hymns in the church. The sweet words included these lines:

My hope is built on nothing less
Than Jesus's blood and righteousness
I dare not trust the sweetest frame
But wholly lean on Jesus's name.
On Christ the solid rock I stand;
All other ground is sinking sand.

Before the service ended, Mr. George W. Peterson, chairman of the board of trustees, announced that the trustees would meet after the service to discuss the future of the church's building plans. The deacon board asked if I would serve as interim minister until a new minister was called. This motion was unanimously approved, which was another challenge because of my other duties at the divinity school and with the Office of Student Life.

During the week, I met with Dean Crawford to get his advice on how to proceed, as serving as intern minister would require another commitment. He promised to be my mentor as I accepted this responsibility, which went beyond my internship. The next week, I met with Keturah to discuss this new role in the church, for which

I was neither prepared nor expecting. Keturah was most comforting and encouraging as we discussed how we would proceed. Her advice was very simple. She expected me to continue to work with the church Sunday school. I would lead the Sunday worship services and other services, including those on Thanksgiving and Christmas.

I had been mentored by some very seasoned ministers, including Dr. A. Edward Davis in Pine Bluff Arkansas, but taking on the role of interim minister was still a challenge in many ways. I informed Keturah I would not be available during the summer months of June, July, and August. She assured me she would make arrangements for my absence.

I asked her how the board had come to the decision to ask me to step in, given that I was new and had not yet finished seminary. She was a very wise and experienced woman and very knowledgeable about the politics of Zion Baptist Church, given that she'd served as the church secretary, as well as the superintendent of the church school. She explained that the church had at least five associate ministers who had been in the church for years. In order to not cause factions in the church, they had selected me as a neutral choice until a new pastor was selected. In addition, during the following months, the deacons would select each of these associate ministers to preach, though I would lead the services. I was relieved that I would not have the full responsibility of preaching during this period of mourning. The deacon board would establish a pastoral call committee to invite other ministers interested in the pastorate to submit their résumés for the committee, to consider their qualifications and determine if the church would allow them to preach.

Keturah asked me to also become active with the Christian Endeavor Society and the Charles Walker Culture Club to encourage the young people to remain with the church during this critical period.

This was the most challenging time in my seminary education, not only because my duties had substantially increased but also because the emotional toll caused me difficulty in keeping up with my studies. I was serving as an interim minister and also carrying out other pastoral duties, including marriages and funerals, except when people would call on other ministers who were more familiar with them and the church. Because of the time requirement and duties, the trustee board gave me a

236

stipend of $200 a month, which was more than I was being paid by my other two jobs. This was very helpful, since my responsibilities required me to have additional funds for transportation and other clothes for special occasions.

The responsibility of heading a very prominent church was exciting and sometimes exhausting. It gave me a very complete experience as an intern. When I would get tired and feel that it was too much for me, I would find comfort by reminding myself that this would end for me when the semester ended, and I would be returning to my migrant ministry for the National Council of Churches on Maryland's Eastern Shore. These new responsibilities increased my need to spend extra hours in the library and study to keep up my work in the seminary.

The first semester quickly passed, and I was unable to visit my parents for either Thanksgiving or Christmas. My parents, although very understanding, were worried that I would not keep up my seminary studies. That was the most important thing to them, even though they knew I was getting valuable experience as an interim minister at Zion. In the four months since Rev. Edwards passed, I had become very familiar with the church membership, particularly with the younger families in the church. I was the age of most of the young people who had just finished college, so relating to them was very easy.

I will always remember Dr. Crawford and Mr. Carey for the understanding and support they gave me during this critical period of my life and study. My ministerial duties ensured that I would not have to work at the post office during the Christmas holidays, which I did not regret. The programs for the young people and the special services during the holidays would take up most of my time.

The church would go through a very difficult period in the several months following Rev. Edwards's death. The plans for building the new church would require restructuring. Although I was not part of the administration, Keturah would keep me informed on what was going on in the church, especially since Rev. Edwards's death concerned the Perpetual Building and Loan Association (Perpetual), where the church had applied for a $200,000 loan to build the church. The church had received $600,000 for the old church property, but this loan was critical for continuing the building of the new edifice. Perpetual was concerned that, because the pastor had died and no new pastor had been elected, the loan was in jeopardy. However, because of the leadership of George W. Peterson, a prominent attorney, Perpetual would not withdraw the loan application and would give time for the election of the new pastor and demonstration that the financial viability of the church was still intact. Peterson would lead the church through these turbulent times, though under withering criticism by some church members.

The funeral of Dr. A. Joseph Edwards was what one could call an ecclesiastical state funeral. He was not only beloved by Zion Baptist Church but also recognized and honored as one of the most prominent ministers in the city. His services were held at the historic Shiloh Baptist Church, founded only a year before Zion in 1863. Rev. Earl Harrison, pastor of Shiloh, asked Rev. J. Randolph of Mount Moriah Baptist Church to give the eulogy.

It was the most moving eulogy I had ever heard. Rev. Randolph was over ninety years of age and still pastored the Mount Moriah, another Southwest church taken by the city through eminent domain. He pointed out how unfair the city had been in requiring these prominent churches to move and disrupting one of the most cohesive neighborhoods in the city. He spoke of Rev. Edwards as one of the most taught ministers in the city, who possessed the most important leadership qualities in the city. His wife, Minnie Edwards, was also praised for the support she had given him during the twenty-two years they'd served Zion Baptist Church.

Rev. Edwards was laid to rest in the newly established George Washington Carver Memorial Gardens Cemetery.

The next year would be pivotal in the life of Zion Baptist. Peterson and his wife, Dr. Gladys Peterson, would prove to be God-sent leaders for such a time as this. The attorney would use his skills to advance the building program, and his wife, a leading educator in the city, would become the cohesive force in the church to encourage the various organizations to work together to advance the work of Zion.

My role was formally established as the interim minister. I worked with the deacon board to make sure the pulpit was covered each Sunday, other services such as funerals and weddings were handled, and other responsibilities were carried out. The diaconate would select the ministers to preach each Sunday, with Communion Sunday carried out by me.

One of the first things the diaconate and the trustees had to do was set another date for the groundbreaking ceremony that had been postponed. The deacons and trustees agreed on the fourth Sunday in October at four o'clock to hold the groundbreaking service at 4850 Blagden Avenue. The service was put together by Keturah, with the support of the deacons. Rev. Kirkland, one of the sons of the church, would preside. Other sons of the church would participate, among them Rev. Thomas C. Garnet, a beloved minister of the church who had overcome blindness to accomplish much, including degrees in liberal arts and a bachelor's of divinity degree from Howard. Rev. Wilbur Henry, who had been recently ordained by Rev. Edwards, would also participate. I was not asked to participate but to assist the other ministers if needed.

This service proved to be spiritual catalyst that was necessary to reenergize the church. The preacher for the service was the Rev. J. L. S. Holloman, pastor of Second Baptist Church and president of the Ministers Conference of Washington, DC, and vicinity. Dr. Holloman was one of the oldest and most respected ministers of the city and a dear friend of Rev. Edwards.

The groundbreaking of the new church in Northwest, Washington, DC, was a very important event, taking place in one of the most prestigious parts of the city, of which the members were proud. Part of this pride was due to the fact that the old church was located in the Southwest—a part of the District of Columbia that, at that time, was one of the poorest areas. This site had been selected by Rev. Edwards and the trustee board because they felt that eminent domain had scattered the membership to other quadrants of the city.

The service, held on a large lot that would support a large and sprawling edifice, was moving and inspirational and dedicated to the memory of the late pastor Rev. Edwards. Dr. Holloman praised Dr. Edwards and Zion's membership for their ingenuity and foresight in building a new church in one of the most upscale areas in Washington. Zion also was the only church removed from Southwest to build a new edifice, rather than purchase one of the "white churches" that had left the area during the "white flight" when whites were leaving in droves to avoid integration. Many black churches bought those overpriced churches, since it was a buyers' market.

The groundbreaking services ended with new energized and positive feelings among the members, especially the young people, since this would be their church for many years.

The next seven months passed quickly. My days were filled with my studies, my work in the chapel office, and the graduate fellowship in the dean of student's office. In addition, my work at Zion required a large part of my time. My duties included visiting the sick, conducting funerals, and assisting in the Sunday services when not preaching. The only reason I was able to juggle so many things was because of my age and energy. At only twenty-three years old, I had a full schedule to say the least. And I found time to continue to see Lucille, who encouraged me and provided a home atmosphere away from the apartment. This was the sum total of my social life and platonic relationship with a female.

Earlene returned to Atlanta where she had received a teaching appointment in the Atlanta Public School System. I continued to correspond during this time and we looked forward to seeing each other. I had planned to go to Atlanta during the Thanksgiving holidays for a weekend. I was very excited about seeing her again, and she encouraged me to come, since she would not be going home for Thanksgiving. I asked Keturah if she thought I could go to Atlanta during thanksgiving to see a girlfriend I had met during the summer when I'd served in the migrant ministry on the Eastern Shore of Maryland. Keturah was very encouraging, especially since she had not heard me mention any girl during our work together. I was glad to get her approval. I did not want to be seen as shirking my duties at the church.

I also received the approval to be away during Thanksgiving from Dean Crawford and Dean Carey and made plans to visit Earlene in Atlanta for the Thanksgiving holidays. Our communications began to increase, with letters and also an occasional call.

I decided to tell my parents I had become interested in a young lady who attended Spelman College in Atlanta and who would be graduating in the summer. Mother wrote me back and was very supportive of my new romance. She knew how disillusioned I had been since my relationship with Joyce, which she thought would color my relationship with other women.

She was right to be concerned. I had not really gotten over Joyce. But I was determined not to expose all of my feelings. Rather, I would look for the qualities I admired in a woman, regardless of whether she and I had a deep love relationship. I reasoned that I could care for someone and even marry her without being deeply in love with her.

Thanksgiving found me in Atlanta with my girlfriend Earlene, for whom I cared deeply and with whom I really wanted to share my life. I can only describe her as being one of the most caring and loving persons I had ever met. Mrs. Taylor, her landlord, was also a very fine woman and told me how lovingly Earlene had spoken of me. This made me feel very special—to know that she really thought I was worthy of her love.

Our three days together in Atlanta were beautifully spent. We revisited the campuses of Morehouse and Spelman, along with Morris Brown College and Atlanta University. We also went to several well-known restaurants, including Pascal's, which still operates today. Although it was thought not to be proper before marriage, we spent the night together at a motel, since we would not dare sleep together in Mrs. Taylor's home.

The three-day Thanksgiving holiday went quickly. I had to leave on Sunday to be in class Monday. Before I left, Earlene and I talked about our work this coming summer with the National Council of Churches. We both were excited about that. We believed we were truly serving a need and making a difference. We also expressed our love for one another and looked forward to seeing each other during the Christmas holidays. I suggested Memphis, since she had not met my parents and my brother, Melvin, whom everyone loved.

The flight back to Washington was rather fast. I arrived early in the afternoon, which gave me time to do personal chores like washing clothes for the week and to prepare for classes the next day. I also checked in with Dr. Crawford to see if there was anything he wanted me to do before Sunday services.

I then talked with Keturah to see if there was anything the church needed, such as a visit to anyone who had been hospitalized since I had been away. Keturah informed me that the speaker for the coming Sunday, Rev. Kirkland, was ill and I had to preach in his place on Sunday. Although I was accustomed to these emergencies, preparing a sermon did require some preparation. There were also some members of the church who were home from the hospital who had asked that I visit and have prayer with them. This I was able to do after classes and before going to the dean of students' office.

Most of the students who had gone away for Thanksgiving were arriving on Sunday for classes on Monday. Going to Baldwin Hall for dinner, I met some of them, and we discussed our visits during the holidays. Most had gone home and talked about the wonderful time they'd had seeing old friends and eating wonderful Thanksgiving dinners with their families.

I did not share with them my visit with my girlfriend Earlene because it was very personal, and I did not feel comfortable talking about my love life and possible marriage.

When I returned to the apartment to resume study for our classes on Monday morning, I found my roommate reading and preparing for his classes. Cameron seemed so laid-back that I could not wait to be a senior and be that confident of my successful completion of my seminary training.

After completing some chores related to my clothes for the week, I started reading for my Systematic Theology class, where Dr. Roberts would lecture on the Trinity and its meaning in the redemptive process. This was of special interest to me because, of all the doctrines or articles of faith, this was the most difficult. The concept of the Trinity was also not easy to accept since we had just completed the chapter about "the sovereignty of God." I finished my reading, looking forward to Dr. Robert's lecture, which would amplify and, hopefully, clarify this doctrine of the church. I turned my radio to WMAL and the program "Music Till Dawn" that would put me to sleep with its soothing sounds by some of the outstanding artists of the day, such as Woody Allen and Duke Ellington.

Monday morning came, and it was back to the daily grind of lectures; note taking; library assignments; and, in my case, reporting to the dean of students' office for any assignments the dean may have for me.

I also checked in with Dean Crawford's office and Lucille to find out what had happened during my absence. After bringing me up to date, Lucille invited me to dinner on Friday, when she would have my favorite dish, rockfish and French fries. I accepted and told her I wanted to talk with her about what was going on in my life and what I had planned for the future. She was somewhat puzzled by this serious talk but said she looked forward to hearing about these new developments.

Ms. Keturah at Zion asked me to come by after school. I readily agreed, since she promised to have one of my favorite dishes, Southern fried chicken, even though she was not from the Deep South. After completing my work at the Office of Student Life, I went to meet with Keturah. As promised, she had the apartment smelling like good home cooking, with the turnip greens and fried chicken giving off a delicious appetizing aroma that only whetted my appetite and made me eager to taste the cooking of the best cook in Washington, Keturah Barnes.

She told me that the young people in the church were interested in my becoming the pastor of Zion Baptist Church. My response was one of astonishment. In addition, I wondered what effect this would have on my time and tenure as an intern from Howard's School of Religion. I explained to Keturah that I had no interest at all in becoming the pastor of Zion for two reasons. First, I had not completed my seminary education, which I believed was absolutely necessary to become an effective minister and pastor. Second, I had expressed to others my goal of becoming a college chaplain after working with Dean Crawford at the Rankin Chapel for almost two years.

She listened to me attentively without interruption and finally said, "This is what the young people your age are saying, and you should know that."

I thanked her and asked her to help me be effective in the work the trustees and deacons had asked of me during the interim period.

Keturah had prepared a dinner that was beyond description and also packaged food to take with me. I thanked her and told her how much I appreciated her and needed her guidance during this critical and sensitive time in the life of Zion. She promised to give me her best advice and guidance and always her prayers and said that, whatever I decided to do in ministry, she would be supportive. I kissed her on the cheek and thanked her for being not only a good mentor but also a friend, notwithstanding our age differences.

While walking back to my Georgia Avenue apartment from Keturah's place, I tried to put together what had transpired during my visit to her home. One thing I was sure of was that I did not want to be considered for the pastorate, regardless how much the young people of the church were interested or supportive.

Keturah continued to encourage me and provided needed information on the state of the church, so I could be more effective in providing the kind of ministry needed during this fragile period in the life of Zion. After talking with Keturah, I was not satisfied with my response about the young people wanting me to become pastor.

I decided to do what I had always done when I needed to make a momentous decision. I would call my father, whom I'd always considered a very wise man.

Back to the apartment, I called home and asked Mother if Daddy was home. She told me he was there, but he was talking to Uncle Hubert. I asked her to have him call me after Uncle Hubert left, as it was important. Mother said she would, but I could detect in her voice concern about my seriousness and need to speak with him.

Daddy came to the phone with his usual greeting. "Hello son, how are you?"

I responded that I was doing well but needed some advice on a spiritual matter. I told him about my work as an intern and also as the interim minister of Zion until the church found a pastor. My concern was that the young people in the church had unofficially expressed their desire for me to become the pastor, and that caused me a great deal of concern and anxiety.

My father spoke with authority, which gave his words strong credibility with me when he asked what the problem was. This stunned me. Instead of giving me the direction I'd thought he would, he had placed the weight squarely on me to answer my own question. I responded that I had not sought the position of pastor and did not feel qualified at this time to become an effective pastor.

My father responded with a very direct question. "Why don't you leave seminary and seek some other kind of calling?"

244

His reply was beyond devastating—to have my father telling you to give up the call and go in a different direction for my life's work.

After a brief debate, he simply said to me, "Son, what did you promise the Lord when your mother was sick unto death?"

Those words put everything in perspective, and I responded by telling him I was willing to do whatever the Lord wanted me to do to further His work here on earth.

After hearing this, my father told me to continue to pray and allow God to direct my path. This was the end of the conversation except to thank him and ask him to pray for me.

After his powerful prayer over the phone, we said goodbye, and I felt as if a huge weight had been lifted. After reflection, I resolved to not be concerned about those issues and concentrate on trying to help the church grow and fulfill the dream of Rev. Edwards and the promises of God. This was the turning point in my preparation and caused me to really focus on my seminary education and not on what the future would be. This resolution enabled me to have peace and joy in my work on campus and grow in my knowledge and understanding of the challenges of the ministry.

The Christmas holidays were fast approaching. Earlene and I had made plans that she would come to Memphis over the holidays to meet my parents, family, and friends. Our relationship had grown tremendously, although I still could not feel the deep romantic love I thought was necessary for marriage. I rationalized that she possessed all the qualities a man could want in a life partner, and deep romantic love was not necessary. I made up my mind to propose to her and hoped she would accept when she came to Memphis.

My schoolwork was progressing well, and I was really enjoying my classes and learning many new things about the history of Christianity, systematic theology, and how to preach. I enjoyed the study of homiletics with a great preacher and teacher, Dr. Crawford. Dr. Wright and Dr. Rice made the Old and New Testaments come alive with their lectures and reading assignments. Dr. Wright was especially interesting, since he used some or most of his lectures to teach us about the occult and his experiences exploring the Hindu and Islamic religions and their relevance to Christianity, as well as our understanding of great religions in the world. This fascinated me and made me look forward to his classes and even the extra class sessions he invited us to attend.

My work in the chapel office and the Office of Student Life kept me busy and provided income, along with the stipend from Zion. This made it possible for me not to think about working at the post office as I had done the previous year. I would also be able to fly home for Christmas and buy Earlene an engagement ring. Things were really going well. I was very grateful to God for directing my paths through all the years.

On December 22, I arrived in Memphis. Gerry and George were waiting for me at the gate. As soon as they recognized me, they ran and gave me warm embraces, with Gerry giving me kisses. We went directly to 1610 Arkansas, where my mother was waiting on the porch as she had done so many times when I was attending Arkansas AM&N in Pine Bluff, Arkansas. Mother came to the car to kiss and hold me, and we shared the sweetest embrace.

We went into the house where my father had been waiting in the living room with Melvin, who I hadn't seen in almost a year. My father stood up, walked over to me, and embraced me, simply saying, "Welcome home, son." His greeting made me feel special.

Melvin also embraced me and said, "I have missed you a lot." This also meant a great deal to me. I had grown up with Melvin more than I had with any of my other brothers.

After we'd talked in the living room for a while, Mother informed us that dinner was ready, though it was not yet six o'clock. I was so happy to see that mother had prepared the dish I'd loved since a little boy— liver and onions, with rice, turnip greens, and hot rolls from Snyder's Bakery. I had gone to pick those rolls up and get every Sunday before dinner. Everything was hot, and the aroma of the food made me even hungrier. We had lemonade to wash it down.

After all of us were at the table, Daddy asked us to bow our heads while he thanked God for "bringing our son back to us safely." My father's prayer was beautiful. He thanked God for our family and my mother, a beautiful woman who God had spiritually healed from cancer in 1956 when I accepted my call to the ministry of Jesus Christ. He thanked God for the work I had been doing for the "least of these," serving the migrant workers in Maryland. Although it was a long prayer, it was the best prayer I had ever heard my father utter.

Everyone, including Daddy, deferred to me as the food was passed around, as was our tradition. After everyone had helped him or herself, I began to eat—which made me wonder why I'd ever left home in the first place. I leaned over to my mother and kissed her on her cheek and said, "I will always love you." This brought tears to her eyes, along with the others at the table.

Everyone ate and enjoyed our mother's superb dishes. When we finished our main course, Mother brought out her favorite cake, a rich pound cake with vanilla ice cream. All of us were full but could not resist.

After dinner, Gerry asked Mother to leave the dishes for her to wash, while she and Daddy talked with me in the living room.

I told them how well things were going and about the progress I was making in seminary, along with my responsibilities at Zion and campus work with Deans Crawford and Carey.

After almost half an hour, my father asked me about my relationship that Mother had told him I had developed and what our plans were. Although I always confided in Mother first, I told them I would be going to Nashville to give Earlene the engagement ring I had purchased in Washington. Both Mother and Daddy smiled and said how happy they were, although they only knew Earlene by what I had told Mother. I also told them she had been raised by her Aunt Ivey Roddy, wife of Dr. Roddy, the principal of Woodstock High School in Woodstock, Tennessee, a suburb of Memphis. Of course, Daddy knew Dr. Roddy, as he was active in civic affairs in and around Memphis.

I also told them Earlene's aunt and uncle had brought her to Memphis to go to Woodstock High School, where they could ensure she would get a better education. Her Aunt Ivey had provided for all of her needs and had taught her some of what she called the "graces" of a young lady. After her graduation, Aunt Ivey and Dr. Roddy sent her to Spelman College in Atlanta. She'd graduated last year and was teaching in the Atlanta school system. I told them she would be coming to Memphis during the Easter holidays to meet them and the family.

Mother and Daddy seemed very happy that I had found someone after my heartbreaking experience with Joyce.

Our Christmas was very traditional, in that we did what we had done through the years. We all went to church for sunrise service and returned afterward for our breakfast since our dinner would not be ready until five o'clock that evening.

On Christmas Day, I called Earlene and let her know that I had told my parents about our pending engagement and future marriage. She was elated and wanted to know what their reaction had been. I told her that they both were very happy and looked forward to meeting her during the Easter holidays.

I left for Nashville the day after Christmas to visit my future wife and meet her parents. I would only be able to stay two days, since I wanted to return to Memphis and spend New Year's Day with my parents and friends. When I arrived in Nashville, Earlene's father was waiting at the Greyhound station to meet me. Mr. Marshall was a big and affable man with a ready smile. We greeted each other, and he asked me how my parents and the family were. I told him they'd asked me to give their regards to him and Mrs. Marshall.

When we arrived at the home, Mrs. Marshall, along with Christine and Curtis, Earlene's sister and brother were in the living room waiting to meet me. After we exchanged warm greetings, Mrs. Marshall served a very tasty dinner of fried chicken, mustard greens, mashed potatoes, and biscuits. It was a most delectable dinner, and I left the table thinking, *Even my mother-in-law-to-be can cook.*

After profusely thanking her and Mr. Marshall for their hospitality, Earlene and I decided to go over to Tennessee State University, where there was a bar and cocktail lounge, even though she did not drink.

When we arrived, it was early evening and the bar was beginning to fill up for the evening. We took a booth in the back, where the music was not too loud and where we could talk romantically, since I was prepared to give her the engagement ring. I asked the waiter to bring two glasses of white wine, along with an appetizer of shrimp cocktail with cocktail sauce. While he was gathering the order, we began to talk about how we'd first met at the University of Maryland, Eastern Shore, in Princess Anne, Maryland, and how, during our migrant ministry, I'd visited her in Cape Charles in a small town called Kiptopeke.

I also asked if she remembered our first kiss. She did, and she reminded me how shocked she had been when I'd spontaneously pulled her close and given her a long passionate kiss. I reminded her that it would not have been long and passionate if she had not cooperated. Immediately following our kiss, which reminded us of our first date, I reached into my pocket, pulled the ring out, and asked her if she would marry me.

After a brief but intent look into my eyes, she said she would—which led to the most passionate kiss I had ever given her.

After our kiss and engagement, we talked about our future wedding plans, which she must have given a lot of thought by the way she outlined the plans. We agreed that she would come to Memphis to meet my mother and father, Rev. and Mrs. Mertie Veazey, who would become her future in-laws. She would make all the plans in Nashville for an early June wedding, since we had to report to our work as migrant minister and day care supervisor around June 15 and would have to spend our honeymoon in Preston, Maryland.

When we returned to Earlene's home, her family were all waiting, as if expecting an announcement—which Earlene immediately made. "Carl asked me to marry him, and I accepted his ring," she told them. Following the congratulations from her family, we decided to take a walk in the neighborhood before coming back to the house for the night.

The following day, I prepared to return to Memphis for the New Year watch night service at Bethlehem Baptist Church, which had been a tradition for many years. Earlene wanted to show me her home church, Mount Pleasant Baptist, one of the oldest in Nashville before I left Nashville. The beautiful church was a stately Gothic structure that had been around since the turn of the century. Upon entering, I saw the wide middle aisle that brides love for their entrance.

Once I had seen the church in which I would be married in less than six months, we returned home, where Earlene's mother had prepared a delicious dinner of fried chicken, lima beans, and mashed potatoes, with homemade ice cream for dessert. After the delicious dinner, we watched television and listened to jazz music for a few hours. We decided to go to bed, since I had a noon bus to catch the following day.

The next morning, I decided to visit some of my longtime friends, Al Jackson, William Hawkins, Gene Miller, and Robert Wesley McGee, all of whom played in our jazz quintet, the Music Makers, in which I played trombone for two years. These were some of my closest friends, especially Al Jackson and William Hawkins, since we'd also lived near each other in South Memphis.

New Year's Eve was especially important to me, since this would be the last time I would see my parents until Easter, when Earlene would visit before our wedding in June. We left for church at ten o'clock to hear the choir before the pastor, Rev. Taylor, brought the New Year message.

My father and I went to the pastor's study, since we would also participate in the service. Melvin and Mother sat in the congregation. This was a very special service for me. I had made one of the most important decisions of my life, which was to select the person I wanted to spend the rest of my life.

The service was very moving. The choir sang with power, and the congregation responded with the Holy Spirit. My father gave opening prayer that was inspiring and uplifting to the congregation and especially to me. Rev. Taylor, the pastor who'd licensed me and subsequently ordained me, preached a great sermon from Isaiah, when the Lord called him and he replied, "Here am I, Lord send me." This message was very significant; I was embarking on a long ministry and needed to rely upon the Lord to give me strength for this journey. The congregation was equally inspired, as the pastor implored them to answer the call of the Lord by reaching out and helping those less fortunate. This impressed me very much, given that this would be the second year I'd be working with the migrant workers on the Eastern Shore of Maryland—work that I found very rewarding.

Finally, the midnight hour was at hand, and the pastor invited those who desired to come and kneel at the altar for our last prayer in the old year and our first prayer in the new year of 1959. Pastor Taylor implored the Lord to bless us and provide for our needs, both physically and spiritually. I was so lifted up. I really needed that prayer. This would be a pivotal year in my theological education at Howard.

After welcoming in the New Year, members embraced each other and wished each other a happy New Year. I was always struck by the warmth and fellowship among members that followed New Year service; it was how I thought church should always be. Rev. Taylor wished me well on my theological education and asked me to keep him informed of my progress. When I returned to Memphis, he wanted me to preach for him. These blessings from my pastor made me feel wonderful.

New Year's Day was the traditional day when we all made New Year's resolutions, which did not last very long. Also, everyone in the South had black-eyed peas and neck bones or pig feet for dinner on New Year's Day.

I called Earlene to wish her a happy New Year and tell her how happy I was about our engagement and future marriage and life together. I spent the rest of the day with my parents. I would be leaving in the morning for Washington to finish my final semester as a middler looking forward to his final year as a seminarian.

My stay was one of the best I'd ever had. My parents were in good health and were happy with their lives. Melvin was doing well and had gotten a part-time job with Mrs. Briggs, who owned Briggs Florist.

I went to sleep early and slept well. Before I got in bed, I thanked God for such a wonderful life and for giving me the opportunities that had come my way during my time at Howard. I really thanked him for wonderful parents.

My ride to the airport with Gerry was nostalgic, as well as inspiring. My sister had always been the sibling with whom I connected the most. We had grown up together after Erwin and Weldon had moved to Chicago and Audrey had left. Audrey, who was eleven years older than me, had remarried a wonderful man Madison Shockley in Los Angeles, California. I never knew her that well because she was away during most of my formative years. Gerry and I talked about my upcoming marriage to Earlene and how I hoped that she and my parents would like her and welcome her to the family. After dropping me off at the airport, she gave me a strong embrace and kiss and told me to do well in school.

My flight to Washington was smooth, both physically and emotionally, because of my realization that everything was working out for me. After arriving in Washington, I went to the apartment I had called home for the past year and a half and found Cameron already back from Buffalo, New York. He told me how much he'd enjoyed his stay at home with his family and friends. Of course, I gave him the news of my engagement to Eva Earlene Marshal of Nashville. I told him we planned to marry sometime in June before going to the Eastern Shore for our work in the migrant ministry. There she would run a nursery for migrant children. I would be the migrant minister to our friends from Florida, who would follow the sun for work throughout the East Coast before returning to home base in Hollywood, Florida.

January 3, 1959, would start another pivotal year for me and for my roommate, Cameron, who would complete his theological education with a BD (a bachelor's of divinity), to later be upgraded to a master's of divinity. Cameron was a good influence on me because of his very intense work ethic. He was also encouraging to me in my seminary work. His father, Dr. Byrd, was a prominent pastor in Buffalo and a civic and community leader—which Cameron would become during his career.

The first day of the new semester was spent meeting with our new teachers and attending classes to learn what would be expected of us during the final semester of 1959. My classes were a continuation of last semester courses, such as Old Testament and New Testament, with new courses like Homiletics, Introduction to Christian Ethics, and Christian Education. Fieldwork and my work with the dean of the chapel and dean of students made for a very difficult semester, especially since I would be serving Zion Baptist in my intern capacity, which required additional preaching and officiating at funerals, weddings, and other pastoral responsibilities. Although this was a heavy schedule, I realized how blessed I was to have these experiences, which would enhance my future ministry, whatever that may be.

The second year was very exciting to all of us. We were helped in our sermon preparations through utilizing what we had learned in Exegesis, which enabled us to interpret the scriptures and relate them to our everyday lives. This was one of the courses in which I excelled; I'd had many ministers, who had brought the scriptures to life, relating them to our everyday lives, though I hadn't realized what they were doing.

Dr. Crawford also taught us how to develop effective sermons and how to deliver them with conviction. We were fortunate to have Dr. Crawford as our teacher. He had studied with and assisted the legendary Dr. Howard Thurman, dean of Marsh Chapel at Boston University. Dr. Thurman was once dean of the Rankin Memorial Chapel of Howard University. Dr. Crawford was an excellent preacher in substance and delivery. I was fortunate to have him as my teacher and personal mentor, since I served as his assistant. Ms. Lucille Stubblefield continued to be a special friend of mine and an excellent secretary to Dean Crawford.

My middler year was perhaps my best year. I had matured and was very serious about my work and study in the seminary. Some of this was due to the fact that I was on the verge of a life-alternating event, my marriage to Earlene that summer. Also, I became very serious as a result of serving as interim pastor, with all the responsibilities of a pastor. However, I was sure I did not want to take on that responsibility as a full-time pastor, with all of the challenging issues that the new pastor would face. Although my workload was taxing, I was energized. My completion of this seminary education was only a year away after this semester, and I could decide what I wanted to do with my ministry. I was still thinking of joining the National Council of Churches as a migrant minister full-time. I also maintained interest in becoming a college chaplain, since I liked relating to students.

The second semester passed quickly, with my academic work and my chapel and student life work both satisfactory and satisfying. Earlene and I had been in communication about the progress of her plans for our marriage and what I needed to do as the groom. She also said she looked forward to meeting my mother and father during the Easter vacation, now only a month away. She planned to come the Saturday after Good Friday so she could attend Easter Sunday service with the family, especially since I would be preaching the Easter sermon at Bethlehem Baptist Church, where I was licensed and ordained to the gospel ministry.

Easter was approaching quickly. I had to take finals in a week, which meant I had to give extra time to my studies, even if I missed time at the Office of Student Life. Although my roommate was a senior getting ready to receive his BD in May, he was immensely helpful, giving me the benefit of his knowledge about the examinations I would be taking. He could not tell me what questions would appear on the exams, but he could give me a broad understanding of what questions might be on them.

My internship was going well, and Keturah was very supportive and helpful during this time. She was an excellent cook, and I spent many hours at her home studying, which allowed me to enjoy some good home-cooked meals rather than dining hall food. I will never forget Keturah Barnes. The love and support she gave me during some of my most critical years was invaluable. She also assisted me in my interim pastoral duties, which were new to me. Her guidance enabled me to navigate all of my responsibilities related to the church.

April arrived and, with it, my plans for going home. That, coupled with Earlene's plans to come to Memphis, made this a very exciting time. Earlene told me she would be leaving the Wednesday before Easter to go home to Nashville and would be coming to Memphis on Good Friday afternoon. Her plan would work out well, since I had to participate in the traditional Seven Last words from the Cross," where each minister preached from one of the seven words. The university would close the Monday before Easter Sunday, which gave students an opportunity to make early plans for Tuesday.

I left Washington late on Tuesday after my last class, allowing me to get to my flight to Memphis at four o'clock that afternoon.

We arrived in Memphis at six thirty that evening, and Gerry and George were waiting at the gate. After our hugs and kisses, George retrieved my bags, and we headed toward the parking lot. The drive to 1610 Arkansas Street seemed so long, with almost every light changing to red as we drove toward South Parkway, which would take us to my street. Our final turnoff of South Parkway onto Arkansas made my heart beat faster, in anticipation of seeing my dear sweet mother.

As we pulled up to the house, Mother was outside with her hands on her hips and her apron on, which told me I was going to have a great dinner. Getting out of the car, I ran and embraced her with all my strength, just holding her for a minute while telling her how much I'd missed her and how much I loved her. During that embrace, I thought about how she had been sick unto death, how God had answered my prayer, and how I had been faithful to my promise to preach for the rest of my life.

We went into the house, where my father reached out and also embraced me and told me how proud he was of me and what I had accomplished. We sat down in the small living room and talked, while Mother went into the kitchen to finish dinner.

Melvin entered the room, and I rose and embraced him. Melvin was a wonderful big brother, although I had to look out for him to make sure he was safe and no one took advantage of his mental challenge.

Daddy talked to me about my future plans after marriage. I told him about the plans Earlene and I had made to return to Maryland to work together in the migrant ministry. He seemed very excited about the ministry and inquired whether he could also serve as a migrant minister. Although Daddy was retired and in his early sixties, I thought this could be an opportunity for him to minister to people who were in desperate need of encouragement through faith. I told him I would speak to Rev. Snyder about his desire to serve and where there were openings. He was quite elated and thanked me for the opportunity, although I had not yet finalized his participation. I felt good just knowing my father still had the desire to help the poor and downtrodden.

On Good Friday, I participated in the traditional services commemorating Jesus's Seven Last Words from the Cross. This service was always moving and inspiring as we remembered His suffering and death on the Cross. This service was traditionally held between 1:00 p.m. and 3:00 p.m., which were supposed to have been the hours when he was crucified. Although I participated, I was not very inspired; this service often turned into a "preaching contest," which took away from the sacredness and solemnity of the commemoration.

The time, however, allowed me time to pick up Earlene on time at the Greyhound bus station. When I met her at the station, it seemed like she would never get off the bus. This caused me worry. Had something happened? Was déjà vu occurring? (I couldn't help but reflect back to what had happened to my engagement to Joyce.)

Nearly all the passengers had disembarked when, finally, my future bride came down the three steps into my arms. We kissed, which embarrassed her in front of so many strangers. We walked toward the car, parked on Fourth Street near Madison, a two-block walk. I inquired why she had sat so far back. She explained that her father was late getting to the station, and the only seats left were in the back of the bus. I teased her by reminding her that it sounded like the old days of segregation.

When we arrived at my home, Mother was waiting on the stoop with her typical apron on and her hands firmly planted on her hips. Mother came down the steps to meet Earlene and, without a word, embraced her like she was one of her own children, which made my heart glad. Earlene also embraced my mother, who would soon be her mother-in-law. Melvin came out to join in welcoming Earlene, who would soon be his sister-in-law. Mother told Earlene that Gerry and her husband, George, would be coming over soon.

When we entered the house, Daddy was sitting but immediately rose. The first thing he said to her was, "How is my daughter?" With that, he embraced her.

Earlene smiled and said, "Thank you, Rev. Veazey."

Melvin followed my mother's lead and also embraced Earlene, which he liked to do anyway. Earlene made him feel very good when she told him I talked about him so much and that she was glad to meet him.

The dinner Mother had prepared was a little different from most of our dinners. My dad liked lamb and, it being Good Friday, had bought a leg of lamb, which Mother had cooked perfectly. We also had green peas, mashed potatoes, and homemade rolls. Daddy came to the table and immediately offered the blessing for the food, asking the Lord to bless Earlene and her family.

When all had dined sufficiently, Mother brought out dessert—apple pie with homemade ice cream. I was shocked. I did not know Daddy and Melvin had made the ice cream while I was away. This reminded me of days past and gone, when Daddy would assign me to churn the ice cream every time he made it, which was too often for me.

Earlene complimented Mother on the dinner, especially the rolls, which mother seldom made. She told Daddy she had not had homemade ice cream, and it was delicious and thanked him for his efforts. I was taken aback. I thought she had set in motion the return to the old days, when I'd spent what seemed like hours churning the ice cream.

After dinner, we excused ourselves to visit friends in the neighborhood, where I introduced her to some people I had known most of my life. First we visited the Petersons, whose sons had attended high school with me. We also went the Bowden's, whose daughter Clara I'd thought had a crush on me but who I'd found too young, being three years younger. We saw my next-door neighbors Mr. and Mrs. Taylor, who had eight children—a difficulty with only the husband working and amazing for this time, when most people were having one and no more than two children. There was also Mrs. Briggs, owner of Briggs Florist, two doors up from us on Arkansas, where Melvin worked delivering flowers in the neighborhood.

I wanted Earlene to meet other friends with whom I'd attended high school who lived in the neighborhood, including my orchestra friends William Hawkins, the saxophonist; Al Jackson, the drummer, whose father allowed me to play with the Al Jackson orchestra; and Carl Johnson, though not a musician, a true intellectual, who became president of the Memphis Board of Education.

I spent Saturday and Sunday giving Earlene a tour of Memphis, including my kindergarten center, elementary school, and the high school from which I graduated. We also went to Coldwater, Mississippi, thirty minutes from Memphis, where I showed her the home of my grandparents, the Jollys, as well as the Henson home of my aunt Winnie and Uncle Virg's not far from my grandparents. We also visited the site of my grandfather Veazey's church, established in 1890, and where the cemetery remained after the church burned down many years before. Aunt Winnie Henson was the only teacher in that area and taught all grades up to the eighth grades.

On our way back to Memphis, we stopped in the little town of Coldwater at a store that bore our name, Veazey-Clark store. The namesake store was always fascinating to me but reminded me that we'd received our name, Veazey, from the lineage of our slave master.

When we returned to Memphis, George and Gerry invited us to go to the Flamingo Club, where the renowned pianist Phineas Newborn and his guitarist brother, Calvin Newborn, were playing. Afterwards Gerry and George dropped me home and then went back to their home, where Earlene would be staying that night.

Easter Sunday morning, we all prepared to go to the Bethlehem Baptist Church, where I had been licensed to preach. Arriving at the church that morning, Earlene was surprised to know that I would deliver the sermon at the service. Many of my friends were in attendance, along with family members who had come to meet Earlene as much as to hear my sermon. I can vaguely remember what I preached, only that it was very short. Rev. R. W. Taylor, the pastor, commented that I would have more to say as I got older.

After the service, members and friends stayed behind to meet Earlene and wish us the best in our impending nuptials. We returned home, where Mother immediately completed dinner and prepared the table. My father asked me to offer the blessing, which I did, especially remembering that it was Easter, which meant new hope through the resurrection of Jesus Christ. The dinner was not unusual for Sunday—fried chicken, mashed potatoes, green peas, homemade rolls, and lemonade. We all immensely enjoyed our mother's cooking and especially the Easter meal.

Following dinner, Earlene and I were invited to George and Gerry's home to listen to music from George's coveted jazz collection. After visiting for several hours, I asked George to take me back to my parents' home for the evening. I said goodbye to my sister and Earlene and promised Earlene I would call her before going to bed. That evening, I had some of the best sleep I have ever had, especially being at home with my parents.

Earlene's bus was not scheduled to leave until noon, so Mother prepared breakfast for Daddy, Melvin, and me. Her breakfast was a surprise, because she had prepared calf's liver with onions, eggs, rice, and gravy. The breakfast was so good and reminded me of all those days when I was attending State and mother would always prepare my favorites, rice and liver. Although this was breakfast, it was very welcome, and I ate with great appreciation.

Gerry, George and Earlene arrived at our house around ten o'clock to visit with Mother and Daddy before leaving for Nashville. They told Earlene how much they appreciated her visit and looked forward to the June wedding in Nashville. We arrived at the Greyhound bus station at eleven thirty and only had time to get Earlene into the station and in line for boarding the bus. As I walked with her to the bus for boarding, we stopped in the line and kissed and held each other. Earlene was somewhat embarrassed but returned my kiss before boarding the bus.

Leaving, I realized I would not see her again until June when I would be in Nashville for the wedding. As the bus drove away from the station, I could see her sitting in the window near the middle of the bus, unlike when she'd arrived in Memphis sitting in the back of the bus.

Once the bus left, George and Gerry asked me to come to their house to listen to some jazz music and have drinks. I welcomed the opportunity, as I had spent most of my time with Earlene, my parents, and dear brother Melvin. George had one of the largest jazz collections of anyone in Memphis. He played John Coltrane, Miles Davis, Sonny Rollins, Sonny Stitt, Phineas Newborn, and local artists like B. B. King and Bobby "Blue" Bland. Although I played with local bands, my music was mostly rhythm and blues, with occasional jazz. After I'd spent several hours at Gerry's, she brought me back home, and I spent the rest of the evening talking with my parents and entertaining some classmates who lived in the community.

I talked with Earlene for over an hour before we said good night and agreed we would talk before she left for Atlanta at three o'clock the next day. My mother and dad had already retired for the night, but I went in to say goodnight and promise my father that I would speak with Mr. Snyder about his desire to join the migrant ministry in the summer. I kissed my mother goodnight and went to bed.

I woke and decided to spend time visiting other high school classmates on my street who I'd not seen since coming home. I was able to see Mildred Nelson, the first person I met when we moved to Arkansas Street; Clara Bowden, who was too young for a relationship back in the day; and Hettye Peterson, who had moved to Memphis from Mississippi and was a beautiful young lady trying to adjust to the ways of the city. I also dropped by to see William Hawkins and Al Jackson.

Earlene called around one o'clock to say she was leaving to catch her three o'clock flight to Atlanta. We hung up with a lingering feeling of excitement about the prospect of seeing each other soon and me assuring her of my love and anticipation of our wedding in June. My flight was not scheduled to leave until six o'clock, which gave me extra time to spend with my family.

Gerry and George arrived to take me to the airport for my six o'clock flight to Washington, DC. The holidays seemed to have been much longer than normal, considering all that had taken placed. I'd finalized my plans to marry Earlene, we'd set a firm date of June 15 for the wedding (her birthday), and we'd both visited my parents. Although I was tired, I was anxious to return to Howard to complete my middler seminary year and prepare to enter my senior and final year as a seminarian.

On my way back to Washington, I thought about my future work. My first desire was to become a college chaplain at a land grant college like Arkansas AM&N. For one, I found students to need spiritual guidance—having left home and the structured religious life provided by their parents and now having the independence to select the kind of spiritual life they wanted. My college days showed me how important it was to keep a spiritual perspective to guide you through the moral turbulence of college life. I also entertained the possibility of becoming a chaplain in the army, although I had my reservations about the use of military interventions. The army was definitely my third choice, with college and hospital chaplaincy my top two choices.

The abrupt announcement by the captain that we were near Washington, DC, and would arrive within thirty minutes broke my musings about the future and brought me back to reality. I needed to think about the end of this semester and plan for our wedding in June.

After landing and securing my baggage, I hailed a Capitol Cab for the ride to 2617 Georgia Avenue, where I found Cameron busy studying for finals that would take place in four weeks. I unpacked and chatted with Cameron about the Easter holidays. Then we both returned to studying, which Cameron was anxious to get behind him, since he would be graduating in May with the coveted Bachelor of Divinity Degree. I was very happy for Cameron and Gus Roman who had transferred from the School of Divinity at Virginia State University and who I had met when we both first came to Howard now two years ago.

Classes resumed on January 3, as well as all my duties in the dean of the chapel's office and with the Office of Student Life, where I had served for almost two years. Mr. Carey had expressed his satisfaction with my work as a counselor.

My friend Carl Anderson was also getting his PhD at this graduation and would become a member of the administration in an exclusive position.

The time for finals arrived and, with it, a time of mixed emotions. We were leaving the intense period of studying, the results of which would determine whether members of my class would become seniors and Cameron and Gus would graduate on time. These were needless fears. We had studied hard, and Cameron and Gus were confident in their final preparation.

Howard's ground crew had already begun preparing the quadrangle for commencement, which had been held on the quadrangle for decades. Each time I passed it, I would think about next year and what it would mean for me and my parents to see me graduate from seminary.

By mid-May, finals had been held, which was quite a relief for me and the other middlers and, most importantly, for the seniors. They were looking forward to the most important day of their career—receiving the bachelor of divinity degree from historic Howard University. This year, the speaker would be Dr. Benjamin Mays, president of Morehouse College, one of the historic and legendary Negro colleges. He would be introduced by Dr. Mordecai Johnson, one of the most outstanding orators of the twentieth century, who could rival the renowned Fredrick Douglass, a runaway slave born only a hundred miles away in St. Michaels, Maryland.

After finals I began preparations to leave for Memphis and prepare for my marriage to Earlene Marshal. The commencement ceremony would be held on June 1, 1960, although the school officially closed on May 27.

I visited with Keturah Barnes and inquired about Zion and when the church was expecting me to preach during the summer. Keturah asked me to let her know my availability after my wedding and when I had to go to the Eastern Short in Maryland to begin my migrant ministry. I assured her I would be available during August, when I would be closing down my work in Maryland. She also asked me to give her best regards to my wife to be.

I left Keturah's to pack. I would leave on June 1 for Memphis in preparation for my marriage to Earlene.

I flew to Memphis, Tennessee, on June 1, 1960, for the last time as a single man, and did it feel strange. The emotions were both high and low, as I realized that my life would never be the same again. During my flight, I thought about what a fine woman I was marrying and how blessed I was to have found her. I also thought about the coming year, which would be my last at Howard University, and what my life's work would be. I had already selected three areas I would like to pursue—college chaplain, hospital chaplain, and army chaplain. Although I had included the army, I really never could see myself in that role because of my aversion to war. I had also contemplated that Earlene and I could work for the National Council of Churches in some capacity related to the migrant work we would be doing on Maryland's Eastern Shore.

The flight to Memphis was the fastest one I had taken since being in Washington, DC. I thought it was because there was so much to do, and everything was on the fast track, even the plane.

I met Gerry and George at the gate, and we retrieved my bags and then drove to 1610 Arkansas Street for my last time as a single man. As she had so many times before, my dear mother was standing on the porch, hands on hips and apron tied around her waist. After getting out of the car, I ran to meet her before she could come off the porch. I embraced her for what seemed like a long time, even though I am sure it was just that I wanted her to know how much I missed her and loved her. As usual, Mother had prepared an early dinner for us. This time it wasn't usual dish of liver and onions, but my second favorite dish I loved for her to prepare—fried chicken, rice and gravy, mashed potatoes, turnip greens, and corn bread only she could make.

I went into the bedroom to see my father and share with him my plans for my marriage to Earlene. I again congratulated him on his appointment to serve as migrant minister for the camps in New Plats, New York. He expressed appreciation to me and Mr. Snyder for the opportunity to serve these vulnerable people. I told him that my work in the migrant ministry had been the most rewarding opportunity I'd ever had. He asked me about Zion's plans for a new minister. I told him I'd preached at the church just before taking my final examinations.

The congregation had received and wished me well in my work with the migrant ministry. He told me how proud he was of me and prayed that I would continue to allow God to lead me and to follow his direction. I thanked my father for all the years he had cared for all of us and supported each of us in our chosen work.

My father had always been an example of courage and integrity. It was not so much what he taught me by words, but the example he demonstrated when I was only twelve years old and he took on a segregated, discriminating, and prejudiced Memphis post office almost single-handedly to bring justice and fairness. Today, employees enjoy advantages that my father made possible. Although he was given some credit for his work, I am here to say, without fear of contradiction that my father did what no other person would dare to do in a Deep Southern state in 1950.

After sharing my present and future plans with my father, I decided to call Walter Martin, whom I considered a brother since I was very young when I was a member of Central Baptist Church, where Walter and his mother were members. I followed Walter throughout my high school years, which meant learning to play the trombone and singing in the high school glee club and other mutual interests. As a result, I was awarded a four-year scholarship to Arkansas AM&N, the school Walter had also attended. I'd sung in the Arkansas AM&N's famous choir, which traveled throughout the country to raise funds and raise the profile of our college. I had also become a member of Alpha Phi Alpha fraternity because of my admiration for Walter. I say this because, when it came to who I would want for my best man, it had to be Walter Martin. He accepted and said he would select the fraternity brothers to serve as ushers and groomsmen for my wedding. This made me very happy.

The days quickly passed. I talked daily to my wife-to-be and made plans for our very special day and her very special birthday, June 15. I told Earlene I had selected my best man, ushers, and groomsmen. We would arrive on June 14 for a six o'clock rehearsal at the Pleasant Green Missionary Baptist Church, where Earlene had been baptized by her pastor, Rev. Porter, who would officiate our wedding ceremony. I made reservations for our wedding party—including my mother and father;

Melvin; and Gerry and George, who would be bringing my parents and brother—to stay at the Holiday Inn near the church.

June 14 arrived, and we all left for Nashville to celebrate the momentous occasion in my life at one o'clock the following day. Walter Martin and my fraternity brothers drove to Nashville in a station wagon owned by one of my brothers. Walter relieved me of so many things that would have been very problematic, including ensuring that Mother, Daddy, and Melvin were comfortable when they arrived in Nashville. Gerry and George had dinner with them and Melvin in their room.

The church was a beautiful Gothic structure and one of the historic Negro churches in Nashville. The wedding party joined in introductions to the coordinator, who would give us instructions for the wedding ceremony. Earlene arrived shortly and I joined her for a moment with the coordinator for last-minute suggestions.

When Rev. Porter joined us, Earlene introduced me and evidently had told him earlier that I was a seminarian at Howard University entering my final year in the fall. Rev. Porter congratulated me and told me he would like me to preach the next time I was in town.

After our brief conversation, the coordinator called the wedding party together to go over all instructions—especially the one to absolutely be on time. Everything was clear for me, except where I would stand and the best man's part in the ring ceremony.

After leaving the church, Walter suggested we go to a club near Tennessee State University for food and drinks and to celebrate my last night as a single man. Everyone agreed. When we arrived, Walter arranged for us to have the back room, usually reserved for private parties. We all agreed to have several bottles of wine; some beer; and, of course, the best fried chicken in the South. After eating and drinking and my friends teasing me with jokes they had heard, we decided to head back to the hotel to rest. After the wedding, they would be returning to Memphis, and I would be taking my bride to Washington on the Southern Railroad's six o'clock train.

June 15, 1960, I awoke to a beautiful sunrise and joy in my heart. I talked to Walter, and it was decided that we all would have breakfast in the hotel restaurant. This would give us an opportunity to have a leisurely breakfast and go back to our rooms and get dressed for the wedding. I called Earlene and told her what a wonderful day it was and how exciting and blessed we were. We said goodbye until we would see each other in the church.

I was the first to arrive at the restaurant for breakfast because I wanted to remind everyone we had to leave for the church no later than eleven thirty in order to be there by noon.

After we had breakfast and chatted for a while, I excused myself to return to my room and get dressed, as well as repack my clothes for my trip with Earlene to Washington, DC. We had to be at the train station no later than five o'clock. I realized that our wedding and reception would not be over until around four o'clock, and Earlene would have to go back home to redress and finish packing. Everything would have to be precise if we were to keep our schedule.

At noon, I arrived at the church with my wedding party. We were asked to remain in the auxiliary room for the coordinator. The coordinator's assistant asked Walter and me to accompany her to Rev. Porter's office to await his arrival.

In the pastor's study, we rehearsed the ring ceremony, which was very brief. The minister asked the best man, "Do we have a ring for the bride?" And the best man responded that he did and then passed the ring to the pastor. I was fairly familiar with the ceremony, having been the officiant of several weddings. I must confess that it was different from the other side.

My nervousness was noticed by Walter, who asked me, "Haven't you done this before?"

"Yes," I answered, "but never on myself."

He broke into laughter. His laughter even helped my nervousness.

Pastor Porter arrived shortly, with great enthusiasm and a very good sense of humor, asking me whether I was ready for my handcuffs. Although this reduced any tension I had, it also reminded me that this was a serious moment that meant my life would never be the same again.

After Rev. Porter finished robing and going over important parts of the ceremony, an usher knocked at the door and informed us that the coordinator was ready for us to come to the altar for the ceremony. Rev. Porter immediately moved from behind the desk and asked us to follow him. Once we have arrived at the altar, he asked us to face him until it was time for the bride to come down the aisle. He had informed us in the study that, when the bride was ready to come down the aisle, the organist would sound a big chord before beginning to play the traditional "Here Comes the Bride."

The organist began to play the music for the bridesmaids and groomsmen to make their way down the aisle. They were beautiful together, the women in their festive gowns and the men in their tuxedos escorting the ladies on their right arms. Next, the organist played another big chord, signaling that the bride was at the door.

After the double doors opened, Earlene and her father Earl appeared, with her on his right arm. She looked beautiful in her floor-length white gown and veil. They stopped several feet before the altar, and Rev. Porter offered a prayer for the occasion and expounded on the meaning and declaration of marriage.

Finally, he asked, "Who gives this woman to be married to this man?"

Earl answered with a strong and firm voice, "I do!"

The pastor took Earlene's hand and brought her to the altar. He asked the maid of honor to take the flowers from her hand and placed her hand in my hand before continuing the ceremony.

After the vows and prayers, Rev. Porter asked for the ring from Walter. The pastor handed the ring to me and asked me to place the ring on Earlene's hand and repeat this vow: "With this ring, I thee wed, and with all my worldly goods, I thee endow."

Although I had repeated this vow several times when I had married couples, it took on new meaning, since I was the one taking the vow.

After a brief blessing of the ring, the pastor asked the bridesmaid to give Earlene the ring, which she placed on my finger. He repeated the same vow with a blessing.

Finally, Rev. Porter began to explain what had taken place and the sanctity of marriage. He finally closed by saying, "I pronounce them man and wife in the name of the Father, the Son, and the Holy Spirit."

The next words were the ones I had been waiting to hear, "Brothers and sisters, would you please stand and greet Mr. and Mrs. Carlton W. Veazey."

The congregation broke into a standing ovation as the organist played a powerful recessional oratorio.

We stood at the door and greeted family and friends who, after passing through the receiving line, were directed downstairs to the beautifully decorated Mount Pleasant Fellowship Hall where the reception was held. The reception was scheduled from two to four o'clock to allow time for us to prepare, including the last-minute packing by Earlene for our trip to Preston, Maryland, by way of Washington, DC, to begin our work as migrant minister and social worker.

At five o'clock, Mr. Marshall took Earlene and me to the train station to catch the Southern Railroad's train to Washington, DC. Once at the station, Mr. Marshall secured a redcap, told him we were newlyweds, and asked him to make sure we got on the train and secured comfortable seats. He then gave the redcap several dollars, which ensured our comfort. We were taken directly to the track and helped onto the train. The redcap found very good seats at the back of one of the cars, where we could have some privacy. We thanked him, and he in turn wished us a wonderful honeymoon, not knowing that we were going to have a working honeymoon in Preston, Maryland, a place he'd probably never heard of.

Settled in our seats, we gave each other a kiss and watched the other passengers board, some with children, which was interesting, and with shoeboxes, which meant they had food for the trip. I was then reminded to ask Earlene if she'd remembered to pack something to eat for our twelve-hour trip.

She replied, "Of course, knowing how much you like to eat." Her mother had packed fried chicken, bread, and pound cake for our trip. Just thinking about it made me hungry, but I restrained myself, given the long trip we had ahead of us.

The conductor called out, "All aboard," at six o'clock, and the train began to move down the track. For the first few hours we watched the countryside. Given the long summer days, it had not yet gotten dark. I had never taken a train from Nashville to Washington, DC. I always returned from Memphis, alone a different route. This train went the eastern route through Kentucky and, from there, to Washington, DC.

We were scheduled to arrive at Union Station in DC at six o'clock in the morning.

Earlene and I shared the highlights of the day and expressed how blessed we were to have so many wonderful family members and friends. We found ourselves getting sleepy, though it was still early. So I held her as I relaxed and closed my eyes and finally fell asleep. We were both very tired and were only awakened after midnight, with the conductor's announcement that we were crossing the mighty Ohio River as we neared Cincinnati.

After we pulled into the station in Cincinnati, the conductor announced that we would be there for one hour for maintenance and new passenger pickup. Earlene thought it a good time to open our shoebox and eat some of the best fried chicken in the South. We purchased a cold Coca Cola and a Pepsi from the vendor moving through the cars. Our snack was very good and satisfied our hunger.

Once the new passengers boarded the train and we began to move out of Cincinnati, Earlene decided to go back to sleep. I found a need to read some of the books I had brought in preparation for the fall beginning of my senior year of seminary.

I have found out during my many years of study that reading is the best sleeping pill ever made for humankind. After about an hour of reading, I fell into a deep sleep and again awoke to the conductor's announcement—this time that we would arrive in the nation's capital in one hour. The conductor asked us to begin gathering belongings in preparation for our arrival. Earlene was already awake and had our belongings together, with the exception of luggage stored in the overhead compartments.

From Union Station, we rode to the Greyhound bus station to catch the nine o'clock bus to Easton, Maryland. There, we would be met by Rev. Snyder and Ken Horner, who would take us to the Preston home of Mrs. Mary Adams, where we would be staying.

Earlene had never been to Washington, DC, and it was an eye-opener for her, since Union Station was just a few blocks from and gave us a view of the US Capitol Building. On our way to the bus station in downtown Washington and only a few blocks from the White House, I pointed out the few government buildings that were on the route.

Although the White House was not on our route, I asked the taxi driver to drive by it since we had time. Earlene was elated to see the home of President Dwight D. Eisenhower in the last year of his presidency. The country was excited about the possibility of a young senator, John F. Kennedy, running against Vice President Richard M. Nixon. I promised Earlene that, when we returned to Washington, DC, in the fall, I would take her on a personal tour of Washington, including all of the monuments and the many museums of the Smithsonian Institution.

We arrived at Union Station and purchased our tickets for the bus to Easton, Maryland. We were then able to relax and talk about our work this summer and our future home in Washington, DC, when I'd completed my final year in seminary. When we were called to board the bus, I suggested we try to sit near the front. On our way to the Eastern Shore, I explained to Earlene that the state of Maryland was divided by the Chesapeake Bay, with Baltimore, the largest city, on the Western Shore and Easton on the Eastern Shore, along with most of the popular beaches. When we reached the Chesapeake Bay Bridge, she was taken aback by its length extending across the bay. I explained that it was a single lane each way, but there were plans to build another bay bridge that would allow more traffic each way.

The trip to Easton was only an hour and a half, and it seemed even shorter, which I attributed to having Earlene with me and my anxiousness to introduce her to Rev. Snyder, Kenneth Horner, and Mrs. Adams.

We arrived in Preston at eleven thirty in the evening and were met by our welcoming party. Rev Snyder was first to say hello to Earlene and welcome her to Maryland, even though he had previously hired her for work in Maryland. Mr. Horner also welcomed her, along with several members of the Preston migrant ministry committee.

After retrieving our luggage, we rode with Rev. Snyder, and the other committee members rode with Kenneth Horner. The drive was rather short, since Preston was only ten miles from Easton.

As we traveled to Mrs. Adams home, I pointed out Mr. Dewey's home. I had told Earlene about Greta Townsend, whom I considered a younger sister. Mrs. Adams's home was a stately colonial a mile from downtown Preston. Mrs. Adams was at the front door to welcome us as we drove onto the driveway. I was first to exit the car and reached back to help Earlene. I introduced Earlene, and Mrs. Adams immediately embraced and congratulated her on our marriage and wished us many years of happiness. Rev. Snyder and Kenneth Horner thanked Mrs. Adams for allowing us to stay with her during the summer.

When they'd left, Mrs. Adams again welcomed us and showed us around the house and to our room and private bath. Earlene was overwhelmed by her hospitality and her beautiful home. It had been a long night and day reaching Maryland, so we decided to retire early. After a refreshing bath, sleep came very easily for both of us, especially since it was a far change from the hard train seats and noise of the engines.

The following morning, I awoke around six o'clock and decided to go outside to reacquaint myself with the surroundings where I had spent so many days the previous summer. From our house, I could see Mr. Dewey's house and also that of his brother Mnason, where had I spent many evenings with his lovely wife and children, especially Greta who we called "Butch."

The air was so clean and clear it gave you the joy of being alive. After walking around the beautiful property, I decided to see if Earlene had woken up and found her sitting up in the bed reading one of her books. She smiled, and we exchanged a good morning kiss.

Mrs. Adams had prepared a wonderful breakfast, for which we thanked her. We waited for Kenneth Horner to pick us up and take us to town to pick up the station wagon the migrant committee had arranged for our use while we were in Preston.

Once we'd completed the necessary paperwork at the local car dealership, I thanked Kenneth Horner and told him I would call him later. Everything began to come back to me as we drove around the small town of Preston. I pointed to the local bank; the First United Methodist Church of Preston; the post office; and, of course, the only supermarket in town, where she would do our grocery shopping, since we had kitchen privileges.

After I'd shown her the various campsites and the day care center near Hurlock where she would be working, we returned to our home for the summer and found that Mrs. Adams had left a beautiful card and gift in honor of our marriage on our bed. It was a handsome sum of money, which we could use. After we'd thanked her profusely, she explained that the migrant committee had assumed the rent payments so that we had complete use of the house without any extra payments. She also said that the kitchen was available for us anytime during the day or night, as she would usually have her lunch and dinner before our return in the evening.

Earlene was tired from the long train ride from Nashville and wanted to go to bed early. Realizing that we had not had any private time together since we were married, we both agreed to go to bed for the night and celebrate our marriage by making love. During our time touring the sites where I would be working, I'd stopped and bought a bottle of Mumm champagne for our special night. Earlene came out of the shower and dressing room wearing a beautiful purple negligee, with a fragrance that excited my desire. I immediately went into the bathroom to shower and prepare for our special night. When I came out, the lights were out, with beautiful candles setting the mood for an exciting night. The mood was further set by tuning the radio to a station from Washington playing a music program called "Music Till Dawn." After several glasses of champagne, we turned to each other's arms and gave in to our sexual desires, pent up since our wedding, eventually falling asleep in each other's arms.

I awakened to the smell of coffee from Mrs. Adams's kitchen and decided to go and say good morning to her. In the kitchen, I found the table set for the two of us and Mrs. Adams saying, "I want to be the first to honor your marriage with this honeymoon breakfast."

I thanked her for her warm thoughts and hospitality. After a few minutes, she asked me to go and bring my wife to breakfast. The word *wife* lingered as I went to bring Earlene to breakfast.

She was awake and listening to music from WMAL in Washington, DC, and said, "How did you find this beautiful music?"

I told her it was the station I listened to every night while studying, and she would hear much more after we got to Washington, DC.

We arrived downstairs to see that Mrs. Adams had adorned the breakfast table with beautiful flowers from her garden. We sat down with Mrs. Adams, and she asked if we would allow her to say the blessing for the morning. We agreed that it would be an honor to have her bless our marriage on this first day after our consummation. The breakfast was good and tasty, with fresh eggs and sausage from local farmers. Mrs. Adams also made real grits, which I used to eat in Memphis.

After breakfast, I left Earlene and Mrs. Adams to talk while I prepared to begin my first day of work by visiting the various camps and crew leaders who had brought migrant workers from Hollywood, Florida, stopping at various places, including Kiptopeke and Cape Charles in Virginia. Will Parker, the crew leader with whom I had worked the previous year, was the first one I met at the Hurlock, Maryland, camp. My relationship with him had been very strained, since I'd challenged him on how he could treat the migrants in such a dehumanizing manner. His response had that he was trying to make a living for his family. The crew leaders lived very well in Hollywood, Florida, and when they went on the migrant tour of the East Coast.

The migrants' journey began by being loaded into an open bed truck with few seats and a tarpaulin covering, for a ride of over a thousand miles during their summer of work. The inhumane conditions were endured as part of the need for employment and the risk one must take for his family. The crew leader's family lived in luxury compared to the migrants and road in a beautiful Cadillac pulling a trailer that had sleeping accommodations, along with a kitchen and a bathroom. The crew leader always invoked his right to provide for his family. And that was just the beginning of the mistreatment and disgusting conditions the migrants endured.

I found the same conditions for the migrants at the Hurlock camp that I'd witnessed the year before even with the promise of better living conditions. First, they still lived in cabins that were converted chicken houses, fitted with several cots with minimal bedding and a wood-burning stove to cook on. Each unit would house five persons, including children. The toilet was an outhouse in the center of the camp, with one water spigot for drinking and bathing. I'd raised these issues last year with the landowner and the crew leaders, who'd promised to improve the conditions.

I had thought that, after the documentary *They Follow the Sun*, by Edward R. Murrow and the favorable response to it, we would have been able to get better conditions from landowners and the crew leaders, who had the ability to negotiate better contracts. This was not to be, which caused me to make the decision not only to try to serve the migrants the best I could but also to take this issue to a new level with the media in Baltimore and DC.

I visited several camps and saw the many people I had met the year before, as well as new migrants.

I then decided to return to the house and take Earlene to meet the couple working at the day care center for the migrant children. Mrs. Adams and Earlene were in a very interesting conversation about Mrs. Adams's husband, who had been dead for several years after many years of marriage. She also spoke very well of Mr. Dewey Townsend, who I had not yet introduced to my wife.

Just before we left to visit the day care center to meet Alvin and Mildred Terry, I decided to take her next door to meet Mr. Dewey. My previous host was a very quiet and self-absorbed man. He spoke very few words, but when he did, they were meaningful and many times profound.

When we arrived next door, Mr. Dewey was sitting on the porch, which we had done together many days and nights. Mr. Dewey stood up and received my wife with unusual affection, which made me very happy, as he was like a very special uncle to me. After inquiring what we would be doing this summer, he wished us well and promised to do what he could to help the migrant workers.

At the day care center at the Hurlock site, Alvin and Mildred Terry met us. They congratulated us on our marriage and welcomed Earlene to the day care center. Alvin was director, and Earlene and Mildred would be assistants who would help care for the children. Earlene received orientation about the day care center operations and told the Terrys about the day care center in Cape Charles, Virginia. They were confident that Earlene would be a help to them with caring for over fifty children daily.

When we left the center, we decided we would have to leave home around seven o'clock to be there before eight o'clock when the children arrived. Alvin was a very efficient director, having worked in this capacity for several years. During the year, he was a teacher in the Portsmouth, Virginia, school system.

When we returned to Mrs. Adams's home, she had prepared a dinner of fried chicken, rice, and greens from her garden. This was a wonderful dinner, and we thanked Mrs. Adams and told her that, beginning the next day, we would prepare our meals if she had no objections. Earlene had earlier stopped by the only supermarket in Preston and bought groceries for the week.

After watching television for several hours, we decided to go to bed and get an early start at seven o'clock, in order to get to the day care center in time. Then I would make my rounds to the migrant camps, including those in St. Michaels and Cambridge. Earlene went to sleep before me, because I wanted to listen to some jazz music first. I had only slept a few hours when I was woken up by Earlene at six o'clock in the morning. I wasn't sleepy or tired, just anxious to get to work.

Since working last summer I had a better understanding of the work and the needs of the migrant workers. I realized that many of the efforts of the previous summer had been accomplished, such as better housing conditions, better pay to the migrants and a greater sensitivity by the religious community of Preston, Maryland. These accomplishments enabled me to have a more effective migrant ministry during this second year. Earlene continued to work with Alvin Terry and his wife at the daycare center. Also, the public health officer with whom I had worked the previous summer was happy that I returned and helped to develop a prenatal program for expectant mothers. The migrant men were also involved in the health program especially since the spike in STDs in the camps during the previous summer. These developments were reported to my supervisor, Rev. Snyder who was greatly impressed with our work.

The months passed quickly and before we realized it was August and we prepared to close down our program. During our last week in August, Mrs. Adams accepted a call from the producer of a television show on WBAL that centered on issues affecting the Eastern Shore in Baltimore, particularly those related to migrant workers. I got in touch with the producer. We discussed the framework for the interview he'd requested, and I accepted that the questions the producer raised were beneficial for the public to understand the plight of the migrants.

I immediately went to inform Earlene that I would have to take her to work early in order to drive to a six o'clock interview I had in Baltimore about the migrant workers. After dressing, we headed to the day care center, where I dropped her off and arranged for her to be dropped off at Mrs. Adams's after work. I would not return from Baltimore in time to pick her up.

Alvin was excited about the television coverage since he knew firsthand the difficulty of the migrant mothers who had to drop their children off at the day care center even if they were sick and needed medical attention. I made note to include his comments during the interview.

When I returned home, I called Rev. Snyder to tell him about the media opportunity to highlight the plight of migrant workers on the Eastern Shore of Maryland. Even though I was sleepy and tired, I stayed up and made notes and calls to the US Public Health Service, who served as my ally in serving the health needs of the women who needed prenatal care. The service was also instrumental in providing the men with examinations for sexually transmitted diseases and prophylactics to prevent unwanted pregnancies.

I decided to rest and sleep for a few hours and asked Mrs. Adams to make sure I was awake by four o'clock to go to Baltimore. I fell asleep after reading over my copious notes and woke when I heard Mrs. Adams gently knocking on the door and calling my name. I answered, assuring her I was awake. It was almost four o'clock, and I decided to take a shower and prepare to leave for Baltimore and WBAL's station.

Mrs. Adams wished me well on my interview and informed me that she had called members of her church to have them watch the interview, as well as other people. That made me nervous but excited about the prospect of this interview getting the coverage needed for change.

I had an exciting drive to Baltimore just thinking how fortunate I was to have this opportunity to highlight migrant worker needs and what could be done to address them. The more I thought about the issues over which I had prayed for two years since I first came to the Eastern Shore, the more I recognized how God had intervened to get the necessary information to the public. I was sure that would raise the social consciousness of the people in the Maryland and the Washington, DC, area.

I arrived at the WBAL television station and was met by a very courteous greeter who asked if I was Rev. Veazey. I identified myself and was escorted to the green room, which was set aside for guests who appeared on various programs. Shortly, an aide came to prepare me for television, which meant checking my dress to make sure my tie was straight and reminding me to keep my jacket buttoned. The most curious thing in the preparation was the application of powder, which they claimed would reduce the glare from the lights. Although I was in a state of shock, I kind of felt like a movie star. After that brief moment of personal grandeur, I quickly remembered the serious and grave issues I had come to discuss and, hopefully, enlist the support of many Marylanders and Washingtonians.

Finally, I was called to the set and introduced by the host as a seminarian at the Howard University School of Religion, the oldest school in the university. He also described my job as a migrant minister with the National Council of Churches. These two introductions made me a proud representative of both. After the introduction, the host graciously said that I had impacted migrant issues on the Eastern Shore and was on the verge of creating the changes migrants had asked for during their many years working on the Eastern Shore of Maryland. He then turned the microphone over to me to describe the issues of the migrants and how they could be remedied. This was more than a blessing, since I could touch on the issues I knew were important and would not involve the host as the person to pose the questions.

I immediately began by reminding the viewing audience that Edward R. Morrow, the renowned commentator of Columbia Broadcasting System (CBS) had produced a documentary titled *They Follow the Sun*. Murrow's work traced the necessary travels of migrants from Hollywood, Florida, to Upstate New York, showing how these migrant workers survived by harvesting crops for our subsistence at the expense of their own and their children's health. Murrow also talked about how crew leaders and landowners profited from the exploitation of migrant workers. His coverage of their plight had caused me to double my determination to do something about this, by bringing to the attention of the people of Maryland and the nation what was taking place in our country—which was a twentieth-century form of slavery.

The anchor, after my commentary of approximately ten minutes without interruption, opened the phone lines for comments and questions from the viewing audience. I expected it to be a diatribe on those of us who had tried to help those who Jesus called "the least among us." To my surprise, the calls were overwhelmingly supportive. Many callers wanted to contribute to support the ministry. I gave them the address of the National Council of Churches in New York where they could send contributions and comments.

The highlight of the night was a personal invitation to meet with Mrs. Dulany, wife of the owner of Dulany Foods, a company that was located in Princess Anne, Maryland and that distributed food on the Eastern Shore and beyond. I was so excited to get this invitation. This was the big break I had hoped for, as it had come from someone from the Eastern Shore and in the food distribution system—someone who would, thus, have considerable influence on the landowners and crew leaders who brought the migrants thousands of miles under deplorable conditions.

When I returned to Preston that evening, Earlene and Mrs. Adams were in the living room with the television still on the station where I had appeared. They were excited and proud of the response from the television audience after I'd answered questions about how I had felt about the interview. I decided to go to bed in preparation for my work the next day, which meant closing down the camps and ministry as the migrants prepared to move on to New Jersey and, later, to Upstate New York. This would include thanking the camp assistants who had helped make my ministry successful.

I also visited Mr. Horner, my strong supporter and a member of the Preston committee. I asked him to convey my appreciation to the committee when they met in August.

Earlene and I planned to leave Preston on August 15 for our new home at Howard University in Washington, DC. Since our departure date was only a few days off, we decided to use the weekend to call on some of the people who'd helped make our ministry so successful.

After stopping to thank Mr. Dewey and his new wife, Dorothy, for their contributions to our work, we crossed the road to thank Mnason Townsend and his wife and children for their support.

We then decided to visit Mrs. Dulany in Princess Anne, about an hour's drive, to thank her for her television support and generous donation. I also wanted to meet her personally and tell her how she had encouraged me in my ministry and that I would stay in touch with her when I returned to DC and Howard University.

The morning of August 15 was beautiful as we prepared to leave for DC. Mrs. Adams had breakfast prepared when we came down at ten o'clock. The table was garnished with flowers from her garden and laden with a wonderful breakfast of fresh fruits, cranberry juice, eggs and sausage, grits, biscuits, and coffee. I had never seen a breakfast like this, even from my mother. At ten thirty, Mr. Horner came to drive us to the bus station in the station wagon before returning it to the local dealer. After we had said our goodbyes to Mrs. Adams, a wonderful lady, we invited her to visit us in DC. She said she would visit and also pray for our success in our marriage and in our ministry.

The ride to Easton was nostalgic for me. I remembered the first time I had come to Preston and how quiet and peaceful it was, which made me wonder how I would ever survive in a place so quiet and placid. My future was uncertain, but I knew that I would always remember the days I'd spent on the Eastern Shore and the wonderful people I'd met and friendships I'd made during my two summers there.

As we drove up to the Greyhound station, I saw Rev. Snyder waiting near the entrance with envelopes in hand, which I hoped to be our last paychecks for the summer. As Earlene exited the car, Rev. Snyder embraced her and congratulated her on our work together with the migrants and their families. I greeted him and asked about his family, whom I had met on other occasions. Kenneth Horner also greeted Rev. Snyder and thanked him for sending us to Preston for the summer. Mr. Horner assisted with our bags as we went to our bus, which was already boarding.

After saying goodbye to everyone, Earlene and I boarded the bus and took the closest seats to the front of the bus, which was my habit.

The bus pulled out of Easton as one o'clock sharp, headed for the nation's capital and our home for at least the next year. Our ride back was exciting. I pointed out places of interest near the Chesapeake Bay, where Mr. Dewey had taken me during my first summer there, such as the many crab and oyster houses, which were the main industry of the Eastern Shore.

The ride to DC was short, and we were soon pulling into the gateway of the capital, New York Avenue, that would bring us to the bus station on New York Avenue downtown. Arriving at the bus station, Earlene and I quickly went to retrieve our bags, which were already being pulled from the outside baggage compartment. Fortunately our bags were among the first brought out by the attendants, which helped us to be first to get a Capitol Cab and head to Howard University and our home on Georgia Avenue.

Our ride to Howard and our new home at 2617 Georgia Avenue was very exciting to Earlene. I pointed out certain places, including one of the oldest churches in Washington, Shiloh Baptist Church. There was the Phyllis Wheatley YWCA, named after the first published African American female poet, who was born in West Africa, sold into slavery at the age of eight, and transported to North America and died in Boston, Massachusetts. I also pointed out the famous Howard Theatre, where all the famous entertainers performed, including Duke Ellington, a native Washingtonian born only a few blocks away. Louis Armstrong and Arthur Prysock were also regulars at the Howard, as were Lionel Hampton and famous singers such as Sarah Vaughn, Etta James, and other popular singers of the time. Finally, we passed the Freedman's Hospital, one of the oldest hospitals, where most Negro doctors got their training.

We finally arrived at the place where I had spent the past two years, which was at the corner. The cab driver helped us with our baggage as we climbed the steps to the apartment building. We had been informed that our keys would be left with Dr. and Mrs. Evans Crawford, the first people I had met when I'd come to Washington.

After I'd knocked on the door, Mrs. Crawford greeted us with a beautiful smile to welcome us to Howard and our new home. She congratulated us on our recent wedding and explained that Dean

Crawford was not home but was looking forward to seeing us. She gave us the keys to the apartment down the hall from them. Mrs. Crawford was kind enough to invite us to dinner when we had finished our shopping for things needed for the apartment.

After returning from shopping, we called Mrs. Crawford to let her know we were back and ask what time were we expected. She informed us that the dean had returned, and we could come any time after six o'clock. It was only four o'clock, so we had time to rest and prepare for dinner. After putting away the things we had bought for the apartment, we relaxed. Then we prepared to go to dinner at the Crawford's

Dean Crawford greeted Earlene with a warm smile and embrace, and invited us into their beautiful apartment. Mrs. Crawford was busy in the kitchen finishing dinner, and Earlene asked if she could help with the preparation. Mrs. Crawford declined and asked us to make ourselves comfortable with Dean Crawford until dinner would be served. The dean was in constant conversation with Earlene, asking about Spelman and Atlanta.

Shortly thereafter, Mrs. Crawford announced that dinner was ready and invited us to please come to the dining room table. The table was exquisitely set, with beautiful china and flowers. The dean asked me to give the blessing. Although I had done this many times in the past, somehow this was different; I was with my dean and homiletics professor, which made me feel I was going to be graded.

After my very short blessing, the food was passed around. We enjoyed roast beef, potatoes, and green beans, with rolls and butter. I must admit that this was a very tasty dinner, which I was thankful for and more than eager eat. We had not eaten dinner since we'd eaten at Mrs. Adams's. But Earlene was very modest in her servings, where I was more than generous in mine.

At dinner we talked about our experiences in Maryland serving as migrant ministers. Dr. Crawford told us that they had seen an article in the *Washington Post* about the conditions that existed and how I had mobilized the community to change them. I explained that the community was very receptive to my appeal. And I hoped that, next year, the conditions would be very much improved.

After dinner, Dean Crawford asked me if I had heard from Ms. Keturah Barnes at Zion and how things were progressing in the church's search for a pastor. I told him I'd heard from Ms. Keturah and was scheduled to preach on Sunday, which was the fourth Sunday and Communion service. He encouraged me and told me that my position in his office would start the first Sunday in September. I thanked him for the opportunity and told him I would be prepared to assist him.

Earlene and Betty Crawford had laid the groundwork for a good relationship, especially when Mrs. Crawford told her that she and the dean had celebrated their honeymoon during their migrant ministry assignment. It was very heartening to Earlene to know that someone else had had that experience beside us. We thanked Dean Crawford and his wife profusely and said good night.

Arriving at our apartment only a few feet from the Crawfords, we immediately prepared for bed. We had been going since early morning to get to Washington and unpack our luggage. We also had a notice that we had other packages from UPS; these were wedding presents we were unable to bring to Maryland, and Earlene's mother had waited for our return to send them to Washington.

After a good night's sleep, awakening in our own place and our own bed was a special treat. Even though it was a very sparsely furnished apartment, we were grateful for having a place we could call home. We spent time going to various stores to get other items we needed to set up housekeeping.

I also wanted Earlene to meet Keturah, since I had talked so much about her. After breakfast, we walked from our apartment to Keturah's home only four or five blocks away. When we arrived there around noon, she met us at the door with the biggest smile and immediately embraced Earlene and me at the same time.

I was glad that we'd arrived around lunchtime, as Keturah always had food, either left over from breakfast or been prepared for lunch. I had never been to Keturah's home when she did not have food. She and Earlene were compatible in many ways, especially since both were elementary school teachers. Keturah told me that, during the summer, many Zion members who were applying for the pastorate had preached, but none had really appealed to the congregation. She reminded me that I was supposed to preach on the fourth Sunday. I told her I was prepared and would be happy when the church finally called a pastor so the congregation could come together to fulfill Rev. Edwards's dream of building the new church on Blagden Avenue. She agreed, saying there were deep divisions developing in the church, which would be detrimental if the wrong minister was called.

Earlene and I said goodbye to Keturah and thanked her for the hospitality and guidance she had given me during my seminary days. She reminded me again that I was scheduled to preach on Communion Sunday. I thanked her again and assured her I would be prepared to lead the service.

Chapter 6

PASTORATE AND POLITICS

I will always remember September 25 because it was the day when I introduced Earlene to Zion Baptist Church, where I had interned for over a year. The people were so kind and supportive and wished us well in our future years. Although I was somewhat nervous, I was reassured by the encouraging words of members, who welcomed me back and welcomed Earlene as well. I preached a sermon on the mission of the church, invoking Matthew when he recorded the words of Jesus, "Inasmuch as ye have done it to the least of these, my brethren, ye have done it unto me." These words had motivated me in all the work that I had done during my migrant ministry. I challenged Zion to be a church where we made a difference in the lives of the poor and "the least of these." I was very emotional about this sermon, given that I had just left a community where inequity existed in the midst of Christians who professed their love for their Lord and Savior Jesus Christ.

After the service, members had arranged an impromptu reception in honor of our recent marriage. Earlene was deeply touched by this and thanked them profusely for their kindness.

We returned home after the church service, happy that we had been received in such a welcoming way. We also met another couple, Rev. Rafe Taylor and his wife, Bennie, and their children. They were wonderful people and would become very good friends and neighbors.

The next day I prepared for registration and for my assignments with Dean Crawford and Dean Carey and my work with them during the semester.

I received a call from trustee George W. Peterson asking if he could come by and talk with me and my wife. Of course I said yes, and we agreed upon three o'clock in the afternoon. He promised that he would not be very long and thanked us for seeing him.

During my time at Zion, I'd had very little contact with Mr. Peterson, except when he would give me my check on the fourth Sunday each month. After I had hung up, Earlene and I wondered why he wanted to talk to us. Could it be that I would no longer be an intern there? Was there some other issue?

We decided to leave this issue alone and let the Lord work out whatever future plans he had for us.

Needless to say, I slept very little during the night, thinking about the meeting with Mr. Peterson the next day. I finally drifted off to sleep and slept until the alarm went off, awakening me at eight o'clock to go to the administration building to register for my final semester as a seminarian.

The day went well. My visit to the administration building officially started off my last year at the School of Religion at Howard University. I also went to the offices of Dean Carey and Dean Crawford to get my semester assignments. After purchasing my books, I went home to be with Earlene and help her with any chores she needed help with.

We visited our neighbor Rev. Taylor and family.

Around three o'clock, I became a little anxious about the meeting with Mr. Peterson, chairman of the board of trustees at Zion Baptist Church. At exactly five minutes after three, Mr. Peterson knocked. Earlene answered the door, graciously invited him to have a seat, and offered him some refreshment, which he declined. I entered the room from the bedroom, greeted him, and thanked him for coming to see us. Although I had seen him many times before, I had not realized how tall he was. I was six feet, and he towered over me, which made him at least six foot ten.

Mr. Peterson was a lawyer for the postmaster general, a very high and prestigious position. He had come to see us regarding a church matter. He was a man of few words, but those he spoke were very direct. He said that some members of the church had observed that I had not applied for the pastorate of Zion Baptist Church, which concerned them very much.

I responded that I did not feel prepared to take on such an awesome responsibility, since I had not completed my theological education. He retorted that the young people of the church had purposely asked that my name be placed in nomination for the pastorate and asked him to convey this message. He asked pointedly whether I would submit my name for the pastorate.

After a few minutes of meditation and reflection I accepted the request and filled out the application, which Mr. Peterson just happened to have with him. He thanked me profusely and told me he looked forward to seeing me on December 9, 1960, at eight o'clock at the Phyllis Wheatley YWCA, where the church meeting would be held for the election of the next pastor of Zion Baptist Church.

We thanked him for coming and asked if he would join us in a word of prayer before he left. I asked God's blessings on Mr. Peterson in these difficult times in the life of our church and to give him strength and courage to lead this church to the Promised Land that Rev. Dr. A. Joseph Edwards had envisioned before his transition.

December 9, 1960, at eight o'clock in the evening will always be a pivotal moment for me in my pilgrimage in clay feet. More than four hundred members were present to vote on who would be Zion's next pastor. I must admit I was very nervous and hoping that this would be over soon.

The house count of members present and eligible to vote came to 475. After the candidates had been introduced, along with their qualifications, the chair began the voting. Since this was a closed ballot voting, the final count was delayed. After all ballots had been tabulated, the final vote count was 360 votes for me; the remainder was scattered among the other candidates.

The moderator, Deacon Richard Chapman, announced that the new pastor of Zion Baptist Church was Reverend Carlton Wadsworth Veazey. Someone moved that the vote be made by acclamation.

Earlene held my hand tightly, which communicated her feelings of pride and thanksgiving.

The next hour was spent accepting congratulations and support for our ministry. Although I was very happy and proud of the confidence they had shown in me, I also recognized the great responsibility I had to fulfill the dream of Rev. Edwards to complete the building of the edifice he'd planned on at 4850 Blagden Avenue NW.

When we arrived home, Earlene and I called my father and mother to give them the good news about the church vote. As the phone rang, I was trying to decide how I would tell them about the historical night at the church meeting. I decided to give the phone to Earlene and let her break the good news. As Earlene told them, I could see she was emotional, and evidently my parents were too.

When she handed me the phone, Daddy simply said, "God bless you, son."

And mother simply said, "Son, we love you very much, and we are very proud of you."

These words coming from my parents still ring in my ears and resonate in my spirit after more than sixty years. The rest of the evening was spent taking calls from members, friends, and relatives from across the country wishing us the best in or new ministry.

Friday, September 2, changed so many things overnight. For starters, I would need to meet with Dean Crawford and Dean Carey to resign, and my duties with both with need to transition to someone else beginning on Monday, December 5, when classes would begin. Along with trying to rearrange my schedule, I needed to meet with the trustee board on Sunday following the morning service.

My final call of the night was to Dean Crawford who had served as my mentor since we met on that August day in 1958 when I first arrived in Washington to begin my theological education. I spoke with Dean and Mrs. Crawford and thanked them for their support during my stay in Washington. They congratulated me and pledged their support in any way they could be helpful.

Sleep came easy that night because everything had gone so well, and I was at peace with God and myself. The following morning, I awakened to WMAL's "Music Till Dawn." I'd been listening to them program for over two years now. It had always been a welcome companion as I read and studied for assignments and examinations.

their

Since I had woken up so early, I decided to work on my sermon for Sunday. It had to be one of reassurance to the members and a vision for the future, realizing we had lost our revered leader who had planned the new edifice and move from Southwest to one of the most prestigious communities in DC. My sermon had to inspire the church to finish the work and complete the vision of our beloved pastor.

As I prayed for guidance and direction in my preparation, I was led to the beautiful words of the Psalm, when David asked, "What shall I render unto the Lord for all his benefits toward me?" This scripture challenged all of us to examine our lives and realize how blessed we were and our responsibility to give back to the Lord in His service for what He has done for us. The notion germinated throughout the day as I continued to put together the ideas for my first sermon as pastor of Zion Baptist Church. This sermon was so important. I had to let the congregation know something about my commitment to the work that Rev. Edwards had left for me to complete.

Earlene awakened, and the first thing she said to me was, "Carl, can you believe what happened last night?"

My response was, "Absolutely," which brought laughter.

Earlene wanted to go shopping for a special dress for her first Sunday as the wife of the new pastor. I decided to stay home and work on my sermon and visit Keturah, who I had selected as my key adviser. After dressing and eating breakfast, I called Keturah and asked if I could come by around lunch for a short visit.

Keturah responded, "You mean can you come and eat?"

I responded with uncontrollable laughter.

Earlene left around ten o'clock to go to Hecht's department store to shop, while I made notes of things I wanted to discuss with Keturah regarding how I should proceed as pastor.

I arrived at Keturah's at twelve thirty. I had spent many hours at her place over the last two years. She answered the door, and I greeted her with the strongest hug I could give her. She, more than anyone else, was responsible for me being and remaining at Zion.

My first question was, "What are we having for lunch?"

She replied, "Chicken noodle soup."

It smelled delicious. She was the best cook after my mother, which is saying a lot, considering I had eaten at many members' homes and the homes of those wanting me to meet their daughters.

I'm ate two bowls of the most delicious chicken noodle soup, which, unlike some chicken soup, did contain some very large portions of chicken. The soup, paired with biscuits Keturah had prepared for breakfast made for a very sumptuous lunch.

After she had cleared the table and sat down with me, I first thanked her profusely for all she had done to advance my ministry and for making it possible for me to have the opportunity to pastor one of the oldest and most prominent churches in the District of Columbia. Keturah and I always had a great rapport and were able to communicate extremely well with each other. After I had confessed my feelings of inadequacy to her, she reminded me that it was neither me nor her who had brought us to this place, but God. Those words were so forceful and penetrating to my spirit that I could only respond with, "Thank you."

Sunday would be my first sermon as pastor, and I asked her what she thought I should preach about. Her only response was that the people needed encouragement and spiritual motivation. While she was speaking these words, the spirit led me to Psalm, which said, "Except the Lord build the house, they labor in vain that build it."

Sunday, September 4, 1960, was a pivotal day in my ministry and my life. When I awoke, I thought the last thirty-six hours had been a dream but a good dream. Earlene was already up and fixing breakfast. Together, we prepared to meet the people at Zion as pastor and wife.

On our way to church, we talked about how our meeting each other and working in the migrant ministry had brought us to a place where we would be challenged to fulfill the new task that the Lord had given us.

Zion had worshipped at the Phyllis Wheatley YWCA at 901 Rhode Island Avenue NW, for the past seven years. When we entered, the ushers asked me to come with them, and the deaconesses asked Earlene to join them during the service. I was taken to the deacon's room, where they had gathered to pray before the service. When I entered, I was met with applause and words of encouragement as the deacons welcomed a new pastor who they had only known for two years.

Deacon Richard Chapman, the revered chair of the deacon board, asked me to lead the prayer in preparation for the morning worship service. I asked the chairman if he would allow me to call on the oldest serving minister of our church, the beloved Rev. Thomas C. Garnet, to offer prayer as we entered the worship hall for our inaugural service under the leadership of a new pastor. Deacon Chapman was kind enough to accept my request, and Rev. Garnet offered a most powerful prayer, asking God to join pastor and people together.

The auditorium of the YWCA was filled to capacity with members, many who had left the church when the old church was demolished by the city under eminent domain. Also, many friends of Zion were there to see this twenty-three-year-old minister called to lead one of the oldest and most prominent churches in Washington, DC. I entered the pulpit and took the pastor's chair, one of the oldest pieces of furniture that was brought from the old church before its demolition. When I stood behind the historic pulpit, which had been in the church for many years, I could feel the spirit of Rev. Edwards and the other five pastors who had preceded me back to 1864.

After thanking God for the opportunity to serve his people and my parents who had brought me up in the nurture and admonition of the Lord, and my wife who had become my partner in ministry going back to the migrant ministry we had shared during the past summer, I took my biblical text for my message from Psalm 127:1. It read, "Except the Lord build the house, they labor in vain that build it."

My theme for the message was "The Church is God's House." The message was meant to remind people that the church was God's house and we are called to serve Him through this house of worship. The message also brought the church to understand that the building and edifice in Southwest, which was illegally taken away from them and their slave and freedmen ancestors, would be redeemed by building another edifice to the glory of God. The message motivated and comforted many in the church, who wondered whether we would ever become the Zion Baptist Church of the past. This rhetorical question was answered through my message that God was planning an even greater Zion, both as an edifice and a spiritual force in Washington, DC.

I reminded the congregation that God had given my beloved predecessor the vision of building a new edifice, which he had advanced against difficult opposition. Rev. Edwards would always be the center of all my efforts in building the new church, since he had labored mightily for its erection and completion. Finally, I reminded the church that the psalmist had said that, except the Lord builds the house, we labor in vain who build it. This related not only to the physical edifice but also to the spiritual church.

My first sermon was well received, and the encouragement from members and friends was outstanding and overwhelming. Receiving these accolades was very encouraging.

However, I realized I had a huge task before me—to complete the legacy of Dr. Edwards and bring together a church that had been scattered because of eminent domain. The building of the edifice was at a standstill; Perpetual Building and Loan had not granted the $150,000 loan because the matching amount had not been raised.

After the service, I met with the board of trustees for the first time. I became reacquainted with Mr. Peterson. As an attorney, he had worked with Rev. Edwards to help bring the edifice project to its present state.

Our meeting was to formalize the agreement between the pastor and the church as it related to compensation and benefits. Ever since Mr. Peterson had come to our apartment that August night, I had developed enormous respect for him and his wife, who had been a strong supporter of my ministry and pastorate.

Dr. Peterson was prominent in her own right. She had risen through the ranks, from serving as principal of Randall Junior High School to becoming the special assistant to the superintendent of District of Columbia Public Schools (DCPS), Dr. Carl Hansen—the highest position any Negro had attained in the public school system.

These two, along with Keturah Barnes, would prove to be the most important people in my young pastorate. In addition, Deacon Morris Robinson, who befriended Earlene and me, would become one of my closest friends and supporters.

At the meeting with the trustees, I was offered $36,000 a year in salary with benefits from the American Baptist Convention. This was acceptable, since I was still in school and Earlene's job prospects were positive; Dr. Peterson would assist her in becoming a teacher in the DCPS. Also, I was allowed to keep my Fellowship with the Office of the Dean of Students, which also provided income, along with my room and board. I would have increasingly more dealings with Peterson as board chair in the days and years to come.

On our return from church, Earlene and I discussed what had transpired that day, including the offer from the board of trustees. Earlene indicated that Dr. Peterson had also invited her to a meeting to discuss employment with DCPS. We agreed to save for a car, which would be necessary, since we both had appointments, and public transportation was not efficient.

Earlene received a call from Dr. Peterson's office requesting that she come for an appointment on the following day. She was elated, and so was I. This meant she would have a chance to continue her career as I launched my career. Everything in our lives seemed to come together in a way that told me that God was with us.

Earlene went to meet with Dr. Peterson. I had scheduled a meeting with Dean Crawford. I wanted to thank him for all his support and get his advice on how to proceed with my ministry, in light of the fact that we were in the process of building a million-dollar church in Washington, DC, which had never been done by a Negro church. Dr. Crawford expressed how proud he and Betty were at my election as pastor of Zion. He pledged to support me in any way he could, saying I could call on him at any time I thought he could be helpful.

Time swiftly passed and arrangements were made for my installation as the seventh pastor of Zion Baptist Church. Dr. Gladys T. Peterson was named chair of the Installation Committee, which consisted of deacons, trustees, and laypersons. The date selected was December 1, 1960. I was asked to name the participants who would install me. I selected Dean Daniel G. Hill, dean of the Howard University School of Religion; Dr. Evans E. Crawford, dean of the Rankin Memorial Chapel; Rev. Jerry A. Moore, pastor of the Nineteenth Street Baptist Church, the oldest Baptist church in the district; Rev. Earl Harrison, pastor of the historic Shiloh Baptist Church; and Rev. E. C. Smith, pastor of the historic Metropolitan Baptist Church, along with all the associate ministers of Zion Baptist Church.

The second Sunday in December came, and many people arrived early for the five o'clock service in the Phyllis Wheatley YWCA. After the morning service, some had their lunch in the neighborhood, since there would be limited seating in the auditorium. My mother and father had been invited by the church, which made the day very special. Earlene's parents had also been invited but could not attend due to Mrs. Marshall's illness.

The installation service began promptly at five o'clock, with the choir processing into the auditorium. The ministers followed them and entered the platform that served as the pulpit. Mrs. Jennie Smith was the renowned choir director of the Zion Baptist Church, having come to the church when she was fifteen years old to serve as pianist. People would come from far and near to hear the Zion Baptist choir under her direction.

I had never experienced a more moving service in my ministry. Dean Hill brought greetings from the Howard University School of Religion. Dr. Crawford brought greetings from the Andrew Rankin Chapel, where I had served as his assistant. Every speaker brought wonderful words of encouragement. The preacher for the installation was Rev. Harrison, pastor of our sister church, the Shiloh Baptist Church. Zion's Rev. Walker had pastored both churches at one time, before electing to give up Zion and remain at Shiloh.

Rev. Harrison was one of the great preachers in the country. His message was outstanding, but the words that remained with me for fifty-five years were these, "Reverend Veazey, you may or may not become a great preacher, but you can become a great pastor." He went on to say, "Your work as a pastor will be long remembered after the words of your sermons are forgotten."

This service would always be a highlight in our lives.

The holidays passed quickly, as we worked tirelessly to raise funds to meet our obligations to Perpetual in order to complete our edifice to the glory of God. My final months in seminary were hectic, in that I was working hard to complete papers and prepare for our final exams scheduled for May 1961. This would mean the close of another important milestone in my life and my pilgrimage in clay feet.

Mother and Daddy planned to attend my graduation exercises, along with Gerry and George, who had been so encouraging and had supported me during my three years at Howard University.

The morning of my graduation arrived and we were on the quadrangle at ten o'clock for our twelve o'clock ceremony. The speaker would be Dr. Benjamin Mays, president of Morehouse College, a premier institution of Negro higher education. I felt very special, since I had taken him to breakfast many times when he came to Howard to speak in the Andrew Rankin Chapel. His message was very relevant. He spoke of the revolution taking place in the country as a result of the civil rights movement led by a young minister from Montgomery, Alabama, who pastored the Dexter Avenue Baptist Church, where the renowned Rev. Vernon Johns had pastored. I had also shared breakfast with Rev. Johns when he'd come to speak at the Rankin Chapel. Dr. Mays gave a moving and inspiring message, which left all of us with a determination to make a difference. My mother and dad were proud, and it made me happy that they could see that their sacrifices for me were not in vain. Receiving my degree, which I wanted to give to my mother, who had been so encouraging to me, along with my father, was the highlight of the ceremony.

My graduation from Howard's School of Divinity led to my next challenge, having been previously elected the seventh pastor of Zion Baptist Church, which was to fulfill the dream of the former pastor, Rev. Dr. A. Joseph Edwards, to build a new edifice. There was one person who was most responsible for the success in building the church—a person who supported me in my leadership in critical days when the building was in doubt. And that was Dr. Gladys Tignor Peterson. She chaired the finance committee, which held the financing of the church in its hands. The committee was responsible for developing the means to raise the funds necessary to meet the requirements of Perpetual. We were tasked to raise over $100,000 before Perpetual would advance the $200,000 needed to complete the building.

Dr. Peterson, who had been influential before I became pastor, worked with me and the congregation in motivating members to sacrifice in order for us to be successful. Dr. Peterson and I agreed we would ask our church members to purchase a "gold brick" for $500 to meet our financial requirements. One has to remember that $500 in 1960 was the equivalent of over $4,000 today. Recognizing also that income was far lower it was a sacrifice for members to give this amount or any lesser amount. Members took out loans from banks and federal credit unions, borrowed from relatives, and took out second mortgages on their homes to build the new Zion Baptist Church. This was unbelievable in the annals of Washington, DC, Negro churches. One of the most inspirational sermons was delivered by Rev. Cameron W. Byrd, my roommate and also intern at People's Congregational Church. His text was from the Book of Psalm, which said, "Come and see what the Lord has done." This sermon gave great motivation to members to give beyond their means.

Dr. Peterson, along with her assistants, including Mrs. Genevieve Johnson, joined with countless others to raise the necessary funds. The church selected McKissack and McKissack as the construction company to build the new Zion Baptist Church which was designed by the architectural firm, Bryant and Bryant. Also participating in the architectural design of the church was our own trustee Mr. Harold Biddieux.

Along with my pastoral duties, I spent part of each day going to the site to check the building's progress. I became a very good friend of the building superintendent of McKissack and McKissack, Mr. Lee Fitzpatrick, who was responsible for the entire building crew. He was a quiet man of very few words but very likeable and very smart. He managed everything, from the foundation to the upper structure, which meant nothing happened in the building process without his approval. When we became friends, he told me that he'd learned everything he knew on the job working for many years in construction, especially with McKissack and McKissack. It was through Mr. Fitzpatrick that I was able to convince Moses McKissack to cooperate and work with the chair of the trustee board, which was under pressure to complete the building by September 1962.

One of the proudest remembrances I have is the fact that everything, from the architects to the construction firm and all of the various subcontractors, were handled by Negro-owned businesses, including the foundation work, the brickwork, the plumbing, and the electrical work. Even the furnishings were provided by Negro contractors. The distribution of funds to contractors was handled by the only Negro bank in the District of Columbia, which was the Industrial Bank of Washington.

One of the saddest things that came out of the building of the first new edifice in the Negro community in many years was the news of a proposal made by a prominent Baptist church in the city. This church had asked that, in the event we failed to meet our commitment to Perpetual, it be considered to take over the building of the church. That meant if we should lose our financial interest, another church would profit from our failure. When I learned of this, I was very angry. It also saddened me to consider that a sister church in the Negro community could take advantage of another church's struggles to advance its own cause. I will not reveal the pastor or the church, but I did convey to the prominent pastor my disappointment in his conduct and made it clear that I would forgive him but would not associate with him again. To this day, I have revealed the neither the church nor the pastor who submitted this proposal.

September 2, 1962, was a historic day I will always remember. It has been almost sixty years since we marched into the new Zion Baptist Church at 4850 Blagden Avenue NW, Washington, DC. The most satisfying moment was when we dedicated the edifice to the glory of God. Silently, I thanked God for Reverend Dr. A. Joseph Edwards, who received the vision and worked tirelessly until his death in 1959 on the day he had planned to break ground for the church we were dedicating today. From that day to this day, I never fail to remind others that this edifice was the vision of Rev. Edwards and that I'd only tried to bring his vision to fruition, for which I am still grateful to God.

The next thirty-three years would be filled with many blessings to our church; many challenges to our ministry; many heartbreaks because of tragedies that brought us to our knees; and finally many failures by me as pastor during my pilgrimage in clay feet. My ministry would be framed on the teachings of my professor of Christian social ethics, my mentor Dr. Crawford.

We were introduced to Dr. Walter Rauschenbusch from Colgate Rochester, who promulgated the new concept of the "social gospel." This immediately appealed to me because it made the teachings of Jesus come alive. He explained the gospel was more than reciting what God had done or what Jesus had done. Rather, it was about sharing what we are called to do as followers of Christ and doers of the Word.

This came to me when I served two summers in the migrant ministry program. Through this experience, I found the transforming power of Jesus Christ through the doing of his words—"As you have done it unto the least of these, my brethren, ye have done it unto me." This verse in Matthew 25 sums up the gospel.

I, therefore, determined my ministry would be one of doing, not talking. This does not mean that there is not a place for preaching the gospel, because it is in the preaching that the Holy Spirit is able to speak to our hearts and give us the grace to do the things Christ calls us to do as His followers.

My ministry would thus have a threefold approach—teaching, preaching, and serving. I would endeavor to have an informed congregation that spoke to the needs of the community. This would be accomplished by the teaching ministry, which would include not only sharing the Word of God but also being informed about the needs of the community, both civic and religious. My future plans were to restore the membership by welcoming those who had left the church during the transition and reaching out to others in the Northwest community who had been displaced from their homes due to the eminent domain ruling.

The government called this urban renewal. My longtime friend and pastor of New Bethel Baptist Church, the Rev. Dr. Walter E. Fauntroy, correctly called it *urban removal* of Negroes from Southwest, Washington, DC, to advance the real estate interest. Negroes were dispersed all over Washington, especially in Southeast, DC. Those with some financial means moved to Northwest and Northeast, where they purchased homes from whites who were part of the white flight that took place during the 1950s as a result of the integration of schools and other institutions.

When eminent domain came to Southwest, Washington, DC, which included the churches, along Zion—which had been in that community for ninety years—every church had to decide what it wanted to do in terms of finding a future location. Many of the displaced black churches decided to buy white church buildings in Northwest, DC. These church buildings had been abandoned as a result of white flight to Maryland and Virginia and many were overpriced. Because of anxiety, the black churches paid prices beyond what they were worth, especially since the white membership had moved and the buildings would only be useful to another congregation. This, to me, was an opportunity to get these churches at a much-reduced price, which would have been acceptable to those congregations who had decided to leave the city for the suburbs. Dr. Edwards was way ahead of his time when he decided that this new Zion would be built by Negro companies, which employed some of the finest artisans in the country.

One of the mistakes Rev. Edwards made on reflection was the selection of the site for the new edifice. It was located in the upper northwest corridor of the city, where affluent whites had continued to live even though, in the 1950s, blacks had begun buying in this area. Nevertheless, the community was mostly comprised of middle-class blacks whose children were grown and had moved away.

Mrs. Turner, who sold the property to Zion, lived on Colorado Avenue directly behind the lot where the church was built. The lot, described as an overgrown swampy area with a spring underneath that would become problematic in the future, sold in 1958 for $37,000, the equivalent to $321,000 today. Despite these difficulties, the real reason this site was problematic was because there was limited opportunity for growth, with very few young parents and very few children in the area. The dividing line between the affluent and the middle class in the area was Sixteenth Street, and because of the perceived differences in economic status, most blacks did not feel welcome to this beautiful Negro church—even though it had come from the southwest quadrant of DC, which was not wealthy or middle class for the most part.

This difficulty, I realized, would have to be solved if the church was to become successful; it remained a challenge throughout the thirty-three years of my pastorate at Zion.

Although the neighborhood was very slow in welcoming us, there were some who helped me break the ice. One of these was Dr. Charlie

Lofton, former principal of the famous Negro school Dunbar High School named after Paul Lawrence Dunbar, a famous Negro poet and playwright of the late nineteenth century and early twentieth century. He was born to parents who had been enslaved in Kentucky. Dr. Lofton proved to be a great help to me and the church, since he was well respected in both the Negro and white communities. There was also Mary Wilson, a prominent schoolteacher in Washington, DC. These two, who lived directly in front of Zion, made me feel welcome, even though I would learn later that the community association had tried to block the building of the edifice in the community. Because of limited parking for the five hundred members we had, I asked the members to respect our neighbors and not block their driveways on Sundays or through the week when he held meetings or other functions.

The year 1962 passed quickly. I had just graduated from the Howard University School of Religion in May 1961 but that all now seemed so far away. Unlike my fellow seminary graduates who were seeking their life's work, I was already buried in work trying to make Dr. Edwards's dream a success. Many times I would see an ex-classmate who would inquire how things were going with such an awesome responsibility as building a church. I was always very casual about answering the question, because it was an awesome responsibility, which I could not adequately express to them.

During holidays such as Thanksgiving and Christmas, we made extra efforts to invite our neighbors to join in celebrations at the church. Some attended, and a few even joined the church. However, the vast majority remained resistant to the church, perceiving it as a disruption to the quiet community.

One day when walking down Emerson Street on the east side of Sixteenth Street, I met a mother who was also walking. I stopped and introduced myself and told her she was welcome to attend the church and bring her children to our Sunday school. To my surprise, she accepted my invitation. Sure enough, she was there the next Sunday with her children, who attended the church school while she attended the adult class.

After the service, she expressed a desire to join but did not understand how to go about doing so. I explained that the next Sunday, when I offered the invitation for membership, she should come to the front and would be received into our congregation.

The following Sunday, she and her children joined the church, and I received them. Two of the children were old enough to be baptized with their mother, and the one-year-old would be dedicated, which is equivalent to baptism.

This experience opened my eyes to the reality that the people on the east side of Sixteenth Street were open to our invitation if we would only ask them. This one experience caused me to challenge the church to invite their neighbors who lived with them on the east side of Sixteenth Street. God blessed this decision, which brought almost immediate results. The church began to grow in members, and I was motivated to introduce new programs, such as a day care nursery, which we had ample room to operate. I asked the trustee board to do the legal work to open the opportunity to the families in our community.

The lead person in this effort was Mrs. Ethaline Swan, a retired supervisor at the Bureau of Engraving, which made the currency for the United States. Mrs. Swan, along with our wonderful chairman, Mr. Peterson, initiated all procedures to obtain the licenses and building changes necessary for us to house over fifty children. Within six months, we were open for business.

This was definitely God sent—when we opened in August 1963, we almost immediately had full capacity, though our fee was $200 a month. The cost was not a problem for the affluent neighborhood, and those who could not afford the fee were subsidized by the United Planning Organization through grants from the Department of Labor and the Department of Health, Education, and Welfare. This was very helpful to our annual budget and also to our efforts to win the community, those on the east and the west side of Sixteenth Street.

I was very proud of our church's ability to have a diversified nursery—with black, white, rich, and poor and parents who really wanted their children to have this kind of experience.

Three years into our marriage, Earlene and I began to have problems, which had been accumulating for several years. At this same difficult time, Earlene stated that she was pregnant, news that should have been received with joy and gladness. However, I had told her right after my election as pastor that I did not want to have children yet. I wanted to wait not only until we had completed the building of the new edifice but also for my ministry to be solidified. Only then would we be in a position to give our child the time and attention I felt was required.

Earlene was very patient during this time. We tried to seek counseling and other ways of resolving our difficulties, which did not happen.

Michael Vincent Veazey was born on February 12, 1963, at Howard University's Freedman's Hospital. Of course our lives changed dramatically. We had been entrusted with a precious life and had accepted this responsibility. However, my planning for Michael's birth had been overshadowed by my attempts to become settled in my pastoral responsibilities.

In the meantime, I had also become interested in city affairs, including the high unemployment in the black community. There was a universal desire to address this problem, since it led to high crime rates in many cities where blacks were the majority. Along with being active in the Northwest Civic Association where Zion was located, I was also recommended to become a member of the District of Columbia Republican Central Committee. Many of my members and friends were curious why I was a Republican, rather than a Democrat. I had to explain that, before 1962, 90 percent of the blacks in the South were Republican because of our allegiance to President Abraham Lincoln, who signed the Emancipation Proclamation. This may sound unbelievable in these times, but one must remember that coming out of slavery was the greatest event we as a race had experienced, and we were grateful for President Lincoln. We supported the Republican Party as our way of being loyal to the party that gave us freedom.

As you may surmise, there were very few Republicans in the District of Columbia. Judge Barrington Parker and Dr. Henry Robinson were instrumental in my becoming a member of this important committee. Among the members was Mrs. Alice Marriott, who served as treasurer and whose husband was J. W. Marriott Sr., founder of the first fast food chain in the District of Columbia. Hot Shoppes were very popular in the 1950s and remained so through the 1970s. They preceded the Marriott Hotel chain, one of the largest chains in the in the world.

The Republican Central Committee also enabled me to meet other influential people who would make a difference in my ministry and civic involvement.

My elevation to the Republican Central Committee was where my political and civic involvement began, although I sought no public position or office. The District of Columbia was governed by three commissioners appointed by the president and confirmed by Congress. Years would pass before I would become involved in city government. However, these contacts brought attention to my ministry, by way of the many people who joined the church because of my involvement.

As a result of the urban removal of Negroes from Southwest, there arose a groundswell of civic interest in the city led by many ministers. Among them were Dr. E. Franklin Jackson of Wesley African Methodist Church, Rev. Dr. Earl Harrison of Shiloh Baptist Church, Rev. Dr. E. C. Smith of Metropolitan Baptist Church, and Rev. C. T. Murray of Vermont Avenue Baptist Church. Rev. Murray had the greatest preaching voice I had ever heard. The most energetic and charismatic of these ministers was a young minister who grew up in Washington and pastored the New Bethel Baptist church, a few blocks from his house on Westminster Street. This young minister was Rev. Walter W. Fauntroy, a graduate of Virginia Union and Yale Divinity School. After becoming pastor of Zion at twenty-three years of age, I became the youngest minister to pastor a major congregation in Washington. Walter welcomed me into the minister's circle. We became close friends and remain so to this day.

One of the most significant events in 1963 took place in August. Dr. Martin Luther King Jr. led the historic March on Washington for equal rights and jobs. More than 250,000 people from around the country attended. Dr. King gave a most powerful speech titled "I Have a Dream," which would become the most celebrated speech since Lincoln's Gettysburg address. My friend, Rev. Fauntroy was the major organizer of the march. Although I was a Republican, this was a march that included a wide diversity of people, rich and poor, black and white, Democrat and Republican. This march would prove to be the turning point in the civil rights movements. And, in turn, it led to a new movement in the city for self-government, led by the ministers of Washington from every denomination.

These aforementioned ministers and many others challenged the city in many areas, among them self-government. No one had ever made an issue of this point in the federal city of Washington, DC. Because Washington was not a state but a district, there was no local input about matters like schools and health. Led by Rev. Fauntroy, these ministers became a force in the city and Congress. DC was governed by three commissioners, none of whom were Negroes. The ministers insisted that one of them should be a Negro so that we would have input in city affairs. This pressure from the religious community helped John B. Duncan, an official of the Department of Interior, become the first Negro commissioner for the District of Columbia. This was giant step toward what would eventually become home rule or self-government. This victory by the religious community was just the start of many others. Since I was new to the city and the political machinations, I was not included with the leadership but supported my friend Walter, who was the moving force behind the ministers' movement.

The year 1964 would be challenging for me in many ways, as Zion was celebrating one hundred years since its founding by the seven freedmen. Not only would this year be historic; in addition, several church members would be turning one hundred years old during the anniversary. Deaconess Smiler, who lived on Constitution Avenue, would turn one hundred before the end of the year. She had taught Sunday school for many years. When I had to become pastor Dr. Peterson had taken me to see her because she wanted to see her new pastor before she died. I will never forget her sweet smile and loving look that greeted me as her pastor. We had prayer together, and she then said a prayer for me and my ministry, which today remains in my spirit.

The year was also a difficult for Earlene and me for many reasons. We had just had a son. Michael was now a year old. Although a joy, he'd had to wear a cast for the first few months because his legs had not formed correctly. I felt so much for him, even though he had no awareness of his condition. Earlene and I were busy keeping him entertained, even as we were having personal problems, which seemingly got worse after our son's birth. I did not think it was because of Michael. But as I had told Earlene, I wanted to wait until things were more settled before we started a family. We tried to keep our relationship in order, despite the difficulty and some resentment on my part.

Unfortunately we grew apart, though maintaining our mutual respect and wanting the best for our son Michael. Tensions were lessened between us due to Earlene's teaching and my planning of the hundredth anniversary of Zion, which kept both of us busy.

This historic anniversary brought back many members who had left during the transition from Southwest. The church was energized by the special events that would be held during September and would culminate on the fourth Sunday, when we would have a special preacher and special music provided by the senior choir under the direction of the renowned Mrs. Jennie G. Smith. She had been playing for Zion since she was fifteen years old.

On the morning of September 27, 1964, the fourth Sunday, the church began to fill up as early as nine o'clock. An anniversary breakfast had been prepared for those who had come early to ensure they had a good seat for this historic service. I arrived early to greet members, friends, and visitors at the breakfast. The preacher for this service would be my mentor Dr. Evans E. Crawford, one of the best preachers in the country. Dr. Crawford had been responsible for my growth and development during my seminary days and had been with me during the three years of my ministry.

Dr. Crawford arrived around ten thirty for the Communion service, which always preceded our morning service on the fourth Sunday. All twenty-two of our deacons were ready to follow me into the sanctuary. The choir, having spent weeks preparing special music for this service, was prepared for the processional, which always immediately preceded the call to worship. The ministers were all seated in the pulpit, including Reverends Thomas C. Garnett, William Kirkland, Wilbur Henry, and Joseph Penn. Dr. Crawford sat in the preacher's chair usually reserved for me, but in deference to him, I'd asked him to sit there. The Communion service was very sacred as we remembered the seven who, through faith, had founded the Zion Baptist Church.

The Zion Baptist choir was absolutely superb, with the singing of Aubrey E. Ballard and Elizabeth Quander leading the choir in singing

"The Old Ship of Zion," a song that always brought the church to its feet. Aubrey was a student of Mrs. Smith at Browne Junior High and had followed her to her church. After my introduction of Dr. Crawford, the congregation stood and sang, under the direction of Mrs. Smith, "The Church's One Foundation." As we sang this beautiful hymn of preparation, my eyes filled with tears. I thought about the thousands of souls who had boarded the old ship of Zion on their way to the glory land.

Dr. Crawford preached one of the best sermons I had heard as he recalled the history of our church being founded in 1864, when President Lincoln signed the Emancipation Proclamation. He also recounted how the children of Israel, under Moses, went out of Egypt into the wilderness on their way to the Promised Land. He challenged us to fulfill our calling; many had not lived to see this day. This was especially challenging for me, as I remembered Dr. A. Joseph Edwards, my honored and esteemed predecessor, whose vision we now celebrated.

A large reception was held following the service in the A. Joseph Edwards Fellowship Hall, named to honor his leadership and vision. Many of my classmates attended, along with members of the faculty. Among them was Dean Hill, who was responsible for my seminary education through the generosity of the scholarships he'd awarded me during my three years at the Howard University School of Religion. I will always be grateful for his faith in me and also for the support and faith of Dr. Dearing King, who had recommended me to Dean Hill. Dr. King would continue to be a very important part of my ministry, due to his immense experience in the ministry for many years.

The day after Zion's anniversary, Earlene and I agreed to seek marriage counseling. We were recommended to a marriage counselor associated with Howard University and attended a very emotional first session. We continued to meet with him, because we desired to make our marriage work. We met with the counselor several times and tried to implement some of his suggestions and recommendations. They did not work, and after several sessions, we stopped our marriage counseling. Our situation seemed to get better during the next few months, but we found ourselves living separately for the most part, although I had not moved from our apartment.

The next six months would be the most difficult time in my life. I was torn between separating from a very wonderful woman and my son, whom I dearly loved, and seeking a new life and maybe a new relationship to help me through this period.

In 1965, a critical year for our marriage, I made the decision that it was unfair to Earlene and me to go through the motions of a marriage. Before I left, we discussed the matter. I told her I would make sure the rent was paid and would also provide her with any money she needed for Michael's care. She was not in favor of the separation but agreed to the terms I had outlined.

As I coped with the loneliness that always follows a separation, there was also a strange sense of peace that I had finally made a decision that would give Earlene a chance to have another relationship and find happiness.

In June 1965, I moved into a furnished efficiency apartment at 1112 "M" Street in downtown Washington, DC. Getting the furnished place made it easy for me to move in with just my clothes. After settling in, I found it difficult living alone. Although I had lived in an apartment with Cameron and Wendell when in seminary, this was quite different. It proved a very difficult adjustment and, indeed, a transitional time in many ways.

My separation, not acceptable in the Baptist church, would cause serious division in the church. I had contemplated this reaction and was ready to accept whatever consequences of my separation that would result, including the congregation rethinking whether they wanted me to continue as pastor.

A church meeting was called to determine my future as pastor. To my surprise, the congregation voted overwhelmingly to retain me, which was very gratifying. This, however, did not resolve all of my problems, since, for the first time, I had no mate. I knew this would create some tension in my life, realizing that there were many young women in the church who were interested in me. I had no intention of cultivating a relationship with any of them, though.

For several months, I lived alone but with the support of my secretary, Helen Robinson, and her husband, Deacon Morris Robinson, chair of the deacon board. I was able to survive with their weekly food and financial help. I will always remember them for their support and encouragement during those difficult days.

After several months—with daily phone calls from parishioners who wanted to know how I was doing (or more correctly *what* I was doing)—I settled down to being a bachelor minister. This was unheard of in the Baptist church. I dated a young lady who was not a member of the church for a short time and this however brief encounter would have ramifications after many years.

One Sunday after service, while sitting in the study, I received a call from a young lady who identified herself as Jean Liggins, the mother of Gayle Liggins, who I had baptized the Sunday before. Mrs. Hazel Adams, her mother, was a member of Zion. I had met Mrs. Adams and admired her for her modesty and kindness toward me. Jean asked whether I was all right and told me how much she'd enjoyed my sermon. I asked her why she'd inquired, and she responded that she had detected something awry in my spirit. This impressed me, as I had been very depressed that Sunday and had struggled through my sermon but did not think anyone had noticed. She also indicated that she was grateful I had baptized her daughter Gayle. I asked if she would like to meet and talk further about my issues. She agreed, and we met in Rock Creek Park at Grove Eight and talked for almost three hours.

The conversation was not only about me but also about the things in which I believed and what she believed. This was a most stimulating conversation, because it had nothing to do with us personally but everything to do with our spiritual development. This greatly impressed me, and we agreed to phone each other or meet for lunch, where we could continue our dialogue. Jean worked for United States Information Agency, which I defined as a propaganda organization. Her only response was a telling laugh, suggesting she knew that I knew what it was all about.

During the next few weeks, Jean and I met for lunch almost every day on the mall or at the East Potomac Park golf course cafe where we could talk. Every day, I learned more about her, and we became closer as a result. I found her a very sensitive person. And even though she had not attended college after high school, she had attended Catholic University and was a well-read person, who greatly impressed me.

During our conversations, I introduced her to the writings of Edgar Cayce, better known as the sleeping prophet with the ability to go into trances and diagnose people with difficult medical conditions.

My compatibility with Jean was amazing, and our connection was very romantic in a strange way. We continued to share our views on extrasensory perception that had been introduced to me by Dr. Leon Wright several years before. Our relationship continued to grow, and we finally reached the stage where we both realized it was more than platonic. We had actually fallen in love. This became somewhat problematic, in that Jean's nine-year-old daughter, Gayle, had only known me as her pastor who had baptized her.

Jean visited me at my apartment at least three times a week, and we shared dinner and intimate time together, which made our relationship very special.

Meanwhile, over the passing months, Earlene and I had scheduled for me to keep Michael on the weekends. This worked well, and Jean was very supportive of me and Michael. I would pick him up on Friday and return him to Earlene on Sunday. During those weekends, Jean would encourage me to take Michael to the zoo or for lunch or dinner. Michael grew very close to Jean, as she always fixed his favorite food— fish sticks. To this day, I still remember one of the most impressive things that Jean did was to tell me to make sure I spent as much time with Michael as I could and not worry about our relationship. This was very important; I had definitely fallen in love with her and wanted to spend as much time with her as possible

Christmas 1965 was very happy, since Jean's family had accepted me and Michael and invited us to spend time during the holidays with them. Michael spent most of the Christmas holidays with his mother and her boyfriend William "Bill" Leysath, who Earlene had met when we lived in the Hampshire Gardens Apartments on Eastern Avenue in Langley Park, Maryland. Bill was employed there. He and Earlene had developed a relationship and had become very personally involved when she and I separated.

New Year 1966 would be a pivotal year for Jean and me. We both felt a special feeling for the watch night service. During the midnight prayer, she came to the altar and took my hand, which I am sure some members noticed with interest. After the prayer ringing in the New Year, she immediately gave me a delicate but pronounced kiss, which I know many members noticed.

During the year, I would meet Jean's aunts—Minyon, Ruby, and Alice—and her only uncle, Bill. The next months were filled with rumors about our relationship and whether we would be marrying soon. Gayle found this rather awkward since many of her friends were inquiring whether her mother would be marrying Rev. Veazey. This was a very difficult period, since we were concerned about Gayle and the emotional toll our relationship was taking on her.

In early 1966 I discussed divorce with Earlene. I met with an attorney friend of mine H. Carl Moultrie, and he advised me to have Earlene meet with him. She agreed and accepted the terms he proposed, which were quite generous. This was 1966, and the terms included child support and other expenses amounting to $500 a month. Although I objected to this unheard of amount, I accepted the terms because I wanted my son to have everything he needed to have a good life. Moultrie filed the divorce papers in March, and the divorce was granted that same month. This was the great news Jean and I had been waiting on.

Several days had passed, and then I asked Jean to marry me. She responded with a very long and passionate kiss. I always told her years later that she never agreed to marry me, and I could not say she agreed because of a kiss.

We were married at her mother's house on Ninth Street NW, at seven o'clock in the evening by my assistant minister at Zion, Rev. Edward A. Hailes. My best man was Deacon Morris Robinson, and the witnesses were Benjamin Hailstorks and Walter Latture. Jean's matron of honor was Shirley Latture, her friend since their teenager years. Mr. Mac Adams and Hazel Adams were family, along with Jean's daughter, Gayle, who was very quiet during the service.

Gayle's reaction was understandable. There had only been the two of them since she was born. Jean and her former husband, Bud Liggins, had had a very difficult divorce. And Gayle was hurt very much by him, in that he did not want a relationship with her. My heart went out to her, and I made a very special effort to let her know how much I loved her as her other father.

Our wedding was very low budget. We were married in her parents' home, with a reception in the dining room with punch and cookies. Our rings came from Sears and Roebuck on Wisconsin Avenue, costing us twenty-two dollars for both. We spent our honeymoon at 337 M Street in Southwest for just one day, Saturday, September 3, 1966.

Sunday, September 3, was a very special day. I would present my wife to the congregation—a congregation she had been a part of since she was a child.

The congregation was amazingly understanding and supportive and, after the service, paused in the rear to congratulate us and wish us the best for the future. I was very pleased that the congregation was so encouraging and willing to accept Jean as my wife.

Our home was in Southwest, and the house number was the same as the church address on F Street, which was 337. This trivia was a good sign that our beginning was being blessed by a greater power and providence. After the service some members had planned a reception for members and friends, which was a joyous occasion for us.

Our new home was conveniently located just twenty minutes from the church through Rock Creek Park. This was bittersweet for Jean, in that her community was once thriving and one of the most cohesive communities in the city, along with the black community in Georgetown. Jean was perhaps one of the very few who had left the old black Southwest and come back to the white Southwest.

This remained our home for the next six years. Jean continued to work for the Voice of America, conveniently located only a few blocks from our home.

We discussed our future as it related to whether we would have a child soon or wait awhile. I had told Jean during our dating time that I wanted one child, since I already had Michael. I know it was presumptuous, but I told her it had to be a girl. This sounded somewhat strange—thinking she could determine whether a child she carried would be a girl or boy. I reminded her of this several times.

Three months into our marriage, she announced that she was pregnant, which made me deliriously happy. This was the day I had waited for and looked forward to—we would be welcoming our new baby in nine months.

Jean had a rather difficult pregnancy because of her anemia and was advised by her doctor, Enos Ray, to take her medication and get as much rest as possible. Her condition was more serious than anticipated; she had difficulty doing household chores that would tire her out. She wanted to fulfill my desire to have a girl, but it was somewhat problematic, with her being thirty-five years old when the baby would be born. Notwithstanding this risk, Dr. Ray assured us that Jean was generally in good health, and there should be no problems.

Members of the church had been very encouraging and supportive of our marriage. When I announced that we were expecting a child, I am sure many started counting the months to determine whether we'd had sex before we were married, which would be a very strange thing today.

The church was in financial difficulty because of the heavy mortgage and other expenses. So I decided to become a special education teacher in Southeast, a rather difficult area because of the poverty and lack of opportunity for many.

The work proved to be just as fulfilling as my days in the migrant ministry. The students with whom I dealt were those other teachers had labeled disrupters and unable to be part of the regular classroom setting. I took it as a challenge to relate to these students, some of whom had been sent to juvenile detention centers for committing crimes but could not be tried because of their ages.

After being assigned the class, I recognized that the one thing that was missing was listening. I decided I would hear the students out and try to appeal to them to use this opportunity to change their lives. My success was due to my ability to appeal to them, and I was also able to develop any plan that I thought would be advantageous. Another thing I did was to give more recreation time, so they would then be able to sit and learn. Some of them definitely had attention deficits.

Later, I accepted a position with the newly founded Opportunities Industrialization Centers (OIC) organization, under the leadership of Dr. Leon Sullivan, the prominent pastor of the historic Zion Baptist Church of Philadelphia, Pennsylvania. The Washington, DC, chapter was established by Rev. David Eaton, a Howard University professor and an ordained Methodist minister. I was given the position of director of the Building Trades Department. Although my knowledge of the trades was limited, I had organizational and administrative experience, having overseen the building of the first million-dollar church edifice in Washington, DC.

I was delighted to have this opportunity. Again it gave me the opportunity to break the bonds of poverty and unemployment. I was also glad to work with David Eaton, for whom I had the greatest respect and admiration because of his commitment to black power, which had come on the scene with Stokely Carmichael and H. Rap Brown. Though many viewed this development as aggressive and violent, this was not the case.

David spoke to the Washington power structure and also to the lethargic black leadership, which was very weak on confronting Washington's white power structure. The efforts of Rev. Fauntroy and Rev. Eaton caused the power structure to begin having conversations that led to funding of the Washington, DC, OIC. It was here that I met Rev. Hailes, who was a part of OIC, as it later became known. Rev. Hailes had come from Massachusetts to Washington, DC, to head the local NAACP. Rev. Eaton appointed him director of Skills Training and Remedial Education, which was headed by a lifelong friend F. Alexis Roberson.

Since Rev. Hailes and I were in the ministry, we became good friends as well as colleagues, and I invited him and his family to Zion. There was an instant rapport between Rev. Hailes and Zion's congregation that prompted me to ask him to become my assistant. He accepted, even though this became a very clumsy because of our work arrangements. While he supervised the department where I served at OIC, I was the pastor of the church, where he served as my assistant. This relationship worked very well because of our mutual interest in religion and the opportunity to advance the social gospel. We became closer, as did our families. His wife, Nettie, and Jean became good friends as they got to know each other through working together at Zion.

Jean was doing much better as we entered the 1967. I was encouraged and looking forward to our new addition to our family, along with Gayle, my newly acquired daughter whom I had baptized and loved since I first met her, before I married her mother. She was partially responsible for bringing us together because, after her baptism, her mother felt comfortable enough to call me—the call that led to our memorable conversation in Rock Creek Park. Although Gayle and I had not become as close as I would have liked, she was trying to reach out in her own way and I encouraged her and welcomed her. I loved my new daughter Gayle, which I would prove in the days and years to come.

My work at the church was going great, and Rev. Hailes was definite an asset, as were other local ministers in the congregation. The work at OIC was also going well, and the community had welcomed and supported it in many ways. The president, Rev. Eaton, was very popular with the city leadership and the black community, which gave us credibility. That translated into generous funding that made it possible to help hundreds of young black women and men to gain meaningful employment to provide for their families. Many of the young women were becoming skilled typists or keypunch operators, which was very much in demand during the 1960s.

The months went by quickly because of our work at the church and at OIC. Dr. Ray had already told Jean to expect delivery in late June or early July. It was already nearing Easter—which would arrive on March 26.

After Easter celebrations, the spring was beautiful, allowing Jean and me to walk many evenings near the Potomac River, was popular with the residents of the Southwest Waterfront.

Summer finally arrived on June 21. Soon, we would welcome our new member of the family. Jean began to tire very quickly and needed to rest often. We spent time going out to dinner at Hogates or Flagship, restaurants on the waterfront. It was a beautiful place to go for an evening of pleasure and delicious seafood. There was also the shopping center on Fourth Street, where the bank, Safeway, People's Drug Store, and a very romantic restaurant/bar called Where Louie Dwells.

Although Jean had begun to feel uncomfortable (which did not include labor pains), we decided to go to the shopping center to the restaurant and bar around eight o'clock. Jean did not drink but did have a Shirley Temple, while I had a scotch and soda. After we had listened to music for an hour or so, she told me she felt labor beginning.

So we returned to 337 M Street to retrieve her bag and drove to the Washington Hospital Center.

On June 30, 1967, we headed to the Washington Hospital Center to meet Dr. Ray and arrived around nine thirty that evening, thinking that delivery would be imminent. Although we kept asking for Dr. Ray, the nurses said he was on his way and to wait for him to make the delivery. The pains would ease and become intense for several hours.

After midnight I was concerned that something would go wrong. I tried reading the paper, drinking coffee, and walking the hallways. Finally, I decided to take a short nap. There was nothing else I could do, it was after two o'clock, and I was extremely exhausted. There was no one in the waiting room, so I decided to lie down on the sofa for a while.

Around seven o'clock, I was awakened by a nurse who said the magical words. "Mr. Veazey, you may come in and see your wife and your daughter."

I cannot explain my emotions, but I do remember the words *your daughter*. God had granted my prayer and given me a little girl. My heart raced as I walked toward Jean's room to see her and my daughter.

She was the most beautiful baby and everything I'd ever desired. She and Jean seemed perfect for each other as they lay there together. My daughter, Caron Valerie Veazey, born on July 1, 1967, at 6:35 a.m. and was everything I wanted. I knew she would be a beautiful girl and woman with special qualities, especially a sweetness I would come to question many times. Even though I was exhausted, I managed to remain at the bedside and relish the sight of my wife and daughter.

An hour passed, and I let Jean know that I was going home to sleep but would return in the morning. Before I left, we called Gayle to tell her that she was now a big sister with all the privileges and responsibilities pertaining thereto. Gayle was excited and wanted to come to the hospital right away. However, I asked her to prepare some food for me, which I could eat at lunch and dinner. She was very good at making macaroni and tuna salad, so I asked her to prepare that.

When I arrived home, I immediately went to bed after giving Gayle a hug and congratulating her on becoming a big sister. She beamed and said she was going to go to the hospital center to see her new sister and her mommy.

When I awakened around eight o'clock that night, I realized my life had changed, and I would become a different man. It is amazing how children can change your outlook and cause you to view things with a different perspective. Caron had brought me joy and happiness, as well as a new sense of responsibility. I was anxious for her brother to see her, as she would also affect his life. They would grow up together, even though he was about five years older.

After calling the hospital and talking with Jean and finding that she and our daughter were doing well, I showered and dressed to return to the hospital. At the hospital, I was told that Jean and Caron could go home in two days. This meant informing Jean's mother, Hazel who was coming to help us make this adjustment, along with Granddaddy, as Gayle called him, who was elated to know he had another granddaughter. A wonderful celebration took place, around Caron's birth, at 337 M Street. Gary Smith, who had been raised by his grandmother Hazel, because his mother was unable to raise him, was there. Gary was a wonderful young man, who had become like a brother to Gayle and would also relate wonderfully to Caron.

After settling down in our small two-bedroom townhouse, we became a family with a new member. Of course, Caron stayed in our bedroom, where we could watch over her and attend to her needs. This required many hours of changing and feeding during her early days. I was a proud father. I now had a girl, which was what I had told my wife I wanted. She had delivered, along with God, who deserves all praise.

Caron chose Jean as the vessel she would come through, according to the philosopher Kahlil Gibran, who said our children come through us, not from us. We will pursue this statement later in our book.

The early years of Caron's life brought joy to both my parents and Jean's parents. Jean was the best mother, exemplifying both love and patience, although it had been many years since she'd had a baby. Gayle loved her baby sister and was very helpful to her mother during those early days.

As we had discussed before we were married, Jean would stay home and raise our daughter. I assured her that I would always make enough money to support our family.

My work with the Opportunities Industrialization Center had given me a new opportunity to make the gospel as relevant as I had preached it was to my church family at Zion. The OIC addressed some real unemployment problems in the inner cities throughout the country.

In this atmosphere of the lack of jobs and opportunities, the civil rights movement reached a dangerous point. There was talk of riots in the city, prompting Rev. Dr. King, in 1968, to call for a Poor People's March in Washington, DC. It was to be a march against poverty and unemployment. Memphis, Tennessee, my hometown—where I had grown up in the midst of discrimination and extreme prejudice—was undergoing a protest by the city's sanitation workers against low wages and working conditions. The city fathers had dismissed these issues out of hand, frustrating the workers to the point they asked Dr. King to come to Memphis to lend his voice and movement to these unfair practices.

Dr. King, after prayerful consideration, decided to go to Memphis to join the sanitation workers in their quest for equality. Dr. King was supported by civil rights workers from around the country, which put increased pressure on city officials to respond to the requests. After a successful march for justice, with participation from many organizations both local and national, a rally was planned at the Mason Temple, built in honor of Bishop Charles Cason, founder of the Church of God in Christ. Mason's Temple was the largest auditorium owned by blacks that was appropriate for this rally. Dr. King was the featured speaker and gave what has come to be called the most prophetic speech of his career. In his speech, he referred to his own death when he said, "I am not afraid of any man. My eyes have seen the coming of the glory of the Lord. I may not get to the Promised Land with you, but we will get to the Promised Land." This powerful but ominous speech left people with mixed emotions.

The next day was April 4. Dr. King and Ralph David Abernathy awakened with the excited feeling that the march and rally the night before had been successful, even though there had not been any response from city officials. The last day in Memphis had been planned to be a celebratory evening, with music and fellowship.

315

In the meantime, we in Washington, DC, had been watching developments in Memphis for a sign that the Poor People's Campaign had new life. At OIC, the day had been typical, with training programs moving ahead and Rev. Eaton motivating staff to do more because people needed urgent relief. We were there late, even though it was after five o'clock; the staff never left at five.

When I was sitting in my office, my secretary rushed in to inform me that there had been a shooting in Memphis, and it was Dr. King who had been shot. Immediately we all gathered in Rev. Eaton's office to assess the situation. At six o'clock, the bulletin came that Dr. King had died at Methodist Hospital of gunshot wounds. All of us knew that this was going to be like throwing gasoline on a fire, which became evident when, on Fourteenth Street, the location of our headquarters, stores were looted and set afire. This pattern followed throughout the black community, including the H Street corridor and Georgia Avenue.

This alarmed the newly appointed government of Commissioner Walter Washington, who served as a surrogate mayor, and the city council, which was primarily black. There was widespread damage throughout the city, and both the police department and fire department were almost helpless.

President Johnson was urged to call for martial law, which meant the federal government would assume governance of the city that was under the leadership of Mayor Walter Washington. The other leaders who would be most affected by this call were John Hechinger, chairman of the city council, and Walter Fauntroy, vice chair of the city council, who had also been a community activist and a lieutenant in the civil rights movement on whom Rev. Dr. King was very dependent.

Rev. Eaton and Rev. Hailes, along with other ministers, appealed to our brothers and sisters not to destroy their own communities. This did not stop those who had become militant and weary of the white promises that were made to better conditions in the black community. This may sound illogical to those of us who are rational. But for those who were looting and destroying the community—where economics favored the white community through stores and other merchants who came into our community to exploit—this was their way of communicating.

Dr. King said, "Riot is the language of the hopeless." This made a lot of sense to those of us who had watched the discrimination, prejudice, and unfair treatment by the power structure. It did not justify their actions, but it did explain how a people could react in such a destructive manner.

President Lyndon B. Johnson sent in the military to patrol the city, especially protecting the major businesses, such as department stores and other large merchants. The riots were continuing in all the large cities—Detroit, New York, Chicago, and Los Angeles, where many deaths occurred due to the reaction of the police department, overwhelmed by feeling threatened and fear that their communities would be taken over by the power structure.

It was almost a week after Dr. King's death before some semblance of order was restored. Much of the credit for this was due to the ministers who Dr. King had enlisted in his efforts to establish an equal society.

The tragedy of this riot was that it took many lives and destroyed the infrastructure of the black community, including major food stores, drug stores, and especially small businesses owned by black entrepreneurs. The rebuilding of the black communities proved to be a major challenge.

Although the black community did not support Nixon in the election, we traditional Republicans urged him to rescue the black community. Art Fletcher, Bob Brown, Samuel Jackson, Jerry Moore, Margaret Haywood, Henry Robinson, Margaret Parker, and I challenged Nixon to provide economic help to rebuild the black infrastructure.

Years went by without support for black businesses under the democratic administrations, and the request we made to President Nixon was met with a very positive response. The small business administration provided millions of dollars to black entrepreneurs to start and enlarge their businesses. The multiplier effect of this meant thousands of our brothers and sisters were hired, receiving meaningful wages in jobs they had not previously been able to access. Several car dealerships were started in the Washington area, with many other businesses started with grants from the Small Business Administration.

On April 1, 1970, as a result of a recommendation by the Central Committee of the DC Republican Party, I was appointed by President

Richard Nixon to a four-year term on the DC City Council. Dr. C. M. Lee of Memphis was also instrumental in my appointment. He'd asked Senator Howard Baker to recommend me to the president.

My years on the council enabled me to assist young officers in the police department, keeping them from being terminated due to minor infractions or no infractions, which was a form of racism. My work with the police department brought me great satisfaction in that, not only could I represent one of the most important functions in the city, which was public safety, but I could also make sure that black officers were treated fairly. Before I left office, the department had one of the first black assistant chiefs, Timothy O'Bryan, who was a first-class officer and a gentleman.

The fire department was also a hotbed of discrimination, also terminating black firemen for minor infractions whites were given reprimands for. My goal was to have a black fire chief before I left office. This was accomplished in my last year, with the appointment Chief Burton Johnson, whose mother, Genevieve Johnson, was one of my strong supporters at Zion.

My final years on the council were spent mainly working with Mr. Kenneth Hardy, director of corrections, which consisted of the DC jail and the Lorton facility for long-term inmates. In the turbulent years of the seventies, crime escalated to historic proportions and our jails and Lorton were strained with overcrowding. Mr. Hardy was ahead of his time and one of the most progressive voices on rehabilitation in prisons. I worked with him in getting larger facilities to alleviate overcrowding and to institute programs of rehabilitation. Thanks to his programs, many young men who had violated the law and were sent to Lorton returned to society with skills to help them provide for their families and become productive citizens. This was the achievement of which I was most proud; it demonstrated we were a city that invested in our young people and believed they were worthy of saving, despite the mistakes they'd made during their younger years. My last year on the council, amid the turmoil of President Nixon's issues with the Congress concerning the Watergate break-in, Jean and I decided to move to Maryland to give our daughter Caron a better education.

During the past eleven years, my father's health had been in decline from Parkinson's disease, with which he'd been diagnosed when he returned from New York serving as a migrant minister for the National Council of Churches in New York. My mother had cared for him for eleven years with only the help of a male nurse named Mr. Thrill, who gave my father the best care and supported my mother in her desire to care for our father and her husband. In 1973, Daddy was rushed to the hospital with complications from Parkinson's and jaundice, all life-threatening. My brothers and sisters rushed to Memphis to see our father and support our mother.

When I arrived, the doctors indicated that Daddy was very ill and not expected to recover. Each night, we visited him in the hospital, realizing that he was growing increasingly weaker and near to death.

The night he died, he asked Mother to have me come into the room. I responded immediately. Daddy looked at me with a long glance and asked me, "Son, have I been a good father?"

This brought tears to my eyes that I would not allow to fall. I answered with a strong and determined voice, "Yes, Daddy, you have been a good father, and I want to thank you for being my father."

When I left the room, I realized I would not see my father alive again.

My mother and I had begun to walk toward the door when she turned and said to him, "Mertie, I will see you in the morning."

I held her as we walked out of the room for the last time.

When we returned to the room where my brothers and sisters were, the family embraced each other. The doctor entered and said, "Mr. Veazey has died." We all cried and held each other as we realized our father had transitioned to a better place.

The funeral was held at the Central Baptist Church, where we had spent most of our lives before moving to South Memphis. Rev. Morrison had died after moving to Chicago to be with his sons, and Mrs. Morrison, who I loved dearly, remained in Chicago after his death and did not return for the funeral. Rev Green, the church's new pastor was very supportive of our family and helped us plan Daddy's funeral. Because of my father's work for equal rights and opportunities for the black employees of the Memphis post office, the church was filled with many of his friends and young men who were able to move up in the post office because of his dedication and work. The postmaster spoke about how my father worked for equality in the post office and even went to Washington to petition the US postmaster general to intervene, which resulted in black employees enjoying the same opportunities as the whites. Rev. Green spoke of how my father supported Rev. Roy D. Morrison as his assistant until his retirement. I spoke of my father as the most influential person, along with my dear mother, in my aspirations to serve the public. Many members of Zion attended, along with others from various organizations with which I had become affiliated during my years of civil service in Washington. The DC City Council sent a resolution honoring my father and speaking of my value as a member of the city council.

I was asked by Bud Krough, assistant to the president, to remain on the city council for continuity. Although I felt a certain obligation to the administration, I felt a greater obligation to Caron's education; I knew this would be the best gift I could give her. At the end of 1973, I resigned from the city council and moved to Olney, Maryland. Jean enrolled Caron in St. Paul's Elementary School, a very exceptional school.

We had a good experience in Olney. We lived on a cul-de-sac, where all of the families knew one another. All of us had children, and we all cared for them and made sure they were safe. This was truly a village. Caron blended with the children, although she was the only African American in the community.

Shortly after our move to Olney, Mother came to visit, like she'd visited all of my brothers and sisters months before. She loved our home in Olney and loved Caron and Michael, who loved her. At St. Paul Episcopal School, Caron excelled in every subject and was considered one of the brightest children in the class. This warmed my heart and made Jean and Mother very proud.

There was one incident I will never forget during that visit. One evening, I heard Caron and Mother talking in her room, with Caron giving instructions that were very humorous. I quietly went downstairs to listen more carefully.

I heard her asked her grandmother, "Did you understand what I just taught you?"

To this, my dear mother replied, "Yes, ma'am, and thank you."

I had to go back upstairs to keep from laughing.

This memory remains with me to this day.

I tried to get Mother to move to Maryland and stay with us, but she said very clearly that, as much as she loved us, her home was Memphis. It was where her house was and her neighbors, church, and flower garden. I never mentioned it again because I could feel her love for her home and friends and church. She returned to Memphis in the late summer of 1978, and I never saw her alive again.

The saddest day of my life was the day Mother died in Methodist Hospital in Memphis on April 28, 1977. It was six o'clock in the evening when I received the call. I was devastated. I had planned to leave the next day to go to Memphis to see her. I had only delayed my visit because Gerry had called me on Sunday and told me that Mother had suffered a heart attack but Dr. Slutsky had said she was doing well. Gerry also said Mother wanted me to come after Deacon Vince Johnson's funeral that Wednesday so that I could stay awhile. That did not matter. I would have stayed as long as Mother wanted me. I had resigned myself to waiting until after Wednesday to go to Memphis on Gerry's insistence.

That day, after the service for Deacon Johnson, I received a call from Gerry informing me that Mother had passed peacefully and was now at rest. I do not know how you can be sad and angry at the same time, but I was. Somehow, I blamed myself for not going that Sunday or Monday. But Gerry convinced me that Mother wanted me to wait until after the funeral for Deacon Johnson to come to Memphis. I have never said this before, and I ask my sister Geraldine to forgive me if I am wrong, but I did not believe Mother said that. I think Gerry was trying to comfort me about Mother's condition and thought, if she made it sound like it was not an emergency, I would not be anxious. In fact, I later found out that Dr. Slutsky had said that the heart attack had been so devastating she would never be able to stand again.

I arrived in Memphis the day after Mother passed. Gerry and I met with the Mrs. Hayes of the T. H. Hayes Funeral Home to make final arrangements for Mother's funeral at Central Baptist Church. Later that day, I learned that Rev. Dr. Henry Greene, pastor of Central, was hospitalized and would be unable to conduct the service. I immediately informed my family that I would conduct the service because, next to her pastor, there was no one I wanted but me. Everyone agreed and met with the organist, pianist, and the soloist Rev. Artis Golden, who had been my roommate at Arkansas AM&N, where we both sang in the choir.

I met with Artis to hear about the last minutes of my mother's life. Artis said that Rev. Greene asked him to go to the hospital for him, since he was not able due to his illness. When Artis had entered the room, my mother was awake and smiled and thanked him for coming. Artis asked Mother if he could do anything for her, and she answered, "Would you pray for me and sing 'What a Friend We Have in Jesus'?"

Artis prayed for her and held her hand. Immediately after the prayer he sang the song she had requested:

> All our sins and grieves to bear,
> What a privilege to carry, everything to God in
>   prayer,
> Oh what peace we often forfeit, oh what needless
>   pains we bear,
> All because we do not carry, everything to God in
>   prayer.

Rev. Golden said that, after the last word, she closed her eyes and turned her head and passed away.

I asked my friend Rev. Golden to leave me alone for a few minutes. When he left, I kneeled down and cried my heart out, partly in grief and partly with joy for the life Mother had lived and the love she had given to all of us.

I thanked Artis profusely for taking the time to be with her, which gave me some comfort. I knew my mother had thought that, in a beautiful and sweet way, my friend was standing in for me.

We lived in Olney until Caron reached middle school. Then Jean and I wanted to move closer to Washington, DC, to be closer to Jean's relatives and other friends. We also recognized that all of Caron's friends were white, which, in the long term, would not be good for her development. Jean found a beautiful colonial in Kensington, Maryland, across from the newly erected Mormon temple.

In the summer of 1979, we moved to 9609 Stoneybrook Drive in order to enroll Caron in Leland Junior High School in our district. This would prove to be a traumatic experience for her. Since she was born, she had been in school with whites, with the exception of the Zion Baptist nursery where I pastored. Caron excelled at Leland, where she befriended both black and white students, which made us very happy.

Caron finished Leland and was scheduled to attend Einstein High School, when the boundary placed her in Bethesda Chevy Chase High School (BCC), a top premier high school in Montgomery County. We had no idea how she would adjust to high school, but we knew she was very bright and had excelled in her academic life to this point. BCC, as it was called, offered a very strong academic program. Since Caron had been an honors student throughout her academic career, she was placed in the honors classes in several areas. This was very gratifying to both Jean and me. And her first year in high school went very well, considering the adjustment she was making to attend school with more black students than she had ever been exposed. I did not realize what a powerful effect having spent her earlier school years among primarily white children would have in her effort to identify with black students.

During her second year in high school, Caron began to fall back in her studies. This caused me great alarm, since I knew what she was capable of achieving. Her black friends included many young people of whom I was very fond and who I'd invited to share our home. Kelly Brockington became one of Caron's best friends, and I was glad about their friendship. But Caron's fondness for the opposite sex disturbed me. She'd met a very nice young man named George, who I liked but not for her. My objection wasn't that he came from a different social and economic background but that he did not impress me as serious young man seeking to improve himself. After noticing that Caron was becoming less interested in her academic work and more interested in her social life, her mother and I decided to take some drastic action in order to give her an opportunity to develop her mind to the maximum in order to become all she could be.

After her first year at BCC, I found a very strong boarding school in Tyrone, Pennsylvania, the Grier School for Girls, which was listed as one of the best boarding schools in the country. Caron was resistant to this change. She didn't want to leave her friends, especially George, who she really felt she loved.

I could understand these emotions for her age, but I knew sometimes you have to step in and make decisions for others, especially if that person is your daughter.

Although I was making a decent salary working two jobs, it was still a big decision. The tuition was $12,000, the equivalent of $23,000 a year in today's dollars, not including the trips and out-of-country tours important for her development.

In the meantime, our daughter Gayle and our son, Michael, were enrolled in Fisk University and Hampton University respectively. Gayle did well her first year but decided to come home and finish at the University of the District of Columbia. Michael had great promise, having graduated from St. John High School, one of the prestigious high schools in Washington, DC. In his second year, he became addicted to drugs and dropped out and returned home.

The tragedy we had to endure was the drug epidemic in Washington, DC, that had reached historic proportions. Although I tried to help him by sending him to some of the best rehabilitation centers in the country and many times thought he had conquered his drug demons, he returned to his habit again and again. Over the next thirty years, he fought these demons, and today he has been successful, even though most of his life is over.

Michael's story would continue to be tragic. His children, Isaiah and Sheriece, would long do well in spite of their absentee father. But tragedy would strike once again when Isaiah, with whom I'd worked tirelessly to make sure he did not fall into his father's pattern, would see his life altered by an unbelievable tragedy. I'll share the story later in this book.

The next two years were pivotal for Caron, allowing her to discover another world she did not realize existed. Caron's experiences at Grier were both a blessing and a curse. She had been thrown into a situation where most of the students came from affluent families. She was not denied anything she needed and was given most of what she wanted. But what she experienced among her fellow students at the boarding school was a different kind of affluence. The kids there were accustomed to having whatever they desired. But Jean and I reminded Caron that we did not have that kind of affluence, and even if we did, she did not need everything she desired. Notwithstanding these problems, she did very well and developed and matured the way we had hoped.

The year 1980 proved to be one of the most tragic and traumatic years of my ministry. Michael had met a young lady, Valencia Nelson, at church. The two had become very close and emotionally evolved. He approached me about talking with her mother, Mrs. Veronica Nelson. Her daughter was worried that she seemed very depressed. I agreed to talk with Mrs. Nelson, and I did call her and ask if I could be of any help. She indicated she would like to talk, and maybe that would help her. I asked if she could come to the church and meet with me. Veronica indicated she would be more comfortable if I came to her home to talk with her. I thought about it and decided that maybe it would be better if I visited her, rather than having her to come to the church. After speaking with her several times on the phone, I agreed to meet her at her home.

This visit proved to be the most tragic decision of my ministry. When I arrived at her home, she invited me in and was very gracious and hospitable, offering me refreshments and snacks. Afterward, she made a deliberate decision to avoid the subject about which I had come to talk with her, the depression. I did not think much about this, and she changed the subject to my son and her daughter, Valencia.

After we had talked for an hour or more, I decided to leave. She asked me to please come back again. I told her I would and set a time in the next week to come back. Although I felt some uneasiness about the visit, I assumed it was because she was a very talkative person and I had not expected this, since she was suffering from depression. The workman's compensation she was receiving as a result of an attack she'd suffered at her school during an altercation between her and a student was ending.

Several weeks passed with weekly visits. During the last visit, she made overtures to me in a sexual way, which I had not experienced before. After a short time, I responded to her advances, which led to a very regrettable sexual encounter. This was the beginning of a tragic end.

Several weeks passed, and I decided to end this regrettable encounter. I told her that the next visit would be my last, and our relationship would end.

In August 1980, I arrived at her home to end the relationship and suggest some other places she could go for help. On my arrival, she was very pleasant, unusually talkative, and very sexually suggestive. I told her that the relationship had to end and suggested several therapists for her to see. As I went toward the door to leave, she cried out to someone in the back room that I was leaving. Two people then came out of the back room in a menacing manner giving me the idea that they had weapons, and telling me to sit down and that I would not be leaving. I was nervous. But I was also confused. I did not understand that I was being kidnaped and held against my will.

After I had sat down, Veronica explained to me that I would not be leaving. Instead, I would be leaving with her the next day to go to Sweden to get married. My confusion turned into panic as I tried to determine what this was all about. During my stay, she forced me to take sexually suggestive pictures, which I resisted but was finally forced to comply by two menacing men who seemed bent on violence if necessary. After this episode, I was held for hours while she waited for me to comply with our leaving for a foreign country the next day. I realized that her possible psychosis was reaching a very dangerous point. Hours passed, and my mind began to contemplate the consequences of my immoral actions and how much I had let my family and church down.

We were on the eighth floor of an apartment building. I contemplated running to the window and breaking the glass and jumping to my death. As I thought about this action, I heard the voice of my mother say to me, "Son, don't do that." Her voice brought tears to my eyes, even though she had died the year before.

After I tried to pray for an answer, something was revealed to me. I later came to understand got the revelation was from the Holy Spirit. I knew that I should feign a heart attack. I had been diagnosed with heart failure some months before. My captors became nervous and told

Veronica they would have to take me to the hospital, as they did not want to be involved in a death. Although she objected, they asked me to come with them and drove me to the Holy Cross Hospital only fifteen minutes away.

When we arrived at the hospital reception desk, the receptionist recognized me and asked in a very loud voice, "Rev. Veazey, what are you doing here?"

I responded that I was having chest pains.

My captors immediately fled, in order to not be arrested for kidnapping.

I called Jean, who had been searching for me. I had been missing since eleven o'clock in the evening, which was when I usually returned home if nothing had occurred. It was now five o'clock in the morning, and when she heard from me she was relieved and upset.

I explained that I would tell her in detail what had happened when I returned home from the hospital. I also called Deacon Robinson, who was not only the chair of my church board but also my friend and had been my best man at my marriage to Jean. He agreed to meet me at home and talk with me then.

I went home, and Deacon Robinson arrived shortly after I did. His presence made it easier to recount what had happened. I knew Jean would be hurt and perhaps he could comfort her.

The following week I met in the chapel with the deacons to inform them of what had happened and offer my resignation. Deacon Robinson opened the meeting with prayer and explained that the pastor needed to talk with the board to get their advice. My speech to the board was the most difficult message I had ever given. I did not hesitate but went directly to the point, informing the board members that, over the past few weeks, I had been involved in an extramarital affair with a young lady named Veronica Nelson. I also told them about how the affair had been revealed as a scheme on her part to extort money and how I had been threatened with violence. I recounted the events of that night when I had contemplated suicide and had been saved by prayer, explaining how the men she had hired to hold me captive had released me at the hospital after I'd informed them about my heart condition.

After my very emotional speech, the board members, who were amazing and very supportive, offered prayers for me and asked me to continue as pastor.

The events that followed were very traumatic. Veronica sent a note requesting $20,000 for the photographs she had forced me to take suggesting a sexual encounter that did not happened. My attorney contacted the Federal Bureau of Investigation, who took over the investigation of this criminal enterprise.

The next few weeks were very difficult because Veronica could not be located. Word finally came that she had been arrested and charged with extortion and kidnapping, as had the men she had hired to keep me from leaving. She was arraigned, and a trial date was set.

As a result of the trial Veronica was sentenced and released to get her business in order. Although justice had been done, I went to the US Attorney's Office to drop the charges, realizing she had a daughter. This gesture was rejected, and the trial and sentencing proceeded.

The judge released Veronica on her own recognizance with the instruction that she was too report on a certain day for sentencing. She failed to report, and a warrant was issued for her arrest. The FBI discovered that she had fled the country to avoid prosecution, thereby committing another felony.

Over a year passed without any knowledge of her whereabouts, although it was thought she was somewhere in Europe.

The US Attorney's office stayed in touch to keep me informed about their progress in locating Veronica and to make sure I wasn't receiving threats from anyone.

One day in late July, I received a call informing me that Veronica had been located and was being returned to the United States for sentencing. When she was brought before the judge, he, for some inexplicable reason, again gave her time to prepare to serve time. Veronica again disappeared, which was very troubling.

Weeks had passed with the FBI searching for her when she called a local black radio station and said that she had been persecuted by the courts because of a relationship she'd had with city officials such as Marion Barry, Carlton Veazey, and others. I knew nothing about these other involvements. However, someone heard she was on the radio and called the FBI, who traced the call from the radio station to an apartment house on Connecticut Avenue NW, where she was living. The FBI proceeded to the eighth floor of the building to arrest. But after the agents had knocked on the door and announced that they were the FBI, she had gone to the balcony and jumped to her death.

This tragedy happened on a Saturday. The local stations reported the story over and over, noting my involvement in her life and also mentioning other people in the city who had allegedly been involved with her. To this day, I cannot describe the sadness and the guilt I felt, although this tragedy was a result of her criminal enterprise.

While preparing for my sermon the next day and knowing my church members were aware of what had happened, I wondered, How I could preach and about what?

I really wanted to ask someone else to lead the service, but somehow I felt spiritually challenged to preach myself. After hours of prayer and meditating, I was led to the text in which Jesus told the story of the prodigal son. This story speaks of the love of the father for his son who had left home and gone to a foreign land, where he became lost and spent his life in sin. The son finally came to himself and decided to return home to his father's house. The interesting thing about the prodigal son's return was that his father never asked him where he had been or why he had left. He simply said to his servants, "Get the robe and the ring, my son who was lost has been found."

This subject of being lost and found was fitting for my experiences in the last year. I had found a wonderful peace in knowing that I had been forgiven, and my loving church affirmed that love that Sunday. I found the strength and courage to declare His word and again ask forgiveness and strength to continue my ministry.

I went to the service that Sunday with a heavy heart and the need for forgiveness. Some may ask why I felt the need for forgiveness concerning Veronica Nelson's death, since she clearly was a part of a criminal enterprise. My answer is that my weakness in the first place led to her untimely end. Yes, there may have been others, and some may feel that she brought this on herself. I cannot take responsibility for anyone but myself, and I will carry that fateful decision to my death.

One of the most amazing experiences came to me after this devastating time. I found not only a sense of renewal but also a new calling to preach with more passion. I also felt called to share with the church my sense that I'd been called to introduce the gift of healing in Zion.

After several weeks, people began to notice the power in our services and that I had been transformed by the Holy Spirit with power in my prayers of intercession and preaching. Our Wednesday prayer service increased over fourfold, to the point we had to move our prayer and healing services to the main sanctuary for more room. This was the turning point in my ministry, which will always have an indelible place in my heart and mind. I was happy and peaceful. I had found the source of the power that Jesus promised when he said he would send the comforter, which was the Holy Spirit.

The church grew in numbers and spiritual power because we relied on the Holy Spirit. The Holy Spirit would take over our services and allow us to experience the power of the Holy Ghost in our lives. This period in the life of Zion was unparalleled in the history of my pastorate. We also started a radio broadcast that reached thousands every Sunday in our "Zion at Worship" every Sunday morning. Every facet of our church program grew, with our twenty auxiliaries matching every city social agency to make the social gospel come to life. I was enjoying pastoring more than I had in the past twenty years.

In December 1990, I celebrated my thirtieth anniversary as pastor of Zion Baptist Church at the Omni Shoreham Hotel, with over a thousand members and friends from around the country in attendance. Mrs. Genevieve Johnson, chair of the event, had been one of my strongest supporters during my thirty years. She had the ability to bring people together and had been appointed by Mayor Marion Barry to chair the Senior Citizens Day held every year at the DC Armory.

I will never forget that night. All of the people there had played a part in my development and any success I had experienced. First among them was my wife, Jean, who had supported me since we met. People often spoke of how much I had accomplished since becoming pastor at twenty-three years of age, which was unheard of in the Washington area. Many times I had spoken about Jean's quiet support and encouragement, which gave me the inspiration to do more. In all the fifty years we were married, she did not complain or try to interfere with my work or my desire to take on more. She did this while raising our daughters, Gayle and Caron. I will always be grateful for her and honor her memory as a truly beautiful spirit.

Those present were members of the clergy of Washington, DC; the mayor of DC, Marion Barry, who had also been a high school classmate at Booker T. Washington High School; and members of the city council, where I had served.

The highlight of the evening was having Rev. Dr. T. J. Jimerson, pastor of First Baptist Church in Baton Rouge, Louisiana, and president of the largest black convention in the United States, the National Baptist Convention, USA, Inc. in attendance. This convention represented more than thirty-three thousand black churches and more than three million members. Dr. Jimerson spoke of my work as chair of the theological commission, the think tank of the convention as it related to theological matters.

We were also honored to be joined by Dr. Benjamin Hooks of Memphis, Tennessee, president of the NAACP, the historic organization with the mission of advancing the progress of colored people (as was the customary way to refer to black people then). Dr. Hooks gave a powerful speech as only he could as a Baptist minister for many years. He was a close friend of my family, and his father was the first black photographer of Memphis, whose business was known as the Hooks Brothers.

After the Friday celebration, we prepared for the anniversary service held on Sunday. Rev. Dr. Jimerson was the preacher for the service. The choir, under Jennie Smith's leadership, brought beautiful music, with beloved sister Elizabeth Quander singing her own version of "Old Ship of Zion" and Aubrey Ballard, my adopted brother, singing "To God Be the Glory" as only he could sing it. To round out the solo trio was Laverne Smiler, who sang one of my favorites, "Jesus Is the Name of My Friend." This was one of the most beautiful services I had experienced.

Finally, Rev. Dr. Jimerson informed the church that he had appointed me as the chair of the prestigious Theological Commission because he admired my accomplishments as a pastor and city official.

The service ended with a beautiful reception in the A. Joseph Edwards Fellowship Hall. This was appropriate, since this edifice was Rev. Edwards's dream, and God gave me the honor of completing his dream. I will always cherish the memory of Rev. Dr. Edwards.

Little did I know what tragic events would come less than twenty-four months after the celebration of my thirtieth anniversary as Zion's pastor, a celebration shared in by more than a thousand—events that would threaten all of my years in the ministry and pastorate.

Chapter 7

CLAY FEET AND FAITH

Mrs. Jean Margaret Veazey, Wife

The year 1991 was a strange one because, although things were going well, there seemed to be some unrest within the congregation. We continued to grow and serve our community, but I discovered that some members were unhappy with the tithing program that required members to give 10 percent of their income to support the church. This was a biblically-based program that I had instituted as part of my plans for the New Year. This program met with instant success, but some members were disgruntled. They felt somewhat guilty, not wanting to tithe and, because there was a certain period set aside for tithers, felt reflected on those who did not tithe. Among them were some trustees, deacons, and deaconesses.

I didn't realize that this program gave some people who opposed me an opportunity to criticize my leadership. As they garnered support, others brought issues they had with my leadership. One who created this dissension in the church was an attorney named James Christian, a young man who I had taken under my wings. Because he had an excellent background, being trained at Harvard, I had elevated him to the chairmanship of the board of trustee. Another duplicitous person was Dr. Robert Owens, chair of the Department of Liberal Arts at Howard University. You will understand why I called him duplicitous as you read this book.

Others participated, including Brother Turner, who owned a business that sold hair products for women. He had joined Zion years before and left after he could not dictate to me or change the program of the church. He joined the Metropolitan Baptist Church, where he also had conflict with the pastor, Rev. Dr. H. Beecher Hicks. He'd returned to Zion with what some saw was a new spirit, which led me to give him another opportunity to serve as president of the Men's Club. He again joined the dissension in the church, allying with Christian, Owens, Bennett, and others of whom I will speak later.

Trustee James Christian, companion to Robert Owens in this evil conspiracy, worked to build a consensus against me and my pastorate. This continued through 1991, when a group of members and officers sent me a letter advising me that they questioned my fitness for the pastorate at Zion Baptist Church and requested my resignation. I sent a letter to the leaders and Christian that, under no condition, would

I submit my resignation or meet with them to discuss it as they had requested. This led to a church-wide rift, with many factions forming and developing an even bigger rift in the congregation. I continued my work as pastor as I had done for the past thirty-one years.

The conspiracy gained new members as some who had differed with me in the past joined with the forces attempting to end my pastorate, including some deacons and trustees. I continued to preach each Sunday, with as much passion as the Holy Spirit led me. Christian and Owens made false charges and sent letters to members without any proof, only their words and lies. This proved to be the most difficult year of my ministry. I was not fighting against an honest disagreement but against charges such as that I had become a dictator and ruled the church without any input from other officials. Everyone knew that these were lies but tended to just overlook them.

A call for the church to meet was initiated by Christian and Owens. They wanted to change the constitution, which called for a two-third's majority of church members voting to dismiss their pastor. Their proposal at this illegal church meeting was to change the requirement to a simple majority of members voting to remove the pastor. This satanic conspiracy by Christian and Owens at this illegal meeting would eventually lead to a meeting of the church that was objected to by members who were supporting me.

They first called a meeting to determine whether there was confidence in the pastor, which was dismissed when members objected to this tactic. After that meeting, they called for a general meeting to determine whether the pastor should be retained in light of the charges brought by the faction led by Christian and Owens. The charges that their pastor had become mean and indifferent to members and was dictatorial were almost laughable, since everyone knew this to be false.

However, it was like Nazi Germany, when Hitler kept saying the same thing about the Jews—so much so that the Germans began to believe the Jews were the cause of their failing economy and then turned on their neighbors and friends simply because Hitler had given those reasons for the problems in their lives.

In August 1992, the church met to determine the future of my ministry at Zion Baptist Church. God had directed me to this church to complete the vision of Rev. Dr. A. Joseph Edwards when I was only twenty-three years of age and in my second year in seminary at Howard University's School of Religion. I had accepted this spiritual challenge and completed the church edifice in 1962, only two years after being elected pastor, addressing all the difficulties of almost losing the church for lack of funds. Also under my leadership the church, the membership that had fallen to less than four hundred when I became pastor had increased to over a thousand.

As we prepared for the meeting of the church to determine my future, some members had solicited the legal assistance of an attorney named R. Kenneth Mundy. Mundy was the best-known lawyer in the city, and he would represent my interest. He tried tirelessly to find a compromise with James Christian, also a lawyer. His efforts were to no avail, with Christian telling Mundy that he and the members wanted me out at any cost.

As the day of the August meeting approached, indifference and downright disrespect was shown to me by some of the officials of the church. On Holy Communion Sunday, marking the death and resurrection of our Lord Jesus Christ, the deacons would refuse to accept the cup or the bread from my hand and would literally turn their backs against me to show their contempt. Although this was very hurtful, I was determined not to allow them to kill my spirit or to allow their contempt to inhibit my pastoral responsibilities. Many letters were written to me and to other members of the church, filled with lies and degrading words about me and my ministry. I had to endure all of this, but my faith in God gave me the courage to fight on. I was reminded of my father's words. "Right has never lost a battle, and wrong has never won one." Those words kept ringing in my ears and gave me the moral fortitude and courage to continue.

Meanwhile, Christian and Owens continued to hold meetings where they told other untruths. For example, they claimed to have offered me a generous retirement package, which never happened.

I told Jean that I would never resign and that they would have to vote me out. She supported me, and I will always be grateful for her support, even if it would cause us disastrous consequences.

August 20, 1992, was the date set for the church meeting to determine my fitness for the ministry and the pastorate. I was in Atlanta, Georgia, attending the National Baptist Convention's annual meeting. As the appointed chair of the theological committee, I reported to the convention the recent developments in theology and how to apply them to our congregations. When I received notice of this meeting, I was very disturbed and somewhat depressed. The church to which I had given most of my life had allowed these men to ask for my resignation without just cause.

When I finished my report before the convention, I returned to the Marriott Marquis Hotel, where Jean was waiting and told her that, because of the tension I felt and anger I had, I was going to exercise. That would give me a chance to reset and relax.

After going to the health club and getting on the treadmill, as was my custom, I noticed a tightening in my chest, which I first ignored. I immediately reduced the speed from five miles an hour to three and finally to two, which did not reduce the tightness and discomfort in my chest. I left the health club and returned to my hotel room, where I told Jean about my discomfort. She gave me several Tums, which alleviated neither the tightness nor the discomfort. After several minutes I told her I wanted to go to the hospital.

Downstairs at the front desk, I described my symptoms to the clerk, who wanted to call the emergency medical services, but I declined and went to get a cab. Once inside the cab, I told the Ethiopian driver to cautiously run every light and to take me to Crawford Long Hospital, the nearest medical facility.

When I arrived in the emergency room and noted that I had a stent in my heart from a recent procedure, the ER staff immediately ran tests. The doctor came into my room and explained that I'd had had a heart attack, but he wasn't sure of its intensity. I vehemently refuted his findings and told him that I had just had a recent examination at Providence Hospital in Washington, DC, and that could not be true. The doctors were very patient with me and called Dr. Quash at Providence Hospital to relay their findings and ask him to speak with me. I was in a very serious state that would require immediate attention.

Over the phone, Dr. Quash said, "Rev. Veazey, you have had a very serious heart attack. Please allow the doctors to treat you."

I hung up and told Jean what Dr. Quash said, and we agreed to allow the doctors to treat me.

The doctors of Crawford Long Hospital, with God, saved my life. They did another stent and prepared me for surgery if I did not improve. I was again informed that my condition was very serious, and the time of my hospitalization was indeterminate. After several days in intensive care, a resident came into my room to examine me and told me how serious this heart attack was. He said the clot that had caused the heart attack missed the main artery, which would have caused instant death. This explanation was the most sobering in my life. Jean was visibly shaken to hear this, and both of us were grateful that God had spared me.

Mrs. Robinson, the church secretary, called after several days to say that she would contact the ministers I had named to carry on my Sunday services until I returned. Little did I know that I would remain in the hospital for eleven days. Jean would remain in the Marriott during that time. Many members sent cards and flowers to the hospital during my stay, and one of my best friends, Robert Plummer, director and owner of John T. Rhine's Funeral Home in Washington, DC, called me every day to inquire about my recovery. We joked about having a funeral director call you every day and inquiring about how you are doing. Bob Plummer was so supportive, telling Jean that, whatever she needed, she should just let him know, and he would take care of it. He was truly one of my best friends since I became pastor of Zion Baptist Church.

Jean was supportive and encouraging and would not allow me to talk about my church issues.

Rev. Dr. Jimerson and the convention's secretary Rev. Dr. Richardson came to the hospital to see me and pray with me and said that everyone at the convention would keep me in their prayers. They both prayed with me and left me an envelope that I thought was a get-well card. In that envelope was a check for $3,000 and a note saying, if I needed more, to please call, and it would be done. This made me feel so much better, in spite of all my troubles both internal and external.

My church secretary, Helen Robinson, would call me daily to let me know about the church. She indicated that some deacons and trustees were questioning whether I'd really had a heart attack. This news extremely upset me. How low they could get? I wondered. And how stupid could they be? Didn't they know they could call the hospital or my doctor to find out? This was all about the plot to discredit me because I had feigned a heart attack when I was kidnapped some years in the past and used my heart condition to get my captors to allow me to go to the hospital. They eventually called Dr. Quash at Providence Hospital, who confirmed that, while in Atlanta, I'd had a heart attack that was life-threatening and required several weeks of recovery.

Even after obtaining a written report, some deacons continued to spread the word that I hadn't really had a heart attack and that this was my attempt to quiet the dissension against me and the campaign to dismiss me as pastor.

I will always be grateful to the doctors of Crawford Long Hospital.

When I returned to Washington after almost three weeks in the hospital in Atlanta, Robert Plummer sent a limousine to pick Jean and me up from Washington National Airport. I will always be grateful to Robert Plummer and his dear wife, Hazel, for their friendship and support during my pastorate. During the next few weeks, I was anxious to return to the Zion pulpit and, hopefully, heal the divisions in the church, which had become wider. I wanted to return the Sunday after coming home, but my doctors absolutely forbade me to resume my duties as pastor, especially conducting Sunday services. After Jean insisted that I listen to my doctors, I decided to take their advice and arranged for other ministers to preach during my absence. Among them were Rev. Dr. Williams of Asbury United Methodist Church and Rev. Dr. Walter Fauntroy of New Bethel Baptist Church.

In the meantime, the dissidents and others continued their campaign against me, causing further division in the church.

When my doctors gave me permission to resume my duties on a limited basis, I returned to the pulpit and preached a sermon aimed at bringing the church together and not allowing the few to divide the many who were interested in having a viable fellowship of Christ called the church. This sermon was received by many but also looked at as a retort against the charges of Christian, Owens, and the others. This did not matter to me. I realized this would be the test of my ministry and would make me listen to what God was saying to me in these circumstances.

The meeting when the church would decide my future as the pastor of Zion Baptist Church continued to be a shock, although my counsel, Ken Mundy, had prepared me to know that my foes felt they had the votes to dismiss me.

The night of the meeting, the church was filled with supporters, as well as detractors who were influenced by dissidents and intent on removing me and selecting a minister who would be willing to accept directions from the officers of the church. My good friend Congressman Fauntroy had said he wanted to come and speak on my behalf, since each side was supposed to be given equal time. When he arrived at the church, he found security guards standing at the door and along the walls of the sanctuary to assure no violence would occur. This church, which was founded in 1864, the year of emancipation, had lowered itself to the point where it had to have security guards to ensure order. Congressman Fauntroy was not allowed in the sanctuary and asked to leave by the security guard captain.

This night of the vote for my dismissal would become indelibly stamped in my mind. The voting process was controlled by dissidents and was inherently unfair, since the members implementing the voting procedures had been selected by them. Also, children as young as ten and eleven were allowed to vote with their parents to ensure that the vote would go their way. Although I had baptized the children as members of the church, no one thought they would be able to vote on such a weighty matter as dismissing the pastor for reasons they did not understand.

When the final vote tally was counted, I was dismissed by less than twenty votes, with all the irregularities and fraud that the conspirators had perpetrated. Some called for a recount, which would definitely have been in order. But I refused to support that and asked my supporters to withdraw their dissent.

I left the church with a broken heart and spirit. That night, I had seen people to whom I had ministered for over three decades turn against me because of some people who wanted to control the ministry and the business of the church without interference.

I arrived home at half past midnight and received a call from Congressman Fauntroy, who told me something I have not forgotten to this day. He said, "Carlton, you will never want anything for the rest of your life."

These were prophetic words. Almost thirty years later, I can say that I am today blessed with everything I need. I will always be indebted to Walter because of his friendship and support through all the years.

The next day, I met with Mundy who expressed his disappointment in the outcome of the vote. He also said he'd file a $10 million suit against Zion for the false charges and jeopardizing my livelihood and future income. He explained that such a case would be difficult to win, considering the courts very seldom interfered with church matters as a result of the Constitution's separation of church and state. However, I learned that, if I'd made a contract with the church many years ago, I would have had legal right to sue for compensation. This I did not do because the culture in which I grew up didn't have ministers signing contracts; they looked upon their calling to the ministry as a divine call and did not require a legal and binding contract to serve a church.

Suffice it to say, I had to sit down with Jean so we could decide where we would go from here.

Although minister friends suggested I could easily pastor another church, I resisted and had actually decided to never preach again. This was one of the darkest periods in my life and my marriage. Although Jean and I had a rather harmonious relationship, these kinds of unexpected traumas in your life cause serious problems—and they did for both of us. I had lost my vocation and livelihood, and she was finding me difficult company. Finally, some members of the church demanded that the church provide me with a severance of six months' salary and health insurance. I found myself remaining in the house, with the exception of going to the Marriott health club for exercise. My sister Gerry observed that after skiing in Pennsylvania at least twice a week, I somehow seemed different when I returned.

Rev. Fauntroy phoned me several days later to inquire about my salary at Zion. I told him my total salary had been over $100,000. He asked me to meet him at New Bethel, where he offered a minimum six-month position as vice president, working with him on a project to assist African countries and offered a salary comparable that of Zion.

Before I began work with Fauntroy, my sister Gerry offered to pay for me to go to Vail, Colorado, to ski on some of the best powder in the country. I arrived in Vail still suffering from the emotional trauma from my Zion experience, but my skiing trip proved to be a turning point in my life. Standing eleven thousand feet on top of the mountain on a beautiful sunny day with the snow glistening, I took a minute to just thank God for being God. I was also grateful that my spirit had begun to return to the joy and peace I had known. I pushed off from the slope and skied with great confidence from one of the highest slopes. I stopped three times to rest and again thank God for another day and spiritual renewal. At the bottom of the mountain, I felt such a spiritual rush that I began to weep uncontrollably—not out of sadness but from the epiphany I had just experienced.

On my return to Washington, Jean informed me that some members who had left Zion as a result of what had happened to me had been calling to meet with me about starting a new church. I told her that I absolutely was not going to preach or pastor again. I had found peace within and was satisfied with my life as it was. Edmonia Johnson, Carrie Leary, Nannie Curtis, Mary Green, and others had been meeting with a friend of mine, the Reverend Dr. Joseph A. Gilmore Sr., pastor of the Mt. Ephraim Baptist Church in Prince George's County, Maryland, for guidance. I did not know that he had offered to pray with them weekly for my return to the ministry and preaching.

Edmonia Johnson and others repeatedly called me, pleading for my return as their pastor. Finally, I agreed and asked Rev. Fauntroy to allow us to pray each Wednesday in his fellowship hall. He gladly agreed. We met for over three months praying together. At one meeting, I asked those who had gathered to stay after the benediction. They were very curious and anxious about what I was about to say. God directed my thoughts and words, which were few, so I simply said that I had heard a second call from the Lord and I would again preach and, hopefully, pastor. There was so much joy in that fellowship hall, along with crying and hugging. They held me and thanked me for allowing God to speak to me.

Others heard the news of my decision to preach again and joined in our weekly prayer services, with participation rising to almost one hundred within a month. This was very encouraging. I also remembered what I had promised God when he'd healed my mother in 1956 after Dr. Lloyd at the University of Tennessee Medical School had deemed her condition terminal.

Each day, I felt a great sense of purpose and peace with my decision to preach again. Several months had passed when I announced that we would hold an organizing meeting after our prayer meeting.

That Wednesday, almost a hundred members came, including some who'd heard about my decision and wanted to be a part of this new church. After the brief prayer service, I announced that the Lord had given me the name of our new church, which would be called Fellowship Baptist Church. I asked them to confirm me as founder and pastor if they so desired.

Immediately, someone moved to make me the founder and pastor of Fellowship Baptist Church. I accepted with gratitude and announced the body of baptized believers in Jesus Christ would be known as the Fellowship Baptist Church. I also indicated that we would have a second organization meeting after our Wednesday prayer service to elect the first officers of our church.

At that meeting, I recommended as officers Carrie Leary, chair of the diaconate; F. Alexis Roberson, chair, trustee board; Nannie Curtis, treasurer; Theresa Chambliss, church clerk; A. Renee McConnell, secretary. Each one of these persons was revealed to me through the spirit, and the vote for them was unanimous.

Later I would announce the members of the trustee board after consultation with the chair and the deacons. The church also authorized me to have an attorney friend and fellow Memphian, Mose Lewis, draw up the constitution and bylaws required for incorporation in the District of Columbia. We also voted to have Rev. Dr. Jerry A. Moore organize the installation service for Fellowship Baptist Church, with consultation with the Rev. Dr. Walter Fauntroy, pastor of New Bethel Baptist Church, where the service would be held.

On Sunday, August 19, 1994, at six o'clock in the evening, the sanctuary of New Bethel Baptist Church was filled with friends from across the city who had known my ministry for the past thirty-three years. Rev. Dr. Moore had been my mentor since I had become pastor of Zion Baptist Church. We had common experiences in the ministry. He was elected pastor of Nineteenth Street Baptist Church at age thirty-four, and I was elected pastor of Zion Baptist at age twenty-three. Nineteenth Street was the oldest church in the district, followed by Shiloh and Zion.

The installation service was a powerful spiritual experience, with Rev. Moore describing our sojourn during the past four years and how God had blessed us to arrive at this wonderful place as Fellowship Baptist Church. Rev. Dr. Fauntroy also congratulated us on our journey and thanked us for allowing him to be a part of our sojourn. We then received the official documents from Mose Lewis making us an incorporated entity in the District of Columbia. We also received from the District of Columbia Baptist Convention and the American Baptist Convention letters confirming our membership in both conventions.

The day's end turned another chapter in the life and ministry of Carlton Wadsworth Veazey, son of Rev. Mertie Veazey and Dolly Veazey and grandson of Rev. George Veazey and Annie Veazey, born in 1860 and 1864 respectively, before emancipation. I am very proud that my grandfather pastored the Enon Baptist Church in Arkabutla, Mississippi, from 1890 until 1930. He died the year before I was born in 1935, and my grandmother died at the age of fifty-seven.

Shortly after our dedication as Fellowship Baptist Church, my dear friend H. R. Crawford, a prominent businessman and member of the DC City Council, offered us a church home at the Roosevelt Hotel building, which had been converted to a senior citizen building that he managed. The Roosevelt was once a thriving and prominent hotel in DC. H. R. Crawford allowed me to worship there for several years without paying rent or any other expenses, in exchange for ministering to its residents.

The use of the Roosevelt was the first of many God-sent blessings as we embarked on our journey. As a church, our mission was to follow the teachings of Jesus Christ as stated in Matthew 25: "Inasmuch as you have done it to the least of these, my brethren, you have done it unto me."

Our services on Sundays and the bible study on Wednesday were well attended. Some people from the Roosevelt came to our services. One of them I will never forget was Charles Walker, who was almost ninety years old and sight impaired and very spiritual. His presence brought a new spiritual vitality to our church. He was ordained as a deacon during his time with us.

After several years worshipping at the Roosevelt, the building was scheduled to close, which meant we had to find another place. God's providence once again visited us. We were able to secure space at the Owl School on Sixteenth Street. This was a godsend, in that it provided us not only with adequate space but also with parking, which was very helpful in that area.

Our congregation grew and many came to be baptized. Among them were the Fears sons, who I had known since their births. Mr. and Mrs. Ernest Fears III joined, along with Ernest Fears Jr., his father. These were some of the first baptisms held at the New Bethel Baptist church. New Bethel was really the sister church to Fellowship because of the close relationship with the pastor.

Our stay at the Owl School lasted for several years, ending when the school could no longer house us due to city regulations and insurance issues. After a meeting with the trustee board, we decided to seek a temporary church home, which we found at my alma mater, the Howard University Divinity School in Northeast. The chapel provided more than enough room for us to meet on Wednesdays and Sundays. After moving to this new location, we intensified our search for a permanent home, asking each member to be a search committee of one to find a home for Fellowship.

One Monday morning after a very spirited service on Sunday, Carlotta Parks, who chaired the hospitality committee called with the exciting news that she had passed a church building at 5605 Colorado Avenue NW with a *For Sale* sign and wanted to know if I would like to look at it. My response was that I would come as soon as I could dress.

When I arrived at the site, my mind went back almost twenty-five years. I had preached at this very church, then St. Luke's Baptist

Church, pastored by Rev. Lucas. I remember well going there one Sunday night to preach as a neighbor and dear friend of Rev. Lucas. This was a very strong sign that the Holy Spirit was speaking to me, and this would be our church home.

The building was in serious disrepair, but I looked beyond that and visualized what it could be. The sign gave a number, which I called. I spoke to one of the officials of the Mennonite church who owned the property. After telling him about our interest and how our new congregation had been looking for a building in that neighborhood, he immediately told me that he would reduce the price from $350,000 to $300,000.

I conferred with the trustee board, and the chair, F. Alexis Roberson, moved that the pastor enter into negotiations with the Mennonite church to determine a final sale price.

When I was at Zion, I had become a member of the American Baptist Home Mission Board, which supported new churches. I asked to speak to someone who could help me get financing for a new church building. I was connected with the loan department for churches, and the young man who answered asked how he could help me. I gave him my name and told him I had started a new church and had found a suitable building for our needs, but we needed $300,000 to buy the building.

He introduced himself as Tracy and asked me if I was the Reverend Veazey who'd pastored the Zion Baptist Church on Blagden Avenue NW. I told him that I was, and he said he'd known me when he served as assistant minister of the National Baptist Church at Sixteenth and Columbia Road. It was this connection that made him confident he could secure the $300,000 loan for us. He asked me to send the church's financial records for the past three years to process immediately. This was another revelation from the Holy Spirit in guiding our church.

Nannie Curtis, our treasurer, was a very smart and intelligent person. She also kept precise financial records. After sending them to Tracy on a Friday, I received his call on Monday, indicating his receipt of our financial records. Since they were of a precision he had never seen, he would have an answer the next day.

True to his word, the next day before ten o'clock, I received a call from Tracy saying that the $300,000 loan had been approved at a very low interest rate and would be available in three days.

I immediately thanked the Lord for His guidance and direction and asked the Holy Spirit to continue to lead us.

After calling F. Alexis Roberson with the good news, I asked her to contact the Mennonite officials and arrange a closing. Realizing that we would need additional money for furnishings and other unexpected costs, I contacted the DC Baptist Convention Foundation to seek a loan for $50,000 that was approved in less than a week.

The Holy Spirit was still guiding us and directing our paths. We held an emergency trustee meeting to select a contractor to renovate the building, with the expectation of having our dedication in September 1999—which put us on a very fast track. After selecting the contractor, we reviewed plans for a congregation that would seat a maximum of 110 people and did not include a choir loft, which would seat another 20 people.

As soon as the contract was signed, every member became excited and began to make huge sacrifices to see a new church edifice erected to the glory of God. Our building was renovated in record time, and the dedication of the Fellowship Baptist Church edifice was held on September 26, 1999.

The dedication was a glorious day, with a full house and some who stood in the narthex to hear the services. Holy Communion was held earlier, which set the tone. And our speaker for the morning service was my dear friend Rev. Dr. Crawford, mentor and father in the ministry, who gave an inspiring message that reminded us that we had gotten to this day through the grace of God.

After the message my good friend Rev. Dr. Fauntroy, who had been so instrumental in our reaching this day, dedicated a tribute to Fellowship through a special selection, "Climb Every Mountain" as only he could sing.

There were many tears and shouts of joy. When the early founders had met in a prayer service led by Rev. Dr. Gilmore, pastor of Mt. Ephraim Baptist Church, they had not envisioned this day. We then paused to remember those who simply wanted God to affirm their faith on this spiritual journey with us, but had not lived to see the completion. We felt assured that they were still among us and encouraging us as we moved ahead.

Our very simple mission as a church of the Lord Jesus Christ was to edify the Lord through worship, study, and being a force for good in the community by supporting those in need, comforting the hurt, and becoming a fellowship where we demonstrated our love for one another through supporting and encouraging each other. This became a true fellowship.

The twenty-two years I pastored Fellowship were the most rewarding and faith lifting I had ever had experienced. I saw miracles in healing, families reunited, children and adults accepting Christ as Lord and Savior, and a congregation that comforted one another in times of sorrow and death. One of the reasons our church members had such a close relationship with each other was due to our small congregation. After pastoring a large congregation numbering over twelve hundred during the sixties and early seventies, I could see the difference and the power of the unique spiritual intimacy of a small church.

One of the differences in our church organization was the respect and authority given to the pastor. Both the trustee board and the diaconate respected my leadership and allowed me to follow the urgings of the Holy Spirit as I led the church in our endeavors.

During my pastorate at Fellowship, I became active in the Religious Coalition for Reproductive Choice, a women's organization whose mission was to ensure a woman's right to determine when or whether to have children according to her conscience and religious beliefs, without governmental interference. This mission grew out of the Supreme Court decision Roe v. Wade, which affirmed a woman's right to have an abortion. One of the reasons the coalition's president, Ann Thompson Cook, asked me to come on as her vice president was her desire to expand the coalition's influence in the black community.

This was a very serious decision for me, not because I did not support a woman's right to choose but because I did not want to accept this responsibility without having a clear understanding of how I would go about explaining this to the black community. I could argue that being a part of this coalition was to the black community's advantage, as black women were subjected to a double standard that caused many of them to die in back alleys trying to induce an abortion through horrific means that often led to death. These attempts were made with clothes hangers, through drinking poisonous concoctions, and by many other unthinkable means. The white women, however, would simply go somewhere and have the procedure done in a safe and sanitary way and return without any embarrassment to family or friends. I had lived through back-alley conditions in Memphis, Tennessee, where I was born, and I had firsthand knowledge of this horrible plight.

After interviewing with Ms. Cook and accepting the position, I put forth several proposals. First I developed my position theologically. Women are born with moral agency as well as men, which meant that they had control over their decisions, as well as their bodies. Most people do not know that the Supreme Court decision of 1974 was not decided on religious grounds. The justices quickly understood that there were too many religious views about this issue. The Supreme Court decided this issue on the constitutional grounds of privacy, which say that there are some things too private for invasion by the state, and a woman's right to choose was one of them. This was the argument I used for many years as I spoke around the country.

Ms. Cook asked me to develop my program to include the black community in our effort to expand this argument. I suggested that we also needed to address the young people, specifically because this generation would change the attitudes people would had on this issue. In addition, I proposed to initiate a program to prevent teen pregnancy, which would prevent even the need to consider the issue of abortion. My first meeting with the board of directors was very encouraging. Each board member expressed appreciation for me accepting the denominations and religious organizations.

I had worked at the coalition for six months when I was asked to attend the Ms. Foundation's annual donors meeting held at 20 Wall Street. Several organizations had been invited to make presentations so that funders could determine which programs they would support. This was my first opportunity to meet people working with other women's rights organizations, who would make presentations.

The other participants and I entered the room to an amazing group. There were small mikes at each place setting. Marie Wilson, Ms. Foundation chair, was the coordinator of the event and opened the meeting, introducing each of us and our organizations. Because I was trying to make sure my presentation was impressive, I read my notes and missed some of the names of the attendees. I was number eight on the agenda. Being so far down the line was concerning. The others would have made their presentations and the funders would have made decisions about who to fund.

When the time came for my presentation, I was introduced as one of the few ministers who led a social justice organization. This was good and also challenging, since I did not know how the funders felt about ministers. When I stood to present, I could feel the intense attention I was getting, not only because I was black but also because I was a minister of a black Baptist church. Some may wonder why this was such a novelty. But as I realized later, some people did not understand how a black Baptist minister could talk about abortion. I used some of my time to introduce myself as a son of a Southern Baptist minister and the grandson of a Baptist minister who pastored in Mississippi for forty years. I noted that my grandfather had been born in 1860 before emancipation and that he had begun preaching in 1890 and had died the year after my birth in 1937. I also spoke about segregation and the unfair treatment of blacks in every facet of life, with my main emphasis on how black women suffered and died as a result of botched abortions and lack of medical care. This was while many white women flew to the islands to have their abortions and vacation and then return to their homes in Memphis and other cities in the South. I then spoke of the need for sexuality education, which was important in our effort to reduce teen pregnancy. My final plea was for funding to establish the Black Church Initiative to provide sexuality education in black churches to reduce teen pregnancy. I received a standing ovation that lasted for several minutes.

The meeting adjourned, and people lingered to talk to one another. A very well-spoken, well-dressed, and elegant woman shocked me by saying, "I really enjoyed your presentation. If I can help you, please get in touch with me."

I was stunned because usually funders would simply write you and ask for more information. Her offer of help was so unexpected that I simply said, "Thank you very much."

After leaving her I went directly to Marie Wilson and asked who the lady who had sat next to me was.

Marie was surprised that I did not know. Her response was, "Carlton, that was Susie Buffett, Warren Buffett's wife."

I told Marie of Mrs. Buffet's offer of financial support for my program. I was in a state of disbelief. I realized how wealthy she and her husband were, and they desired to provide financing for my program.

Upon my return to Washington, DC, I imparted to Ms. Cook the news of Susie Buffett's offer of support. She was elated and expressed satisfaction with my presentation. I thought we should call Mrs. Buffet right away, but Ms. Cook thought we should wait and call later.

The next day I was insubordinate and called the Buffett Foundation in Omaha, Nebraska, and asked to speak to Mrs. Buffett. I was instead connected to her son-in-law, Allen Greenberg. I introduced myself and told him of my meeting with Susie Buffett at the funders meeting in New York. He informed me that Susie had told him to expect my call and to help me any way they could. Allen asked me how much money I needed to launch my program.

I was lost for words, though I had thought about first steps. They would include a listening tour in select cities. I would meet with ministers throughout the country to determine their interest in my proposal to reduce teen pregnancy in our communities and to introduce the issue of pro-choice, which I found beneficial to black women.

When Mr. Greenberg asked me again about the amount of money, I responded that we would need at least $150,000 to accomplish these first steps. He assured me he would discuss this with Susie, and I would hear from them shortly. I left the call elated and grateful to God for once again bringing people into my life to fulfill my mission.

I told Ms. Cook what had transpired in my conversation with the Buffett Foundation attorney. She was excited that we had received a positive response in such a short time.

Within several days, I received a handwritten check from Susie Buffett on her personal account for $150,000. This money would allow me to travel around the country introducing our programs and inviting various ministers and other leaders to Washington, DC, and the Howard University Divinity School for our first summit. There we would address blacks and the pro-choice issue, as well as the need to reduce teen pregnancy in the black community.

Meanwhile, Fellowship Baptist Church was growing and thriving as new members joined and visitors continued to come from the community and also Zion Baptist Church, my former church. I traveled a great deal because of my obligations at the coalition, which meant that many Sundays I was away. I always asked other ministers to lead the services.

Ernest and Patricia Fears had joined our church when we worshiped at the Owl School. Patricia's father had served as my assistant minister for many years before becoming pastor at Mt. Moriah Baptist Church. Patricia, whom we had baptized many years before, expressed an interest in the ministry. After I had licensed her, I asked her to serve as my assistant. I also told her that attending seminary was mandatory, not for me but for herself. I asked her to prepare to serve during my absences. This was a blessing for me and the church, in that she was known and loved by the members.

Ann Cook resigned to pursue other areas of work on women's issues and suggested that I should submit my name for president. I was elected the first black person and the first man to head up the coalition made up of millions of people in twenty-six religious denominations and organizations. It was a signal honor and opportunity to enlarge my ministry on a national and international scale. The board offered its total support, especially after Ms. Cook told them that, due to my presentation to the funders in New York, the coalition was one of the leaders in the movement, especially in impacting the black religious community.

As my travels increased, with speaking engagements and fundraising, my church was very supportive, allowing me to be away while still paying me a full-time salary with benefits. Rev. Fears carried on her duties in an admirable way, which made my work travel easier.

I did, however, meet with the trustees to make sure the business of the church was intact. F. Alexis Roberson, a treasured friend since our days at the OIC, made me feel very comfortable with the running of the business of the church.

Black Church Initiative attracted hundreds of youth leaders and churches to be a part of this innovative program, which was religiously based and consistent with the values of the church. Rev. Leslie Watson was our first director and did an outstanding job recruiting ministers and youth leaders across the country to participate. After our months of listening meetings and speaking about the efficacy of the pro-choice movement, we received our first funding from the Buffett Foundation for over $3 million a year, the largest grant ever received by the coalition. During my first year, the budget went from $1 million to over $5 million. We had more organizations join the coalition as a result of our new work and exposure through the media. This undertaking by our organization brought local and national attention. We were not only embracing the pro-choice message but also addressing the teen pregnancy issue devastating the black community.

The first organizing meeting for the National Black Religious Summit on Sexuality took place at the Howard University School of Divinity, which was once the School of Religion. Over three hundred ministers, youth leaders, and religious educators met to discuss how to formulate a program sensitive to pastors and the theological concerns of the black religious community. This meeting brought people together from every facet of community and political life and proved to be an outstanding beginning of a movement to improve the outreach of our churches and provide our young people with the knowledge to have a life with a future. Many of the ministers embraced this movement and spoke glowingly of how this would transform the sexual norms within the church. After three days of meetings, workshops, debates, and moving worship services, we left to take this message back to our respective communities.

Some of the notables in attendance were Rev. Dr. Jeremiah Wright of Chicago; Rev. Dr. Gus Roman, president of the Lott Carey Convention; Rev. Dr. Evans Crawford, dean of the Andrew Rankin Chapel at Howard University; and many other national leaders who committed to supporting and making this movement one that would transform religious education throughout the country. One of our movement's most dedicated and loyal allies was Dr. Joycelyn Elders, MD, the US surgeon general who spoke openly of the need for sexuality education and was subsequently dismissed by President Clinton for her stance on sexual issues.

The Buffett grant led to many organizations taking notice, which meant additional funding from organizations such as the Ford Foundation, the Soros Foundation, the Rockefeller Foundation, and many other prominent foundations that supported abortion rights issues and sexuality education.

During my leadership of the coalition, I had several unbelievable experiences. I received a call from a woman from Florida, who asked me to come to Florida to talk more about Black Church Initiative. After I had gone to Florida and spent the afternoon speaking with her about the high teen pregnancy rate, which was twice that of the white community, she assured me I would hear from her. Several weeks later she sent a check for $1 million with a promise of more as we continued our movement. This happened several times as we moved throughout the country, especially the South, home to the most fundamental religious churches.

The coalition became one of the most prominent organizations of the pro-choice movement, which meant more publicity and recognition that helped us to spread our message. There were television appearances throughout the country and speaking appearances in all sections of the city, even in those places known to be anti-choice communities.

However, during the Republican Convention, we were harassed and challenged by so called "pro-life" organizations. After several years I had serious threats made against my life as a "baby killer." All of this made me more determined to speak for women and social justice. Some in the black community even accused me of genocide and threatened to eliminate me.

Much of my success has to be given to my fine staff, who supported me in many ways. I especially appreciate their sensitivity to my pastoral duties. Among them were Esther Huggins, my first assistant, and Sonya Crudup, the chief operating officer, who made it possible to travel extensively throughout the country to raise money and fulfill speaking engagements, which raised the coalition's profile. Leslie Watson must be given great credit in helping me to formulate the Black Church Initiative, one of the strongest programs of the coalition.

The coalition's programs were so effective that my friend Frances Kissling, president of Catholics for Choice, invited me to go to Beijing, China, on a mission for the United Nations to speak about the so-called one-child law that limited couples to having one child. I will never forget going to the province of Landau several hundred miles from Beijing, where I interviewed a couple in their twenties. When I asked them if they agreed with the one-child law, they responded that the government was trying to be responsible, remembering the recent famine. They also indicated that the one-child rule was not a problem for them, since they had not finished university and wanted their child to have the opportunity to get a higher education. This very important trip informed me about the debate, and I will be always grateful to Frances Kissling.

I am also, grateful to Frances for inviting me to go to South Africa to report on the HIV/AIDS pandemic and how we could assist this country with our programs. This trip was welcomed, since President Nelson Mandela had been elected and faced this difficult challenge. Besides hearing him and Bishop Tutu speak, I was taken with the beauty of the country, especially the city of Cape Town. I can say that out of all the cities I have visited, including those in Europe, Cape Town was the most beautiful I had seen. Table Mountain was right in the middle of the city, giving it a majestic feeling.

While touring Table Mountain, I met some young women who were very kind. After introducing themselves, they asked where I was from. I told them I was from the United States and was interested in addressing the HIV/AIDS pandemic in their country. They were very excited about my program and said they would like to help in any way they could. Cindy Leroux introduced herself and her friend, whose name I don't recall, and said they wanted to welcome me to South Africa. Cindy also said she was interested in working with us to address the HIV/AIDS issue in her country and the pandemic on the continent. I was impressed with her knowledge and her commitment, since she had just finished high school and was focused on going to college. We exchanged information, which let her know I was staying at the Virginia and Alfred Hotel.

I returned to the hotel and received a call from Cindy, saying that her parents would like for me to come to dinner as their guest for the evening. I was taken aback by this generous invitation but accepted, since I had found Cindy to be a very informed young lady and because of my desire to learn more about South Africa in general and Cape Town specifically. I arrived at the Leroux home, which was located in a very middle-class section of the city, where I was greeted by Mary and Peter Leroux, along with their son. This setting was in stark contrast to the townships, with its shacks and shanties, that we had seen riding from the airport.

Peter told me they were considered colored, which in the days of apartheid was considered a step above blacks. This caused great friction before apartheid and also since apartheid had ended. This was because apartheid was based on a color test that made light-skinned Africans "colored" and dark-skinned Africans "blacks." And, of course, the whites were "Afrikans."

Mary was a great cook and had prepared a wonderful dinner of fish and chicken, with assorted vegetables fresh from the local gardens. I really enjoyed the meal, but more than that, I felt I had found a family in South Africa to whom I could relate if I were to establish a program in Cape Town I had discussed such a program with Frances Kissling, my sponsor of this trip. After dinner, I had a long discussion with Cindy to determine her interest in joining the coalition as director of our South African Initiative, which would help reduce incidents of AIDS and prevent teen pregnancy in South Africa.

After several days of discussion, Cindy agreed to accept the responsibility. I informed her it would be several months before I could officially offer her the position, but I was sure that, after finding a funder, she would be my choice to lead this program.

The rest of my trip was very enlightening, especially hearing President Mandela speak in Cape Town and Archbishop Tutu introducing him.

I returned to Washington, DC, from South Africa and was very encouraged to work harder than ever to extend our Black Church Initiative throughout South Africa to combat the pregnancy rate in the townships. We established a department to address these issues that was led by Leslie Watson, a very talented organizer who had worked with Jesse Jackson in his movement and campaign for president. Our funding for the South Africa Initiative was assured, and Leslie was busy preparing to bring our South Africa delegation to our next National Black Religious Summit on Sexuality at Howard's School of Divinity, scheduled for the summer. She hired a very talented staff and coordinators throughout the country. There was energy and excitement throughout the organization, with our board hailing this as one of the most exciting movements since the Supreme Court affirmation of Roe v. Wade in 1974.

Our staff had continued to address the issues of our mission, which were to ensure a woman's right to determine when or whether to have children based on her conscience and religious beliefs, without governmental interference. We were the only religious organization that supported a woman's right to choose, with the exception of the Catholics for Choice, a very strong organization that supported us, even though we were a Protestant organization.

My efforts to introduce the coalition ministers of many denominations were challenged in many ways. First, I had the difficulty of getting the ministers to understand that the major tenet of the religious coalition was in line with the theological thought of Protestantism, which was the doctrine of "free will." This was in direct contradiction to the religious right, which said that God was opposed to abortion based on the fact that the embryo was a human being and desired the right to be protected. My answer to them was that the embryo was not a human being. Therefore, they could not use that argument that this was taking a human life. I continued to challenge them in my speeches, while they cried out and called me a baby killer because I supported a woman's right to choose as the Supreme Court had ruled in 1974. These same people who allowed a child to come into the world would then "abort" the child through lack of heath care, lack of educational opportunities, and a system that saw many youth going through the criminal justice system. One may not define real abortion as I have described it, but the fact of the matter is that this is real abortion.

My work with the coalition continued to be a success, with new churches joining every week. Our influence extended nationwide, and our funding continued to increase, with some private donors bequeathing us millions of dollars. This work made my ministry very relevant. Our work was saving many lives through our support of women and programs to help youth to have meaningful lives.

Everything in my life seemed to be going very well. I was grateful for a renewal in spirit and the opportunity to make a difference in the lives of people. However, Jean and I had experienced very difficult times in our marriage and with our children, especially my son, Michael, who had been in and out of rehabilitation programs that did not seem to reach him for several years. I prayed and worked as hard as I could to get him restored so that he could have a meaningful life. It would be several years that Michael would live on the streets, where drugs were exchanged, and participate in the life that goes with it. I prayed to God to give me the strength to support him and restore him to his former self. As a minister, I felt very sensitive. I preached that all things were possible with God, and my son was a victim of drugs—a situation that seemed to have no resolution.

One day I was talking with Dr. Lewis Kurtz, a member of Zion and a personal friend with whom I had shared my son's problem. He had recently lost his wife at a relatively young age. He said words to me that I will never forget. "Reverend, it rains on both sides of the street." Immediately I remembered the word of the Holy Scriptures: "It rains on the just and the unjust." Dr. Kurtz brought me back to remembering the Holy Spirit, my guide throughout my life.

In addition, when I was in Cape Town, South Africa, monitoring our program there—which was necessary for continued funding—I received a difficult call one early evening. Jean had called to tell me that our daughter Gayle, who suffered from asthma, had suffered an attack and had been taken to Greater Southeast Community Hospital. She needed to go immediately.

I tried to comfort her. Then I spoke with my chief operating officer, Sonya Crudup—who handled all arrangements, including those related to emergency situations. Sonya changed our itinerary, and we left that night to start our journey home. We were able to leave that next morning, traveling through Paris, and were back in the United States America, a fourteen-hour flight away, as soon as we could make it. The entire time, I was thinking about Gayle and my dear wife Jean, who had to bear all of this grief alone.

I arrived at the hospital around six o'clock in the evening and went directly to the critical care unit. There, I saw Jean with sadness I had never seen on her face, even when her mother whom she loved dearly, passed. There are some moments where words are inadequate, and the only things you can do are embrace and allow your spirit to speak to someone else's spirit.

After going into the room where Gayle was on the ventilator—the doctor had declared her clinically dead—I kissed her lips and held her hand and wept, which was the only response I could find in my spirit.

Cindy Jenkins then said a prayer. I held her hands for a minute and took Jean's hand and left the room. There was a sense of finality, as well a sense of new beginning for Gayle.

The service was a one of the most beautiful I had witnessed. The choir sang beautifully, and her friends spoke so personally. Gayle had, at one time, worked for the Lorton reformatory, a district agency in Lorton, Virginia. To my surprise, all of the directors for whom she had worked were in attendance, which was a great tribute to her. Also her coworkers from the DC Department of Employment Services turned out in large numbers, causing the church to overflow. Rev. Steve Tucker, the pastor where she had attended, was so gracious and supportive in allowing us the use of the facilities.

After Gayle's interment, Jean and I vowed to make sure Gayle's daughter, our granddaughter, would always be cared for and loved as much as we could, though we knew we could never replace her mother. My granddaughter's father, Rodney, was very supportive. We knew he would also make sure that their daughter would always be loved.

Caron, our youngest daughter, took her sister's death very hard. Actually, she had looked at Gayle as another mother, since there was almost fourteen years between them. After the services and the love of so many friends from both Fellowship Baptist and Zion Baptist, we tried to go on, with the assurance that Gayle was on another level, experiencing love, care, and spiritual growth.

Days passed, and we continued to grieve. But we had Saudia to consider and to help move on with her life as her mother had desired. Fortunately, Saudia had attended Maryland State University on the Eastern Shore in Salisbury, Maryland. Although she did not complete her degree, she was able to secure employment and work on her dancing, which she had perfected to the point that she could teach and perform in various genres around the city. The family was proud of her and impressed with the strength she had demonstrated during her mother's passing.

Saudia's mother had left her the townhouse in which they'd lived, along with generous insurances that provided her the opportunity to establish herself as a productive citizen.

Saudia's aunt Caron, who was in New York working for Sony Records as vice president for Global Marketing, helped her to secure employment. This allowed her to explore other areas of employment while she continued to perfect her dancing skills and seek opportunities in the theater.

I was satisfied knowing that Saudia was well on her way to developing her life in New York. I turned my attention back to Jean, who was still grieving deeply. She would sit for hours looking at Gayle's picture and playing Lionel Ritchie's "Hello" over and over as she thought of Gayle and her new life beyond this world. Some of the lyrics of the song were:

> Because I wonder where you are
> And I wonder what you do
> Are you somewhere feeling lonely?
> Or is someone loving you?

I was very concerned about her and tried to comfort her as much as I could. She tried to carry on as best she could, but she never returned to her old self.

During this period, Jean had recently been diagnosed with kidney failure, which required her to visit the nephrologist monthly for tests and receive injections to slow the kidney disease. This helped her because she turned her attention to her health, which was important to her.

Fellowship Baptist Church was continuing with productive programs, such as the food pantry and the diaconate program assisting the poor in our community. I was very pleased and grateful that the church had allowed me to pursue other areas of ministry, including the Religious Coalition for Reproductive Choice. Through my involvement with the coalition, I had traveled throughout the United States and to many countries to represent the coalition, particularly Cape Town, South Africa. I'd spent many weeks away from the church, but my congregation had supported me, viewing my work as an extension of the church's witness.

In the meantime, years passed with little or no contact with Zion Baptist Church, where I had served for thirty-three years. During my service there, I had improved every facet of the church's life. Membership had increased from four hundred to over fifteen hundred during my tenure. The mortgage on the church had been paid off, as well as the mortgage of the Family Life Center, which served as a senior center for members and friends in the community. This senior program was funded by the city and administered by Ms. Lavern Rouse.

Zion had moved on and selected a new pastor, Rev. Dr. Emil Thomas, from California, who remained there for eleven years and resigned suddenly as a result of some differences with the board of trustees. The church was without a pastor for many months causing many members to leave.

Zion finally called Rev. Dr. Keith Byrd, an associate pastor of First Baptist Church of Brentwood, Maryland, where a classmate of mine, Dr. Perry Smith, was pastor. I was invited to participate in the installation of the pastor but declined. I was still healing from the pain and hurt I had experienced at Zion during my later years and ultimate departure.

Seventeen years passed before I would ever worship at Zion again. Reverend Byrd invited me to preach, which I accepted with much prayer and trust in God.

I returned to the pulpit of Zion Baptist Church in September 2009, with the church filled to capacity with many friends and members in attendance. Among them were Rev. Dr. Evans Crawford and Rev. Dr. Gus Roman, one of my roommates in seminary who had pastored four prominent churches on the East Coast, including churches in Baltimore, Philadelphia, and New York. At that time, Gus and I had both pastored for over thirty years, with the majority of my years spent at Zion during his tenures in the four churches. This was a very emotional day for me. I had not stood in that pulpit in seventeen years.

So much had happened in the intervening years. Jean's family had been a member of Zion for four generations, her grandmother at one time serving as organist. Her mother and father, Hazel and Mack Adams, had passed on, along with all of her aunts, Alice, Mignon, and Ruby. Her one uncle, William Brooks, the only surviving member of the Brooks family, refused to leave Zion; his family had been one of the longest serving families of the Zion Baptist Church.

Jean found it offensive that many members she knew I had helped beyond my pastoral duties had turned against me. They had been swayed by rumor and the power play of Trustee James Christian and Deacon Robert Owens, who both had many times expressed their fondness for us both.

Pastor Byrd led the worship service with dignity and Christian love. He expressed appreciation for my thirty-three years serving as the seventh pastor of the Zion Baptist Church. Deacon Edward Hightower, in his introduction of me cited all of my accomplishments as pastor of Zion Baptist Church, including leading a dedicated membership at the age of twenty three. I had ordained Deacon Edward Hightower. I'd also recommended him for the office of treasurer after the death of my god-brother Benjamin Hailstorks, who had served as the second treasurer under my leadership. His mother, Helen Robinson, was my secretary until my departure and subsequently died after I left the pastorate. Helen was one of the most dedicated officers. All the members had loved and admired her for her efficiency and attention to detail. I could not have had a better secretary, and I dearly loved Helen.

I had prayed about my sermon. I wanted it to be helpful and not hurtful. I was directed to the scripture in the book of 2 Kings, where the Lord told the Israelites to remember when they came into this new land what he had promised to their fathers, Abraham, Isaac, and Jacob. The Lord admonished them that, when they came into this new land with houses they hadn't built, wells they didn't plant, and vineyards they didn't plant, when "you have eaten and be full, then beware lest thou forget the Lord thy God that brought you out of the land of bondage into this land of promise." My subject was "remembering not to forget," which was about remembering those who had passed on—who had made this day possible through faith in God and their sacrifices, which God honored.

There was no recrimination in my sermon, only the warning not to forget the Lord, who used seven freedmen and the thousands who followed to continue the work of God for over a hundred years.

Rev. Dr. Byrd was very effective in leading this service. Just before closing, he asked the congregation to stand with the officers of the church and join him in prayers for forgiveness of me and Zion, which I really appreciated.

Although I did not speak of forgiving those who had despitefully used me, as the Lord's Sermon on the Mount instructed, I had forgiven those who had done dastardly things against me and my family—which ranged from denying my family any severance pay, refusing to pay my retirement, and canceling my health insurance. These acts caused me much pain and anguish, which only the Lord removed after I had forgiven my enemies.

After the pastor's prayer, members streamed toward me to tell me how happy they were that I had returned to Zion to preach once again. Some cried right before me, asking me to forgive them. This was an amazing experience that I will never forget until my transition, when I hope to have my services at Zion with Pastor Byrd officiating. I ask that Fellowship Baptist be adequately represented during the service, with Rev. Patricia Fears assisting Pastor Byrd. Rev. Fears represents the bridge between these two congregations, since her father, Rev. Dr. Edward Hails, served as my assistant before becoming the pastor of Mt. Moriah Baptist Church. Many people lingered to thank me for services I had rendered to their families, such as dedication of their children, visitations when they were in hospitals, and officiating weddings and funeral services for their loved ones. These memories brought back days of joy and sadness. But I also felt gratitude, in that I was able to carry out the mission of my ministry.

After this celebration, many members felt comfortable to invite me to bring remarks at Zion for their loss of loved ones. Although I sometimes had reservations about certain members who had joined the opposition during the difficulties that led to my dismissal as pastor, I did not let that interfere with my supporting them in their loss.

I made the decision to step down from the presidency of the Religious Coalition for Reproductive Choice in 2015, after the most fulfilling experience of my profession. Over the past fifteen years, summits had brought together thousands of adults and young people to discuss issues of sexuality. The membership and the board of directors had been so supportive in every way that it was difficult but necessary for me to step down. It was time for me to support my wife, who had developed kidney failure and was on dialysis three times a week, four hours a day.

Jean demonstrated unusual courage during this time. The coalition's generosity enabled me to focus my attention on her. Its support was evidenced by a resolution that resulted in the coalition retiring me with a severance of $200,000. I was relieved of any duties and allowed to take any job I wanted without penalty. Although I was offered support from the White House in finding employment, I decided to use that time to support Jean in what I did not realize would be her last year before her transition.

In August 2015, Jean and I made a momentous decision at the urging and with the support of our daughter Caron, who had suggested we sell our house on Stoneybrook Drive in Kensington, Maryland, and move to Leisure World of Maryland in Silver Spring, Maryland. She recognized that our house had become too much of a burden on the two of us. We were nearing our eighties, and trying to maintain a large house had become too much, even with the help of our housekeeper, Molly. Colleen Lee, who we had met through Deaconess Edmonia Johnson, a dear friend and member of the church, made arrangements to sell the house and assist us in acquiring a new home in Leisure World, a popular and beautiful retirement home. It was also only five minutes away from DaVita Dialysis Center, where Jean had dialysis, making its location very convenient for us both. On many days, Jean would drive herself. I found this very courageous and believed it demonstrated her desire to live, which I had doubted a few months before.

The day we visited Leisure World with Colleen, we had just about given up when the property manager told us about some low-rise condominiums that had just been built in 2014. We looked at all available condos and were very impressed with several. The manager asked if we would like to see the model condominium. We both replied that we would.

When she opened the door, Jean let out a loud, "Wow," and began looking at how beautifully the place had been furnished. I also was very impressed with the location, which was facing Georgia Avenue, where we could see the traffic coming and going, as well as cars entering the complex. The glass front was quite impressive, giving the place the feel of being larger than it was. The furniture and pictures, along with the tastefully appointed bedrooms, added to our desire to live there.

After a few minutes, I turned to Jean and asked if she liked the condo. Her answer was a strong, "Yes," with a big smile on her face.

The only question was whether we could afford it.

Without talking to Caron who had encouraged us to move, I took the leap of faith and told Jean we would buy it. Seeing her face register joy and happiness was worth all of the sacrifice we had to make. Caron agreed that, if Mommy liked it, we could buy it. The purchase would never have happened without her support and help.

We went to the settlement in Olney, Maryland, coincidentally the city where we had purchased our first house on Hedgegrove Terrace thirty-six years earlier. After signing what seemed like an eternity of papers, I asked Jean to write the check that amounted to more than a half million dollars. I had never written a personal check for that much, and we thanked the Lord for allowing us to have this beautiful home for the remainder of our days.

We went directly to house, located at 15000 Penfield Circle, Unit 412, in Silver Spring, Maryland. We could not carry out the ritual of the husband carrying the wife across the threshold and thought it better to refrain, since both of us had gained a few pounds since our marriage almost fifty years ago.

We thanked God for such a beautiful home, and we recognized the generosity of our wonderful daughter Caron, who had made it possible for us to move into what we both hoped would be our last home together. I had told Jean that, although I wanted to move back to Washington, I would agree to this beautiful place in Leisure World. I also told her that, if she outlived me, this home would be hers, free of debt and without any mortgage for the rest of her life. If she transitioned before me, I would be moving back to Washington, DC, since I'd always wanted to move back after Caron finished high school. In the meantime, we agreed to be happy while we had this opportunity to enjoy one of the most beautiful homes we had ever owned.

We settled into our new home, with Jean driving herself to dialysis during the summer and early fall. When the weather began to turn during the fall, I drove her and picked her up, which I was more than happy to do. The only reason I agreed to let her drive at any time was because she said she felt better when she could drive. This I could understand, as she had been very independent before I'd met her. I knew that being able to do some things for herself would help her to adjust to her dialysis and build her confidence.

Every morning, I would find Jean on the enclosed porch looking out on Georgia Avenue, watching the many people going to work and leaving from the Leisure World complex. There was also a beautiful fountain surrounded by several flags—those of the United States, American, Maryland, and Leisure World.

When fall passed to a beautiful but uncomfortably cold winter, I would offer to drive her to the clinic, which she would sometimes decline. As the weather began to turn colder with some precipitation from time to time and as her health grew increasingly more problematic, I insisted on driving her and picking her up from the dialysis center. During those years, I got to know many of the patients and their families. The close-knit group allowed us to form a semblance of a family that was very supportive. Jean was quite popular at the clinic because of her genuine love for the friends she made.

In early winter I recognized that, although we still had the services of Molly, our housekeeper, we needed a caregiver to help Jean with her personal care needs. I sought help from care service groups including

366

Visiting Angels, and after several weeks of their service I asked one Rose Ahu to consider working full-time to do the things that Jean would prefer that Rose do instead of me.

Rose and Jean were very compatible personality wise, and Jean was satisfied with her care. As autumn turned to winter and the visits to the dialysis center became more difficult, while I was still pastoring my church fellowship, I hired a driver who would come on the days when I was not available. Rose's husband, Nelson, was also helpful in emergencies.

Caron's management of, and travels with Pharrell Williams, a recording artist, increased which prevented her from visiting as often as she desired. But during her frequent calls, I assured her that her mother was very well cared for. Caron and her husband, Louis, decided to come home for Thanksgiving, which made her mother very happy.

On Thanksgiving Day, I went to lead the worship services as the church met to give God thanks for all the blessings of the year. We also decided to get our dinner catered, although I would have to pick it up after church before returning home. After church, I went to a popular restaurant to pick up our dinner for five, which included all the trimmings and dessert. Caron and Lou were staying at a nearby hotel. They had arrived the Wednesday before Thanksgiving.

Upon arriving at the condo, I found Saudia, our grandchild, already there, helping "Mama" get dressed for dinner. After putting the dinner on the counter in the kitchen, Lou and Caron arrived to heat and prepare the meal. Saudia was helping, as was Jean, with both asking if anyone needed help and making sure they could find everything they needed.

Dinner went well. All had plenty to eat and much remembrance of the past, especially our beloved Gayle, Saudia's mother, Granddaddy and Grandma Adams; and the many hours we'd spent together on holidays in our Kensington, Maryland, home. I especially recalled the many hours of sitting with Granddaddy on the patio, listening to him recall the days when he played in the Negro League. Founded in the late twenties, the league became a major league representing the talented black players who had no chance of playing in the white National League or the American League. Both were all white and black players had no chance of playing in either, regardless of how talented they might have been. Granddaddy also knew a lot about Washington, DC, especially about Southwest. The area was largely populated by blacks. It was home also to some Italians and Jews, who dominated the business in the community, even though many blacks had business and social clubs. One black business owner of note was Bruce Wahl, who was very popular and served as an usher at Zion Baptist for many years.

The year 2016 entered with our family enjoying our new home but concerned about Jean's declining health. She had started to have problems in other areas of her body. Rose would work twelve hours a day, preparing her for the night and then returning early in the morning to prepare her for the day. I thanked God every day for our daughter Caron, who supplemented our resources so that Jean could receive the services she needed.

Rose's schedule was to arrive early in the morning and prepare Jean for me to take her to dialysis at nine o'clock. Shortly after the New Year, we discovered that additional help was needed. Jean was becoming less ambulatory and now needed total assistance. Rose suggested that we hire her niece, Estelle Ahu, who we found well qualified with good references. Rose and Estelle had certified nurse's assistant licenses that were certified by the State of Maryland.

Although this arrangement was costly, Caron and I remembered that Jean's one request was that she not be put in a nursing home. Her morale was boosted when she learned that Rose and Estelle would be there to care for her, and I would transport her to dialysis.

I learned a lot about my wife, even though much of it I had already known. Jean was, indeed, a strong woman spiritually, with a strong belief in the afterlife and how we prepare for it here on earth. She endured her illness with this belief. Only someone who has been through long-term dialysis or has cared for someone who has can understand how difficult it is on the person, as well as the caregiver and spouse. Many days I assisted her into the clinic with my heart breaking, watching her struggle with my assistance to get to the door and get equipped for dialysis, with catheters going in her arteries to circulate her blood. Because she was on blood thinners, she was always cold and asking for blankets, which we provided. A television was attached to her hospital chair to make her comfortable during the procedure.

Months and years passed with Jean's dialysis procedure repeated three times a week for fifty-two weeks without fail. And on the appointed days when she did not dialyze, it meant dialysis two days in a row. I cannot adequately describe how difficult dialysis was. But it was what stood between her and death. The only remedy was a transplant. But age and overall physical condition determined who would be eligible, and Jean had congestive heart failure, which disqualified her for transplant. She decided she would do dialysis, although in her heart, she would have not agreed except for her family, who she loved and who wanted her to try dialysis. Before she started dialysis, I assured her that, if she felt she could not continue, I would agree. I had always known that Jean valued quality of life over living a long time.

The summer of 2016 was very difficult. Jean was frequently hospitalized for ancillary problems, such as bladder infections, frequent for those who have compromised health. This further weakened her, and several times she refused hospitalization, saying she just could not go through those procedures again. She also began to plead with me to let her rest from dialysis, which I did on occasion. It was clear to me she was just too weak for the three-hour procedure, which would also weaken her. This decision was not easy. I knew when Jean did not go to dialysis. It meant she would have to make it up with consecutive days, which were also very hard on her body.

During the month of August, she became very alone in her thoughts, even though she was looking forward to our fiftieth wedding anniversary. Colleen was invaluable to us during Jean's illness. And Jackie Johnson Reeves, the daughter of Edmonia Johnson, one of Jean's best friends, was instrumental in helping to arrange the fiftieth wedding anniversary celebration.

As September approached, invitations were sent to friends and some members of our church and Zion. The date was set for September 2, 2016, at our home in Leisure World. Many friends came, including many of her very close friends, among them Shirley Latture, who had been her maid of honor at our wedding held at Jean's parents' home at 4904 Ninth Street NW. I remember the date so well because September

2 was on a Friday, and I was looking forward to presenting my wife to the church the following Sunday, which I knew would be a surprise to the congregation.

The large room was decorated tastefully with the assistance of Vicey Grey Frazier and the wonderful caterer who made the afternoon special with special additions to the menu. Minister Bonnie Burnett and Judith Allen brought joy to us and the attendees with special music, including "The Wind beneath My Wings" and other beautiful songs.

Rev. Frank Tucker and his wife Brenda attended, although Brenda was also suffering with kidney failure and dialysis. She brought much encouragement to Jean during her sickness. Rev. Tucker offered a powerful prayer that brought tears to many eyes, including mine.

Jean's greatest joy was to hear childhood friends and relatives speak of their years growing up and their adult years together.

Our daughter Caron; grand-daughter Saudia; and Shirley Latture, her maid of honor, also spoke about their many years together.

After everyone had spoken, I was called upon to say some closing words. My marital journey of fifty years with Jean was difficult to put into words. What I wanted to tell Jean was that I loved her and was grateful for her supporting me throughout our marriage. Although she knew how difficult marriage to a minister was, with all my responsibilities and other areas of work, I wanted to tell everyone that she had been a faithful and supportive wife in all my endeavors. She was also a great mother to Gayle, Michael, and Caron Valerie, on whom she doted and whose life and future she strongly influenced.

After the singing of "The Lord's Prayer" and benediction, the celebration ended as I had wanted, with joy and evidence of happiness among the friends and family.

Jean showed a marked change in her spirit after the celebration. She seemed to go to dialysis with such sadness it broke my heart to see her struggle. She was very quiet and sometimes unresponsive to Esther or Rose. I tried to get her to talk, but she wanted to be left with her thoughts. I realized that some thoughts are the private domain of the person having them and only to be shared with God.

She struggled through dialysis for the next three weeks, and I would privately shed tears seeing the physical and spiritual struggle she was going through.

One evening during the latter part of September, when we got home and Rose was about to prepare her for rest after her three-hour dialysis, she asked Rose to allow the two of us to be together so that we could talk. Rose left the room, and I sat beside her bed and heard her say words that ring in my ears today even as I am writing. "Carl, I am not going back again," she told me.

As I held her hands, I did not speak. Finally, I said to her in the calmest voice I could muster, "Jean, do you know what that means?"

She answered in the strongest voice I had heard from her in a long time. She said the final words, "Yes."

We held hands for a minute, and I kissed her and then called Rose back into the room to prepare her to rest before dinner.

That evening, I called Dr. Barry Hecht, who had been Jean's doctor for over forty years. Dr. Hecht said he was sorry, but Jean's decision was understandable; each patient must decide his or her own course of action. Although I thought his reply rather academic, I also recognized that this was a reality to him. He asked me to call hospice care at Montgomery General Hospital for help to prepare me for the next days.

The next day, I called hospice and explained that I had talked to Dr. Hecht about my wife's desire not to continue dialysis and he had suggested I call for help preparing for her eventual transition. As a pastor for over fifty years, who had helped members prepare for their loved one's transition, I'd thought I knew how they felt. I realized that, not until my wife was the one about to transition, was it possible to put myself in the place of someone letting go of a loved one. This was the difference between sympathy and empathy. Only when you have walked in the other person's shoes can you know the experience.

I thank God for hospice care. The team arrived near the end of September and introduced themselves. Although I do not remember their names, I do remember there being a nurse, a minister, and a contact person during this period. The minister asked Jean if she would like to participate in our conversations, but she very pleasantly declined. The three-person team explained they were there to help Jean be as comfortable as possible and that they worked as a team to provide any medicine for comfort, with the minister offering spiritual solace to Jean and me. The nurse explained the effects on Jean's body when she withdrew from dialysis, which had exchanged her blood and provided new blood to help her organs function, especially the lungs. I don't think Jean was listening, and Rose told me she had fallen asleep.

The nurse brought out of a bag with several vials containing morphine and Valium. She explained first that there is no way to predict how long Jean could live, but it usually took between five days to two weeks. She also told Rose and me that there would come a time when Jean's lungs could not handle the fluid, causing her to experience the feeling of not being able to breathe. When that happened, I should take one vial of morphine and squeeze its syringe, which would give her relief from the sensation as the lungs filled to capacity. If Jean showed evidence of anxiety, I should use the vial of Valium that was activated as soon as it was squeezed into her mouth. This was very difficult, but I tried to listen carefully. I did not want Jean to suffer in her transition.

Although I thought Jean would be somber the day after our meeting with hospice, I was surprised. She seemed relieved and was also happy to know her baby girl, Caron, was on her way to see her, along with her husband, Louis. It seemed that she was in another place, anticipating their arrival that Thursday.

When Caron arrived, looking very pretty and bright, she immediately went to the bed and embraced her mother for the longest time, as if they were in silent communication. They shared many ideas about spiritualism, so I know they must have been communicating with each other without words. Finally, when they looked at each other, her mother exclaimed, "My beautiful baby."

And Caron responded, "Mommy, I love you."

I left the room to be with my thoughts and tears.

Thursday and Friday were filled with joy, and everything was positive. That was not planned but came as a result of Jean insisting on being happy and the rest of us enjoying each other. While Caron and Louis were visiting, Saudia came to share with them in caring for Jean. Saudia was very tender and loving, reminding Jean of her oldest daughter, Gayle Michelle, who had transitioned ten years earlier. Every day, she would look at Gayle's picture and listen to Lionel Ritchie's "Hello." Colleen had also gotten Caron's picture framed and placed on the wall, where she could see it while lying down to rest.

On Saturday, October 1, 2016, Caron and Louis arrived at our home early, and Caron relieved Rose in caring for her mother. They listened to music and talked about the funny times in Caron's childhood.

Jean had always accused me of protecting Caron. Once, she and her mother had a strong disagreement about something, with Caron refusing to go to school. Jean, becoming exasperated and realizing I was home, told her to stay home, since her father was home. Feeling sorry for her, I'd suggested we do something, and she asked if we could go down to the Potomac River and paddleboat. I had agreed, and we'd had a really nice time. When Jean returned from work and before she could inquire about Caron's day, Caron said with glee, "Mommy, Daddy and I went paddle boating down at the Potomac and had lots of fun, didn't we, Daddy?"

Her mother did not approve of this at all. She claimed she was trying to raise Caron right, and I was undermining her efforts. This was not true, but we did enjoy a day together.

This sort of banter between Jean and Caron went on Saturday, along with them sharing music and eating together. Although I was not home at the time, Caron said when she and Louis returned to their hotel to rest, they told Jean they would return the next day, Sunday.

After they left, I thought about one of the happiest days we had spent with Caron and Louis. It was December 26, 2011, in Long Island, New York, where we had gone for the marriage of our daughter Caron Valerie Veazey to Louis Robinson. Only they knew why they selected the day after Christmas. The small wedding consisted of only family and friends, including Louis's mother, Ms. Isabel Robinson; his children, Eddie, Nicole, and Sammy; his brother; and close friends. What made it special was that they had asked me to officiate. I was very proud, but I think I was more nervous than at any other event, though I had performed hundreds of weddings during my ministry. However, this was my daughter's wedding, and I wanted it to be perfect, which it was. Caron was glowing and beautiful, and Louis was dressed very handsomely. The ceremony took only seven minutes, since they had requested the expedited version. I can assure you it seemed like more than seven minutes. The emotional time came when I had to pronounce them husband and wife. My little Veazey girl was now Mrs. Robinson. Her mother and I shed tears of joy, realizing Caron was sharing her life with someone she loved and who loved her. These were the kind of memories that ran through my mind as I watched them together.

Sunday began uneventfully, with my decision to stay home, since I had given notice to the church that I would be retiring. The Pulpit Committee had been hearing ministers preach for the past month. One of the finalists for my position, Rev. Robinson, would bring the sermon on this Sunday and I had planned to attend. However, I awakened that morning and decided I would not attend church and would instead stay home with Jean. Rose would be there when Caron and Louis came. My routine had been to get up late, have breakfast, and watch television. I passed through the hallway and asked Rose how Jean was doing and whether she'd had breakfast. Rose assured me she'd had her breakfast and was resting.

I returned to the bedroom to read the Sunday paper and watch my favorite talk shows but instead went back to sleep and awakened around two forty-five in the afternoon. I went to talk to Rose and inquire about Jean, who was asleep.

Around three o'clock Rose called to say that Jean seemed to be struggling to breathe, which I confirmed. I immediately remembered that she could be helped by giving her the morphine. I went to the refrigerator and retrieved the syringe, with no thought these could be her last moments with me.

I said, "Honey, open your mouth. I am going to give you something to make you feel better."

She raised her head slowly, with Rose's assistance, and I gently squeezed the syringe of morphine into her mouth. She closed her mouth, but I could detect some restlessness after she took the morphine, as the nurse had previously directed. So I went back to refrigerator and got the syringe of Valium.

Rose raised Jean's head, and I said, "Honey, open your mouth. This will make you feel better."

She did, and I squeezed the syringe of Valium.

374

I was concern as to whether I was doing this correctly and needed to get further instructions. I asked Rose to hold Jean's hand while I called hospice to get further instructions. Jean's care team had specifically instructed me not to call the EMS or 911.

Before the phone could ring to connect me with the hospice office, Rose called out to me desperately, saying that she thought Jean had transitioned. When I saw Rose crying and holding Jean's hand, I knew that her pilgrimage was over, and she had arrived at her new home.

I put the phone down and told Rose to let me hold Jean's hand and asked her to call the hospice. As I held my wife's hand, it felt so strange in my hand. I felt something was missing. It wasn't just the limpness of her hand but the clear realization that her spirit had departed. This brought me a sense of sadness but also a feeling of gratitude that her struggles were over.

When Rose reached hospice, she was told that a nurse would be sent right away, but I could check her heart to see if there was any beat. I did this, and as I knew, there was no heart beating. One thing I did was to gently close her eyelids. After I kissed her goodbye, I pulled the covers up neatly around her and asked Rose to sit with her until the nurse arrived to confirm her death.

I returned to the bedroom, sat, and cried, which I had wanted to do many times in the past. But I had wanted Jean to stay strong and realize she was being watched over by a loving God.

My mind then immediately turned to Caron and Louis, who had left the night before with the expectation of seeing her mother alive again. I prayed for guidance before I called, and God directed me to talk to Louis and just ask them to come over because I wanted to tell Caron and be with her when she found out that her mother had transitioned. Louis said they would arrive shortly. One of the things I admire about my son-in-law is that he is very calm, which is good for both of them.

I heard the doorbell ring. When I opened the door, I embraced Caron, and she said through her tears, "Daddy, why didn't you tell me?"

I didn't answer because there was no answer, except that I had done what I was directed to do.

Caron approached her mother's bed slowly and reached down and kissed her and cried out, "Mommy," in such a mournful way it started my tears again to flow. Saudia, who had arrived, also wept, realizing both her mother and her mama were gone.

Saudia stood by Jean's bedside until attendants from Rhines Funeral Home arrived. After the nurse had completed her work and given the attendants permission to take her to the funeral home, I asked everyone to go with me to the hearse waiting outside to say goodbye. I led them out as we followed the attendants carrying Jean's earthly remains to the hearse.

After we watched them place her in the hearse, we returned to the apartment where we were met by the pastor of Zion, Rev. Dr. Keith Byrd, along with Rev. Robert Tolson and Rev Patricia Fears. All expressed their condolences for my family and offered continued prayers.

Rev. Dr. Byrd rendered a closing prayer, and then everyone left except family members and our caregiver Rose; her husband, Nelson; and Estelle. We talked at random about how cheerful Jean had been over the previous days, and Caron recounted how she and her mother had recalled so many past experiences, which had brought laughter and, sometimes, sad memories.

After several hours, Rose and her family left but promised they were available for anything we needed for the services. I told them we would never be able to repay them for their devotion to Jean during the months of her illnesses.

The rest of us decided we would meet in the morning to start planning Jean's final rites. Everyone was gone except Caron, as Louis had returned to the hotel to allow us to spend some private time together.

Later that evening, Caron entered my bedroom and asked if we could talk about her mommy and our lives together. She really wanted answers to such questions as what it was like being married for fifty years, what our best years had been, and what had been the most challenging.

I went back to the days after her mother and I had just gotten married. During our engagement period, I had told her mother that I wanted one child—a girl. It was very presumptuous of me to determine what sex I wanted, but I had told Jean that I had seen the little girl I wanted and she possessed all the qualities I wanted. She was a child who was beautiful inside and out, a child who would have an innate spirit of kindness and generosity, and a child who would be compassionate, with a spirit of justice. I knew that no child would have these things evident at a young age but would develop these spiritual qualities as she grew in age. After Caron was born, I was amazed that not only did she look the way I'd thought she would, but I also felt as she grew that her spirit was developing into exactly the kind of person I knew she would be.

After all of the questions and discussions for four hours, Caron called Louis to pick her up, and they left me alone for my own time with thoughts of Jean and me and what our lives had meant to each other.

On October 3, 2016, I was still awake at daybreak remembering our lives together. Finally, I fell asleep shortly thereafter and did not wake until noon.

A sense of renewed energy swept over me to start preparations for Jean's memorial services, to be held at Zion Baptist. Pastor Byrd had been so kind to offer along the church, along with his services. Of course, Fellowship Baptist was our church. It was where we held membership, and we were founding members. We realized, though, that our church could not accommodate the anticipated crowd. So we agreed to Rev. Byrd's offer to hold the service at the church where I had pastored for thirty-three years.

I needed the help of certain people to prepare the kind of service I wanted Jean to have. It would be a very beautiful service of readings; words of comfort from some of my close friends; and music from friends who were artists in their own right, who would sing for Jean songs that mirrored her life. Among them would be "I'm Blessed," sung by Minister Bonnie Burnett; "I Won't Complain" (New Bethel); and the processional "Let the Church Say Amen" by Andre Crouch. The hymn would be "Great Is Thy Faithfulness."

When I had called Vicey Frazier earlier for her help with the program, she'd replied, "Whatever you need, I am here for you and the family." Her response made me feel very good. Next, I called J. T. Rhines Funeral Home, which had been owned by one of my closest friends for over fifty years. After his death, he'd left instructions that Mr. Pickett and Mr. Smith, his faithful employees and trainees, would be offered ownership, which meant they would carry on his tradition of service of the highest standards. Since I had made prior arrangements with Mr. Smith, he knew that Jean would have the same kind of cherry wood casket I had selected, along with the other arrangements left to them.

The one thing Jean had insisted on was that there not be any viewing, which had been a tradition in the black community. Aside from the viewing for the family and very close friends viewing her with the funeral directors, the casket was not opened again. The funeral program with the order of service was prepared by me, with the assistance of Vicey Frazier.

The morning of October 7, 2016, was a beautiful day with bright sunshine to begin Jean's day, which the Lord had blessed. We arrived at the church around ten o'clock to receive friends and relatives who had come from near and far to honor the memory of Jean Margaret Blanford Veazey, who had transitioned to another level of existence—a level she had earned because of her spiritual growth in this life.

As the people came around to greet us, each spoke in glowing terms of Jean and her magnetic personality. Many of Caron's friends spoke of how much Caron loved her mother, who had introduced her to the spiritual life and engaged her in reading material to help her develop spiritual values and practices.

The choir was in full voice, consisting of members from Zion and soloists from Fellowship and New Bethel. Just before the service was to begin, Louis, Caron's husband, told me that Pharrell Williams and his parents, Mr. and Mrs. Pharrell Williams, had arrived with some of the staff from California. The members were so kind to welcome them. They were all deeply respectful and supportive of Caron; it touched my spirit in a very special way.

The ministers came to the pulpit, and a young minister I had baptized gave the call to worship that began the service. The choir was directed by Judith Allen, the renowned and longtime church choir director—famed Duke Ellington High School choir director, former minister of music at Zion Baptist, and organist at Fellowship. After the call to worship and the prayer came the reading of the scripture by young ministers, one of whom was baptized by me as a child.

Many of Jean's friends were there. Those who spoke were Myra Coates, Shirley Latture, and Mansfield Coates Jr. Jean's childhood friend Joan Ashton was scheduled to speak but was hospitalized. Joan visited as often as she could during Jean's illness, although her health was frail.

I will never forget the beautiful and melodious voice of Minister Burnett as she sang, "I'm Blessed." Viola Bradford from New Bethel sang another one of Jean's favorites, "I Won't Complain." The song brought tears to my eyes as I thought about what Jean had been through for seven years. I stood and raised my hand in honor of God, who had given her strength to persevere.

Jean was a valuable part of our church founding, along with Edmonia Johnson, who with Jean's assistance as a conspirator helped persuade me to accept the call of God to organize Fellowship. I accepted and, together with the original charter members organized the Fellowship Baptist Church.[1]

Speaking on behalf of Fellowship Baptist Church was the chair of our board of trustees, F. Alexis Roberson, who knew Jean throughout our marriage, dating back to our work with the OIC. Jean and I spent

---

[1] Charter members of Fellowship Baptist Church: Hazel Adams, Gloria V. Anderson, Maureen Barnes, Rashelle Brooks, Miriam S. Catlett, Vernell L. Catlett, Jerrel L. Catlett, Miles Chambliss, Naima Chambliss, Theresa B. Chambliss, Carolyn Clary, Salone Clary, Mignon Coates, Nannie B. Curtis, Gloria Davis, Mary Fowler, Thelma Gardiner, Mazzie Gaskins, Audrey Gooden, Aaron K. Green, Mary B. Green, Geraldine V. Greene, Mary Hawkins, Janet Helms, Cutura B. Hill, Jay Dianne Johnson, Margarete Johnson, Edmonia C. Johnson, Benjamin H. Johnson Jr., Mae Jones, Lawrence T. Jones, Whittier Jones, Myka Kirkland, Cynthia Kyle, Carrie L. Leary, Gayle Liggins, Ruby Lipscomb, Virginia Littlejohn, Sheena L. Lopez, Frenchi Mack, Dorothy M. Mahoney, Andrea Renee McConnell-Mack, Gwendolyn E. Mebane, Dortha Mercer, Larnell Nealy, Nadine Nealy, James Pegram, Carolyn Rudd Pegram, Jeanne Peyton, Lucille Praither, Lisette Privado Carol A. Releford, F. Alexis Roberson, La Verne Lee Rouse, Arthur Scandrett, Ruth Gloria Sheppard, Joan Shorter, John Shorter, James Roy Smith Sr., Turner Speller, Tracey Speller, Henrietta Speller, Arthuryne J. Taylor, Everett L. Thomas, Kimberly E. Thomas, Inetta W. Tibbs, Melvin Tibbs, Carlton W. Veazey, Jean Veazey, Maxine Warren, Kristen N. Wheeler, Sadie K. Wheeler, Jerrel L. Wheeler, Frank S. Wheeler III, Marcia A. Williams, and Naomi Woodfolk.

times with Alexis and Chuck for dinners and special occasions honoring Alexis. In her remarks, she spoke of how easy Jean was to talk with and her stylish dress. She also admired how Jean carried herself in the role of "first lady," a title she wore with ease and how she made everyone feel comfortable. She continued to speak about Jean's unwavering support of her husband that was evident in her never complaining about my long hours and how she had been so pleased to see the Lord bless us with a new edifice. Alexis's remarks were very comforting to all of the family, especially me and my sister Audrey, who is now ninety-two years old.

I had invited several ministers, including Rev. Dr. Roman; Rev. Dr. Fauntroy; and Rev. Dr. Frank Tucker, pastor of First Baptist Church, where his uncle Lemuel Tucker had pastored before him. I had known his uncle and wanted to welcome him as his uncle had done when I was first called to Zion Baptist Church. Rev. Tucker was a very special friend and supporter of my work. He served as the chair of the Black Church Initiative when I was president of the Religious Coalition for Reproductive Choice. These three ministers, along with other ministers present, were very supportive and comforting. In the audience was my former roommate, Rev. Dr. Cameron Byrd, who had been a close friend for many years.

When it was my turn to go to the pulpit, I asked Caron and Saudia to join me as we spoke on behalf of the family. Our son, Michael, was present but did not join us because he had special emotional issues. I stood for what seemed like an inordinate amount of time. When I finally opened my mouth, all I could say was, "Jean was a good woman." The words almost made me collapse in tears as I thought about what I had just said. She was not only good to her children in every way; she was also good to her grandchildren, nieces, nephews, cousins, and the entire family. She was a good wife, who always supported me quietly through sunshine and rain and was always there, reminding me of my call to the ministry and the promise I had made to God to answer the call. She was good to my mother and father in many ways. Our daughter Gayle preceded Jean in death, but there was not a day that she did not talk with her in the spirit and play Lionel Ritchie's song, "Hello."

I asked Caron to speak. She gave a heartwarming and loving speech about her mommy and how she had learned to be spiritual through her.

She also said, in the most gentle and sweet way, "Mommy, I will always love you," which brought me to tears.

Saudia, on whom all of us doted as Gayle's daughter and who had accepted her mother's death and was carrying on in her absence, spoke of her "mama" in such a sweet way. You could feel her grandmother's spirit, which made all of us feel for her.

Rev. Dr. Byrd had not known Jean very long. But the first time she'd met him, she had said to me privately, "I really like him." And she had wished him all the success at Zion, in spite of the pain some of the members had caused not only me but also her. After all, she and her family were fifth-generation of members of Zion. Rev. Dr. Byrd's presence at our home when Jean died was spirit sent, as he had a certain presence that expressed genuine concern and love. Although he did not know her in terms of her religious experience, I had told him that, since Jean and I met, she had brought a special feeling and understanding of God that not only intrigued me but also made her attractive to me (alongside her physical appeal). His eulogy was excellent. He captured the essence of her, which was her spirit. The brief times they met, he would always comment that she not only made you feel comfortable; she also had an aura that told you she was spiritual. He spoke about her telling him how much she enjoyed his sermons. What I liked most about his eulogy was that he did not try to get too religious about her, because she was not religious as much as she was spiritual. I will always be grateful for his very kind eulogy.

I was again comforted by the choir as Rev. Dr. Byrd gave the benediction and led us out, and the choir sang my special song by Andre Crouch, "Let the Church Say Amen." The song was so meaningful, especially the words, "God has spoken, let the church say amen." Indeed, God had spoken. And Jean had heard him and answered, "Yes, Lord, thy servant heareth."

The funeral procession moved slowly toward the Washington Beltway on our way to the Maryland National Memorial Cemetery in Laurel, Maryland, for the final service of interment. Jean and I had purchased our joint plots at the cemetery several years ago while I was pastor of Zion; I had asked the church to purchase a large plot of land that would become known as the Zion's Garden, which would serve as the final resting place for many members of our church. Our family had purchased plots, and here many members of the Brooks family had been buried. The first buried there was Jean's nephew Gary Smith, a wonderful young man whose life was cut short by a fatal motorcycle accident. Jean's father, Mac Adams; her mother, Hazel; our daughter, Gayle; my brother, Melvin; Jean's uncle, Bill Brooks; aunts Alice White and Mignon Coates; uncle, Mansfield Coates; and aunt, Ruby Lipscomb were all buried in Zion's Garden. We laid Jean to rest in our plot.

After the brief graveside service, we greeted one another as Caron lingered at her mother's grave.

Most of the family remained at Zion, where a repast had been prepared for the family and friends. I did not attend and went home to Kensington. I needed some time alone to reflect on my life without Jean and what I would do in the future. We had agreed that, if I was to predecease her, she would remain in the condominium that was paid in full at the time of purchase, and, if she was to predecease me, I would move back into the city. I had wanted to return to DC ever since Caron finished high school. We had remained in Kensington so that Jean would be near her nephrologist, Dr. Hecht, and because she was in love with our home, which she had chosen thirty-five years ago.

I sat in the living room of our condominium, which we had only shared for one year and one month, and remembered how happy Jean had been when she knew we would be moving into this lovely home. The condo had been specially decorated by Colleen, and Jean had loved it, although she'd lived to enjoy it only one year.

Sitting there, I thought about the first time Jean had mentioned death, which was strange, since she had been doing reasonably well with her treatment at the time. She stopped me in the hall and said, "Carl, I am dying."

Lost for words, I'd held her tightly and, without another word, kissed her on the cheek and walked with her to the living room.

That was the last time we mentioned death until two weeks later when the hospice team came to visit after Jean had made the decision to wait on her transition to her next life.

Although the condominium was very comfortable, I wanted to move as soon as possible to the city, to continue whatever life was in store for me. Colleen, who had been helpful throughout our several moves, was encouraging and supportive.

Several weeks passed as Caron and I talked about the future without her mom. I told her I wanted to move as soon as possible so I could start to focus on the future. This may seem odd to some. But I had also resigned from the pastorate at Fellowship, concluding fifty-five years of pastorate, which included my thirty-three years as pastor of Zion. The strange thing was, seemingly, everything was coming to a close, which included my retirement and Jean's transition.

Sonya Crudup, my chief operating officer when I served as president of the Religious Coalition for Reproductive Choice, was very supportive and helpful during the trying times I'd been through, including the last days of Jean's illness. I asked for her suggestions as to where I should move in the downtown area. She took me to Southwest and other areas, where many new buildings were being built. We found a place in the area of the "old" downtown Washington, before the renaissance of Washington. New buildings were being erected in every quadrant of the city. The old downtown Washington had been home to Hecht's, Kann's, Lansburgh, and Garfinckel's. All of those stores had been torn down, and the downtown had moved to Connecticut Avenue. Lansburgh had been replaced with a large apartment building covering almost a square block from Seventh to Eighth Streets and the cross streets D and E.

I moved into a new apartment in November 2016, thanks again to Colleen and Sonya. I found myself in a beautiful place and filled with gratitude to God for all his blessings.

The question in my mind was what David asked God in Psalm 112. "What shall I render unto the Lord for all His benefits toward me?" This question haunted me day and night until one day, while awaiting my appointment with my massage therapist Jamila, I was greeted by a young lady serving at the front desk. I asked if she had attended college.

Her reply was, "Yes, sir. I attended Villanova University and have a degree in English and journalism."

Instantly, I asked if this was the only job she had.

She responded, "No. I am doing this to supplement my income." She told me that she worked for one of the largest accounting firms in the city.

Although I was rude, in that I didn't remember ever asking what her name was, she formally introduced herself as Kimberly Jackson of Washington, DC. She had attended public schools in DC and had received a four-year academic scholarship to one of the most prestigious and outstanding universities in the country.

It was during our conversation that I told her that, fifteen years ago, I had begun writing a book about my life and what I had learned after sixty years in the ministry but could not quite get it to come together. Then I asked her if she would like to assist me in writing my book.

She immediately answered, "Yes, sir."

That was the beginning of a relationship that has lasted almost two years. It has been almost a year and a half since we started this pilgrimage in clay feet, which has been the most therapeutic and spiritually enlightening experience I have ever had.

Now that I am nearing the end of this pilgrimage, it is time for me to reflect on some theological beliefs that are not found in any seminary textbook but, rather, developed over sixty years of accepting a new life in Christ Jesus. I joined the church at the age of nine because I loved everything about Jesus and wanted to be like Him. The simplicity of this confession has always made me realize the power of religion and especially the Jesus of history and the Christ of experience as set forth by Dr. Harry Emerson Fosdick. Through all of my seminary days and pastorates, I have always had searching questions about my faith— questions I realized could be answered by no one but me.

My preaching was not complete because some things that I read in the Bible I could not accept, and I have constantly searched for answers about these things. What I plan to do in the pages I have left is to set forth some of these questions and give the answers that I believe are dictated by the Holy Spirit, upon which I have depended throughout my ministry and especially as I write this book.

When I first accepted the pastorate of Zion Baptist Church, I had not yet finished Howard University's School of Divinity. My studies were not complete, but my father told me to go forth and depend upon the Holy Spirit, which would guide and teach me those things I needed to know to pastor.

Since Jesus established the church on the faith of Peter, who declared, "Thou art the Christ, the son of the living God," the church has been in a constant state of flux, in character as well as in practice. The Pentecostal experience as the church was confirmed, and to this day we have been trying to be the church that Christ left us through His precepts and examples.

One of the teachings of Jesus as it related to salvation was in the act of doing. Teaching, an integral part of Jesus's ministry, should always lead to action. The Sermon on the Mount was not only a beautifully written teaching document, which contained words of life and wisdom; it was also a call to action for those who truly believed. The Council at Nicaea, which laid the framework for the Catholic (general) church, determined what books would be included in the New Testament. An example of the Council's power would be its decision to exclude the gospel of Thomas from the New Testament because of the *faithlessness* of Thomas who did not believe the bodily resurrection of Jesus until he could confirm the wounds of the Crucifixion. This is controversial to this day.

The council set forth the belief systems for the church as it grew and became more organized. The first church at Rome became known as the Roman Catholic Church, with Peter as the first pope of the church. Many books have been written about the papacy, with all of it faults, failures, graft, and sin. The books on this period of Christianity are too lengthy for me to do justice. However, the one thing I recognize from the beginning of the Catholic Church is "organization." I will elaborate more as we come to the church of today and how it has changed in many ways and also become more like the early church. This is evidenced by the choice of the papacy (with all of its graft and failures) not to include in the record the writings of some disciples who also had an account of Jesus and the gospel, such as the Gospel of Thomas.

Before the church at Rome, the record by the church fathers detailed how Christians went from house to house praising and worshipping God through Jesus Christ. This was the purest form of the church, because they tried to live out the teachings of Jesus in their daily lives and not what government dictated. Pentecost was an example of what power was in the first church, with all of them speaking in different tongues but each understanding the other. Also the church was responsible for each other, even in their daily needs. Remember that they had all things in common; everyone was cared for. What a contradiction in our message, with homelessness and hunger affecting a large portion of our population.

After Martin Luther nailed his Ninety Five Theses on the door of the church at Wittenberg, Germany, the Protestant Reformation was born. This courageous act by Luther represented a major change in the Christian world, in that it ushered in other denominations, such as the Lutherans, Episcopalians, Methodist, Baptists, and the many other denominations we see today.

I return to my original thesis that the power of the church was diminished by the very character of the institution—the word *organization*, which suggests group, rather than the individual. And because of this, the church has taken on the very character of the society it seeks to convert. When the early church met from house to house, they had one mission and one mission only—to spread the word of this new gospel of Jesus Christ. This weekly meeting of the early Christians was only to make sure that the needs of their brothers and sisters were being met and to share their Christian experiences. Other than these times, they were all preachers, teachers, and messengers of the "Good News." This is what is needed and missing in today's church. The power of individual witness has been lost in the corporate religious complex, which has caused the gospel to become materialized for the profit of the leaders, not unlike the days of the Roman papacy and its graft.

This has also caused us to lose the power of the individual witness in our everyday lives. The right thing is not determined by our religious convictions but, rather, by what the majority thinks. This is evidenced by today's political scene, where we have a president who has defamed the office and diminished our values with the support and active engagement of the religious right, which in my estimation is neither "religious" nor "right." As I write, there are thousands of mothers, fathers, and children, even babies who came from Central America because of the violence and living conditions in their country. They arrived at our southern border and were instantly arrested and their children taken and placed in cages like animals. But we still worship every Sunday as if nothing has happened. Still, as I write, thousands of babies and young children are not accounted for and may never be. Where are the followers of Jesus Christ who were adamant about the treatment of children? I could go on and on with other instances of the church of Christ and its failures because we established group thought, rather than having each person be responsible for his or her witness to God.

I cannot fail to recount my own experience growing up in the Deep South, where, in places like Memphis, Tennessee; Mississippi; and Arkansas, segregation, discrimination, and violence ran rampant through the cities and towns in the south. The last lynching in Memphis was in 1936, the year I was born. We were given second, third, and fourth hand books to study, while the white students were given the most advanced books to study. Our saving grace was that our teachers, like professor Blair T. Hunt, one of the great principals of the South; Dr. (Papa) Lowe; Lucy Campbell; Robert Wesley; and McGhee and others, made up for our deficient books. Many of our teachers attended schools in the North, such as Michigan, Columbia, Harvard, and Yale, and returned home to teach us. It was this religious commitment I grew up understanding.

These instances of the impotence of the Christian church feeds only on the concept that the church has lost what Jesus called "the salt," which has lost its savor. The church can also be judged by how we treat the hungry. We live in a world where everyone can be fed and hunger could be a thing of the past, but due to greed and selfishness, this possibility has not been achieved. This is true not only in the United States but also throughout the world. When 10 percent of the population controls 90 percent of the wealth, what else needs to be said? This is a far cry from the day of Pentecost, when the church was born and the church members all had "everything in common." Some may say that this sounds like socialism. Regardless of the politics, this is what Jesus calls us to do in his directive to minister to the "least of these."

Another area of spiritual embarrassment is the idea that only those who are Christians are spiritually legitimate, which means all other religions are false. Again, this is a misreading of Jesus's words. He said, "I am the way, the truth, and the life." According to my New Testament professor, Dr. Leon Wright, the Greek actually reads, "I am a way shower," giving a completely different reading that does not allow the arrogance of some to claim that Jesus is the only way. After hearing Dr. Wright explain this difficult scripture, I am inclined to accept the term *way shower*, which allows for God to have other expressions and pathways to Him. The arrogance of this verse is not consistent with what we know about the teachings of Jesus.

When I was in undergraduate school at the University of Arkansas at Pine Bluff, Dr. Tillman Cochran, my sociology professor, introduced me to a powerful book by William James, *Varieties of Religious Experiences*. The book opened my mind to the evolution of religion and how humankind found it in different forms and in different parts of the world. This was a radical thought for a young boy brought up in the religious tradition that held the only legitimate religion was Christianity. Today, young people reject out of hand this belief because it flies in the face of research and history. They have also discovered the commonality of religion, which to them is closer to the truth, especially after reading a powerful book by Peter Gomes called *Reading the Bible with Heart and Mind*, which speaks to the development of the Bible, the underpinning of the Christian religion.

Young people in the twenty-first century see wars of religions, with our president declaring the Muslim religion to be a religion of violence. They see some religious groups rejecting all other religions, holding to their limited views of the world, which fails to recognize that God is not as small as our minds. They see such groups fail to ask the question about how, when, and where religions evolved in various parts of the world. Many young people see the faults in this way of thinking. My heart is made glad when I see young people honestly explore these issues.

There are many reasons young people are leaving the mainstream denominations. One is because of what one of my professors suggested. "We are answering questions that no one is asking." This was an astute observation, which is evidenced by what young people consider to be the irrelevance of the message of the Christian church.

I have said enough about the demise of the church as we know it. Now let us turn our attention to what the future holds for the "disorganized" church. One of the least talked about Christian attributes is the gift Jesus the Christ left us before his ascension, which was the Holy Spirit. Before Jesus left, He promised the disciples he would not leave them comfortless but would send the Holy Spirit. This is spoken of in the book of Acts, where the people were all overtaken by the Holy Spirit and spoke in different tongues but understood each other. This was the indwelling of the Holy Spirit, which is not raised to the level it should be in our pilgrimage in clay feet. Young people will develop the spiritual art of meditation, which is the most powerful thing the individual can do in his or her desire to develop spiritually, our only purpose for being on earth. This ability to meditate will assist us in accessing the power of the Holy Spirit, which Jesus said would guide, teach, and assist us in becoming more Christ-like. This is not a corporate function but an individual act that increases one's awareness of the God and his son Jesus Christ. This art was perfected by the great Howard Thurman, the spiritual sage who taught us through his writings to learn to access the Holy Spirit in one's daily life for growth and strength.

The power of meditation is a private act that leaves you alone with the Holy Ghost, which means you have spiritual intimacy with Jesus. This does not require preaching but an ability to listen with the third ear to the Holy Spirit. The power of this act is the fact that it does not need corporate involvement, which actually detracts from your ability to hear what God is saying to you through his son, Jesus Christ. This idea may be disturbing to many who have learned to depend on corporate worship for their development, which in fact detracts from their development.

The "church" as we know it will diminish, but the power of the Holy Spirit will increase. That is something this present generation has found helpful, although it needs to be refined and tethered to the religious grounding we all need. What will happen to preaching? one could ask. Meditation will be the new church, and the Holy Spirit will be the preacher or communicator that will guide us and teach us those things we need to develop.

The one thing that will last from the relics of the present-day church will be the music of the church, whether anthems, hymns, or the present gospel music. I have some knowledge of music, having grown up in the church, where I heard the musical compositions of some of the most prolific gospel music writers, such as Lucy Campbell, Thomas Dorsey, and others, who made the Gospels come alive and ushered in the power of the Holy Spirit. Music is a universal language that everyone understands. Throughout my years as a seminarian, student, and minister, I have been convinced that the inspiration for jazz, gospel hymns, and anthems comes from the same source. The Holy Spirit provides the inspiration for the creativity for each of these artistic endeavors. The voices of Mahalia Jackson, Aretha Franklin, and Ray Charles, who covered both jazz and gospel, attest to the truth that the Holy Spirit is not confined to what we call the sacred. The secular and sacred are really the same, except what our ears, hearts, and minds receive. The spirit that moves us is the same.

How can one listen to George Frederic Handel's *Messiah* and not realize that this is otherworldly or the Holy Spirit at work? The technical ability to put together such a powerful, intricate, and moving contrapuntal composition speaks of only the Holy Spirit at work. Listen to Lucy Campbell's "Touch Me, Lord Jesus" or Thomas Dorsey's "Just a Closer Walk with Thee." Or who could listen to Miles Davis, Lester Young, or Art Tatum and not realize that they are listening to something that is otherworldly or from the Holy Spirit? The inspiration of the gospel singer and the saxophone artist comes from the same source. The inspiration of great preachers comes from the Holy Spirit. The reason I make these observations is that this is the way the new generation will understand their religious connections, which will usher in a change to the way we worship.

My final observation concerning the church and the theology we have accepted for centuries, which I am about to challenge, was a result of one of my members, a trustee named Nannie Curtis. Nannie was a friend I had known for over fifty years. She had supported my ministry as much as anyone I have known. Nannie always asked me, "Rev. Veazey, why don't you preach about the afterlife and what heaven and hell are?" She died before she heard me share my thoughts about these subjects.

Although I had delivered hundreds of eulogies over my fifty-five years in the pastorate, I usually preached the typical sermon, which suggests that those of us who were believers in the Lord Jesus Christ, after death, went directly to heaven. I never preached a sermon where I consigned anyone to hell. This was due to the fact that I never believed that a loving God would send someone to a place of so-called fire and brimstone, which I could not believe because it would be impossible for a spirit to burn. This I will speak to more directly as we pursue the afterlife that Nannie Curtis had asked me for years to explore.

I stated earlier that my seminary years were very formative years and caused me to raise questions that I had not been spiritually courageous to pursue until now. You may remember that our pilgrimage begins at birth and does not end until the transition we call death. Again, the inspiration for the following spiritual principles came from the teaching and inspiration of Dr. Wright, professor of the New Testament and a practicing spiritualist. My belief is that we come to this earthly plain called earth for only one purpose, and that is spiritual development, not fortune or fame.

Jesus admonished us, "Be ye perfect as your heavenly Father is perfect." I understand this to mean that everything we do "should" be directly related to our spiritual development. Jesus Christ as our way shower or the way is our model, and through following him, we develop spiritually. We will also develop spiritually through our everyday endeavors of work, family, relationships, and many other phases of life. Amassing money and worldly goods does not mean spiritual growth. Rather, it is how we use these material things for our spiritual development that makes the difference. Education is also a means of developing spiritually. Even our status in life, whether we are rich or poor, allows us opportunities for spiritual development. Everything in life allows us to develop, even though some experiences may be negative. Some of these ideas I did raise with Nannie Curtis, although I never concluded the end of this argument as it related to the afterlife.

The most crippling thinking that the church has promoted has been the shibboleths that we incorporated into our theology that have been devastating to our spiritual development.

No one accepts the teachings and ministry of Jesus the Christ more than I do. I have been following his teachings in my way as I make this pilgrimage for over seventy-three years. As I look back over my pilgrimage, I realize that all of this has been a growing process for my spiritual development, which, again, is the only reason for our existence. All of the sacraments, creeds, ordinances, or other religious experiences are only for our spiritual development.

The Christian church has been responsible for the lack of spiritual development of many in the church because of ordinances that are not understood in the context of their growth and spiritual development. Let us take the ordinance of baptism in the Baptist church, where I have served for two-thirds of my life. Baptism is necessary for salvation, as we have been told, and the act of baptizing is only to publicly demonstrate what we have accepted spiritually, which is to bury the old self and rise with a new spirit. When this is not properly understood, we give people a false sense of security around their spiritual development, the only reason for our coming to this earth. Even the doctrine of salvation, which proclaims that, to achieve eternal life, we only have to profess Jesus as Lord and believe on him. This simplistic formula for salvation causes many not to become serious about their development but to rely solely on the "blood" of Jesus to save them.

The writer of the book of James says it succinctly when he proclaims, "Faith without works is dead." All of these observations, among others, suggest that what is important in this life are those things that work for your spiritual development as you prepare for your next level of development, which we will move toward immediately.

The fourth Sunday of October 2016, I preached my last sermon at Fellowship Baptist Church, titled "There Is No Heaven." Needless to say, there was an eerie silence in the congregation after hearing the title. When I had allowed a sufficient time for the "dramatic pause," I asked the congregation to listen carefully to me. Two weeks after my wife of fifty years had transitioned, the first statement I made was, "Jean is not in heaven. She is on a higher level because of the spiritual development she achieved while here on earth."

Jean was a believer in Jesus the Christ as a way shower. Jean tried with all of her might to grow spiritually in order to achieve a higher level of existence corresponding to her earthly spiritual growth. This will not be her final destination, and she will continue to grow and learn and develop where she is as she moves toward the oneness with God that is the ultimate destination.

I ask all of my minister friends who question this understanding of the afterlife, "What do you think Jesus meant when he said, 'In my father's house are *many* mansions'?" (my emphasis). Not one has ever given an adequate answer. This is mainly because we have not understood that the challenge of earth is to prepare ourselves for a higher level, where we can continue to grow toward an even higher level of existence.

I continue to be dismayed with the church in these challenging times when the president of the United States fails to recognize the humanity of our country and the values for which we stand. This is evidenced when observing the horrific events on the southern border of our country, where many have come fleeing the violence in their country and we respond by kidnapping their children, which will damage them for the rest of their lives. One would think that those of us who remember the words of Jesus about how we treat children would rise up in righteous indignation at the sight of a little child crying for her mother, from whom she has been separated, maybe not to see again.

Where is the church? Where are the Christians? Where is the Christian rage? The silence is deafening, and the message to our young people is that the values we espouse in our worship services are just empty words. This is why I say that the days of the church as we know are numbered.

Many of my friends disagree with this with strong convictions. The evidence is all around us in the decline of the Protestant church's membership rolls. This is also evident in the Roman Catholic Church, with the closing of churches across the country due to lack of attendance and interest from young people.

Another area in which I cry out for a response from the people of God and followers of Jesus the Christ is the economic disparity that exists today. The fact is that 90 percent of the wealth in this country is controlled by 10 percent of the people. The s rich are getting richer, and the poor getting poorer. And these inequities fly in the face of what we as Christians profess. The early church, as I stated earlier, "had everything in common." In other words, they tried to make sure that everyone was provided for, especially the women and orphans.

It is my belief that, if we rightly understood that we are here for spiritual development—which is evidenced by what you do and not to what church you belong—the world be a different place. Until we understand we do not need the organized church to develop, we will continue to be anemic in our spiritual development. The real church will not be the edifice where we meet and gather to worship, but the streets where we live and work and make a difference in the lives of our brothers and sisters around us. We must preach accountability as followers of Christ. When Jesus told the story of the lawyer who had been raised by the rich young ruler, Jesus asked which of the three had shown compassion on the stranger on the Jericho road. The lawyer answered, the Good Samaritan. To this, Jesus gave this directive: "Do this and live."

This is the same admonition Jesus gave us concerning those who are hungry, naked, lonely, strangers, sick, or in prison. These are his words: "Inasmuch as you have done it unto the least of these, *my brethren*, you have done it unto me" (my emphasis). These are the ones to whom he will say, "Come inherit the kingdom prepared for you." I believe this is the same as moving to a higher level of existence, which comes to those who are spiritually developed.

These observations have been hewn from the rock of experiences, both good and bad. These criticisms of the church come from what I have come to understand from fifty-five years of pastorate and the shared experiences of many other pastors. No one person has a monopoly on the life and meaning of Jesus the Christ. However, we all have the responsibility of sharing whatever truths we have come to see through the prism of our personal and pastoral experiences.

As I enter into the twilight of life and my calling as a gospel minister, there is one other observation I want to reemphasize. I began this book observing that we come to this planet for one reason and one reason only—not for fame or fortune but simply to use our experiences and achievements to develop our spiritual lives. Too long have we offered our congregations the easy passage to the sublime place we call heaven.

With my last sermon at Fellowship Baptist, "There Is No Heaven," I was warned by my friends and associates that what I was preaching could be devastating to some. There were those who had believed in this easy passage to a sublime place and had made no effort to prepare, except to repeat the shibboleth, "We believe in the Lord Jesus Christ as our Savior." I believe this also, but I also believe His saving me is to show me how to develop spiritually in order to move to a higher level of spiritual existence when we transition from this earthly existence. This is that *what* Jesus meant when he said, "In my father's house are many mansions." There are many levels of existence, and our earthly development will determine our level of existence after our transition. This to me is spiritually sensible and relates to a just God.

Now, let us turn our attention to those who do not develop their spiritual lives while here on their journey. I do not believe in a God who would banish a part of his creation without the possibility of redemption. Therefore, hell is not a part of my theology or religious belief. Persons who do not develop their spiritual lives, when they transition, become earthbound spirits, bound to the earth, trying to learn and find redemption in other people's lives. The danger in this is, because of their need for negativity, they find persons who possess these qualities and become part of their lives, looking for improvement. Of course, this, which is called demonic possession, doesn't happen. The person in whom they reside has the possibility of improvement, which would mean the possessor would also improve. This could prove to be their deliverance if the possessed continues to grow spiritually until his or her time of transition.

This also can be dangerous for those who allow themselves to become the object of demonic possession. All of us are candidates for this kind of possession if we allow negativity or other evil attitudes to take possession of our lives. This is not a new phenomenon. Many psychologists, psychiatrists, and other persons who have studies mental and psychological development will attest to cases that defy diagnosis and can only be explained through supernatural means, which borders on the Catholic doctrine of exorcism. This practice is not accepted by many in the medical or theological field.

Those of us who are familiar with the Bible, particularly the New Testament, will remember Jesus casting out demons. The man who was possessed and tried to kill himself is one example. Biblical and historical lore will attest to the fact that there were many cases of demonic possession during the time of Jesus. I am not trying to get you to accept this. I'm only using it as a means of explaining why there is always the possibility of redemption.

The church, therefore, has missed an opportunity to help one live a spiritually productive life by only giving people church conversion, which is a formula for entering the pilgrimage, without helping them to understand why the journey is important. Although I waited until this time in my life to share these beliefs, I feel obligated to allow the word of truth to come out as the Holy Spirit directs me.

Finally, as I come near my pilgrimage ending, I also feel the mist from the Jordan, which means that, in a few days, we will be crossing over to another dimension of spiritual encounter, where we will experience new opportunities for growth. What I am about to share is very personal, and I debated within myself whether to share this experience. After much prayer and meditation, I have been urged by the Holy Spirit to share with you the last traumatic experience I have had on this journey. As many family members and friends know, I have always used alcohol socially for the most part, but also as a kind of sedative to help me through tense times. This may sound strange for a minister and follower of Christ to admit. However, I share with the apostle Paul the experience of beseeching God to deliver me from the "thorn in the flesh," which in many ways has tormented me, even when I knew not. I prayed many times for deliverance. But as I have preached many times, the Bible says to us, "Behold I stand at the door and knock." God has always been ready to deliver me, only if I had been ready for deliverance. I share with the apostle Paul when he said he prayed three times for the "thorn," as he called it, to be removed. God's answer was, "Paul, my strength is made perfect in your weakness."

Strange as it may seem, my malady made me search even more for God's grace and mercy. Without my thorn, I would have become very proud of the gifts that God had bestowed upon me. Whenever I felt that I was self-sufficient, my "thorn" would always be present to remind me of my dependence. The burden of alcohol was present in my marriage for fifty years, during which time Jean pleaded for me to get some help. Strange as it may seem, I knew why I was being tested through this demon of alcohol and that only God would and could deliver me. I am sure you are mystified by the spiritual logic, but please be patient as I try to explain my understanding of this burden.

During these years, I was able, through God's promised strength, to do many things and lead many organizations and churches. Everything that God led me to do was always extremely successful from the time I assumed the pastorate of Zion at the age of twenty-three, an appointment to which God gave good success. My years working with CBOs (community-based organizations) like OIC, my appointment as a member of the District of Columbia City Council and vice president of the Religious Coalition for Reproductive Choice, and my God-given final opportunity of leading a new congregation have all been a part of God's plan for me. As for the people who God allowed me to meet along my journey, it was always clear to me why they were sent.

Permit me to share an illustration of how my life has always been directed by an unseen hand but through an undeniable spirit, which was God. I must share with you may confrontation with my most difficult spiritual moment. After Jean's death on October 2, 2016, I moved back downtown in November, with help through my adjustment from Colleen and Sonya. My beautiful place was right in the center of the city, but something was missing. I became lonely and began to drink excessively. After several months, I realized that this had become uncontrollable and called my daughter Caron to tell her that I needed help. She immediately told me to prepare to leave in a few days to get therapy through a recovery program in California. I had some embarrassment with confessing my weakness to her, but she had known for many years and had discussions with her mother about my plight.

Caron arranged for me to go to Tres Vistas Recovery center in San Juan Capistrano, California, for at least thirty days. My traveling companion, who she had arranged to escort me, was Ron Armstrong. Ron arrived in Washington, DC, on May 17, 2018. We flew to Tres Vistas Recovery. After Ron left, I was introduced to Dr. Headrick and his medical staff by Amanda, his chief of staff, who then administered a physical and blood work. Next, Kyler, one of the counselors, drove me to the recovery center. I arrived at the center, which looked like a large mansion, around eight o'clock in the evening. Once inside, I was introduced to Nate and Jeff, the only two males in the program. I was very upset about the arrangements, even though it had everything I could possibly want or need. I complained and informed the staff that I would not be staying and would be leaving in the next few hours. Nate and Jeff pleaded with me to give the recovery center a chance. For the next few hours, I tried to find everything wrong with the center I could and called Caron in Los Angeles to tell her of my decision to leave. She was quite disappointed that I was not pleased with the arrangements, and I really couldn't put my finger on what was wrong, except I did not want to be there. This was strange. I was the one who'd called Caron and told her unequivocally that I needed help. Nate, Jeff, and Dr. Headrick persuaded me to stay until the next day. I reluctantly agreed.

That night was the longest night I'd ever had. My desire to drink was not a problem, although I had been without alcohol, with the exception of one drink on the plane, for almost twelve hours. After reading and talking to some friends, I drifted off to sleep that was some of the best sleep I'd had in quite some time.

When I awakened in the morning, Stephen, the administrator of the building, came to the door to tell me that the chef, Brian, wanted to know what I wanted for breakfast. I replied that I wanted eggs, bacon, toast and coffee. He informed me that breakfast would be ready in fifteen minutes, and I immediately prepared myself to go to the dining room for my first meal in Tres Vistas.

Brian greeted me with a very pleasant, "Good morning," to which I replied with a very monotone, "Good morning," which was part of my rejection wearing off. After breakfast, I returned to my spacious room with plenty of closet space. The rooms were double, and Nate and Jeff roomed together.

After breakfast, I sat down to chat with several of the residents, including Alexis, Nate, Jeff, and Robert who had just arrived. I found out that the recovery center only accepted six residents at a time, to maximize the care to each. The more I found out about the Center, the more I realized that Caron had selected, with the advice of Ron, one of the most exclusive and effective recovery centers in Southern California.

I met the ten staff members, not including the two chefs, and my first day got off to a much better start, after I had met and talk with the other residents, including three females named Alexis, Mayson, and Timea. We bonded and became family, which made our therapy that much more effective. After planned and prepared therapy, we were able to spend the day reading, meditating, and sharing conversation with each other. Not only did this make us closer as a "family"; it also gave us insights about one another, while enabling us to find out more about ourselves through others.

I became acclimated to this routine and looked forward to each day the longer I was there. Dr. Headrick was an outstanding resource. He could relate to our experiences as a result of his own addiction some thirty-eight years earlier. I looked forward to spending time with him each day he came to visit.

I was an anomaly in the program, in that there had never been a minister in recovery at Tres Vistas. My title did not make any difference to my friends, and we could discuss anything without the fear of being insulting to one another. This freedom, in itself, given the openness it afforded, made recovery so much more meaningful.

I finished detox after one week. It amazed Dr. Headrick that I had no reactions and needed no medication to assist me in my recovery.

Although this was a thirty-day program, the days went by rapidly. I had been at the center for two weeks, when Nate announced that he would be leaving, since he had finished his thirty-day recovery. This caused me some unease, because Nate and Jeff were the only males besides me, even though we had great relationships with the females in the program.

The day Nate left was very emotional. There was a short gathering, where we all expressed how his friendship had positively impacted each of us. This was done by passing a special coin around to each of us as we spoke our last words to Nate before his departure. Each person emotionally expressed appreciation for what Nate's presence had meant to him or her.

Finally, Nate was able to express his appreciation, which was emotional and filled with wisdom as he related to each of us. The words that resonated with me were when he said as he left us that he could say that he'd had his last drink. Those words resonated with such power that, during my remaining days at Tres Vistas, each day I would make them my prayer.

One week before my departure day, I became somewhat anxious. I anticipated what life would be like when I returned to Washington, DC, with my friends. Although my coming to Tres Vistas was no secret with my friends, I wondered what would be different about me when I returned. Each day I had been at Tres Vistas, I would try to spend as much time with residents and staff as I could, realizing that I may never see some of them again. Dr. Headrick allowed me to move my departure day up to Friday, June 15, because I had a speaking engagement and had made the progress necessary for my release.

June 15 was both an exciting and a melancholy day for me. I would be leaving around two o'clock to return to Washington, DC, after almost a month, with a new attitude, as well as a clean and sober body that I had not had in years. My Morning Prayer was one of thanksgiving as I remembered the Bible verse, "Every good and perfect gift comes from God." After the wonderful breakfast that Chef Francisco had prepared, I went to therapy as usual. We would not meet for my "coin out" until eleven o'clock, one hour before my departure for the airport. The morning was uneventful, except Chef Francisco expressed how much he had enjoyed me being there, which made me feel very good.

Everyone gathered in the television room for my coin out at eleven o'clock. Amanda began by telling the group how we'd met when I had arrived in Dr. Headrick's office on May 18 after being brought to the office by Ron Armstrong, my counselor and traveling companion. Amanda also talked about my first impressions of the center and how I had demanded to leave but, after the intervention of my daughter Caron and staff, had decided to give it one night. The rest, she said, was history.

Amanda then asked Dr. Headrick to speak because of his time limitations. He too expressed how appreciative he was of my decision to stay, because I had brought some positive things to the program. He also indicated that I was the first minister and pastor to partake in the program.

Each person said very nice and encouraging things to me, and I remember that meeting very vividly to this day.

Caron's office had arranged for a car service to take me to the Los Angeles Airport. After I had boarded the plane, the attendants came around to find out what I would like to drink. I answered in the clearest voice I could muster, "Water, please, with lemon."

There is nothing wrong with water, but I think I made too much of a deal out of it. During the flight, I also had several glasses of ginger ale, which I found very satisfying. My seatmate, a wonderful lady from Washington, DC, who was retired but very active in art and worked in several museums, kept me occupied during my flight. The flight seemed very short to me, which may have been because I was so excited to return home with a "new me."

Arriving at my apartment, I called Sonya and asked her to have dinner with me to celebrate my return and sobriety. We selected the Prime Rib Restaurant on K Street, where I'd been eating for the last forty years. It was indeed a wonderful homecoming, and I had so much to share with Sonya about my recovery and how I viewed the rest of my life.

After dinner, I felt very tired, which I attributed to the excitement and anxiety from such a long and emotional day. The next several days, I walked a lot near my apartment located one block from the major government buildings and called the federal triangle. I was also downtown near all the restaurants on Seventh Street and the Verizon Center, where the Washington Capitals hockey team and the Washington Wizards basketball team played.

That Saturday, I spent most of the day preparing to preach at the Bethlehem Baptist Church, where my friend Dr. James Coates was celebrating his sixtieth anniversary as pastor. This preaching engagement was very important to me. At the time I'd accepted, I'd had no idea I would have just spent almost a month in recovery before the engagement. The timing made it very important, as my sobriety would make my message different. I thought about the life of Rev. Dr. Coates since we left seminary over fifty years ago and wanted to reflect on his ministry in one of the poorest and neglected parts of the city. His ministry was truly a commitment to the calling of Jesus to care for the "least of these," which he had done faithfully for more than sixty years.

My sermon was about "remembering not to forget," which was taken from a scripture in the Old Testament, where the children of Israel had come into the Promised Land and God warned them to not forget who had brought them out of the land of bondage in Egypt. The scripture actually reads, "When you come into this land that the Lord promised to your fathers, Abraham, Isaac, and Jacob, with cities that you buildest not, wells that you diggest not, trees that you plantest not, when you have eaten and are full, then beware, lest you forget the Lord thy God who brought you out of the land of bondage." My subject, "remembering not to forget," spoke to the sin of ingratitude.

Rev. Dr. Coates had sacrificed much to serve the Lord in this area where he was most needed—not in areas where he would be comfortable and compensated adequately.

I preached for him several times since but do not plan to continue this practice. When this book is done, my plan is to travel and speak about *Pilgrimage in Clay Feet*. I want to raise the awareness of those like myself. I will encourage others to work to continue developing their spiritual lives and to use every opportunity to do that with whatever means God has given them. And I will share that we can also continue our spiritual development through the negative things we have brought into our lives, which can be redeemed through using those negative things as means of developing an even deeper spirituality.

Closing Words of Gratitude

In closing I want to thank God for a beautiful life he gave me through my wife and children. Jean brought a deeper meaning of love, which she demonstrated to me with her patience, understanding, and forgiveness. Gayle died early but accomplished much in her short life. Michael has struggled in his life for fifty-six years as a result of negative decisions but remains a good soul who is trying to find its way. Caron, who I specifically asked God to send, challenged her mother and me but developed spiritually and used her development to accomplish much. But she never forgot the primary purpose of her life was to develop spiritually. My second-oldest daughter, who I discovered late in life, has been a blessing to me and to her community, advocating for social justice.

I am grateful for my grandchildren, Saudia, Isaiah, Sheriece, and Johanna, and my one great-grandchild, Zion, in whom I see the seeds of spirituality even at his tender age of seven.

The one grandchild I set apart is Isaiah Veazey, now incarcerated and getting psychological assistance because of his schizophrenic psychosis. I know that even in his condition he is here for his spiritual development. I am encouraged not only because of the wonderful doctors and therapist who are treating him but also because, since his incarceration, he has read almost all of Dr. Howard Thurman's books, which to me is a sign of his awakening spiritual connection and development. I pray daily for his aunt, whose life he took during this sickness. I pray God's love and mercy on his dear aunt's soul and the soul of my dear grandson as he works out his soul's salvation.

Finally, as I prepare for my exit to the next level of spiritual development, I am trying to redeem the hurts and pain I have caused and the lost opportunities God has given me. I hope you will strive to reach a higher level of spiritual existence and also help someone else on his or her pilgrimage in clay feet.

CPSIA information can be obtained
at www.ICGtesting.com
Printed in the USA
BVHW031451020719
552053BV00012B/2/P